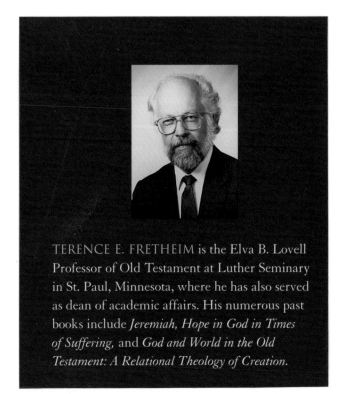

TERENCE E. FRETHEIM is the Elva B. Lovell
Professor of Old Testament at Luther Seminary
in St. Paul, Minnesota, where he has also served
as dean of academic affairs. His numerous past
books include *Jeremiah, Hope in God in Times
of Suffering,* and *God and World in the Old
Testament: A Relational Theology of Creation.*

ABRAHAM

Studies on Personalities of the Old Testament

James L. Crenshaw, Series Editor

ABRAHAM

TRIALS OF FAMILY AND FAITH

TERENCE E. FRETHEIM

The University of South Carolina Press

Published by the University of South Carolina Press
Columbia, South Carolina 29208

www.sc.edu/uscpress

Manufactured in the United States of America

16 15 14 13 12 11 10 09 08 07   10 9 8 7 6 5 4 3 2 1

Library of Congress Cataloging-in-Publication Data

Fretheim, Terence E.
    Abraham : trials of family and faith / Terence E. Fretheim.
        p. cm. — (Studies on personalities of the Old Testament)
    Includes bibliographical references and index.
    ISBN-13: 978-1-57003-694-1 (cloth : alk. paper)
    ISBN-10: 1-57003-694-2 (cloth : alk. paper)
    1. Abraham (Biblical patriarch)   I. Title.
    BS580.A3F74 2007
    222'.11092—dc22

                                                                2007007193

This book was printed on Glatfelter Natures, a recycled paper with 50 percent
postconsumer waste content.

CONTENTS

SERIES EDITOR'S PREFACE

Critical study of the Bible in its ancient Near Eastern setting has stimulated interest in the individuals who shaped the course of history and whom events singled out as tragic or heroic figures. Rolf Rendtorff's *Men of the Old Testament* (1968) focuses on the lives of important biblical figures as a means of illuminating history, particularly the sacred dimension that permeates Israel's convictions about its God. Fleming James's *Personalities of the Old Testament* (1939) addresses another issue, that of individuals who function as inspiration for their religious successors in the twentieth century. Studies restricting themselves to a single individual—for example, Moses, Abraham, Samson, Elijah, David, Saul, Ruth, Jonah, Job, Jeremiah —enable scholars to deal with a host of questions: psychological, literary, theological, sociological, and historical. Some, such as Gerhard von Rad's *Moses*, introduce a specific approach to interpreting the Bible, hence provide valuable pedagogic tools.

As a rule, these treatments of isolated figures have not reached the general public. Some were written by outsiders who lacked a knowledge of biblical criticism (Freud on Moses, Jung on Job) and whose conclusions, however provocative, remain problematic. Others were targeted for the guild of professional biblical critics (David Gunn on David and Saul, Phyllis Trible on Ruth, Terence Fretheim and Jonathan Magonet on Jonah). None has succeeded in capturing the imagination of the reading public in the way fictional works like Archibald MacLeish's *J.B.* and Joseph Heller's *God Knows* have done.

It could be argued that the general public would derive little benefit from learning more about the personalities of the Bible. Their conduct, often less then exemplary, reveals a flawed character, and their everyday concerns have nothing to do with our preoccupations from dawn to dusk. To be sure, some individuals transcend their own age, entering the gallery of classical literary figures from time immemorial. But only these rare achievers can justify specific treatments of them. Then why publish additional studies on biblical personalities?

The answer cannot be that we read about biblical figures to learn ancient history, even of the sacred kind, or to discover models for ethical action. But what remains? Perhaps the primary significance of biblical personages is the light they throw on the imaging of deity in biblical times. At the very least, the Bible constitutes human perceptions of deity's relationship with the world and its creatures. Close readings of biblical personalities therefore clarify ancient understandings of

God. That is the important datum that we seek—not because we endorse that specific view of deity, but because all such efforts to make sense of reality contribute something worthwhile to the endless quest for knowledge.

James L. Crenshaw
Duke Divinity School

PREFACE

Scholarly studies of the story of Abraham have long been available in Genesis commentaries, Pentateuchal research, and more specialized analyses of individual texts and themes.[1] The last two decades or so, however, have seen an explosion in the breadth and depth of "Abrahamic" scholarship.[2] The renewed attention given to these narratives has been sparked by several emerging interests and concerns, from the role of women to an intensification of Jewish-Christian-Muslim inter-relationships, prompted especially by events in the Middle East. As a result, interest in the Abraham story has reached beyond scholarly circles (whether in Hebrew, Bible, or history of religions) and caught up the larger culture. One thinks of the appearance of Abraham on the covers of *Time* and *Newsweek* magazines, with accompanying stories of no little sophistication, or of the best-selling book by Bruce Feiler, *Abraham: A Journey to the Heart of Three Faiths,* with associated "salons" that were held across the United States in the first years of the new millennium. This renewed interest in the story of Abraham shows no signs of subsiding. Indeed, the intensification of the dialogue among the three major religions will mean an ever-increasing attention to these chapters in Genesis.

Abraham and his family have, of course, been given significant consideration by religious communities through the centuries. This interest can be tracked in several ways, from the history of biblical interpretation through an analysis of the history of art. The Akedah in particular has been given attention. Special appeal has been made to Abraham as the recipient of divine promises and as a paradigm of faithfulness to God.

The story of Abraham and Sarah, Hagar, and Ishmael is portrayed primarily in Genesis 11:26–25:18. These narratives focus on Abraham, depicting various episodes in his life, from his birth (11:26) to his death and burial (25:7–10). Abraham is also the most frequently mentioned Genesis character in the balance of the Old Testament (forty-two references) and in the New Testament (eighty-five references). Sarah is less frequently mentioned and is not present as a character in key texts (for example, Gen. 15; 18:16–19:38; 22); yet, she appears episodically throughout the narrative, from the beginning to the end (11:29; 25:10), and five times in the balance of the Bible. Hagar and Ishmael appear in only three chapters (Gen. 16; 21:8–21; 25:1–18; cf. 1 Chron. 1:28–31; Bar. 3:23), but they are integral to the proper telling of the larger story.[3]

Abraham is the "first" of the Genesis patriarchs and has become the progenitor of three major religious traditions (Judaism, Christianity, and Islam). As such, he has lived up to the meaning of his name ("the father of a multitude," according to Gen. 17:5). Abraham's story is followed by narratives of his son Isaac and his grandson Jacob/Israel (25:19–36:43), whose twelve sons are the progenitors of the twelve tribes of Israel. The complex interrelationships of the sons of Jacob are told in the so-called story of Joseph (37:1–50:26), which sets the stage for the exodus and accompanying events.

This study is primarily concerned to develop the theological issues that center around the figure of Abraham, especially in Gen. 12–25. Issues related to putative literary sources and possible historical and social backgrounds will receive only introductory attention.

THE BASIC STORY LINE IN GENESIS 12–25

Little is known of Abraham prior to his call (12:1–3). Genealogical references establish Abraham's lineage as a descendant of Shem, and more specifically, Eber (or the Hebrews; Gen. 11:10–26). Later genealogically related texts are concerned to show that he is ethnically related to various Arabian (25:1–6, 12–18) and Aramean (22:20–24) groups, "the children of Lot" (Moabites and Ammonites, 19:30–38; cf. Deut. 2:9, 19), as well as the descendants of his son Isaac (Jacob, the progenitor of the twelve tribes of Israel, and Esau, the progenitor of the Edomites, Gen. 36). Abraham's Mesopotamian origins are made clear by the several references to Ur of the Chaldeans (probably south of modern Baghdad), from which the family of his father Terah traveled to Haran (in southeast Turkey) on their way to Canaan (11:31; 15:7; cf. Josh. 24:2). There they settled until the death of Terah (11:32), at which point God's command to Abraham calls him, in effect, to complete the journey to Canaan.[4] Continued family links with Haran are evident in the search for a wife for Isaac (Gen. 24) and in the Jacob story (Gen. 29–31). Abraham's birth and early years in Ur are minimally noted (11:27–31; 15:7; cf. Neh. 9:7; Acts 7:2–4). Joshua 24:2–3 implies that God brought Abraham out of an idolatrous situation in which his father served other gods.[5] It is not altogether clear whether Abraham also did so (see Isa. 51:2); that he was a monotheist is certainly not stressed in the Genesis narrative. Later Jewish literature expands upon this early life, linking him, for example, to a vocation in astronomy, for which Chaldea was famous. Two specific pieces of literature from the early centuries C.E. (*The Testament of Abraham; The Apocalypse of Abraham*) draw Abraham into the sphere of apocalyptic interests.[6]

The Genesis texts have a special interest in the journeys of Abraham and his family; over the course of the narrative they are brought into contact with every major part of the land of promise and with every neighboring people. Initially, he moves through the land, from Haran to Shechem to Bethel to the Negeb, and finally to Egypt (12:4–20). After negotiating over land with Lot (at Bethel), he settles in the Hebron area (13:1–18), from where he engages in military activity in protection of Lot, who lived in Sodom (Gen. 14). The latter text represents Abraham as a person of considerable wealth, with the capacity to engage in military engagements with neighboring peoples. The resultant blessing on the part of the otherwise unknown priest-king Melchizedek (14:18–20) demonstrates that God can work through "outsiders" to bless the people of God.[7] God's promise in 12:3, "I will bless those who bless you," assumes that the nonchosen have the powers of creational blessing.[8]

The next major section in the story of this family focuses on the son that God has promised (implicit in the promise of nation and name in 12:1–3). The issue comes to the fore in questions addressed to God by Abraham (15:1–2), to whom God responds with the promise of a direct heir (15:3–5), though without explicit mention of Sarah. Abraham's response of faith (15:6) is followed by still further questions (15:7–8), to which God again responds with a unilateral covenant focused on the unconditional promise of a land (15:9–21). After an apparent fulfillment of the promise of a son in the birth of Ishmael through Sarah's slave girl, Hagar (16:1–16), God moves to a more precise promise of a son with Sarah as the mother, though with special consideration for the future of Ishmael and his family (17:15–20). The "covenant" with Abraham, the first instance of which had focused on the land (15:7–21), is now *recharacterized* as being "between me [God] and you" (17:1–8). This "everlasting" covenant introduces a heightened sense of the relationship between Abraham (and his family) and God. Notably, the covenant is marked by the rite of circumcision (17:9–14) and by new names for each of the major characters: Abraham (from Abram, 17:5), Sarah (from Sarai, 17:15), and even God (17:1, El Shaddai). Remarkably, this newly minted name for God means that God's own identity from this time forward is linked with this family. God binds the divine self to this identity and God's commitment thereto will not be compromised. Indeed, God's very future will be shaped by this association, for God will be forever known as the God of Abraham.

The cycle of stories moves through several problematic incidents, from Abraham's repeated endangerment of Sarah (12:10–20; 20:1–18) to disbelief in God's promise on the part of both Abraham and Sarah (17:15–18:15), toward the fulfillment of the promise of a son through Sarah (21:1–7). The story of Sodom and Gomorrah (18:16–19:38) provides a catastrophic interlude that illustrates the more *global* concerns of God evident in the specific choice of Abraham and family. Among them: that blessing may be mediated to "outsiders" through the intercessory activities of the Abrahamic family and that God takes moral evil with great seriousness, exhibited not least in a lively concern for justice and the plight of the innocent. This story is also illustrative of the different directions for life that are possible in view of choices made (in this case, Lot). This story of disaster exhibits a remarkably interactive relationship between Abraham and God (especially 18:22–32; cf. 15:1–11) and God acts to deliver Lot (and his daughters) because "God remembered Abraham" (19:29).

The next section (21:9–22:19) is climactic, consisting primarily of two parallel stories regarding the potential loss of the sons of Abraham, first Ishmael to the wilderness (21:8–21), then Isaac as a burnt offering (22:1–19). Yet, both sons are delivered, as "God was with the boy" Ishmael (21:20) and the angel of the Lord stops Abraham from completing the sacrifice of Isaac (22:12–14). Moreover, to both sons God makes remarkably similar promises regarding continuing life and community (21:13, 18; 22:15–18). Both Isaac and Ishmael return to bury their father (25:9) and the fulfillment of divine promises to both sons is reported (25:12–18, 19–26). The narrative concludes with accounts of the death of Sarah and Abraham's purchase of a burial plot (Gen. 23)—an initial installment of the gift of land, the procurement of a wife (Rebekah) for Isaac (Gen. 24), a notice regarding Abraham's third family (25:1–6), and the report of Abraham's death and burial (25:7–11).

Abraham's three wives bear him eight children. In addition to Sarah, Hagar is given by Sarah to be his "wife" (16:3), and she bears Ishmael. After Sarah's death, Abraham takes another "wife," named Keturah (25:1), who bears him six additional children. Gen. 25:6 refers to both Hagar and Keturah as "concubines," probably because of their secondary standing within Abraham's household. This reality is recognized in that their children are less than full heirs of Abraham, as they are given gifts and "sent away" (25:6). At the same time, these children were a part of the fulfillment of the promise that Abraham would become the father of a multitude of nations (17:5–6; see 25:2–4; 12–18). Besides Isaac, however, only Ishmael among Abraham's other children is the recipient of promises (17:20; and 16:10; 21:13, 18). Remarkably, God thereby makes commitments to those who stand outside of the family of Abraham and Isaac.

Some tension exists in the narrative regarding Abraham's wealth and social standing. On the one hand, the general image of Abraham in the story is that of a nomadic shepherd of modest means (cf. his ability to travel with apparent ease). On the other hand, in Gen. 14 he has an army of 318 soldiers in his retinue and in Gen. 23:6 he is called "a mighty prince" by occupants of the land of Canaan. Moreover, many servants were part of his household (14:14; 15:2; 17:12–13, 23–27; 18:7; 24:2, 35, 59). Estimates range as high several thousand people, including women and children. The one servant named (Eliezer) was perhaps the leader of this group of servants, and would have been Abraham's heir in the absence of his own children (15:2–3); he is probably the servant commissioned by

Abraham to seek a wife for Isaac (Gen. 24). It is not clear at what point these servants were acquired, but at least some of them (probably including Hagar) were given to him by Egypt's pharaoh (Gen. 12:16), along with other gifts that certainly advanced his wealth, if it did not establish it in the first place (the pharaoh, too, seems to acknowledge Abraham as a person of considerable social standing). Abraham's status was also recognized by Abimelech, who further increased his wealth in the wake of this negative encounter (20:14). Elements of both a settled and a nomadic culture seem to be combined, perhaps reflecting a complex history in the transmission of these texts.

OVERVIEW

Chapter 1, "The Universal Frame of Reference: A Key to Understanding Abraham," seeks to relate the story of Abraham in Genesis 12–25 with preceding chapters 1–11).[9] Chapter 2, "The Abrahamic Narratives: Literary and Historical Perspectives," surveys basic literary and historical issues raised by the story of Abraham. Chapter 3, "Abraham: Recipient of Promises," addresses what I consider to be the most important theme of the story of Abraham, namely, God's promises, both to Abraham and Sarah and also to Hagar and Ishmael. Chapters 4–6 focus on the issue of the "Other" or the "Outsider." Genesis 12:3 envisages three possible relationships that the chosen family might have with the Outsider.

- Those who bless you.—Outsider as *gift*. Blessing with respect to the outsider does not travel in only one direction, from the chosen to the outsider; the outsider also has the capacity to bless the chosen. Both directions will be evident in these texts.
- The one who curses you.—Outsider as *threat* to the chosen family.
- Through you all the families of the earth will be blessed.—Outsider as *challenge* to the chosen family. How will this family fare in taking up this responsibility?

Several of the stories in chapters 4–6 address such relationships, though in different ways and in a fashion that is more often ambiguous than precise; these "outsiders" have a significant and varied impact on the chosen family over the course of their journey.

In chapter 7, "Isaac: Birth, Endangerment, and Sign of the Future," centers on those narratives that have to do with Isaac. Chapter 8, "Memory and Tradition," seeks to track the story of Abraham through the rest of the Old Testament, the Deuterocanonical and Pseudepigraphical books, the New Testament, and, more briefly, the Qur'an.

ACKNOWLEDGMENTS

The figure of Abraham has long captivated me. Preparations for my commentary on Genesis and other publications have regularly brought me into close contact with this individual and the characters around him. Theological issues that are raised in these Genesis chapters, by Abraham and about him, have often been my own issues. His theological journey has in many respects been a mirror of my own. My personal life experience has intensified that connection. Our son-in-law, Veli Gul, is a Muslim and that has thrown me back into the Genesis texts, those about Hagar and Ishmael in particular, with renewed energies. I have come to see that the common roots we share in the family of Abraham may be capable of fostering closer relationships and deeper conversations among us and among others in our respective religious traditions. I hope that this modest volume may in some small way contribute to that conversation. I dedicate this book to him.

This book would not have been completed without the help of many people. I wish to express appreciation to my students at Luther Seminary, who have kindly tolerated my slow pace of teaching this story over the years and helpfully interacted with this material in an earlier form. Pastors and laypeople in several settings have thoughtfully responded to portions of these chapters. I owe a special word of thanks to student Susan Peterson-Koesterman, who responded to most of these chapters in a way that often prompted further reflection, and to my colleague Arland Hultgren for his comment on New Testament sections. I owe a special word of gratitude to the series editor, James L. Crenshaw, who kept the pressure on for the book's completion and made helpful suggestions along the way. Finally, I express my love and appreciation to my wife, Faith, whose constant encouragement and support has helped me stay the course.

ABRAHAM

CHAPTER I

THE UNIVERSAL FRAME OF REFERENCE
A KEY TO UNDERSTANDING ABRAHAM

A s with any effective literary work, the way in which the book of Genesis begins is important for a proper interpretation of all that follows, not least the story of Abraham. Genesis (indeed the Bible) begins, not with the chosen people, but with the creation of the universe and the ordering of families and nations. The book of Genesis sets the story of Abraham and Israel's other ancestral figures (chapters 12–50) deeply within the context of the entire creation (chapters 1–11). In other words, the opening chapters of Genesis catch the reader up in a universal frame of reference.[1] The story of Abraham will not be properly understood apart from this universal context.[2]

In the study of Genesis it has long been the practice to drive a sharp wedge between Genesis 1–11, the "primeval history," and Genesis 12–50, the "ancestral history."[3] The exact dividing point between these "histories" has been disputed (from 11:10 to 11:27 to 12:1), but good reasons for such a division are rightly claimed. The narrator's eye moves from "the whole earth" (11:1) to focus more specifically on the progenitors of Israel. Genesis 1–11, which has had the world as a stage, is immediately narrowed down to a village in Mesopotamia, to a single family, to the mind and heart of a single individual—Abraham (12:1–3). At the same time, the difficulty that scholars have had in precisely establishing the precise break point should alert readers not to make the break sharper than the text itself does.[4] The story of the Tower of Babel (11:1–9) places the narrative story in Mesopotamia, which is the geographical context for the beginning of the story of Terah's family (11:27–32).[5] In some ways, the line of Shem (11:10) could be seen as the response to the catastrophe that was Babel.

But even those scholars who sharpen the break between Genesis 11 and Genesis 12 often note that 12:1–3 is a fulcrum text, linking Abraham with key themes of the immediately prior chapters. For example, Abraham's calling by God is presented in 12:1–3 as having a particular relationship to "all the families of the earth." Those "families" have been identified in Genesis 10 as the descendants of Noah's three sons—Japtheth, Ham, and Shem (10:5, 20, 31), survivors of the flood. Genesis 10:32 summarizes the point of interest: "These are the families of Noah's sons." It is with reference to these families that God bespeaks both a promise and a vocation (12:2–3): all these families will be (and are to be) blessed in and through Abraham and his descendants.[6] This global observation is of crucial importance in understanding the story of Abraham; yet, the story of Abraham has often been seen largely in terms of a "salvation history"; that is, God's election of this family narrows God's activity in the world largely to matters of sin and redemption.[7] The result has been a common neglect of the creational themes that fill subsequent texts, including the story of Abraham.

More recently, especially under the impact of literary and canonical readings, there has been a renewed interest in the integrity of the book of Genesis as a whole.[8] Among other matters, such a perspective recognizes that the world stage remains very much in view throughout Genesis. Abraham is deeply rooted in that earlier history (evident in the genealogy in 11:10–26) and his family and their descendants will find themselves in continuing contact with the peoples of that larger world throughout Genesis 12–50. The divine choice of Abraham to "all the families of the earth" (Gen. 12:3) is repeated in contexts relating to each of the major ancestral figures—Abraham, Isaac, and Jacob—and at key junctures in their lives (18:18; 22:18; 26:4; 28:14).[9] It seems clear that the narrator ties these two parts of Genesis together in ways that are rich and deep. Too sharp a distinction between these two major sections of Genesis will not serve the interpreter well.[10]

That God's choice of Abraham constitutes a universal strategy also helps relate the ancestral stories in Genesis 12–50 to the rest of the biblical material. In Janzen's language, "It is the distinctive function of the ancestral narratives in Genesis 12–50 . . . to sustain the literary and theological connection between Genesis 1–11 and Exodus-Revelation." The "elective particularity" of Genesis 12–50 "is placed in the service of the wider story of God and all creation." With its focus on "individuals and families amid other families and nations, Genesis 12–50 offers every individual and family a gate of entry into the story for themselves" (Gal. 3:29).[11] God's work in the world is not narrowed down to a select few, but through these ancestors that divine activity is opened up to the world. The promises of God are, finally, applicable to all the families of the earth.

Genesis 17:4–5 will express this theme in somewhat different, genealogical terms, namely, Abraham as the "father of a multitude of nations"; Sarah, too, will give rise to "nations" (17:15–16), with her descendants giving birth to peoples that extend well beyond Israel, for example, her grandson, Esau/Edomites. In these terms, the family of Abraham and Sarah will have a creational impact by expanding the world of nations.[12] The effect of this reality will be that the "families of the earth" blessed through the chosen family will include many of their own descendants. Across the centuries this intergenerational reality has become increasingly complex, as many of those very descendants have established themselves in related, but significantly different, religious communities (including Christianity and Islam).

At the same time, for all the universal connections, Abraham is not a new Adam; he steps onto a world stage that is not in tune with God's creational intentions. The downward spiral that began in Eden plunged the world into a cosmic catastrophe, and the postflood world seems once again on the way into a profoundly negative future, not least the fragmentation of the human community (Gen. 11:1–9). This very theme introduces the story of Abraham, if on a much smaller scale: not much of a future at all seems to be in store for the family of Terah, with early death, barren wives, and interrupted journeys (11:27–32).

GENESIS 13 AS AN ILLUSTRATION

Close links between Genesis 13 and material in Genesis 1–11 may help illustrate this point, evident especially in the use of certain words and themes. For example, the word "beginning" and the phrase "he called on the name of Yahweh" (13:3–4) recall Genesis 1–11 (1:1; 4:26), as does the reference to the "well watered garden of the Lord" (13:10; cf. 2:6; Exod. 3:8). Given Abraham's well-being and wealth, and his settlement in the Promised Land, a claim is being made that God's basic creational intentions are being realized in him. At the same time, the words "evil" (ra') and "sin(ner)" (ht') are used for the first time early in Genesis (for the people of Sodom, 13:13; cf. 4:7; 6:5; 8:21). And the strife between "brothers" Abraham and Lot (cf. 13:8, 11) recalls the story of Cain and Abel (4:8–11). The Sodomites are the first historical people for whom the language of wickedness and sin is used and they are the first to experience the floodlike destruction (sht) of divine judgment as a result (13:10; cf. 6:12–17; 9:11, 15). These words for sin/evil/destruction are used only in these texts in the Abraham cycle, though Abimelech will use synonymous language to refer to the actions of Abraham (20:9–10), showing that the chosen family itself is caught up in the world of sin and its effects.

The reference to the destruction of Sodom and Gomorrah (13:10) also serves to note the drastic change in the ecology of the area within the lifetime of Abraham (19:24–25). The reference to Zoar also is anticipatory of this cataclysmic event (13:10; 19:22–23, 30). In some sense the Sodom story, begun here, is seen as a continuation in history of the interweaving of human choices and cosmic disaster sketched out in Genesis 3–8. Lot's beautiful land will become an ecological wasteland; and these effects are related to the wickedness of Sodom (13:13). The reference to Sodom's destruction (13:10), which assumes that readers know the Sodom story, does not imply that Lot moves into a situation already doomed before his arrival, but suggests a close link between human sin and the environmental future of the area.

These links between Genesis 13 and Genesis 1–11 mean not only that God's creational activity is manifest in the life of this family, but also that the forces that make for evil and chaos hover near and threaten its future (cf. 4:7). Abraham lives in a world in which the forces of wickedness are very much a reality and sin will powerfully intrude upon his life and the life of his family. Specifically, Lot's integration into the Sodomite orbit of life serves as a reminder of negative possibilities for the people of God. The wickedness that was described as characteristic of humankind as a whole (Gen. 6:5; 8:21) has now intruded into the very heart of the family chosen by God to reclaim that creation. This experience should serve as a reminder for the community of faith that the choices its members make with respect to the land, and socio-economic issues more generally, have a potentially negative environmental impact—on the human community and on God's blessings of the land.

A key purpose of this material in Genesis 13 is to show that the world to which Abraham is vocationally related is a world like that described in Genesis 3–11. These textual links of a global sort are an indication that this ancestral story is to be interpreted through the lens provided by the opening chapters of Genesis. This exercise could be repeated with each chapter in the Abraham story.

In the face of these negative developments, it is important to say that Abraham's world is still the "good" world that God created. God did not abandon the creation to the consequences of its own sins within that "primeval" time and that divine commitment continues into Abraham's world. Though they may be endangered, there are still gardens that look like Eden (13:10). The genealogies that regularly punctuate the narrative, both before the call of Abraham (4:17–26; 5:1–32; 6:9–10; 10:1–32; 11:10–26) and after (22:20–24; 25:1–6, 12–18; 35:22–36:43) testify that life, however troubled, continues. Recall that God's covenant with Noah has given the postflood world the shape of a rainbow; God's promise insures its future—for God keeps promises. This global promise positively affects the entire world of which Abraham is a part and, more particularly, makes possible God's promises to Abraham and his family.

The narrative shift to Abraham does not mean a new world or even a new divine objective for the world. God's goal of reclaiming the world remains in place. What comes into clearer view is the means by which God will move toward this objective, namely, in and through a specific family, the family of Abraham and Sarah. In so describing the matter, Genesis 12–25 does not recharacterize the God of Genesis 1–11 or the divine intentions. Indeed, the image of the creator God who makes promises and who graciously and providentially acts in judgment and salvation in a fractured world continues to be sharply evident in Genesis 12–25. But now, God determines, from within those basic divine ways of relating to the world, that the best way in which the creation can be reclaimed is for God to act in and through a specific family. At the same time, this divine decision does not reduce God's work in the world to a salvation history; God's work in creation continues apace independent of the chosen family and will play an important and gracious role in ongoing world developments.

God's call of Abraham, then, may be described as a divine strategy in the service of a universal purpose, namely, the redemption of all the families of the earth
that had fallen under the sway of human sin and its disastrous effects, issuing in
a new creation (on Genesis 12:3 see below). Readers might wonder why God
chose this particular approach. Why would God not simply snap the divine fin-
gers and save the world in a moment? It would have saved a lot of trouble and
included everyone. We do not know why God chose this strategic alternative from
among those possible, but it may be surmised that only such a way could honor
the integrity of the relationship between God and world to which God was
committed. We also do not know why God chose Abraham rather than another
person or family. One might surmise that God saw certain gifts in Abraham that
prompted the divine choice; yet, the text does not probe such matters (unlike for
Moses in Exod. 2:11–22). But the text makes clear why God chose Abraham: so
that the human and nonhuman creation might be blessed and again be enabled to
live in tune with the original divine intention. God's choice of Abraham is an initially exclusive move for the sake of a maximally inclusive end that encompasses
the world. In more modern terms, election is for the sake of mission.

This universal frame of reference can be tracked through the story of Genesis
12–25 in connection with several key themes.

THE PRESENCE OF GOD THE CREATOR

In these texts, God is confessed as the creator of the earth, both by outsiders
(Melchizedek, 14:19) and Abraham (14:22), as the "Judge of all the earth" (18:25;
cf. verse 18), and as "the God of heaven and earth" (24:3) and more briefly as "the
God of heaven" (24:7).[13] Such a global understanding of God's presence and activity is necessary if the matters relating to the larger world of which this family is a
part are to make theological sense. In other words, these claims regarding God
connect well with the opening chapter of Genesis and its testimony to God as creator of heaven and earth. The "earth" and its inhabitants remain in clear view in
the midst of the story of a specific family.

These texts also witness to God's presence and activity independent of the chosen family, and hence provide what is probably the most basic dimension of the
universal frame of reference of these chapters.[14] The stories of Hagar and Ishmael
are a prime example. Indeed, God enters Hagar's life at precisely that point when
her exclusion from the chosen family has taken place (16:7; cf. 21:17). While
her contact with the family of Abraham is important, God's attentiveness to Hagar
and Ishmael comes more in spite of what that family has done than because of
their concern for outsiders and their welfare (an all-too-common experience). The
testimony is clearly stated: God appears to Hagar, converses with her, and makes
promises to her that are worded much like those promises given to Abraham
(16:10–11; 17:20; 21:13, 18).

Another example is God's appearance to Abimelech in a dream, wherein God takes the initiative and communicates with the outsider (20:3–6). Indeed, God engages the outsider in dialogue, and this bears positive fruit in the life of all concerned. It may be disconcerting to the reader that God engages such a one apart from the ministrations of the community of faith, but this story makes clear that God does not run a closed shop on who receives a word from God and who can engage it.

A somewhat different witness to the work of God as Creator can be discerned in the story of Sodom and Gomorrah (18:16–19:29). In and through divine messengers, God is present and active in these cities and is understood to mediate their destruction in and through elements of the natural order (19:24–25).

These texts serve to remind the chosen people that Israel's God plays an important role in the life of "unchosen" persons and places. Such "outsiders" have experienced God, even if they have not realized that it was God. The text specifically witnesses that Hagar does realize the nature of her experience (16:13). She knows that God has been active in her life in both word and deed outside the boundaries of the community of faith. And the word of God she has experienced is especially remarkable in that God is portrayed as a Creator who makes promises to those who do not belong to the chosen people (16:10; 17:20). The chosen people cannot confine God's presence and activity—even words of gospel and promise—within their all too often oppressive and narrowly conceived structures of life and worship.

BLESSING

Blessing is a key theme in the narratives that follow, with many direct (nearly ninety occurrences) and indirect references.[15] Blessing shapes the life of this family in varying ways as well as the lives of many outsiders whom they encounter. Because blessing is basically a matter of creation,[16] it testifies to God's work as creator. This divine creative activity of blessing is ongoing and provides life-giving, life-enhancing benefits for all creatures in every sphere of existence, from spiritual to more tangible expressions. Blessing is most evident in fertility and the multiplication of life, from herds and flocks, to field and forest, to new human life; it embraces material well-being, peace, and general success in life's ventures (see the list in Deut. 28:3–15).

Blessing is given creationwide scope from the beginning of Genesis; it includes human and nonhuman creatures (1:22, 28) and it continues into the post-sin, pre-Abrahamic world (5:2; 9:1) and, in turn, into the ancestral world. God is portrayed in Genesis 12–25 as one who has a history of blessing Abraham, promised in his initial calling (12:2–3). God's blessing work is most commonly evident in and through the ordinary, everyday workings of this family rather than in extraordinary events (though they are not excluded). One can commonly speak of blessing as God's effective, but unobtrusive activity behind the scenes bringing goodness and well-being into every sphere of life.[17] At the same time, blessing is not always evident; even the chosen family will, for example, suffer famine. God has so created the world that it is not a risk-free place; the natural order, with its interplay of law and chance, does not work mechanistically and human behaviors can also adversely affect the functioning of that order.

Inasmuch as blessing belongs primarily to the sphere of creation, nonelect peoples are not dependent upon the elect for many forms of blessing; it rains on the just and the unjust and families continue to thrive (cf. Matt 5:45).[18] Genesis 12–25 makes clear that God is active for good in the lives, not only of Abraham and his family, but also of outsiders such as Abimelech, Hagar, and Ishmael. The genealogies of the nonelect, for example, those of Ishmael and Esau, (25:12–18; 36:1–43), also demonstrate this point. Various human and nonhuman agents mediate these blessings from God. Indeed, the nonelect may even mediate blessing to the elect, a point stated in general terms (12:3; 27:29) and illustrated, as we shall see, several times in the larger narrative (12:16; 14:18–20; 20:14; 26:12–14). The divine election of Abraham does not entail exclusive access to the goodness of God's creation; indeed the "nonchosen" have gifts to give to the chosen.

Blessing is used throughout Genesis to encompass two realities. The first comprises God's specific, constitutive promises to the elect family, initially through Abraham (son, land, many descendants, nationhood; 12:1–3, 7; 13:14–18; 15:4–5, 18–21), and not mediated by the nonelect. I call them "constitutive" because they are community-creating, without which Israel would not have come to be. These promises are called "the blessing of Abraham" in 28:4 and are repeated to Isaac (26:3–4, 24) and Jacob (28:13–14; 35:10–12). The identity of the son who is to be positioned to receive the constitutive blessings (and related responsibilities) becomes a key matter for consideration in the narrative. Will it be Abraham's firstborn son, Ishmael, or will it be Isaac?

The second reality comprises the general, creational realities of which we have spoken, such as fertility and various forms of prosperity and success in the social, political, and economic spheres. These blessings can be mediated and experienced by all of God's creatures, independent of their knowledge of God (see below).

To relate these two types of blessings is not simple. The creational blessings are life-enabling and life-enhancing, but they are finally not sufficient for the fullest possible life. The chosen family is not given implicit permission to neglect these creational dimensions of blessing; rather, the particular vocation of this family is to bring focus and intensification to those blessings as they bear upon issues of redemption. The constitutive blessings mediated through the elect bring focus and intensity to the blessings of creation, make them more abundant (30:27–30), and decisively give new shape to both the human self and the larger community. Through relationships with this family, life for individuals and communities will become even more correspondent to God's will for goodness and well-being in creation. The larger issue at stake in these divine choices is a universal one: the reclamation of the entire creation in view of sin and its deleterious effects upon life.[19]

The (potential) mediation of God's constitutive blessing to "outsiders" in and through the chosen family becomes a centerpiece of these chapters.[20] Readers should especially note the numerous contacts made between Israel's ancestors and the "nonchosen" peoples. Abraham, for example, is brought into relationship with virtually every people in Israel's socio-historical context, from Egyptians (12:10–20), to numerous Near Eastern nations, including the king-priest of Jerusalem (14), Hagar and Ishmael (16; 21); Arabian tribes (25:1–6), Sodom and Gomorrah (18–19), Moabites and Ammonites (19:37–38), Abimelech and the Canaanites/Philistines (20:1–18; 21:22–34). The interest in these peoples on the part of the narrator is, most basically, that Abraham interacts with them. Or, in the case of Sodom and Gomorrah and Lot's sons, Moab and Ammon, Abraham makes their future (potentially) possible through intercession (19:29).

Abraham's contact with these peoples is not forbidden or discouraged in the narrative; in fact, it seems to be encouraged. Even a cursory reading shows that remarkably little polemic is directed against these outsiders in the Genesis text (Sodom-Gomorrah is the exception).[21] In fact, as will become evident below, these "nonchosen" folk will often play a positive, if at times critical, role in Abraham's life and God's economy. The reader may observe the several ways in which Abraham relates to these peoples as one who is charged to be a mediator of God's special blessing. The way in which Abraham interacts with these individuals and groups, whether negatively or positively, carries an important word about the nature of the vocation of the chosen family and God's larger creational designs. Sometimes the chosen fulfill their responsibilities to the outsider in exemplary ways (Abraham's intercessory activity on behalf of Sodom and Gomorrah); at other times, they alienate the outsider and frustrate God's purposes to be a blessing to all families (Abimelech in Genesis 20). It remains uncertain the extent to which these ancestral encounters with outsiders are intended to be models— negative or positive—for ancient readers in one socio-historical context or another (for example, Babylonian exiles). But, quite apart from authorial intention, these ancestral encounters have often so functioned.

PROMISE

While blessing is central in Genesis, it is inadequate and incomplete without promise. Promise is the most basic category with which the ancestral narratives work.[22] God's promises to Abraham have deep levels of continuity with the creational blessings he experiences. But what he is promised is something more, something beyond what the creation—human and nonhuman—is able to provide. Within creation, blessing is powerful, life-enabling and life-sustaining, but finally insufficient for the fullest possible life. The promises bring blessing into the sphere of redemption.

God has a promissory relationship with the universe before any covenants are made with Abraham. God makes a covenant with Noah, indeed with all creatures (Genesis 9:8–17; cf. 8:21–22); it is in fact a promise to them. With this particular promise God is committed to the future life of the world; without this promise the creation would not be preserved in the wake of continued human wickedness and its effects. The point may be stated in these terms: the "creator God has a relationship of love and faithfulness toward the earth and says a fundamental and irrevocable 'yes' to *this* earth and *these* human beings."[23] This global covenant will stand forever and be as good as God is, and so human beings can rest back in its promises. This covenant will remain in force regardless of how human beings respond to it. Even more, God will uphold this covenant independent of the community of faith, quite apart from Israel's life and mission; all human beings, whether persons of faith or not, are enveloped within this divine promise.

This universal covenant is revealing of God's most basic way of relating to a post-sin world—from within a committed relationship, in patience, and in mercy. Even more, the covenant with Noah and all flesh provides the context within which other covenants become possible. Indeed, it provides the grounding for the promises to Abraham and Israel (the links with the covenant with Abraham in Genesis 17:1–8 are especially to be noted). The universal character of the Noah covenant provides the umbrella under which the covenants with Abraham find their place, revealing that their scope has universal implications. In other words, this universal promissory reality generates more particular promises to serve the divine strategy, which now will focus on the redemption of the world. The covenant promises that God makes with Abraham (Isaac and Jacob) are as firm and good as the universal promises God has made, and they have a comparable purpose, namely, to serve and preserve life for all.

By calling Abraham in language filled with promises (12:1–3), God brings him into the new day provided by promise. This divine word newly constitutes Abraham. God's new commitment to the relationship with Abraham that promising entails, makes for a new identity for the one who now responds in trust and obedience. Abraham now takes into his life the character of the promises made; he is now one whose future looks like this. The future is not yet, but because it is promised by one who is faithful to promises, his very being takes on the character of that future, though not apart from his own faithful response to the word of God that created his faith in the first place. More generally, it is significant that the promise stands at the beginning of Israel's ancestral story. Israel will forever understand itself to be constituted and shaped by the promises that Abraham receives from God.

Even more, it is God's promise as promise that is key here, quite apart from the fulfillment of particular promises, though there are such. What counts finally is their continuing status as promises, which can then be appropriated by the community of faith in later generations as still applicable to them and their future.

Strikingly, God chooses not to make Abraham the sole recipient of divine promises. God makes repeated promises to Hagar and Ishmael (16:10–11; 17:20; 21:13, 18). The language is remarkably similar to the promises given to Abraham and Sarah (cf. 12:2; 17:15–16), though "covenant" is used exclusively for the line of Isaac. God is thus shown to make promises, as Creator, with those who are not a part of the line of "chosen people"; in this respect Hagar and Ishmael stand in the train of the promises to Noah and all flesh. These promises to Hagar and Ishmael show that God continues to have a promissory relationship with the larger world. Though the chosen people can rest back in the promises they have received, they cannot confine God's promises to themselves. Such texts witness to the fact that "God has not exclusively committed himself to Abraham-Sarah."[24]

OUTSIDERS AS THOSE WHO BLESS AND TEACH THE INSIDERS

The God-given vocation of the chosen family is not stated in any simple way. Their concern for the outsider is certainly not to mediate blessing to peoples who have heretofore not experienced blessing. Readers can see that outsiders experience the blessing of God just by virtue of their life as creatures in God's good world. The regular interweaving of stories about outsiders in Genesis 12–25 shows that God's life-giving and life-preserving work in creation extends well beyond the borders of the chosen family. The textual space given to the genealogies of outsiders is ample testimony to their experience of such creational blessings (for example, Ishmael in 25:12–18; Esau in 36:1–43). Even more, Genesis 12:3 clearly anticipates that such outsiders have the capacity to bless those who belong to the chosen family ("I will bless those who bless you"). Abraham and his family are the beneficiaries of such blessing activity in several encounters with outsiders. Examples include the pharaoh (12:16) and Abimelech (20:14).[25]

GENESIS 14 AS ILLUSTRATION

Genesis 14 may be examined more closely as an important witness to this point. Melchizedek blesses Abraham (14:18–20) and God mediates blessings to Melchizedek (and others) in and through Abraham by ridding the country of its predators. The net effect is a triangular repetition of blessing, from God to Abraham to Melchizedek (representing the nonchosen), and then back again from

Melchizedek to Abraham to God ("blessed be God," 14:20). Significant religious links are thus made between the progenitors of Israel and at least some elements of the Canaanite populace.

Genesis 14 has been integrated into Abraham's story for several reasons: It gives the chosen family a role in the world of nations, which links up with the designation of God as creator. This chapter exalts Abraham "as a great and powerful prince who encounters victoriously the united kings of the great kingdoms of the east."[26] But, more importantly, it signals that God's call to Abraham (12:1–3) has a purpose that spans the globe. This chapter and the Table of Nations (10:1–32) have many ties; together they enclose Genesis 11–13, placing Israel's beginnings in Abraham within a universal context. Even more, Melchizedek and Abraham are represented as worshipers of the same God. Melchizedek's God language, El Elyon (it probably carries the sense of "God of gods," 14:19–20) is not represented as new to Abraham, indeed he claims it as his own in the oath he swore prior to his encounter with Melchizedek (14:22). Abraham also claims that *Yahweh* is another name of El Elyon. Hence, the name Yahweh is thematically linked with the considerable knowledge of God, even theological sophistication that Melchizedek already has.

Interestingly, while Abraham and Melchizedek share the understanding of God as creator, Melchizedek confesses their God as both creator and redeemer (18:19–20) in a way that Abraham had not (14:22). Hence, it may be said that Melchizedek is represented as Abraham's teacher regarding the activity of their common deity. It is notable that it is God the Creator, maker of heaven and earth (*qānāh*; Ps 139:13; Deut 32:6; Exod. 15:16), who is confessed as the Liberator. Already existing confessional language for the Creator, evident in both Abraham's earlier oath (reported in 14:22) and in Melchizedek's blessing (14:19), is pressed into doxological service for this moment of salvation. The God who is confessed as creator of heaven and earth (not simply of human beings) is central to the faith of both principals from this early period; from the narrator's point of view, this confession is not understood to be a later theological development. That both individuals worship God with this language also indicates that some commonality in the faith was understood to exist between the progenitors of both the later Israelites and Canaanites. This text is witness to the knowledge of God the Creator, indeed a Creator who liberates, outside of the chosen family. The chosen community would understand that such witnesses have been made possible by the work of God the Creator within these "nonchosen" communities *independent* of the chosen family.[27]

Another teacher of Abraham in these stories is Abimelech (20:1–18). Melchizedek's knowledge of God is matched by Abimelech's knowledge of sin and issues of justice (20:9–10). Abimelech engages in a dialogue with God (20:3–6) regarding theological matters at stake in God's statement to him, and with no little sophistication. He has a keen sense for truth and justice and moves theologically with God in ways that properly discern the will of God at work in this situation. Abimelech next moves to a theological confrontation with Abraham (20:9–10). Without introductory niceties, with no fear as to how this prophet might react,[28] and claiming no divine authority, Abimelech pronounces Abraham guilty and functions as his teacher, indeed his confessor: "What have you done to us? How have I sinned against you, that you have brought such great guilt on me and my kingdom? You have done things to me that ought not be done. . . . What were you thinking of, that you did this thing?" Readers may be uncomfortable that an outsider speaks such a prophetic word to one of God's own prophets, calling him to account for his behavior. The word of God is thus delivered to Abraham by an outsider who had come to some keen theological understandings independent of his relationship to the chosen family.[29]

THE PLACE OF THE HUMAN

God's entrusting of human beings with significant responsibilities in God's creation is a universal claim. The high role given to the human is evident throughout Genesis, from the assignment of dominion (1:28) to the role that Joseph plays in the world (41:57). Divine activity does not entail human passivity in working toward God's purposes for the creation. Human sin does successfully resist the will of God and has disastrous consequences for the life of the world. But this reality does not occasion a divine pulling back of the high role given to human beings (for example, Gen. 3:23–24 exhibits no change in the divine commission of 2:15; cf. Psalm 8). The family of Abraham, in whom God places much confidence in mediating blessing, is a supreme example of such a divine way of working in the world.

Importantly, God does not perfect people before deciding to work in and through them. This means that God's work in the world will always be associated with realities such as deception or patriarchy, which to one degree or another will frustrate the divine purposes and issue in mixed results. Human beings are finite as well and hence will make mistakes. At the same time, the faithfulness of individuals is important for the effectiveness of God's work in the world; the text's witness to Abraham's faithfulness is clear and unequivocal (Gen. 15:6; 22:15–18; 26:3–5). Yet, through thick and thin, God will remain committed to promises made and will work through their failures to bring about life and well-being for as many as possible.

This more general understanding of the human is important in assessing the characters in the story of Abraham. One scholarly tendency has been to demonize some of the characters (for example, Sarah efforts to obtain a child through Hagar,

16:2) or to whitewash them (Abraham often and, more recently, Sarah) or to agonize over the moral issues (did or did not Abraham violate Sarah in passing her off as his sister). The narrator, however, seems to have no particular interest in this direction of thought. God does not measure morality before making choices or persisting with choices made; God's choices seem often "disengaged" from their behaviors.[30] It is striking that God's testing of Abraham (Genesis 22) does not entail a moral issue; rather, a specifically religious issue of trust is raised. Indeed, it may be claimed (at least in modern terms) that God calls upon Abraham to violate a certain "moral value" to demonstrate a religious value. God works in and through people of all sorts, people who have both gifts and character deficiencies. At the same time, this way of working reveals a deep divine vulnerability, for it links God with people whose reputations are not stellar and opens God's ways in the world to sharp criticism.

CHAPTER 2

THE ABRAHAMIC NARRATIVES
LITERARY AND HISTORICAL PERSPECTIVES

Critical Approaches to Genesis 12–25

Two issues may be raised briefly in the context of genre and structure: the type of literature represented in Genesis 12–25 and the structure of these texts.[1]

TYPE OF LITERATURE

The story of Abraham consists primarily of two types of literature, narratives and genealogies. Ten genealogies provide the basic structure of the book of Genesis as a whole. The story of Abraham is enclosed by genealogies, two at the beginning (Shem, 11:10–26; Terah, 11:27–32) and two at the end (Ishmael, 25:12–18; Isaac and Rebekah, 25:19–20). Two other genealogies are included along the way: the genealogy of Nahor, Abraham's brother, whose granddaughter was Rebekah (22:20–24) and the genealogy of the sons of Abraham and his wife Keturah (25:1–6).

The historical value of the genealogies and other aspects of the story of Abraham is the subject of much debate (see below). Their original life setting was probably the family or tribe, those most interested in such matters, within which they were transmitted orally over the generations. As for their purpose, at one level they track the "pedigree" of the Abrahamic family for social and political purposes. At another level, they have a theological function, showing that God's creative activity of blessing continues apace in this family—generating new lives, ordering them into families, and preserving them through the generations.

In terms of narrative, the Abraham cycle is rather episodic in character, making the flow of thought often difficult to discern. It is not as sustained a narrative as that of Jacob and especially Joseph. This development coincides with the characterization of the chief personalities, with Abraham least well developed (but more than Noah); Jacob and particularly Joseph are more fully portrayed. Moreover, the God who is rather directly engaged in the life of Abraham is depicted in more unobtrusive ways in the remainder of Genesis, especially in the Joseph story. What that might mean is uncertain, but the more direct divine engagement with Abraham may be a way of grounding the story of this family, and the chosen people, as firmly as possible in the divine initiative. The sheer existence of this family and their ongoing life is a God-generated reality.

The specific form of the Abrahamic narratives is difficult to assess. It is generally agreed that they are not historical narrative, at least in any modern sense. At
the same time, they present some features that are commonly associated with history writing, for example, the movement through time with some chronological
references; as such, they do have a "history-like" character. Generally speaking,
the literary vehicle may be said to be that of a story of the past, richly informed by
ongoing appropriations of this material by succeeding communities of faith. This
theological and kerygmatic interest of these later generations—with their fundamental concern to speak ever anew a word of/about God to members of the chosen people—suffuses these narratives.

A more specific formal designation to describe the type of narrative represented
in Genesis 12–25 has been difficult to discern and scholarly assessments vary.
Efforts to speak of saga or legend or folktale or myth have not been particularly
helpful or fruitful, though motifs in the narratives may echo usage in such genres.
The designation "story," though its has the disadvantages of imprecision and
ambiguity, is perhaps most helpful in that it reflects how these narratives commonly functioned in the community. That is, these stories are told in such a way
that they could become the stories of successive generations of the people of God.
Indeed, as we shall see, the Abrahamic stories will often anticipate later stories
from Israel's long history with its God. By and large, the world reflected in these
stories is ordinary and familiar, filled with surprises and joys, the sufferings and
troubles, the complexities and ambiguities known to every community. This
strong interest in concrete and everyday matters in these stories, relating to the
family in particular, has suggested that the language of "family narrative" may be
especially appropriate.[2]

At the same time, readers are urged by the narratives themselves to observe that
they are not simply concerned with human words and deeds. The texts witness
that God is a key character in the story and has become deeply engaged in the life
of this family, dysfunctional as it may be. To take this reality into special account
might mean that the designation "theological narrative/story" would be particularly appropriate. Such a designation does have the virtue of recognizing that these
are stories wherein both God and human beings are active characters.

STRUCTURE

Numerous efforts have been made to discern the structure of the Abraham narratives.[3] While a certain chiastic ordering has been discerned, with a center in the
two covenant chapters (15, 17), care must be used so as not to overdraw the parallels, combine disparate elements, or neglect overlapping structures or stories—
for example, Genesis 16 is often neglected in such efforts. It seems best not to
impose a precise arrangement on the Abraham narrative, but to discern more

modest structures from within the flow of the narrative itself. Readers should be prepared to observe structures that do not fit established patterns. In terms of basic content, the promise of the land centers the first part of the narrative (chapters 12–14) and the promise of a son centers the last part (chapters 15–22), with chapter 15 inverting the two themes (15:1–6 centering on the son; 15:7–22 on the land). Genesis 23 returns to the land promise and Genesis 24 to the son's story.

The most striking literary feature of the Abraham narrative is the doubling of key elements over the course of the narrative.[4] This characteristic brings greater coherence across the larger story and promotes an ongoing mirroring effect, but without a chiastic or other precise arrangement. Each "retelling" of the story invites the reader again and again back into prior texts, inviting comparison and contrast. All along the way, readers are invited to take another look at Abraham (and his complex family as well) from a different angle of vision and from a different place in their journey with God. What might such differences in perspective say regarding the development of God's purposes in and through these progenitors of Israel?

The most basic structure of these chapters may be laid out as follows. This structure is not precise and has some overlapping elements throughout. One of the more remarkable dimensions of this structure is the interweaving of material regarding chosen family and "outsiders." The episodic character of the stories and the absence of a sustained narrative focused on the chosen family is a matter needing attention for a proper appreciation of the story of Abraham.

GENEALOGIES ENCLOSE THE NARRATIVE

Two genealogies begin the narrative and two genealogies conclude it: 11:10–32—Abraham's ancestors (Shem, 11:10–26; Terah, 11:27–32); and 25:12–20—Abraham's descendants (Ishmael, 25:12–18; Isaac/Rebekah, 25:19–20). It may be noted that the Jacob story is also bracketed by genealogies (25:12–20; 36:1–43). These family listings highlight the particularity of the fulfillment of the divine promises to Abraham as well as ongoing life-giving and life-enhancing work of the Creator. Notably, these genealogies are not solely concerned with the chosen line of Isaac. Abraham is indeed the father of a multitude of specific nations, reaching far beyond the line of Isaac.

GOD'S CALLING AND TESTING OF ABRAHAM (TO UNSPECIFIED PLACES)

Two narratives—12:1–4, initial call, and 22:1–19, call to sacrifice Isaac—embrace the core dimensions of the narrative regarding Abraham. Genesis 22 begins with language that is similar to that of the beginning of God's call of Abraham in Genesis 12. In effect, given the history of Abraham with his God to this point in the narrative, will he still respond to God's call in comparably trusting ways?

ABRAHAM'S ENDANGERING OF SARAH

The repetition of the theme of Abraham's endangering of Sarah—in 12:10–20, in Egypt, and 20:1–18, in Philistia—highlights Abraham's continuing failure to respond well to life's crises. This feature of the narrative thereby rejects any attempt on the part of the reader to think that Abraham is "getting better and better" in his relationship with God and others. In fact, the divine testing of Abraham (22:1) follows shortly upon the second of these instances (20:1–18), thereby suggesting that God is troubled by such a pattern in Abraham's life.

STORIES PERTAINING TO LAND

Two stories involve the land promise—13:1–18, dividing up the land with Lot and his family, and 23:1–20, purchase of land as Sarah's burial place. The divine promise of a land for Abraham and his family stands near the beginning of the Abrahamic narrative (12:7, "To your offspring I will give this land"). The working out of the details of that promise is evident, particularly in the interchange between Abraham and Lot (13:1–13), issuing in God's closer specification of the land promise (13:14–18), which in turn will be formalized in God's unilateral, unconditional covenant with Abraham in 15:7–21. This dimension of God's promise will return in Genesis 23, where Abraham's purchase of land for a burial plot for Sarah constitutes the first formal possession of the land (though see 20:15).

STORIES PERTAINING TO LOT AND HIS FAMILY

The remarkable concern of the narrative for Abraham's nephew Lot is one of several illustrations of the interest in branches of this family that are not specifically associated with God's covenant with Abraham, also evident in the stories of Hagar and Ishmael and the sons of Keturah (25:1–6). Worth considering are two stories of Abraham's nephew Lot—13–14, Abraham gives Lot property rights and provides protection, and 18:16–19:38, the story of Sodom and Gomorrah (protecting Lot again). Lot increasingly moves toward outsider status in the narrative. In other terms, the "outsider" is given a prominent place in both structure and theme throughout a narrative that is essentially devoted to the establishment of the chosen people of God. In other words, Israel cannot be understood in isolation; it finds its place in God's economy only in relationship to those who are not chosen. God's presence and activity in the world, as we have seen, are not confined to the chosen family.

A FOCUS ON GOD'S COVENANTS WITH ABRAHAM

It is common to understand that these covenantal texts—15:1–21, promise of son (15:1–6), and covenant regarding land (15:7–21), and 17:1–22, covenant with Abraham (17:1–8) and promise to Sarah (17:15–22)—formalize God's promises to

Abraham and his family and constitute a center for the Abrahamic stories. Strikingly, they bracket the story of Hagar and Ishmael, who, on the one hand, stand outside of the covenant with Isaac (17:20–21), but, on the other hand, are given repeated divine promises (16:10–12; 17:20; 21:13, 18). The reader is thereby invited to discern just how the Abrahamic covenants are related to God's promises to the family that stands outside the chosen line.

HAGAR AND ISHMAEL

Once again, significant portions of the narrative are centered on members of Abraham's family that stand "outside" of the line of the people specifically associated with the "covenant." These include 16:1–16, Sarah, Hagar, and the birth of Ishmael; 17:15–27, the exclusion of Ishmael, yet with promises and circumcision; 21:8–21, banishment of Hagar and Ishmael with continuing promises; and 25:12–18, the genealogy of Ishmael. That the narrator would devote so much material to individuals who seem to constitute a "dead end," from the perspective of both God and Israel, is remarkable. The "outsider" is thereby given an ongoing role in the story of both God and Abraham that must not be downplayed—for God keeps promises.

THE ELECTION AND BIRTH OF ISAAC

That God's covenant is established with Abraham's son Isaac, and not with any of the "outsiders" who appear in the story, is a key claim of the narrator, as is evidenced in 17:15–22; 18:1–15, annunciation of Isaac's election and birth; 21:1–7, birth of Isaac; and 22:1–14, the endangerment of Isaac. At the same time, that claim is not presented to the reader by means of a sustained argument, as if to demonstrate that Isaac is an obvious divine choice or that there is something that the human principals have accomplished that leads God to this choice. In fact, both Abraham and Sarah respond to the divine promise of Isaac with incredulous laughter (17:17; 18:12–13). That the fulfillment of the promise of Isaac is narratively delayed, suspended in the air of chapters dealing, once again, with outsiders (18:16–20:18) again shows their importance for the chosen family.

STORIES RELATING TO ABIMELECH

Once again, an outsider plays a significant role in the development of the narrative, as seen in 20:1–18, interaction of Abraham, Abimelech, and God; and 21:22–34, covenant between Abimelech and Abraham. Abimelech's importance is especially related to his encounter with God, his confrontation with Abraham, his testimony regarding God's presence with Abraham, and Abraham's establishment of a covenant of peace with him.

THE END OF THE OLD AND THE BEGINNING OF THE NEW

The transition for the old to the new is marked by 24:1–67, the search for Rebekah, who succeeds Sarah as matriarch, and her marriage to Isaac (these dimensions of the story signal the beginning of the fulfillment of the promise with respect to Isaac); and 25:1–11, the death and burial of Abraham, yet in the wake of even more progeny.

SOURCE AND TRADITION

As with the book of Genesis generally, the Abrahamic texts are usually seen as a composite, drawn from various sources and edited over the course of many centuries. The classical source-critical consensus spoke primarily of three interwoven sources (Yahwist [J], Elohist [E], Priestly [P]); some texts, such as Genesis 14, were left unassigned. The repeated stories in Genesis 12–25 (outlined above) have provided some clues as to the nature of this editorial process. So, for example, God's establishment of the covenant with Abraham in Genesis 15 has been associated with the Yahwist, while the covenant in Genesis 17:1–8 has been linked to the Priestly source. Or the endangerment of Sarah in 12:10–20 is identified as Yahwistic, while the parallel in 20:1–18 has been associated with the Elohist (cf. also Isaac's endangerment of Rebekah in 26:1–11). These sources were gradually woven together by editors over five hundred years or more, from the United Monarchy (tenth century) to the postexilic era.[5]

The common assumption is that these authors and editors told and retold these stories over the centuries, shaping them to speak to ever new generations of Israelites. So, traditionally, the Yahwist is associated with the concerns of the United Monarchy (David, Solomon), while the Priestly writer has often been understood to address Israel in Babylonian exile.[6] With an increasing concern these days for the final form of the text, efforts have been made to relate the present Pentateuch to the concerns of the Jewish community in the postexilic period.[7] However one resolves these particular hypotheses, it is likely that an ongoing "rolling" body of Abrahamic material was continually supplemented and used again and again to speak to communities of faith over many centuries (like a snowball that picks up additional snow as it rolls down a hill). As such, these texts are hermeneutically layered, with many possible settings in view over time, though they are difficult to sort out.[8]

This long-prevailing consensus regarding source divisions has come under sharp challenge from several perspectives over the last generation in particular. Few scholars doubt that Genesis consists of traditions from various historical periods, but little consensus exists regarding the way in which they were brought together in their present form. From within the source-critical perspective, the nature, scope, and dating of the sources have been regular subjects of debate. For example, difficulties have especially been associated with the Elohistic source, and so it has been common to speak of JE as a composite epic source. Moreover, during the heyday of source criticism, the Priestly source was usually thought to have been worked out in independence from the earlier J and E segments, with distinctive perspectives on Abraham.

In more recent studies, however, P is often understood to be the redactor of the Abrahamic cycle, drawing upon JE and other materials and putting them together essentially as we now have them.[9] This would mean that, while the P sections were the Priestly writer's special contribution, they were shaped with a view to what is now present in the JE sections, and were never intended to stand by themselves. From this perspective, the P understanding of Abraham is to be found only in Genesis 12–25 as a single whole (with a few scattered references in chapters 26–50). The various differences among the sources may then be understood, finally, as internal qualifications. A theologically coherent perspective on the story of Abraham, which the P writer presumably had, is to be found in these fourteen chapters in interaction with one another. In effect, these chapters together become the canonical perspective on the story of Abraham; indeed, given the speculative nature of efforts to discern the original scope and context of the JE material, Genesis 12–25 together constitute the only perspective on Abraham of which we can be certain.[10] The differing theological voices of the tradition, woven together, have become a more sophisticated theological perspective on Abraham and more closely approximate the understanding that Israel, finally, discerned regarding Abraham and his family.

As has been implied above, newer literary approaches have called into question many of the assumptions and conclusions of the source-critical consensus. These newer strategies focus on issues of literary criticism rather than literary history, on the texts as they stand rather than their history prior to their present shape. As a literary entity, the text now exists in its own right and has a life of its own; this approach honors the text as text, with its own internal world that needs attention.[11] The most fundamental task is to examine the amazing variety of the text's literary features to see how they work together to form an organic and coherent whole. Special attention is given to such matters as language and style, surface and deep structures of the text, rhetorical devices, narratological features such as repetition, irony, plot, depiction of characters, and especially point of view (of the narrator and the characters). These newer literary approaches have contributed significantly to our understanding of these texts; finally, however, they should be used in conjunction with other approaches, though just how that should be accomplished has been much debated.[12] We will seek to be attentive to the various literary studies of Abrahamic texts as we move through the volume.

HISTORICAL ISSUES

Historical issues with respect to the Abrahamic narratives are complex.[13] These ancestral stories are narratively placed in the time before Israel's sojourn in Egypt and the Exodus. As noted above, the literary vehicle used in these texts is that of a story of the past; Israel understood these ancestral figures as part of its pre-Exodus heritage. At the same time, the narrators' interests were not those of a modern historian. For example, they were not focused on issues regarding the historicity of these texts, seeking to discern whether or not the events portrayed really happened or to reconstruct a history of this era. It seems clear that these narratives are not a straightforward account of what actually happened in some ancient time and place. They portray matters that would normally not be a part of any public record (Genesis 14 is something of an exception, but is highly enigmatic); rather, they portray the complex relationships of the life of a family in which God is regularly and directly involved. At the same time, Israel, if pressed, would no doubt have stated that these traditions preserved authentic memories of pre-Exodus times and places, and that the men and women in these texts were actual persons. The genealogical materials show some such chronological interest on the part of the narrators, though these details are notoriously difficult to interpret. It seems clear that the Bible does not, finally, tell us very much about the historical context of Genesis 12–25.

Although the ancient writers were not concerned to reconstruct a history of this early era, modern scholars have picked up that interest, working with biblical and extra-biblical data, seeking to discern "what actually happened." This task has been made especially complex by the nature of the texts themselves as well as by the difficulties in assessing the import of extra-biblical parallels.[14] In the late nineteenth century, Julius Wellhausen could say that "we attain to no historical knowledge of the patriarchs." A later stage in Israelite history is reflected in these Genesis texts "like a glorified mirage."[15] A significant shift in historical reflection occurred about a half century ago, when William F. Albright could speak of the "substantial historicity of patriarchal tradition."[16] Though a few scholars still want to make claims comparable to those of Albright,[17] the decades since have seen this assessment shift back toward the pessimism of Wellhausen, especially as a result of the work of Thomas L. Thompson and John van Seters.[18] Ronald Hendel's approach is somewhat softer: "there are some bits of data and historical arguments that show the antiquity of at least some aspects of patriarchal traditions."[19] Citing the names of certain places and persons, he wants to speak of texts where "history and imagination intermingle." But, finally, "We do not know when or if any of these persons ever existed in history."[20]

At the least, scholarly reconstructions of this ancestral period have had mixed results. Various ancient Near Eastern parallels to ancestral names, customs, and modes of life have been overdrawn at times; yet, the parallels may be sufficient to claim that these texts carry some authentic memories of a second millennium setting and that they are not simply a product of ancient imaginations. The historical task remains exceptionally difficult and Abraham and his family remain elusive figures at best (the earliest known possible extra-biblical reference to the name Abraham exists in a tenth century Egyptian text set in the Negeb, a familiar setting for Abraham in the biblical texts). In a general way, it is common to date the time of the ancestors in the first half of the second millennium (2000–1500 B.C.E.).

ABRAHAM AS THE PROGENITOR OF ISRAEL

One particular historical issue relates to the narrative positioning of Abraham as the progenitor of the Israelite people. The matter is complex and disputed. Contrary to the canonical arrangement of Israelite ancestors, Jacob would seem to be the progenitor of Israel rather than Abraham. It is Jacob, not Abraham, who is given the name Israel; it is Jacob who is the "wandering Aramaean" in the historical credo of Deuteronomy 26:5–9. For these and other reasons, it is often thought that Abraham may not have been literally the "father" of all Israelites. Rather, his story was prefaced to the story of Jacob because of his relationship to certain southern tribal groups (later known as Judah; note Abraham's special connections to Hebron, Beersheba, and other southern areas, though he establishes altars across the land: see Gen. 12:6–8). At some point, these groups were integrated into the main Jacob-Joseph tribal association (in the north, later called Israel) and their progenitor was in time given an honored place in the classical genealogical framework. The unification of northern and southern tribal configurations under David and Solomon (ca. 1000–920 B.C.E.) is commonly suggested as a time for such an interweaving of these traditions.[21]

In this plausible reconstruction, Abraham was the literal progenitor of only some of the tribes that constituted the Israelite people. The construction of the Abraham-Isaac-Jacob genealogical framework, then, enables the major tribal groups that made up the Israelite peoples to be related to a single ancestral heritage (compare the way in which, say, the pilgrims and practices such as Thanksgiving function similarly for Americans). This literary and cultural linkage of ancestral figures, while not literally genealogical, does recognize the complex roots of Israel's foundations and stakes a claim with respect to the continuity of their various historical experiences and their faith in the same God.

"The remembered past is not merely a glorified projection of the present, but a conflation of past and present in which history, folklore, and ethnic self-fashioning are thoroughly entangled. . . . The present and the future are built into the structures of the past, and hence its memory is both familiar and compelling."[22]

ABRAHAM PREFIGURES ISRAEL'S HISTORY

While the effort to track the origins and development of the Abrahamic narratives has often been pursued with larger bodies of texts (such as J or P),[23] such work has also been pursued at the level of individual texts. And so, for example, the three texts that speak of the endangering of Sarah/Rebekah (12:10–20; 20:1–8; 26:1–11) have been closely studied with an effort to determine how they might be related to one another.[24] Such efforts have not brought agreement on their relationship nor borne significant fruit in helping to unpack the texts in their present context.

From another angle, it has been common to observe that several of the stories in the Abraham cycle have significant parallels in other Old Testament texts, especially the book of Exodus (see below for detail). Many of the stories in Genesis 12–25 adumbrate Israel's story. Indeed, the overall structure of Israel's history may provide a grid to which the various Abrahamic stories are related, so that the flow of thought in the Abrahamic story parallels the flow of the history of Israel. Those responsible for transmitting the Abrahamic stories have certainly integrated these links at some point in the history of these traditions, though it is not clear when and how this development took place.[25] This is a major task; we only point out a few of these links.

Abraham's journey to Egypt (12:10–20), departure therefrom, exchange with Lot, and the conflict in the land of promise (Gen. 12:10–14:24) has many parallels with Israel's later journey to and from Egypt and initial settlement in the land.[26]

- Abraham goes down to Egypt because of famine (cf. 42:1–5; 43:1, 15; 47:4, 13). To "sojourn (*gûr*)" (12:10) is also used for the later descent into Egypt (47:4). In 26:1–3 God tells Isaac not to go down to Egypt and sojourn there. Is it not yet the appropriate time?
- Egypt is both life threatening and life enhancing.
- The use of a ruse (12:11; Exod. 5:1–3).
- Sarai, like Moses, is taken into Pharaoh's house.
- Conflict with Pharaoh.
- Plagues on Egypt (*nega*ʿ; cf. Exod. 11:1).
- Enrichment/despoiling in Egypt, with belongings listed in detail, enabled by the Egyptians (12:16; cf. Exod. 12:35–38).
- "Take and go" (*lāqāh; hālak*; 12:19 and Exod. 12:32).
- Let Abraham/Israel go (12:20 with Exod. 11:1, 10; 12:33; *šālaḥ*); "go up" from Egypt (ʿ*ālāh*; 13:1 with Exod. 12:38; 13:18). Also to be noted are the parallels between Abraham being "brought out" of Ur of the Chaldeans by God (*yāṣāʾ*;15:7) and God bringing Israel out of Egypt (12:17, 42, 51).

- Abraham's journeying in "stages" toward the promised land mirrors Israel's wilderness wanderings (13:3; Exod. 17:1; Num. 10:12).
- Lot's being "with him" with "flocks and herds" (13:5; cf. Exod. 12:38).
- Lot compares the Jordan valley to "the land of Egypt" (13:10) as do the Israelites during the wilderness murmurings (Exod. 16:3).
- The strife between the herders of Lot and Abraham (merîbâh, 13:8) also is characteristic of the Israelites during their wanderings (Exod. 17:7; Num. 27:14). Israel encounters the descendants of Lot along the way (Deut. 2:9–19).
- Looking out over the land of promise (13:14–15) finds parallels with Moses (Deut. 3:27).
- The repetition of the promises of land (13:14–18) anticipate the situation after the next Egyptian sojourn. Generally, the promises are repeated over the course of chapters 12–25 to assure readers from later generations, perhaps especially exiles, that the promises of God still stand, no matter the experience.

Anticipations of the period of the conquest and the judges (and beyond) are also evident in Abraham's life. The theme of strife in Genesis 13 and the references to Bethel and Ai (Gen. 13:3) and to Canaanites (12:6; 13:7) recall the early narratives in Joshua. The violence of Genesis 14 is also a part of a larger pattern wherein Abraham is seen to mirror the early history of Israel in his own life, especially the conquest of the land, the period of the judges, and the Davidic Empire. The six peoples listed in 14:5–7 (from the region around the Pentapolis of 14:2, 8) are among those encountered by Israel on its journey to Canaan. For the four kings (14:1, 9)—representing the world powers known from that era—to have conquered these peoples means gaining control of routes and lands that are integral to Israel's later move into the promised land. Abraham, in conquering the kings, not only frees the peoples there, but clears that region of powerful outside forces. More basically, Abraham, as military leader in the same area with respect to many of the same peoples, prefigures later Israel. In effect, Abraham takes over the promised land by conquest.

There is a formal similarity of the story in Genesis 14 with those of the judges. In this way Abraham is identified as a savior figure for Israel. Continuities with the Gideon story are especially strong. The three hundred men of Gideon (Judg. 7:7) face a situation not unlike that encountered by Abraham's 318 men, and the liberating effect is comparable. Moreover, the link between Abraham and Melchizedek (Gen. 14:18–20) anticipates later relationships between David and the Jebusites of Jerusalem (Ps. 110; 2 Sam. 5:6–10); compare also David's campaign against the Amalekites (1 Sam. 30).

The fact that the covenant now follows in Genesis 15 is certainly not fortuitous. The way in which the covenant is addressed parallels the covenant with David.

God chooses Abraham (12:1–3); God chooses David (1 Sam. 16). God saves Abraham from Egypt (12:10–20); God saves David from his enemies (2 Sam 5:24–25; 7:1). Abraham worships God (12:7–8; 13:18); David worships God (2 Sam. 6:15–17). God establishes the covenant with both (15:18; 2 Sam. 7). The consistent order is this: election, deliverance, faith/worship, and covenant. God's choosing and saving actions constitute the foundation of the covenant; God establishes the covenant with those who have faith, evidenced not least in worship. The covenant does not establish the relationship; it becomes a moment where God formally obligates himself to promises spoken to faithful ones. The covenant with Abraham prefigures the covenant with David, with whom God's promises to Abraham find a renewed realization. Abraham's own history parallels that of David.[27] There is a sense in which it is appropriate to speak of David as a new Abraham.

Ties with the Exodus events are also evident in the stories of Hagar and Ishmael. Certainly it is not an accident that the language used for Sarai's (and tacitly Abraham's) mistreatment of Hagar ('ānāh, 16:6; affirmed by God's echo of this language in 16:11) is also used to speak of Israel's oppression by Egyptians (Gen. 15:13; Exod. 1:11–12) and in commandments binding on Israel (Exod. 22:21–22). Given the prefiguring concerns played out in Genesis 12–15, Genesis 16 may reflect how the Israelites, or any peoples who have been delivered, can quickly turn to a denial of their own history.

The story of Sodom and Gomorrah also has links to the Exodus: the outcry of the oppressed, the environmental disasters (plagues), the fate of the Egyptians, and Israel being brought out (yāṣā'; like Lot, 19:16).[28] Another parallel is the Sodomlike encounter in Judges 19:22–30, a text heavily dependent upon Genesis 19.[29] In the latter text, the sexual abuse comes from Israelites, not foreigners. While the inhospitable mistreatment of others in the two stories has similar components, the focus in Genesis on divine judgment through a natural disaster and the preservation of a remnant push the story in somewhat different directions.

This story probably also has links to the disaster that befell Jerusalem at the hands of the Babylonians in 587 B.C.E. The dialogue between Abraham and God with respect to saving the cities of Sodom and Gomorrah because of the number of righteous within it (18:16–33) might be related to questions raised in the wake of the fall of Jerusalem. Why would God, in effect, condemn the righteous in order to pass judgment on the wicked? Should not the righteous in the city mean that God would save the city for their sake? Jeremiah is asked by God to search Jerusalem to find even one such righteous person (Jer. 5:1).

Comparable parallels to the fall of Jerusalem and the exile are suggested by the story of the binding of Isaac (22:1–19). Faithful Israelites, like Abraham, have been put to the test in midst of a judgment that has killed many of their children. With the loss of so many children, is there a future for Israel? What happens to

God's promise to Abraham if that happens? It is as real a question for this later generation of Israelites as it was for Abraham. To have God's promises so regularly punctuate the Genesis narrative would have been important for an exilic audience, so tempted to despair (cf. Isa. 49:14). It is striking that the promises to Abraham—land, nationhood, name, descendants, presence—are so attuned to the exiles' future as a people. That "descendants" are referred to thirteen times in Genesis 17 alone would not be missed. Like Abraham, they would be living short of fulfill-ment; but promises generate hope in God's possibilities. The key would be their trust in the God who keeps promises. Once again, such parallels with their asso-ciated questions suggest that the Abrahamic narratives at times have been edited with a view to later events in Israel's history.

Finally, God's "bringing out" Abraham from one land to another (15:7) prefig-ures more than Exodus. Similar language is used by the prophets to speak of a new bringing out of Israel by God (Jer. 16:14–15; 23:7–8; Ezek. 34:13). Abraham pre-figures the return of the exiles from that same far country to the land promised them. The specification of boundaries in Genesis 15:18–21 proclaims to exiles that the promises of God with respect to this expanse of land are still in place (cf. Lev. 26:44–45).

The story of Abraham is portrayed so as to prefigure the story of Israel. Abra-ham is the father of Israel in more than a genealogical sense; Israel's story plays out Abraham's story one more time. What Abraham does, his descendants do; he anticipates Israel's history in his own life.[30]

THE RELIGION OF ABRAHAM AND THE ANCESTORS

One dimension of these texts often cited in this discussion is the nature of the reli-gion of the patriarchs.[31] The religious (and other) expressions of these chapters are often distinctive from later Israelite practices.[32] From this it seems clear that later Israelites in retelling these stories did not simply read their own religious lives back into these texts. At the same time, the perspectives of these later tradents is certainly reflected in these texts; this may be evident in that nothing in these texts seems to be theologically incompatible with the later faith of Israel. One apparent memory of worship practices from pre-Exodus times includes refer-ences to the worship of God under various forms of the name El (El Elyon, El Shaddai, El Olam, El Bethel), referred to as the God of my/our/your father(s), the God of Abraham, the God of Isaac, and the God of Jacob (Gen. 16:13; 21:33; 33:20; El is the name of the high god in the Canaanite pantheon, and the generic term for deity).

Some traditions understand Yahweh as a name for God revealed only at the time of Moses (Exod. 3:14, 16; 6:2–3) and that El was an earlier name for God. The ancestral texts, however, generally understand El to be an alternate name or epithet for Yahweh. For example, Abraham understands Melchizedek's "God Most High (El Elyon)" to be identified with Yahweh (14:18–22). Or Hagar responds to "the Lord" (Yahweh) who had given heed to her affliction (16:11) with the new name, El Roi (16:13; cf. 17:1, Yahweh with El Shaddai). The likely suggestion is that the presence of the name Yahweh in these texts reflects the later retelling of the stories of Abraham in Yahwistic terms.[33] Hence, the frequent use of Yahweh in Genesis is anachronistic in some ways, but it conveys an important theological conviction: the God whom the family of Abraham worshiped under the name El is to be identified with the God worshiped later under the name Yahweh. The revelation of the name Yahweh to Moses meant a genuine advancement in the understanding of God that the ancestors had, but at the same time manifested considerable continuity thereto and without significant contradiction.

This ancestral God was understood to be a personal deity who accompanied this family on its journeys, providing care and protection. The conversations between God and the members of this family are described in terms that would be characteristic of everyday personal interactions (see, for example, the discussion between Abraham and God over the future of Sodom and Gomorrah, 18:23–32). The personal nature of this God-family relationship is evident also in the almost complete absence of religious institutions independent of family life—for example, no temple, priesthood, sacrificial system, Sabbath keeping, or dietary regulations (all important for later Israel at one time or another). The Genesis texts exhibit no concern whatsoever that Abraham, the founder of Israelite faith, is so nonobservant regarding such practices.

A closer look at 12:4–9 is illustrative. Worship is obviously an integral part of Abraham's life; his worshipful activity presupposes practices in place before his call. His journey through the land seems not to be associated with the founding of sanctuaries, but, rather, building altars at known sacred places (without personnel or buildings), marked by trees (12:6–7; 13:18; 21:33; cf. 35:4; Moreh is probably a well-known site), pillars, or stones (28:18, 22). The later association of these natural markers with idolatry (cf. Exod. 23:24; 34:13; Deut. 12:2; 16:21) is not evident in these texts. Abraham's altar building is part of a personal and familial act of worship, probably with sacrificial acts (cf. 8:20; 22:13). These acts of worship seem to be expressions of gratitude to God for the promise (each is built "to the Lord," cf. 13:18). "Invoking the name of Yahweh" (cf. 4:26; 13:4; 26:25) refers to worship generally. These forms of worship, then, are on the move, not tied down to priests or sanctuaries, and integrated with daily life. The altar also functions as a marker that continues to exist beyond Abraham's presence, perhaps a public sign of God's promise of land. Abraham's journey is paradigmatic for that made by Jacob in Genesis 35, including attention to trees and altars.

Moreover, strikingly, given the divine strategy of which we have spoken, Abraham has no special concern for introducing the content of the faith to outsiders. Religious life consists basically of this God and this family, though the creational dimensions of which we have spoken are evident. It is not that God's activity was considered limited to this family, but that is the focus. Worship practices are evident, but they are practiced independent of existing (Canaanite) shrines and they revolved around the particular needs of the family, with the patriarch undertaking whatever priestly responsibilities might be called for (for example, building an altar; sacrificing; praying; blessing; tithing; see 12:7–8; 13:4, 18). In the one instance where Abraham does engage in such worship activity (the covenant-making ritual in Gen. 15:7–21), it is God who gives the instructions (Jer. 34 indicates that this ritual was a practice familiar to at least Israelites of a later time). The one reference to prophecy (20:7) is used, not to lift up Abraham in a critical role against religious practice, but for purposes of intercessory prayer on behalf of outsiders.

Notably, as we have seen, these texts assume that "outsiders" have knowledge of God and no distinction is drawn between their God and that of Israel's ancestors; or at least their understanding of God does not come under criticism. The legitimacy of the worship of non-Israelite individuals is at least implicitly acknowledged (see, for example, Mechizedek, Gen. 14:18–20). Moberly speaks of "the ritual simplicity and 'ecumenical' openness" of the religion of the ancestors.[34] Remarkably, no signs of idolatrous practice are evident among the outsiders, and hence no related criticism; the one text in Genesis that raises issues of idolatry seems to confine the matter to insiders (35:2–4), and they are not said to have been influenced by outsiders. At the same time, it is made clear that some residents of the land were grave sinners, and, finally, deserving of destruction (13:13; 15:16). Notably, only one other text understands that the religion of the ancestors was originally idolatrous (Josh. 24:14), and that before the journey to Canaan in Genesis 12; such a perspective plays no role in the Genesis presentation of Abraham and his family (contrast the Quranic presentation of Abraham, where the patriarch's monotheism is sharply on display).[35]

If the religious life evident in these texts constitutes at least in part an early form of the relationship with God that continues into Israel's later life, this perspective and practice might have contributed to its highly personal and relational character. Aspects of this continuity might include the prominent use of familial images for the God-people relationship and a continued focus on the family in contrast to, say, the state or religious institutions.[36]

CHAPTER 3

ABRAHAM

RECIPIENT OF PROMISES

12:1–9; 13:14–17; 15:1–21; 17:1–21; 22:15–18.

D ivine promises are one of the most remarkable dimensions of the Abraham narrative. They occur in almost every chapter (they continue throughout Genesis, but are less prominent in chapters 25–50).[1] The call of Abraham sets this promissory tone and direction in place (see below) and the narrator returns to it again and again. Most of the promises are spoken directly by God, in the first person. The majority of the promises are spoken to Abraham; two are spoken to Hagar. It is instructive to list these divine promises; they give an excellent sense for the prominence of this particular divine word in the story of Abraham and his family:

Genesis 12:1–3—Blessing, nation, name. Blessing of those who bless Israel.

Genesis 12:7—land

Genesis 13:14–17—land, numerous offspring

Genesis 15:1—Your reward shall be very great.

Genesis 15:4–5—heir, numerous descendants

Genesis 15:7, 18–21—land

Genesis 15:13–16—Israel will be brought out of Egypt (which will be judged) and brought into Canaan, and Abraham will die in peace at an old age.

(to Hagar) Genesis 16:10–12—She will give birth to a son and will have numerous offspring.

Genesis 17:2–8—numerous offspring, land, God will be God to them.

(regarding Sarah) Genesis 17:16—blessing, son, numerous offspring, multitude of nations, kings.

(regarding Isaac) Genesis 17:19, 21—covenant as an everlasting covenant

(regarding Ishmael) Genesis 17:20—fruitful, exceedingly numerous, twelve princes, great nation

(regarding Sarah) Genesis 18:14—have a son

Genesis 18:18–19—great and mighty nation, all nations blessed through him

(regarding Ishmael) Genesis 21:13—great nation

(to Hagar) Genesis 21:18—great nation

Genesis 22:15–18—blessing, numerous descendants, possession of gates of their enemies, other nations gain blessing

Genesis 24:7—land

It becomes clear from such an extensive listing that God's promises play a central role in the story. Indeed, without these promises, the story would be something quite other than what it is. The promises are spoken about several people, including chosen as well as nonchosen (Ishmael). The promises focus on several themes (descendants, name, nation[s], kings, blessing) and the promises for chosen and nonchosen are remarkably similar. Covenant language distinguishes the promises for the line of Isaac from that of Ishmael. The promises are unilaterally declared by God, with no prior conditions stipulated (for example, the character or moral stature of the recipient). God makes the decision to make these promises as a strategy in the service of a universal purpose, and we are not told why God chooses Abraham rather than someone else.[2]

The promises spoken by God have creative capacity; they generate the power to respond positively to the command. The promises are also stated in unconditional terms throughout, though more sharply in some contexts (for example, the promises to Hagar; the promises in Genesis 15). To speak of unconditional promises is not to claim that human response is irrelevant, but God's word of promise does generate that response, so that the human party cannot claim an innate capacity to come into a relationship with God. At the same time, while faith is a divine gift, the word from God is resistible, though God does not roll over at the first sign of resistance; a divine persistence to "hang in there" with this family through thick and thin is basic to the nature of this relationship (cf. Moses in Exod. 3–6). Even in the face of continued resistance, it is important to state that God's promises will never be taken back; they will never be made null and void as far as God is concerned. People can remove themselves from the established relationship and its sphere of promise and fulfillment, a move that God may honor. But, when the textual claim is made that the promise is "everlasting" (17:1–8), it means that those who believe can absolutely rely on the promises and know with certainty that God will ever be at work to fulfill them on their behalf. God so commits the divine self to these promises that, even in the wake of massive Israelite idolatry, Moses can appeal to them as still binding for God (Exod. 32:13).[3]

Initially we take a literary-theological look at the call of Abraham (Gen. 12:1–9) and then move to the two covenant chapters (15; 17).

12:1–9: CALLED BY GOD WITH PROMISES

God's speaking, in particular God's articulation of a command accompanied by promises, constitutes the generative event of the story of Abraham. Everything in Abraham's story follows from God's word to him in 12:1–3. Without those divine words, there would be no preserved story of Abraham, or at least no story as we know it. At the same time, Abraham's trusting response to God's word also decisively shapes the story that follows. A comparable rhythm of divine word and faithful human response is also evident in 15:1–21 and 17:1–27. This rhythm provides the focus for the story of Abraham in a way no other aspect of the story does. We will take a look here at the primary contexts in which this rhythm is evident.

The genealogical and geographical notes in 11:27–32 introduce the call of Abraham in 12:1–3, and anchor Abraham in the story of the nations in Genesis 1–11. Abraham and his family do not come onto the world scene out of the blue; they have deep familial connections to all the nations of the world. Even more, this family is linked thereby to God's cosmic purposes and activity. The God who – speaks to Abraham in 12:1 is not even introduced; it is assumed that this is the God who created the world and who has been engaged in the life of all peoples of the world in the previous chapters.

Genesis 11:27–32 also helps readers respond to an oft-asked question: How is it that Abraham responds so positively and without hesitation to a life-changing command from God (12:4)? Moses' response (Exod. 3–6) seems so much more realistic. Indeed, Abraham even has to assume that the command comes from God (though the narrator does tell the reader). This silence may indicate that verses 1–3 are the narrator's summary of the call rather than an actual report thereof.

These introductory verses inform readers that, when the call came to Abraham in Haran (in southeastern Turkey), he and his family had originally begun a journey to Canaan from their home in "Ur of the Chaldeans" (11:31; probably the ancient Babylonian center south of modern Baghdad). They had settled in Haran, however, for reasons unspecified. Abraham's immediate response to God's call may assume that he understood this to be the continuance of a journey that was originally intended to go all the way to Canaan. Indeed, Abraham may have had a sense that the call of God was somehow behind the initial move of his family to Canaan , (as 15:7 suggests; cf. Acts 7:2–4). At the end of chapter 11, the reader is left with Terah's death, his uncompleted journey to Canaan, the death of one of his sons, the barrenness of Abraham's wife Sarai, and an orphaned grandson (Lot). Hence, the word of God (12:1–3) enters into a point of great uncertainty for the future of this family. Readers may wonder whether the father's death (11:32), always a disruptive event in a family's life, may have prompted such an openness in Abraham to move on. Parallels between 11:31 and 12:5 show that Abraham completes the journey begun by his father Terah.[4]

    11:31 a. Terah took Abraham . . . and Lot . . . and Sarai . . .
           b. and they went forth . . . to go to the land of Canaan
           c. and they came to Haran and settled there.
    12:5   a. Abraham took Sarai . . . and Lot . . .
           b. and they went forth to go to the land of Canaan
           c. and they came to the land of Canaan.

These parallels show that Abraham's move was not a total break from the past, but continues a journey already begun. God explicitly enters into the picture in the midst of a journey that has been begun and halted, but certainly God has been present in this family's life from the beginnings of their journey from Ur (as God claims in 15:7).[5] Abraham's "going forth to a new life is not to be explained only in terms of God's action, nor only in terms of human social aims and values and scripts, but in terms of their mysterious interaction. The similarity between Terah's agenda and Yahweh's call of Abraham suggests that God works in and with the forces and circumstances of human life."[6]

At the same time, God's extensive promises to him in 12:2–3 were certainly the most critical factor in generating his trusting responsiveness. Indeed, no other motivation is stated besides the efficacy of the word of God in his life. God's command in 12:1 does not stand independent of the promises that follow in 12:2–3. That is, God's word of promise creates Abraham's trusting response (as God's promises in 15:1–5 will create his faithful response in 15:6). In other words, Abraham's obedience is not a "naked" obedience, dependent only upon his internal resources. The promises from God are the decisive reality in engendering the trust needed to obey the command. It was certainly possible for Abraham to resist God's word, but it is not possible to know what steps God would have taken had Abraham not trusted God enough to leave (cf. Moses in Exod. 3–6).

This time Abraham leaves all but his immediate family (including his nephew Lot)[7] behind in Haran. The barrenness of Sarai, so prominently stated at this point (11:30), will become a central theme for the story that follows, as will Abraham's relationship with Lot, whose enigmatic place in this family is explored at key points (chapters 13–14, 18–19). Links with the family in Haran continue through the story of Abraham (22:20–24; 24) and Jacob (27:43–28:7; 29–31), as both Isaac and Jacob return to marry members of their family (Rebekah; Rachel).

As we have seen, Genesis 12:1–3 are universally considered to provide the key, not only for the story of Abraham, but for the rest of Genesis; indeed, the references to "great" name and nation also anticipate Israel's later history as a people. It is a fulcrum text, thoroughly theological in focus, especially written to link chapters 1–11 ("all the families of the earth") with the stories of Abraham and his family that now follows. Abraham is here showered with promises, the fulfillment of which he will only begin to see; yet his response will shape a future beyond his own life (26:4–5, 24). These promises are brought into play in the following narratives again and again in various formulations, with the implied themes of descendants and land made more specific; further imperatives will also play a role (17:1; 22:1).

The words from God include both command and promise; the promises are the central word, not least because they will enable the fulfillment of the commands. The passage may be outlined as follows:

12:1—*Call and command.* God appears without introduction and commands Abraham to leave—in increasing levels of intimacy—his country, his clan, and his home in order to journey to a land God will reveal to him (cf. 22:1–2). Verse 4a reports Abraham's positive response to the divine directive.

12:2—*Promises, with a concluding challenge.* This verse consists of a series of three cohortatives that express with emphasis the intention of the divine speaker with respect to Abraham and his family. God will (note the recurrent "I"): make Abraham a great nation, bless him, and make his name great (notably, while these promises assume a land, the actual promise of land does not occur until 12:7, when Abraham is actually on the land). The initial placement of the promise of "a great nation" may signal a central interest; this is in essence the promise of a new community that will be blessed and given a new name. This promise moves beyond Abraham as an individual and brings Israel as a nation-people (*gôy*) into view. To speak of a promise of blessing is not to anticipate a one-time future event, but an ongoing reality for the future of Abraham's descendants. Sometimes, interpreters will speak of covenant in connection with these promises, but covenant, which is a formalization of promises made, will not take place until Genesis 15 and 17 (see below).

The imperative in 12:2b could express either result or intention ("so that [and] you will be a blessing") or retain its imperatival sense ("[you are to] be a blessing"). In either case, it indicates that God's fulfillment of the three prior promises will enable Israel's life to take the shape of blessing in the world. The "other" is in view here: Abraham and his descendants will be a blessing to others. This clause is also preliminary to the language of blessing in 12:3.

How these promises are to be related to Sarai's barrenness (11:30) sets up a key issue for the narrative that follows, though the promises at this point do not necessarily involve Sarai in the fulfillment. Lot possibly could come to mind for Abraham, but God's promises are so open-ended that the point seems to be the absence of calculation on Abraham's part and his simple trust that God will find a way (Abraham's first concern about heirs is expressed in 15:2).

12:3—*The gift, threat, and challenge of the outsider.* This verse, while it initially continues with God as the subject of the promise, actually introduces a new direction of thought related to the outsider. To encounter the outsider may mean that Abraham's family will be blessed ("those who bless you"), that they will be cursed ("the one who curses you"), and that they present a challenge ("through you shall all the families of the earth be blessed").

God's promise that "those who bless you" will in turn be blessed is a promise for those outside the chosen community; the promise is related to Abraham and his family only indirectly. Notably, as we have seen,[8] the nonchosen have the power and the gifts to bless the chosen, and God here anticipates that kind of future for Israel (for example, the Egyptian pharaoh and the king-priest

Melchizedek, 12:16; 14:18–20). Those who treat Israel in life-giving and life-sustaining ways here receive a promise of blessing from God. In other words, the
"outsiders" are encompassed within the promises of God from the beginning—
before Israel blesses them.

The phrase, "the one who curses you I will curse," makes two shifts, to the singular and to an imperfect verb. This language is not another free-standing promise, but a note on the previous promise, namely, that should any person (the
subject is singular) treat Israel with contempt they will reap the consequences of
their deed (Deut. 7:9–10; 5:9–10). To put the matter positively, part of Israel's
blessing is that they will be protected (though certainly not in any absolute sense)
from those who mistreat them. Cursing is not a divine objective of the same order
as the others; but is conditional on the mistreatment of Abraham and his descendants. The first word for curse (*qll*) has reference to any form of mistreatment, the
second ('*rr*) refers to the divine mediation of the consequences of such behaviors.
In Genesis 16:4–5, Hagar will show contempt (*qll*) to Sarah and God will respond
by commanding Hagar to return to Sarah rather than exacting the curse.

Genesis 12:3b shifts to the perfect tense, and "families" is the subject of the
verb (outsiders are once again in view). The translation is difficult; passive, reflexive, or middle translations are possible. For example, New Revised Standard Version (NRSV) has changed the Revised Standard Version (RSV) reflexive ("shall
bless themselves") to the passive ("shall be blessed"; so also New International
Version [NIV]), as in the other texts where that form of the verb is used (Niphal;
18:18; 28:14). The reflexive translation makes Israel's role less active, namely,
Abraham's blessing will become so commonplace that people will bless themselves
by invoking his name or by desiring to be so blessed (48:20).[9] It is, in effect, a
promise of recognition by the nations of the earth that the descendants of Abraham have been blessed by God. When the Hithpael (reflexive; middle) form is
used, the NRSV shifts to the middle voice (the response of the other is more in
play), "gain blessing for themselves" through Abraham's offspring (22:18; 26:4).
Whatever the translation, and the issue seems to be undecideable, the blessing
received by Abraham has the objective of being extended to all the families of the
earth. Westermann (who prefers the reflexive translation) agrees: "God's action
proclaimed in the promise to Abraham is not limited to him and his posterity, but
reaches its goal only when it includes all the families of the earth."[10]

The final phrase in 12:3b represents the objective of all the previous clauses.
God's choice of Abraham will lead to blessings for all the families (note the corporate focus) of the earth. God's choice of Abraham is an initially exclusive move for
the sake of a maximally inclusive end. Election is for mission (in the broadest
sense of the term).[11]

Genesis 12:4b–9 report Abraham's silent, but active and positive response to
God's call, reviewing his travels to and through the land he has been shown (by

unknown means). During this journey, he is accompanied by God, builds altars, and worships God. Abraham's faithful and worshipful response is thus given emphasis at the onset of the story, and to that theme the narrator will often return. Indeed, Abraham's fidelity will be seen to be important for the shape that God's promised future takes (22:16–18; 26:4–5, 24). God's promises in 12:1–3 are not left floating above the life experience of the recipient, for when Abraham reaches Canaan, God informs him that this land will be given to his descendants. New promises of God emerge in view of new times and places and are directly related to the life situation of the recipient (cf. 15:2–5). The reference to the Canaanites (12:6; 13:7) is commonly considered an anachronism, but it is probably a generic term for all pre-Israelite inhabitants of the land (cf. 15:19–21). Given the basically positive view of Canaanites in Genesis (though see 15:16), this reference probably pertains more to 12:3b than to later problems; at this point the future seems open-ended.

That Abraham trusts the promise and moves from Haran to Canaan will certainly mean a new level of meaning and life for him and his family. But it is also the case that the God who commands and promises will be forever changed as well. Having made promises, God can be counted on to be faithful to promises made. And so this means that God will be committed to a future with the one who has faithfully responded. The issue presented by the narrative is now not only a matter of human faithfulness, but one of divine faithfulness to specific promises. And so God will never be the same again. By the divine word, God has created a new family for both Abraham and God. This action creates for both participants a new world and a revised way of being in that world.

THE COVENANT IN GENESIS 15

Genesis 15 narrates the first recorded dialogue between God and Abraham. Strikingly, Abraham's only words to God are questions—regarding offspring and land—and they come in response to divine promises. The chapter has two segments (15:1–6, 7–21), which have similar structures: divine promise (verses 1, 7), Abraham's questioning (verses 2–3, 8), and God's response with reassuring words and deeds (verses 4–5, 9–21). The phrase, "the word of the Lord came" (verses 1, 4), so common in the prophets, occurs only here in the Pentateuch (cf. Abraham as prophet in 20:7) and, together with its visionary context, gives to the promises a special status. The first biblical instance of prophetic language has to do with promise, not with critique and judgment.[12]

The divine promise in 15:1 is God's response to Abraham's actions in chapter 14 and confirms the judgment of Melchizedek.[13] Abraham had refused any spoils, but God, Abraham's shield (as in "deliverer," 14:20), now sees to Abraham's "reward" in recognition of Abraham's faithful action on behalf of others, including the king and people of Jerusalem.[14] The uncertain nature of God's promise of reward prompts Abraham's question in 15:2–3: "What good will spoils be, if I cannot pass them on to my children?" Abraham's repeated concern turns the issue to a promise that remains unfulfilled, namely, God's promise of offspring (12:7; 13:15–16). The issue is not whether there will be an heir (Eliezer of Damascus—a difficult Hebrew phrase—could be adopted), but whether the heir will be from Abraham's own line, a matter of great importance in that culture. God had promised "seed," not simply "heir."

God speaks directly to Abraham's concerns, with "heir" repeated and word order designed to emphasize the point. No, Eliezer will not be your heir. Yes, one whom you father will be your heir; indeed, your "seed" will be as numerous as the stars in the sky. The reference to the stars is a rhetorical move to make a point about the promise in the face of his questions: God keeps promises. The image of the stars does not center on issues of power, but on stability and, repeatedly, on sheer numbers. This rhetorical shift from dust (13:16) to stars also suggests stability and perhaps security (Jer. 33:20–26 for its use for David's offspring; cf. 31:35–37).

Unlike Abraham's questioning response to God's promise in verse 1, Abraham now believes God.[15] That is, Abraham rests back in the arms of the one who has given the promise, trusting that God's word is good and true without having any concrete evidence that God's promise would come to pass (Heb. 11:1, 8–12).[16] Abraham's faith has been enabled by what God has just said; indeed, God's word has created Abraham's faith. Abraham's faith has not been generated from within himself or through his own resources. More specifically, this faith-event occurs because God particularizes the promise for Abraham by addressing the specific situation opened up by Abraham's question. Abraham has expressed some very particular needs having to do with the future of his family, and God responds directly to those questions. Not just any word from God will do; interestingly, the promise of verse 1 did not issue in a statement about Abraham's faith. God has now put the promise in relation to the need, and in a particular rhetorical fashion. The promises of God are so spoken that Abraham comes to believe that there is nothing so difficult in the present circumstance that will prevent God from seeing the promises through to completion.

Abraham's faith was "reckoned to him as righteousness." Or so it has most commonly been interpreted (including the New Testament, Gal. 3:6–9; Heb. 11:8–12).[17] But it is possible, in view of the indefinite reference of "he" (see NRSV footnote), that the "he" is Abraham rather than the Lord and that Abraham believes that God is righteous. The verb "reckon" likely has a cultic background wherein the priest formally declares that a gift has been properly offered (Lev. 7:18; 17:4).[18] In response to Abraham's faith, God in effect functions as a priest and formally declares that Abraham is righteous (cf. Ps. 106:31). Righteousness (*tsedeqāh*) often has reference to the doing of justice to a relationship in which one already stands (cf. 18:19; 38:26); but in this context, righteous is what Abraham becomes by virtue of God's declaration in view of his faith. God declares that the God-Abraham relationship is "right," that is, in good order.[19] Given such a divine evaluation, God makes clear that the faithfulness of human beings is of central importance. At the same time, what Abraham says and does in the wake of this divine reckoning is not a matter of indifference to God, though God's promises will not be compromised.

Abraham proceeds to request a sign, that is, some concrete indication that God's promise of land shall become a reality (15:8). The reader may well ask: what has happened to the faith of Abraham, so amply evident in 15:6? Should faith be seeking signs? It becomes evident here and in the larger narrative (see, for example, 18:23–33) that believing and questions do not necessarily stand over against one another (Exod. 3:11–12). It is not unnatural to faith, or unbecoming to believers, that their questions persist in the midst of belief. Indeed, given the just-announced declaration of righteousness, Abraham's questioning is seen to be not only appropriate, but characteristic of a person of faith.

While Abraham's question in 15:2 had focused on God's giving, this question focuses on Abraham's knowing. That God responds directly to this new issue of knowing is clear from the language of verse 13: "*Know* this for certain" (cf. 24:14). A key point: Abraham's knowing will come not only from what God says, but also from what God now does. God's response to Abraham's question is a rite, in the preparation for which Abraham is engaged. Abraham will "know this for certain" because *God,* rather than the usual human being, goes through the rite and submits the divine self to its terms. While extra-biblical parallels to some of the details exist,[20] the only other biblical reference to the rite is Jeremiah 34:18–20, where participants in a covenant walk between dead and divided animals and thereby invoke death upon themselves should they be unfaithful to obligations they have assumed. This rite was established for the formalization of a solemn oath or promise, which is what "making a covenant" entails in this context (verse 18); this covenant is a life and death matter. God's promise is presented as a ritual event in which God participates, involving both God's word and God's deed; the entire rite constitutes a divine answer to Abraham's question.[21]

Abraham falls into a deep sleep, and all is dark and foreboding (Job 4:12–16), perhaps to shroud what God does. The effect for Abraham is a seeing and a knowing, which penetrates to the deepest recesses of Abraham's being. God, whose presence is symbolized by the smoke and fire, actually passes through the divided animals (verse 17). In this act of self-imprecation, God in effect puts the divine life on the line, "writing" the promise in blood.[22] God alone participates in the ritual, indicating the unilateral character of the promise. The only obligation in this covenant is what God takes upon the divine self (royal grants in the ancient Near East are a possible parallel).[23] In the midst of this ritual, God speaks a word about the future, for Abraham personally (verse 15) and for his descendants (verses 13–14, 16). Then, in conjunction with God's passing through the divided animals (verse 17), God proclaims an unconditional promise to which God is absolutely committed (verses 18–21): life on a land they can call their own. God's word is as good as God is. This announcement is prefaced by reference to a long delay (400 years) before the fulfillment (verse 16b). The sins of the Amorites (Canaanites) will not have "yet reached its full measure"; that is, it takes time for sins to have their full effects (Exod. 20:5; note the reference to the fourth generation).[24] The story of God's people during those four centuries will be such that they will have to live with God's promises through dark and complex times. Abraham receives no immediate fixes, no instant gratification; the faithful often have to live with delay.

A few words about covenant may be helpful at this point. The covenant in this text bears close similarities to the covenants with Noah (9:10–17; 6:9) and David (2 Sam. 23:5; 7:8–17) in terms of stability, eternality and unconditionality. In all these cases, God establishes the covenant with one who has faith (15:6). In this context, covenant means a promise under oath, solemnly sworn, not an agreement or contract, and the making (literally, "cutting") has reference to the rite with cut animals. The covenant is unilateral, declared and sworn by God at God's own initiative. The promise grants the land (with specific boundaries) to Abraham's descendants. It is now theirs; it is not a future gift. This covenant, then, is a sworn formalization of a prior promise given by God (12:7; 13:14–17).[25] God, by partici-pating in this ritual, enters into that promise at a depth not evident heretofore, at least from Abraham's perspective. This kind of divine involvement comes in response to Abraham's question. Abraham thereby moves God to take steps to assure Abraham of the irrevocable nature of the promises. God's promises had been irrevocable before, but, given the divine participation in the rite, Abraham should now "know" how deeply God has entered into this commitment.

This covenant is a promise that God will never nullify. The covenant-promise is by Yahweh, as God places an obligation upon the divine self (and hence it is not strictly "legal"). Yet, it is also with a faithful Abraham, though not in a contractual sense. Making and keeping promises to Abraham on God's part entails a relation-ship of consequence, an ongoing tending of the promise as it relates to the life of Abraham and his descendants. Yet, while the promise is an everlasting one, partici-pation in its fulfillment, as we have seen, is not guaranteed to every person or gen-eration. The promise is always there for the believing to cling to, knowing that God is ever at work to fulfill it, but a rebellious generation may not live to see it. Faith is not a condition for the giving of the promise, but one can by unbelief leave the sphere of the promise. "Unconditional" promises do not make faith irrelevant (22:15–18; 26:5).

Abraham's response to God's unilateral promise is not recorded. In any case, Abraham's faith in God (15:6) is more than matched by God's faithful response to Abraham. In swearing by the divine self, God does justice to the relationship with Abraham and thereby shows forth the divine righteousness. Abraham trusts God and God can be trusted. Abraham can be assured of God's faithfulness.

The meaning of its several details remains open given the virtual absence of proper names in Genesis 15:13–16, and the ambiguity with respect to matters of timing. This being the case, the use of "plan of God" language for this text can be used only in a general way as well.[26] There is no divine effort to lay out the future with precision. As such, it opens up the text to generations of the people of God other than those of Abraham. The text becomes available to speak of comparable ways in which the people of God will experience life in the world, often as exiles and sojourners, whether oppressed or under just judgment. This text also speaks to the way in which God will be involved in the lives of God's chosen people through the generations: judging iniquity, delivering from oppression and exile, and giving them a home in which to dwell.

THE COVENANT IN GENESIS 17

God also establishes a covenant with Abraham in Genesis 17. This text is structured as a typical theophanic narrative, within which the word of God is predominant: (1) God's appearance in human form (as in 16:7; 18:1); (2) self-identification (El Shaddai); (3) a word to the recipient, including commands as well as promises. The basic content of the covenant that God establishes is in verses 4b–8; (4) Abraham's response to the word (initially, verse 3a; then, verses 17–18), which occasions a more emphatic and particular divine word (verses 19–21), after which God departs; and (5) a report of Abraham's obedience to God's command regarding circumcision (verses 23–27).

The interpreter is naturally faced with the question: Why are there two accounts of a covenant with Abraham?[27] Is the covenant in Genesis 17 a literary variant of the covenant in Genesis 15, or a renewal of it, or a revision of it (that is, the next stage in its development), or a different covenant altogether? In terms of literary origin, the two chapters may be parallel accounts (commonly ascribed to the Yahwist and the Priestly writer), but they are now interwoven into a single narrative fabric and efforts must be made to discern the sense of them together. The significant elements of overlap between the covenants in Genesis 15 and Genesis 17 indicate that this divine commitment is not altogether new, whatever new elements may be present (see below).[28] Both covenants are alike in that they entail a divine commitment to promises made; whatever the relationship between the covenants, the promises of Genesis 15 remain intact, so that the promises of Genesis 17 are in significant part a divine confirmation of the promises in Genesis 15. The covenants are also similar in that they follow

upon expressed difficulties—either questions asked (by Abraham, 15:7–8) or familial turmoil experienced (issues relating to Hagar and Ishmael, 16:1–6). At the same
time, genuinely new elements appear in Genesis 17. What are these new elements?

The focus of the covenant in chapter 15:7–21 was on the promise of land
(15:18). Though that promise was for "your descendants," the exceptionally
strong link between Abraham and his "descendants" in Genesis 17 (repeated 13
times) is a new element, or at least a new formulation (verse 7). Also, the "covenant"
is now, for the first time, specified as "everlasting" (17:7, 13, 19), though the designation of eternality for the promise of land in 13:15 certainly assumes some such
understanding of the covenant with Abraham's descendants, the land's occupants.
In addition, some new phrases appear: "between me [God] and you," "to be God
to you," and "I will be their God." This repeated language gives a heightened sense
of the centrality of the relationship between Abraham (and Sarah) and God (Exod.
6:7). In addition, a more global understanding of covenant is evident (a "multitude" of nations),[29] and the promise of "kings" is also a new element (17:6, 16;
35:11). Why these new elements?

Most likely, the covenant in Genesis 17 is viewed as a revision (more than a
renewal) of the earlier covenant in view of the "events" of chapter 16, which suggest that Ishmael is the fulfillment of God's promise of a son.[30] Indeed, thirteen
years have passed between 16:16 and 17:1, during which time Abraham lives with
what 16:15–16 suggest is a settled matter (Abraham himself seems to think so,
17:18). It may be that the Ishmael experience only serves to create a narrative
delay in the always-in-place fulfillment of the promise in Isaac; yet, Ishmael's place
in the narrative is more substantial than stylistic (given the promises made to
him). More likely, during these thirteen years, everyone—including God—lives
with Ishmael to see what opens up regarding the future; it is finally discerned (for
reasons unknown) that Ishmael will not do. Whatever the reason, God views it
important to move in new directions toward fulfillment of the promise of a son,
this time with Sarah as mother (17:19), not simply with Abraham as father. This
promise of a son by Sarah, and the specification of promises for her, is also one of
the new elements in Genesis 17 (verses 16, 19).

The newly intensified relationship that God establishes is given special standing by being accompanied by new names for all participants: Abraham, Sarai, and
God. The new divinely given name for God is El Shaddai (17:1, "God of the mountains" or, possibly, "God of the breasts"). The common translation "God Almighty"
(from Greek and Latin renderings) is an unfortunate abstraction, for it unpacks
(and hence limits) the concrete image of mountains (or breasts) in a univocal way.
Mountains mean more than almightiness (for example, Ps. 36:6; the translation
"breasts" would emphasize nourishment, see Gen. 49:25). The concrete image
should be retained in translation or (as is usual with names) transliterated. As

Hagar gave a new name to God in 16:13 in view of a new experience with God, so here God reveals a new name for the divine self that is congruent with this new moment in the life of God with this family. The newly shaped promises identify a somewhat different future that God will have with this family. God's very identity is now bound up with this family—for an eternity.[31] God will be forever known as the God of Abraham and God's very life will be everlastingly caught up in the life of this family.

This new divine identity in correlation with newly shaped promises is also recognized in the new names given to both Abraham and Sarai. The new names signal a recharacterization of their relationship with God (not a change in person or character). The two names Abram/Abraham and Sarai/Sarah are commonly considered dialectal variants, but they are changes. Both names mark significant new directions in their place in God's purposes. The text (Gen. 17:5) understands Abraham's name change to reflect less focus on his ancestry ("exalted father") and more on his heritage ("father of a multitude"). God promises that Abraham will be "fruitful" (commanded creationally in Gen. 1:28 and fulfilled for Israel in Exod. 1:7). The personal relationship with God lifted up in this covenant immediately moves out to encompass a relationship to the nations. The focus of Abraham's new name is certainly on God's promise, but it also is a more explicitly outward-looking name, drawing others onto the scene of God's activity.

Sarah/Sarai means "princess," and how the new name marks her newly characterized role is unclear. In any case, for the first time, she is given promises similar to those of Abraham: promises of blessing (twice), nations, and kings (17:16), and the promise to her of a son is repeated in verse 19. That these promises are repeated for Sarah is important (even though spoken to Abraham). Sarah is not subsumed under Abraham, finding her importance for the future only through him. Sarah is a genuine coparticipant in the covenant promise—and God so states the case, clearly. In other language, mother Sarah is associated with posterity as much as is father Abraham (in that culture it is the father who is commonly so identified). It is striking that this word about Sarah immediately follows the word about the circumcision of males. Given her standing in view of God's promises to her, it is not unimportant that the promises are given to one who is not circumcised. The promise is not made dependent on her obedience, except in the sense that sexual activity on her part will be necessary for a child to be conceived and born.

As with the covenant in Genesis 15, this revision of the covenant is not an institution or a social structure or a treaty; it is the formalization of an already existing promise of an ongoing and intimate relationship between God and this family and their descendants. Covenant equals promise formalized by God. God proceeds to make or establish the covenant on the divine initiative; this is not a decision

made by Abraham (or any other human party). At the same time, God establishes
the covenant with a person who has faith and has been declared righteous (15:6;
the same pattern is evident in covenants with Noah, Israel, and David). In other
words, a "right" relationship between Abraham and God already exists ("relationship" is a more comprehensive word than is "covenant").[32] Abraham does not now
have to do something else for the covenant to be established.

What, then, does it mean for God to begin with imperatives (17:1)? Again,
God's commands assume a relationship with a person whose faith and righteousness have been unambiguously stated by the narrator (15:6). Abraham is commanded to walk before God, that is, to be loyal to God (as Noah did, Gen. 6:9; cf.
5:22–24; Ps. 15:2; 101:2; Prov. 20:7). The narrative later testifies that Abraham has
done this (24:40; 48:15). The second imperative specifies the consequence of
obeying the first command: he will be blameless (unreserved faithfulness in every
aspect of the relationship, but not sinless; so also Jacob, 25:27, and David, 2 Sam.
22:24; cf. 1 Kings 3:6). Blameless is understood in the sense of integrity, not per-
fection. Inasmuch as walking before God is already characteristic of Abraham as a
righteous person, it is not something that he now must begin to do. Moreover,
inasmuch as walking before God does not take place in a moment or a single act,
these divine imperatives do not specify conditions for receiving the covenant; they
are imperatives with respect to continued relationship within the covenant. Abraham's falling on his face (17:3) does not express an agreement to walk before God
or even intent to do so; it implies that Abraham's faith exists, for this is a worshipful response to a God who speaks to him in this way regarding such momentous
matters.

The use of the word "everlasting" with respect to the covenant that God makes
(verses 7, 13, 19) and the land (verse 8; cf. 13:15) has to do with the promises
from God's side. God will never annul or break the covenant. The language does
not specify that Abraham must walk before God in order for God to keep the
covenant; Abraham and his descendants never have to wonder about God keeping the commitment made. If those to whom such promises are made, however,
do not walk before God (that is, remain faithful) they can remove themselves from
the sphere of promise, but what it takes to determine how or when this might happen is not presented for human judgment. Indeed, such a major sinful act as the
idolatry of the golden calf proves not to be such an instance (Exod. 32:13).
Goldingay helpfully states: "Although the covenant involves a walk before Yhwh
with integrity, evidently it is not exactly dependent on it. It issues solely from
Yhwh's desire to make it, and the same dynamic makes the covenant a perma-
nency . . . When God makes a commitment, it stands . . . Neither divine fickleness
nor human perversity can imperil the covenant."[33]

What, then, of the imperatives: "keep my covenant" and "every male among you shall be circumcised" (17:9–10). First, Abraham and his descendants (including Ishmael) are commanded to "keep (*šāmar*) my covenant." Generally speaking, "to keep" is more closely specified in 18:19 and 26:5, and involves more than circumcision (cf. Exod. 19:5, referring to this covenant[34]). In these contexts, "to keep" is doing justice to being faithful to the relationship with the promising God. That understanding also seems to be the case with "keep my covenant." Genesis 17:10 does not identify covenant and circumcision (shown by verse 4), but is rather an instance of synecdoche (the part—circumcision, for the whole—covenant).[35] As 17:11 states, circumcision is "a *sign* of the covenant between me and you." Genesis 17:13b helps clarify the issue: "My covenant shall be marked in your flesh as an everlasting pact (Tanakh)." Circumcision is an enfleshed sign of the covenant, an enduring mark of the flesh is a sign of God's everlasting covenant. Circumcision creates an external, but hidden mark of group identity that persists in the face of the efforts of others to dismiss or devalue the covenant of which it is a sign. As a sign of faithfulness to the covenant (verse 11), the physical act itself is not primary. Though external, it is not a visible sign of belonging. But it is a sign of belonging for the individual male as well as a sign for the community, who in seeing to such a practice are thereby being true to God's command.

This understanding of circumcision does not make the covenant bilateral;[36] circumcision is a response to God's establishment of the covenant, a sign of an already existing reality (17:11), not a means by which the covenant is implemented. It is a sign of faithfulness to the covenant from the human side (different from the rainbow in 9:12–17; it resembles the Sabbath of Exod. 31:16–17). God will never be unfaithful, yet human unfaithfulness can lead to severe consequences (verse 14). The male will be "cut off" from the people; no action by court or cult—execution or excommunication—is in view; the matter is left up to God (Lev. 20:1–6). But it is important to note that they are members of "his people" before they are or are not circumcised. Even though women may be included in the covenant community only by virtue of being members of a household where the males are circumcised, it is notable that they are not said to be cut off. It is possible that the covenant promises would continue to be applicable to them, which in turn could have led to the later metaphoric use of circumcision (see below) as a way of including females. This later development would be in line with God's promises to Sarah (17:16, 19).

The relation between the two clauses in verse 14 is important; the last is not causally related to the first. And so neglecting circumcision is not the essence of the breaking of covenant, such neglect is a sign of unfaithfulness. An act of omission is a sign of an act of commission. Moreover, practicing circumcision is not the essence of keeping the covenant. Being faithful to the relationship with God entails more than circumcision; the way one's life is shaped is important. Hence, there is never an appeal in the Old Testament to circumcision as a guarantee of God's favor and blessing. Other traditions will speak of judgment on circumcised ones with an "uncircumcised heart" (Jer. 4:4; 9:25; Ezek. 44:7–9; cf. Deut. 10:16; 30:6). The sign of circumcision in and of itself is insufficient. It can become an empty sign.

Circumcision is common among Israel's neighbors (and beyond), often as a rite of passage (Jer. 9:25–26; God assumes that Abraham knows the rite). It is striking that God does not create a new rite that would set Israel apart from its neighbors (also the case with Christian baptism). Rather, God takes an existing practice from the larger culture and "baptizes" it for use within the community of faith. As such, circumcision does not function as a rite of distinctiveness from other peoples or cultures. Notably, the repeated reference to slaves (verses 12–13, 23, 27) indicates that presence in the covenant community is what matters, not racial stock or social standing or even membership in the chosen family. Circumcision is a democratizing move, at least for the males.

As a mark on the body, circumcision is linked with the command to walk before God, which entails all aspects of the life of the person. The relationship with God is not simply a spiritual journey; it draws in the bodily dimensions of life as that to which God lays claim. It is commonly suggested that the sign of the circumcision of the penis is particularly related to procreation and the promise of descendants (17:4).

God's word about circumcision (17:9–14) is followed by promises regarding Sarah (17:15–16; see above). Abraham first responds by speaking and laughing "to himself," as will Sarah (18:12; yiṣḥāq, a play on the name for Isaac ["he laughs"] is a continuing theme, 18:12–15; 19:14; 21:6, 9). It is the laugh of incredulity because of their age as potential parents (verse 17; cf. 18:12). While Abraham responds by falling on his face in obeisance in verse 3, here he falls on his face in laughter (he is the subject of no verb between these "falls"). His immediately expressed concern is for Ishmael (17:18) suggests that he is pleased with Ishmael as the fulfillment of God's promise of a son, and sees no need to proceed further (verse 18). No good reason exists to consider Abraham's laughter of a different kind from Sarah's in 18:12, a text which demonstrates that Sarah was not told what he here learns.

God does not discipline Abraham, but simply says "no," and speaks of a new son, to be born of Sarah and named Isaac, with whom God will establish the covenant. At the same time, God is responsive to Abraham's concerns about Ishmael. God speaks promises regarding Ishmael similar to those given Isaac, including nationhood and royalty (21:13, 18; 25:12–16 lists the twelve princes). That

Ishmael is specifically excluded from the covenant line means that his circumcision (which now follows in 17:23) does not in itself constitute membership in the covenant people.[37]

Isaac is the chosen one by God's own decision. The gender-specific future reference (17:19; cf. 18:14) links up with 21:1 and a significant level of divine involvement to bring about this result, the details of which are not provided (what would be the options for the divine working?). This series of events is not testimony to absolute divine foreknowledge, but an instance of God knowing what God will do. After the conversation, God leaves the scene, and the narrator repetitively reports that Abraham follows through on the divine command, himself wielding the knife for all male members of his household. The person who circumcised the 99-year-old Abraham is not noted. The circumcision of Ishmael, "his son," is noted three times, others twice (verses 23–26). The response to the covenant is fully fulfilled by Abraham for his own generation.

Abraham and his family are surrounded with divine promises. The issue for them is not to see the fulfillment of all these promises in their lifetime, though it is important to have sufficient taste of fulfillment to show that the promised futures are on track. Faith will inevitably mean living with promises as promises, short of fulfillment. As the reference to nations and kings in 17:20 implies, the promise "has a more universal application in that a larger segment of humanity looks upon Abraham as its spiritual father," including Christians and Muslims (John 1:13).[38]

CHAPTER 4

ABRAHAM AND OUTSIDERS I

THE ENDANGERING OF SARAH

Genesis 12:10–13:1; 20:1–18

P eople of faith have always had a somewhat mixed sense of how to relate to outsiders, those who stand outside their communities. Certainly such persons are to be embraced in any understanding of "mission." Yet, it seems the people of God have not wanted to link God too directly or positively with the lives of such outsiders, lest the advantages of being religious seem too few or one's missional zeal be blunted.

A number of texts in the story of Abraham prompt reflection with respect to God's relationship with outsiders. These texts prevent easy assumptions regarding God's presence and activity in their lives. God is at work among them; indeed they are surrounded by divine graciousness, though they may not recognize it or name the experience for what it is.

This work of God has, of course, often happened independently of the words and deeds of the elect, and no doubt often in spite of them. Abraham, the chosen one, all too often brings trouble rather than blessing to outsiders, not attending very well to the call to be a blessing to all families. Indeed, the deeds of God's elect have often led to the suffering of such peoples; that they have responded with as much magnanimity as they have is amazing. Though the chosen may complicate and frustrate the divine work, they cannot finally stymie it. God will find a way to move around them and often through outsiders in working toward the divine goals.

Abimelech's role as prophet and confessor with respect to Abraham deserves recalling. We may find it unsettling that an outsider functions as a prophetic voice to an insider. Once again, listen to what Abimelech says to Abraham: "You have done things to me that ought not be done. What were you thinking of, that you did this thing?" That sounds like Amos or any number of prophets. It is ironic, then, that Abraham is anachronistically called a prophet only in this text, and that by God himself. The outsider prophet indicts the insider prophet, calling him to account for his behavior. The people of God are all too seldom willing to hear a critical word from an outsider as word of God to them, bringing them up short regarding their practice of truth and justice. Perhaps they think that they cannot be called to account by such persons on moral issues. But many outsiders have consciences just as sensitive as insiders, and often more so; the people of God do not have a corner on discerning good and evil in our life together.

In view of the call to be a blessing to all families, one issue the people of God face is the attractiveness of the faith they present to outsiders. They so often wrangle among themselves—one thinks of the culture wars and the religious wars at home and around the world. One consequence may be that outsiders find the faith quite unattractive and the call to be a blessing is blunted and blurred.

The people of God are living in a society that is increasingly pluralistic and secularized, They will be surrounded more and more by such outsiders. How will they relate to these other persons and families of God's world? What kind of claims will they make for themselves? Like Abraham, the children of Abraham are called to be a blessing to all families. How is that best done in this new context?

We have seen that Genesis 12:3 envisages three possible relationships that the chosen family might have with the "Other" or the "Outsider" or the "Unchosen."

- Those who bless you—A Gift
- The one who curses you—A Threat
- Through you all the families of the earth will be blessed—A Challenge

In the chapters that follow 12:3, outsiders are often presented as a blessing, as a threat, and as a challenge.

We begin with the stories about Abraham's endangering of Sarah and the role of outsiders therein. This story is a thrice-told tale and has received considerable scholarly attention, particularly from a literary perspective.[1] The first story is narrated in 12:10–20. In Genesis 20:1–18 Abraham will again seek to pass Sarah off as his sister in the face of a perceived threat from outsiders. This text is more closely marked by dialogue and theological reflection. Isaac acts in a similar way with respect to Rebekah (26:1–11). Many scholars think that this is a single story retold in somewhat disparate ways and set into the narrative at different points by later redactors in view of changing religious and cultural contexts.[2] In the present form of the text, however, each of these stories are understood as distinctive, though their functions within the narrative are not unrelated, particularly with respect to the chosen family's relationship with outsiders.

ABRAHAM AND SARAH IN EGYPT, GENESIS 12:10–13:1

The story of Abraham's entry into the land of promise begins with a problem—a severe famine (12:10; other land problems will occur in chapters 13–14). This problem with the land, which he has just been promised (12:7) and has been exploring, will occasion his first encounter with outsiders—Egyptians. Abraham no sooner receives the promise then he has to leave it behind with all the attendant uncertainties; what is promised is not something that he is able to settle into.

A gift is offered him by God and almost immediately it fails him; land is a precarious gift indeed. While the promise of land is something upon which Abraham can depend, the gift itself is not so dependable. The fruitfulness of the land is not guaranteed as the gifts of God can become something other than what they were created to be (cf. Gen. 1:11–12, 29–30 with the thorns and thistles of Gen. 3:17–18). Abraham must move out of the land of promise in order to survive. It would have been no demonstration of faith in God to not take appropriate action and wait for God to perform a miracle.[3] This trek is but the first of a number of such journeys away from the land of promise for this family, often into alien and dangerous territory (for example, Gen. 42:5; 43:1; 47:4).

Abraham seems not to have anticipated fully the dangers he or Sarai would face until he is at the Egyptian border (12:11). He thinks (he does not know for sure) that Sarai is key to his own personal future; indeed, it is because of her that his life will be spared (verse 13).

Abraham's first words in the narrative, spoken to Sarai, are difficult to understand (verses 11–13). Abraham asks that Sarai conceal the nature of their relationship, because the Egyptians might kill him to procure such a beautiful woman (the text puts her age at sixty-five). The issue is probably not that Abraham lies; his claim in 20:12 that Sarai was his half-sister may be correct. This presupposes a situation where adultery is forbidden, but a murder might be arranged (cf. David and Bathsheba). Even then, it appears that Abraham does not order Sarai to say that she is his sister, given the use of the particle $n\bar{a}$ in verses 11, 13, which gives the command of verse 13 ("Say") more of the sense of an entreaty ("I pray thee," KJV) in view of the perceived danger of the situation with which they are confronted. And so Abraham's word to Sarai is couched in language that trusts that she will recognize the rightness of his request. This suggests that Sarai responds, not because she has been ordered to, but because she sees that this is the right thing to do in this circumstance. She acts in order to save Abraham from a perceived life-threatening situation. Her acquiescence is the key to Abraham's future.

Many readers sympathize with Abraham's equivocation; after all, he not only comes to Egypt with hat in hand, he understands his life to be in danger as well. Faced with such a dilemma, and preparing for the worst, he puts life ahead of honor. Other readers have pronounced his actions cowardly and lacking in integrity. This is also the judgment of the Pharaoh (12:18–19). At what price does he seek to assure his personal safety? A repeated focus on self fills his speech. He puts Sarai at the disposal of his personal concerns, life for himself at the potential expense of Sarai's honor. In fact, as his sister, one is given to wonder whether she is even more likely to be taken; he seems to risk losing her altogether.

The truth probably rides the cusp between these two views. One might argue that Abraham had few options, none of them perfect. He chooses to enter into a situation fraught with danger and ambiguity and devises a careful strategy, albeit imperfect, self-serving, and dishonoring of Sarai.

Abraham is sometimes judged because he makes no reference to God, that he should have appealed to or shown confidence in divine help as he faced this dilemma. But this direction of thought is not helpful. Characters in Genesis often make decisions and pursue actions without specific reference to God, and without being judged for it; indeed, Abraham seems to be rewarded (12:16). Human strategies are not in and of themselves out of order; in fact, "the narrator presents his character in a world where natural crises arise with no relation to the divine, and where the person of faith makes independent decisions in response to them"[4] The narrator speaks not one word of Abraham's faith in God or his lack thereof. The interest centers on the way in which he handles a problem in daily life, with all of its complexities and ambiguities. Moreover, the alternative could be viewed as tempting God to provide miracles (cf. Exod. 17:1–7) or assuming an unreal divine protection plan.

The reason why the narrator gives Sarai no voice in this story is uncertain. It could be reflective of the patriarchy of the time. Yet, because Sarai is later given a powerful voice (16:2; 21:10; as are other women in Genesis), her silence is likely to be purposive. It could be a characteristic of her relationship to Abraham or she chooses to suffer silently, tacitly agreeing to risk her honor and her life for Abraham's sake—the report of her voice in 20:5 suggests the latter. It is striking that Abraham has no response when Sarai is "taken" (contrast Abraham's response regarding Lot in 14:14).

Sarai is now the one around whom the story unfolds. While she is given no voice (nor is God) and her feelings are never noted, she acts (as does God) in such a way that the end result is good for Abraham (and for God). She is referred to thirteen times, moving from being Abraham's wife to his sister to "the woman" to Pharaoh's wife and back to Abraham's wife. This focus on Sarai should be allowed to have its full interpretive import. It is because of her that Abraham feels threatened, that things may go well with him, that his life may be spared (verse 13), that Pharaoh is "good" to him (verse 16). Even more, God acts because of her, afflicting Pharaoh (verse 17). God is not said to act because of Abraham, but because of Sarai. While Sarai has not been named the mother of the son to this point in the narrative, God's action here anticipates that choice; it is, in effect, because of God's eventual promise to Sarai that God acts here "because of" her (12:17).

The fact that pharaoh does take Sarai, and her beauty is touted, seems to indicate that Abraham's fears are not baseless. Sarai is so praised that she is taken into the Pharaoh's house to become his "wife" (verse 19; cf. 16:3); the lack of any marker to distinguish the use of "wife" for Abraham and for the pharaoh in verses 17, 19 means they have the same force. Abraham had failed to anticipate that

Pharaoh himself would enter into the picture, let alone take Sarai for a wife. If it had been any Egyptian but Pharaoh, he may have thought he could negotiate as Sarai's "brother" (cf. 24:55) and been able to have her returned to him. The reference to "wife," as well as the time that passes (verse 16), makes it possible, even likely, that the marriage is consummated (to deny this seems a case of special pleading). Genesis 20:6 explicitly states that Abimelech did not have sexual relations with Sarah; that that is not the case in this text invites the reader to wonder.

The question remains as to what the pharaoh would have done had Abraham not passed off Sarai as his sister. Pharaoh says that he would have acted differently if he had known she was his wife (12:19); indeed, when he finds out that Sarai is Abraham's wife, he returns her to Abraham and lets them go. At the same time, the narrative suggests that Pharaoh acted this way because of the plagues (12:17); readers are left with the sense that it was this divine action that led to pharaoh's next moves. Notably, the conversation with Abraham that Pharaoh reports (12:18–19) is not related by the narrator in 12:14–15. The parallel with Abimelech (20:9–10) suggests that he would not have taken Sarai if he had known she was Abraham's wife. Yet, readers are not informed.

Because of Sarai ("for her sake"), Abraham is treated well by Pharaoh. It is not made clear why it is that Pharaoh deals well with Abraham for Sarah's sake (12:16), an action that occurs before the plagues occur. That it may be a payment to Abraham for Sarai is possible, though that does not necessarily carry the idea that Abraham bartered with the pharaoh for her.[5] In any case, prosperity comes to Abraham at the expense of Sarai; indeed, Pharaoh makes Abraham a wealthy man (cf. 24:35; 16:1 implies that one slave was Hagar). He is preserved from the effects of the famine and the actions of the pharaoh, but it has cost him the (temporary) loss of Sarai and it has cost Sarai her honor and dignity. Notably, Abraham does not reap the full negative effects of his behavior, which happens because of Sarai (verse 16) and Pharaoh (verse 20). No mechanically conceived moral order is at work here; human activity can cut into the act-consequence spiral and ameliorate its effects.

Pharaoh's action is inappropriate with respect to Sarai, even though he participates unknowingly (cf. Abimelech in 20:3–6). The result is that his action brings the divine judgment in its wake (objective guilt). While the identity of the "great" plagues is unknown, diseases are probably in mind (Ps. 73:5, 14; 2 Chron. 26:20). That God acts "because of Sarai" (verse 17) shows God's focus on delivering her from this situation. God's action constitutes the turning point in the story. It is not stated how Pharaoh comes to understand the link between his actions toward Sarai and the plagues. Yet, the immediate juxtaposition of the plagues and his interrogation of Abraham shows that this understanding is a matter of his own insight (note his threefold mention of "wife").

The text helps illumine the correspondence that exists between act a quence. The act of the pharaoh and its consequence occur within the creation. The unnatural relationship of the pharaoh to Sarai has natural effects, namely, disease.[6] The consequence is intrinsic to the deed. Yet this interplay is not understood in a deistic way as God midwifes the consequences. God delivers Pharaoh into the hands of his own iniquity, the fruit of which is disease (Isa. 64:7; Jer. 6:19; 21:14).[7]

One might well wonder about the fairness of these effects, given both the bless- ings that Abraham receives and Pharaoh's unwitting activity. It is Abraham, not Pharaoh, who has occasioned this problem, as Pharaoh discerns (verse 18). He rightly blames Abraham, not Abraham's God, putting the fault where it belongs. But the workings of the moral order are not mechanistic, but a loose causal weave (see more on Abimelech below). This has been true generally throughout human history. People do experience great disasters in life "through no fault of their own." They also experience great benefits.

It is not insignificant that Pharaoh asks Abraham exactly the same question that God asked Eve in the garden (3:13; similarly of Cain, 4:10), and that he "sends away" (šālaḥ) Abraham and his family in a way not unlike God does Adam and Eve (3:23). Abraham may have experienced shame and dread at being peppered by the (nonjudicial) questions of an angry emperor, but the narrator makes a different point. Just as Sarai had no response to Abraham in verses 11–13, so Abraham has no response to Pharaoh in this, the only other dialogue. Abraham is reduced to silence too.

THE ROLE OF OUTSIDERS

The Egyptians present a threat to Abraham, or at least a perceived threat, but he does not respond in a way that is helpful or exemplary, endangering his wife Sarah and occasioning a plague on the Egyptians.[8] Yet, the Egyptians become the channel in and through whom blessings can flow to the chosen family. At the same time, when God becomes involved in the aftermath of that unfortunate encounter, the situation may be turned around. As we have noted (see chapter 3), the Exodus story may provide a structure for the narrative. The text is bracketed by Abraham's descent to and return from Egypt (12:10; 13:1) and numerous elements of his sojourn in Egypt parallel Israel's later experience.

The relationship of this text to "outsiders" introduced in Genesis 12:3 is complex and ambiguous. On the one hand, the Egyptians are perceived to be a threat to Abraham and to his future, and Abraham's premonitions may be on target in that the Egyptians do make the anticipated judgment regarding Sarai's beauty. At the same time, the reader is given to wonder whether Abraham is fully justified in expecting the worst from the outsider. On the other hand, the Egyptians "bless"

Abraham with many gifts of great value (12:16). Even after the ruse is discovered and Sarai is returned, Abraham is allowed to keep all the gifts and go on his way. From the generous, if not uncritical, way in which Pharaoh responds when the ruse becomes known, even if under some duress, it seems unlikely that he would have mistreated or killed Abraham—if he had known the truth from the beginning of the encounter. God's action (the plague) is critical in enabling a positive turn of events, but before that occurs, the "outsider" pharaoh has become the mediator of considerable blessing on Abraham and his household.

Abraham's actions are ambiguous as well. Is Abraham overly motivated by self-interest, concerning which Sarai is a convenient means to preserve his own life? Or is he, in view of common knowledge regarding the predilections of rulers to collect wives, primarily concerned with the safety of Sarai? Or do both rationales come together here? Janzen states the issue well: "The question is: When should faith interpret the motives of other social groups on the basis of one's own fear and suspicion, and when does such suspicion merely perpetuate and intensify a human drama driven toward evil by fear, defensiveness, and manipulation? When is faith called to break this vicious cycle by a social interpretation arising out of trust, and to accept the risks of such an interpretation?"[9]

Abraham and his family are sent away from Egypt abruptly and ignominiously, escorted to the border; yet, Pharaoh exhibits a remarkably generous spirit. While the plagues no doubt prompt this treatment of Abraham, Pharaoh also acts toward Abraham in a way more liberally than he would have to. Pharaoh not only lets Abraham off the hook, but lets him keep all the possessions that he had accumulated because of the ruse (12:20). Ironically, Pharaoh proves to be more of a behavioral model in this instance than Abraham, alleviating the negative consequences that might well have befallen Abraham. Pharaoh unknowingly serves God's purposes in this situation.

This more positive portrayal of the Egyptians appears throughout Genesis (cf. chapters 39–50). This depiction is remarkable, given what is to come in Exodus (though see Pharaoh's daughter, Exod. 2:1–10). The Egyptians are not the embodiment of evil, they are not destined to a certain way of being. Other futures are available to them. A comparison with the plague stories in Exodus brings out a notable contrast. While plagues are visited upon the Egyptians in both texts, the reasons differ. In Exodus, the conduct of the Egyptians themselves stands front and center as the rationale for the plagues. In the Genesis text, it is Abraham, God's own chosen one, whose behavior leads to Pharaoh's action which, in turn, leads to the plagues. Abraham brings a curse rather than a blessing upon the nations (12:3). In his very first contact with outsiders, Abraham fails in his response to the call of God and the relationship with the Egyptians is deeply problematized. When this action toward Pharaoh is combined with the later oppression of the Egyptian Hagar (16:6–11), the text may suggest that the chosen family is at ✓ least in part a "teacher" with respect to later Egyptian oppressive practices.

Abraham is not inevitably the bringer of blessing to the outsider. In this case, he has so comported himself that the "other" is not blessed, but suffers. How chosen ones such as Abraham respond to others is shown to have great potential for ill as well as good. If Abraham is any indication, the most basic root of these problematic ways of relating to outsiders, finally, seems to lie in a deeply rooted centeredness in self. In addition, just because the Egyptians are not believers (cf. Abraham's claim about Abimelech's fear of God, 20:11) should not occasion suspicion or a lack of basic human trust. That benevolent behavior is possible on the part of unchosen outsiders is testimony to the continuing work of God the Creator in the lives of all people. The chosen should be able to recognize these wide-ranging positive effects of God's creative work, and seek to join hands with such persons in working toward God's goals of a reclaimed creation.

Finally, readers should note the way in which the outsider Pharaoh functions as Abraham's teacher, even confessor: "What is this you have done to me?" (12:18). Abimelech will call Abraham to account more fully and in a more theologically sophisticated way (20:9–10), but Pharaoh's questions and charge give evidence of a basic sense of truth and justice, bringing an appropriately sharp critique against God's own chosen one.

ABRAHAM, ABIMELECH, AND THE SINS OF THE RIGHTEOUS, 20:1–18; 21:22–34

Once again an outsider receives focused attention in the story of the chosen family. The chief character of this text is King Abimelech, whose dilemma and its resolution is referenced at the beginning and end of the story (20:2–3, 18). God speaks only to him in this chapter, and it is toward his Abraham-provoked plight that readers, even those sympathetic to Abraham and Sarah, finally gravitate.

In its present context, this text provides a return look at Abraham after all that has happened to him in chapters 12–19. How might he fare in a situation comparable to the one he faced in 12:10–20? In a nutshell, Abraham seems not to learn very well from his life experience or from his developing relationship with God. In 20:1, Abraham journeys (nāśā') and sojourns (gûr) for the first time since 12:9–10, a text that introduced the previous story of the endangering of Sarah. Now Abraham, for reasons not stated, sojourns in the city-state of Gerar (in the southwestern corner of Canaan in what became Philistine territory, see 21:34). King Abimelech of Gerar, like Pharaoh, presents a comparable threat to Sarah. Once again Abraham responds in a way that endangers Sarah. Abraham seems to be intimidated by royal types.[10]

The connections with the preceding chapters on Sodom and Gomorrah are especially strong: issues of human and divine justice, sin and consequence, and

Abraham as intercessor. Links with the following chapters (especially 21–22) have long been noted,[11] and Abraham and Abimelech have a return engagement in chapter 21. The focus on the closing of wombs at the end of the narrative (20:18) leads into the story of the conception and birth of Isaac (21:1–7), wherein God's action and Abraham's expressed paternity reinforce the concern expressed in 20:4–6. The story is structured in terms of three dialogues: Abimelech with God (verses 3–7), with Abraham (verses 9–13), and with Abraham and Sarah (verses 15–16).[12]

The narrator's immediate reference to Abraham's repeat performance (20:2) is striking, though we later hear of Sarah's apparent concurrence (verse 5) and Abraham's stated rationale (verses 11–13). This way of beginning the story strongly suggests that the reader is to conclude that the patriarch has not learned from the previous experience. Abraham's action once again seems to be a deliberate endangerment of Sarah, placing her life and well-being in jeopardy. It is not clear from verse 2 to whom Abraham is speaking when he refers to Sarah as his sister, and, unlike 12:11–13, gives no reason for saying it (and there is no reference to her beauty). That Abraham's behavior is inappropriate is more apparent here than in 12:10–20, as the dialogue between Abimelech and God makes clear, Sarah's acquiescence notwithstanding. Moreover, Abraham once again fails to consider the effects of his actions on outsiders. In spite of all the divine words and deeds in his life up to this point, they seem to make no difference in his decision-making. These actions may well provide some of the backdrop for the divine testing of Abraham in chapter 22 ("after these things," 22:1).

That the narrator gives Sarah only an indirect voice could be reflective of the patriarchy of the time. Yet the voice given women in Genesis, including Sarah's earlier initiatives (16:2; 21:10), intimates that Abraham's later reference to her "kindness" may be right (verse 13)—though "long-suffering" may be a better word. As in chapter 12, Abraham has no response when Sarah is "taken" (unlike at the taking of Lot in 14:14).

Various reasons have been given for Abraham's behaviors: he still prefers Ishmael; he does not believe God's promise of a son through Sarah; he will gain further wealth as he did in Egypt; or even that Abraham wants Sarah's son to be the progeny of Abimelech—or is at least nonchalant about that happening. It is likely that, given his prior experience in Egypt, he knows that that is at least possible. Sarah would be ninety years old or so by this time, and one wonders about her attractiveness to Abimelech, but the extended lives of the ancestors need to be kept in mind. The text remains unclear regarding his motives, but that it is an unfaithful move on his part is clear.

When Abimelech finds out that Sarah is Abraham's sister, he "takes" her, presumably to be a part of his harem. God immediately enters the situation to protect

Sarah, speaking to Abimelech in a dream—a medium of divine revelation and no less real or personal than a direct divine encounter (see Jacob's dream in 28:10–22). Indeed, Abimelech and God carry on a conversation within the dream.

Challenging God's announcement of his impending death, Abimelech claims innocence in view of his ignorance of Sarah's relationship to Abraham. Abimelech is not passive in the face of a divine decision that he deems to be unjust and refuses to resign himself to his own death. He sharply questions God and flatly claims innocence and integrity of heart (cf. 17:1; Ps. 78:72; 24:4), expecting God to acknowledge his innocence if justice is to be served. He places his action in the context of his general loyalty to interhuman relationships. His question in verse 4, "Lord, will you destroy an innocent people?" is much like the query of Abraham in 18:25, "Lord, will you destroy an innocent people?" The dialogue makes clear that more than Abimelech's personal future is at stake; the very future of his community is in jeopardy (verses 7, 9, 17–18). God responds positively to him by acknowledging his innocence. Indeed, God has been so active in Abimelech's life that he was prevented from touching Sarah. God may have accomplished this effect through the sickness from which he is later healed (see verse 17), or possibly by working in the deep recesses of his mind. Such a saying is theologically difficult. That is, if God can enter into people's lives and at will prevent them from sinning, then human sin becomes a divine choice, occurring when God chooses not to hold them back from doing so. A more likely interpretation here would be that Abimelech does not sin because he is responsive to God's work in his life, which is not an overpowering reality. When sin does not occur, then the confession is that God's work in one's life and thought has been the enabling reality.

Though God announces that Abimelech is a dead man because of what he has done (verse 3), verse 6 makes it clear that God, having prevented him from sinning, knew he was innocent. This means that the divine death announcement in verse 3 is not a forensic judgment, but a matter-of-fact statement regarding the moral order and its consequences for Abimelech. That is, deeds have consequences just by virtue of their having happened (objective guilt, as with Pharaoh in 12:17), and people reap those effects quite apart from their intentions or their knowledge of what they have done (an observable reality then and now). Hence, no divine acquittal is given (or necessary) in verses 6–7. Rather, God gives attention to the effects of the deeds apart from questions of guilt or innocence.

The announced consequences for Abimelech, then, are intrinsic to the deed; God does not introduce a judgment from the outside. Yet, God did create and continues to oversee the world in such a way that it functions like this, so that ultimately one could speak of divine responsibility. The negative effects of Abimelech's unwitting deed on his entire community, and not just on himself, is a general truth about God's creation. People do experience disasters in life "through no fault of their own." They also experience great benefits through no credit to themselves. This lack of retributive exactitude is a sign of looseness in the causal weave of things. And, because of the seamless web of life—the interconnectedness of things—those who are innocent are often caught up in sin's effects or, for that matter, the wicked are caught up in the effects of righteous acts. So the lack of fairness bends both ways, but some such world order is necessary in order for there to be such realities as novelty, surprise, and serendipity. One might well wonder about the fairness of the effects on Abimelech, given both that Abraham occasioned the problem and that Abimelech's sin was unwitting. This is the issue Abimelech raises with God, though it is noteworthy that he puts the blame where it belongs—on Abraham, not God.

The references to the effect of Abimelech's deed upon his people lift up the communal impact of an individual's sin, a reality insufficiently recognized in the all too common individualistic understandings of sin and guilt. Words for sin can refer to any point on a continuum from the sinful act (the first reference in verse 9) to its far-reaching effects (the second). An innocent person, indeed an entire nation, has been caught up in the effects of the sin of Abraham. These linkages witness to the seamless web of life, the interconnectedness of all things; those who are innocent are often caught up in the consequences of the sinful deeds of others (from personal abuse to wars).

This looseness in the causal weave also means that divine or human activity may be able to ameliorate the effects of sinful deeds (for example, Abraham's prayer, 20:7, 17), but what in fact can be done will vary from one situation to another. God's statement to Abimelech recognizes the unwitting character of the situation, and also attends to the consequences of the deeds upon Abimelech's community. We learn from verses 17–18 that Abimelech's death would have been caused by a malady that was capable of being healed and that the women of his household were unable to conceive. In preventing Abimelech from touching Sarah through an illness, God has prevented a worse deed from occurring and even more serious effects. So the situation is not as bad as it might have been. In view of God's action, possibilities for Abimelech's future are more hopeful as a result.

Another theological issue is raised here, namely, the distinction between acquittal and salvation. Abimelech could be forgiven for the sin committed unwittingly and thereby be personally restored; but, forgiveness, however positive the results, does not wipe out the effects of the sin with one stroke. Those effects have to be dealt with in other ways, the results of which are often called salvation, in both the Old Testament and New Testament.[13] Generally, God forgives sin, but "saves" from the effects of sin. Where there is forgiveness there is also life and salvation, but forgiveness does not comprehend all that is entailed in salvation. Further work is needed to deal with the effects of the sin that have reverberated out from the sin. In Isaiah 40:1–11, for example, God announces that exiled Israel is forgiven double for all their sins, but salvation in any full sense still lies ahead in the return from exile. In a contemporary situation, an adult may be forgiven for the abuse of a child, but the effects of that abuse will need considerable attention over the months and years ahead before healing occurs. From a biblical perspective, such healing is comprehended within the sphere of God's salvation work. For both testaments, God's saving activity occurs within the spheres of both creation and redemption. While the prayers that are the vehicle for healing do come from within the community of faith, God is engaged in other ways in the healing of people, often quite apart from any link to persons of faith (for example, through the medical community).

God specifies that two things must happen for the situation to get turned around for Abimelech and his family if their deaths are to be avoided. He is to restore Sarah to Abraham, and the prophet Abraham is to pray for him.[14] The identification of Abraham as a prophet protects him from any precipitous judgment on Abimelech's part, for it makes his life dependent on Abraham's intercession. But it also shows the divine concern for Abimelech, providing a means by which he and his family can be brought safely through this crisis. But, it is not enough that he restore the situation to the point where it started. He also has to consider all the effects that his action has let loose (for example, the sickness of his wife and female slaves, verse 17). Prayer is deemed necessary in order to deal with such realities, and becomes then a vehicle for divine salvation in the comprehensive sense.

Abimelech reacts to God's word in two basic ways (20:8–10). One, he gives a report to all his servants, which generates fear among them over the potential consequences. This gesture is not an act of repentance, for Abimelech does not believe he has done anything wrong and proceeds to indict Abraham. Two, he confronts Abraham and in effect conducts a judicial inquiry, using knowledge regarding Abraham's complicity that Abraham does not know he has. Interestingly, Abimelech does not reveal the source of his knowledge regarding Abraham's sin and claims no divine authority for what he has to say. Given what Abimelech knows and has suffered at Abraham's hands, he shows notable restraint and magnanimity toward the one who has caused him so much trouble.

Abimelech pronounces Abraham guilty and, using assertions and rhetorical questions, seeks to elicit a confession from Abraham. The charges he brings against Abraham are accurate and to the point: "You have done things to me that ought not to be done. . . . What were you thinking of, that you did this thing?" Abimelech's sin language is accurate and reveals the essence of the problem. He has not sinned (ḥāṭāh) against Abraham, but Abraham has brought a "great guilt" (ḥeṭāʾāh) on him. Abimelech accurately discerns that it is Abraham's sin that lies at the root of the problem, and its effects have reached out through Abimelech's unwitting deed and begun to engulf his entire kingdom. Gerar faces a disaster due to Abraham's unrighteous action. The righteous may be forgiven by God for such sins, but their long-term effects may be devastating indeed.

Abraham responds by admitting that he did what he did, but he is very defensive and seeks to justify his actions (20:10–13). He gives three reasons:

First, he had determined with certainty (*raq*) that there was no fear of God in this place and so had to protect himself (cf. 12:10–20). In view of what Abraham has done, and what the reader has learned about Abimelech, this reason is highly ironic. The "fear of God" is indeed to be found in this place. Not all cities, or indigenous peoples, are like Sodom. To fear God is to be in tune with the basic order of things as God has created them, including interhuman relationships, with all that that means in terms of basic human values such as life, truth, and justice. It is Abraham who has not exhibited the fear of God. This experience lays the groundwork for the later testing of Abraham's fear of God, where God tests Abraham on precisely this issue (22:12). To seek to make fine distinctions between Abimelech's fear of God and Abraham's fear of God misses this point. Abimelech's life conforms in basic ways to God's purposes for interhuman relationships, and this is amply evident in this story.

Second, Sarah is his half-sister, who became his wife (a permissible practice, later forbidden, Deut. 27:22). It is difficult to determine whether Abraham's claim is a fact, though it would seem that the genealogy of Terah in 11:26–30 would have made this clear were it actually the case. The irony is that Abraham's response does not speak to the point being made. Abraham had not given Abimelech sufficient knowledge for him to make a proper decision regarding Sarah. Abimelech's reference to Sarah's "brother" (20:16) is probably deeply ironic and keeps Abraham's deed front and center.

Third, Abimelech was not a special object of this kind of behavior on Abraham's part. Abraham had done this often—at every place where they had sojourned (readers will recall one such instance, 12:10–20). Moreover, Abraham's focus on Sarah's showing kindness (*hesed*) to him has a deeply self-serving ring to it (20:13), focusing on his welfare rather than on Sarah's. If he does testify accurately to Sarah's kindness, this is witness to Sarah's long-suffering selflessness on behalf of Abraham. Even more, Abraham lays the blame back on God for making him wander (not the full truth of the matter); this argument also has a self-serving ring, an Edenlike move that seeks to lay the blame on God for what has happened. This rationalization suggests a less than trusting relation to God, let alone an inability to develop strategies for life that take the well-being of outsiders into account.

Given Abraham's rationalizations, Abimelech's response is remarkably magnanimous. He restores Sarah and gives Abraham a significant sum of money for the purpose of her exoneration (literally, "covering of all eyes") within her family (shame is the issue addressed). It is her vindication, a public demonstration that Sarah has not been wronged and hence can be held in honor within her community. Given his action with respect to Sarah, Abimelech "is the only one who could effect her acquittal."[15] As such Abimelech manifests a concern for Sarah and her welfare that Abraham has not exhibited. Abimelech also gives Abraham animals and servants, and offers them a place for living in his own land (the Promised Land). This member of the indigenous peoples of the land offers some of his land to this recent, not very trustworthy immigrant; indeed, Abimelech offers him his choice of lands, as Abraham had earlier offered Lot (13:8–9). It is to be noted that Abraham is not consigned to the poorer land nor are he and his family herded together into reservations. And we learn in 21:34 that Abraham took up residence there.

By these actions, Abimelech again shows that he is indeed one who possesses the fear of God, whose actions are in tune with the Creator's purposes. One could conceivably say that he acts purely out of self-interest in view of what God has warned him about Sarah's restoration and about his need for Abraham's prayers (20:7). At the same time, his sharp questioning and critique of Abraham shows that he does not coddle Abraham for fear of offending "a prophet" (and God had informed him, 20:7). And he believes the word of God about the need for Sarah's restoration and acts on it in ways beyond what was divinely called for.

The question might be raised as to the connection between Abimelech's actions with respect to Sarah, his own sickness, and the closing of the wombs in Abimelech's household.[16] The perspective of the narrator is that there is "a dynamic cosmological relationship among the physical order, the moral order, and God. . . . This connection means that immoral behavior under the judgment of God may result in a catastrophic convulsing of creation in the realm of that immoral behavior."[17] While Abimelech is innocent, his actions (objective guilt) have had cosmological consequences. This includes his sickness as well as that of the women in his household. Bruckner says it well: "Abimelech has been caught in a web of cosmological consequence. He must rely on a prophet to restore his health, not because he is guilty, but because he is sick. He is sick, not because he is guilty, but because he has become the victim of a lie and has unwittingly participated in a violation of the created moral order."[18]

Even with all of Abimelech's gifts and concern for the individuals involved, especially Sarah, it is only Abraham's prayer interceding on Abimelech's behalf that enables the healing (cf. his intercessions for Sodom and Gomorrah, 18:22–33; Num. 12:13; 21:7). Though Abraham is responsible for the trouble, God responds to his prayer and heals Abimelech and his wife and female slaves so that they can once again bear children (the identity of the illness is uncertain). Notably, God does not heal directly, but works in and through the prayers of Abraham. The

prayer of a righteous man may avail much (James 5:16), but here it is the prayer
of an Abraham whose righteousness has been brought into question (in the sense
of doing justice to the relationship), and his prayer proves to be effective. The
righteous one (Abimelech) needs the prayers of the unrighteous. God doesn't perfect people before working through them to carry out the divine purposes. Other
biblical texts will speak of means that God uses in addition to prayer (for example, 2 Kings 20:7), but prayer is shown here to be a powerful vehicle through
which God works to heal.

The narrative returns to the relationship between Abraham and Abimelech the
Outsider in 21:22–34 (cf. his contact with Isaac in 26:1–33).[19] That Abimelech is
a character in two different chapters in the Abraham cycle is not unparalleled (see
chapter 2). This second encounter suggests that the relationship between Abraham and the outsider (especially those in Canaan) is a matter of some consequence, as does the immediately prior story of Hagar and Ishmael. Isaac's birth
(21:1–7) occurs in the midst of a world filled with such relationships with outsiders. The story also highlights Abraham's first acquisition of land in Canaan (cf.
chapter 23), a renewed concern in view of the new son.

In this second encounter with Abraham, Abimelech interprets Abraham's relationship with God in religiously insightful and theologically accurate terms: "God
is with you in all that you do" (21:22; cf. the comparable language of the narrator
in 21:20). Abimelech expresses his concern (22:23) that the basic human loyalty
(ḥesed) he has shown to Abraham be returned to his family (and to the land).
Abraham swears that he will do so. Abraham then complains to Abimelech about
the seizure of a well, a key resource in a drought-ridden world (21:25). Abimelech
replies that he had not been informed until this moment. This exchange concludes
with a nonaggression pact-covenant, according to which the two agree to main-
tain a relationship of integrity (21:27–31).[20] Among the animals that Abraham sets
apart for the ritual, he includes seven ewe lambs that are to serve as a "witness" in
their future relationships that this well that had been seized was in fact Abraham's
well. Both Abimelech and Abraham agree to the terms of the oath, and Abimelech's
return to his territory is a sign of his agreement.[21] It is in view of this sworn oath
with the ewe lambs that Beersheba is said to have received its ambiguous name
(either well of seven or well of the oath).

Abraham plants a tree at Beersheba as a permanent sign of the treaty and worships God (21:33). The epithet used for God (only here)—El Olam, the Everlasting God—may express a confidence in God's tending to this relationship after the
death of the present participants. Abraham sojourned for an extensive period of
time in Abimelech's land (21:34). This note testifies both to the effectiveness of
the treaty and to Abraham's continuing alien status in a land included in the
promise (15:18–21). Abraham's worshipful response to the "political" covenant

of reconciliation with Abimelech creates a link between peace-making events of everyday life and the worship of God. Abraham does not reserve God-talk for explicitly religious matters; he thereby recognizes that God has been involved in social and political life, enabling justice and peace in a situation filled with strife.

THE ROLE OF THE OUTSIDER

This text has been commonly neglected in teaching and preaching, perhaps because the story gives such a favorable impression of a person who stands outside the community of faith. That Abimelech is a Canaanite complicates the issue even more. Generally, Genesis is positively disposed toward the indigenous inhabitants of Canaan, remarkable in view of later conflicts.[22] On the other hand, a mixed portrayal is given of Abraham, though efforts to excuse him are legion. Given the fact that the religious communities look to Abraham as the exemplar of what it means to be a person of faith, this text has proved to be somewhat embarrassing.

Abraham is an immigrant, not unlike the relationship of many families to this continent, about which we so lustily sing: This land is my land. As indigenous peoples, Abimelech and his family might be said to be an ancient counterpart to the Australian aborigines or the Native Americans. The text may also ask readers to ponder whether, in this respect, Abraham's sins have become theirs. Though as far as we know, Abraham and later Isaac at least kept the peace treaties made with Abimelech.

It may be helpful to list the several ways in which the text lifts up the person and activity of the outsider Abimelech. Given the portrait that emerges, readers might properly wonder whether he provides a model for the community of faith.

1. God is present and active among outsiders; indeed they are surrounded by experiences of divine activity—both judgment and salvation—whether they realize it or not.

2. God takes the initiative and communicates with the outsider. The word of God is here heard in an unexpected place and by one who is not a "person of faith." "The Canaanite king hears the voice that speaks as God's voice because it says what he recognizes to be just and valid."[23] Even more, not only does God hear the words of the "pagan," but engages the outsider in dialogue, and this bears fruit in the lives of all concerned. We may find it disconcerting that God engages such a one apart from the ministrations of the community of faith. But this story makes clear that God does not run a closed shop on who receives a word from God and who can engage it.

3. The sharp, direct questioning on the part of this nonchosen one counts with God. It affects the shape of the future of all characters (including God). Abimelech evidences genuine courage in such a confrontation, both with God and later with

Abraham. And God responds positively to Abimelech's challenge in ways that open up possibilities for life rather than death (cf. Gen. 31:24; Num. 22:20). This is a dialogue and it is similar to that between God and Abraham in Genesis 18:22–23. Religious questioning on the part of the "unchosen" ones is not only a matter that God treats seriously but one in which God himself directly engages, albeit through less than "orthodox" channels (such as dreams); but it is no less real for that, and God will use comparable means with Jacob and Joseph.

4. Abimelech has a keen sense for truth and justice and moves in ways that properly discern the will of God in this situation. Abraham-like suspicions about such outsiders are common among all of Abraham's heirs. This text encourages readers to recognize that daily life has often been positively informed and undergirded by the wisdom, insight, imagination, and common sense of the Abimelechs among us. God often makes use of such persons to make the divine will known, to be of assistance in daily life, and to further the divine purposes for the world.

5. Abimelech, the outsider, exemplifies the fear of God in how he speaks and acts in this situation, both with God and with Abraham. Abimelech acts with a faithfulness that works itself out in his daily life in terms of truth and justice; God himself speaks of the integrity of his heart (20:6). The insider did not believe that an outsider could be a "God-fearer" (20:11), but the narrative shows that Abraham does not properly assess the outsiders' relationship with God or their character.[24] Whether such "insiders" recognize the transcendent reality at work is another matter, of course. A challenge of the chosen community is to speak with "outsiders" in such a way that they can make connections with the God experiences they have already had, enabling them to move toward naming that experience for what it in fact has been.

6. Abimelech, the outsider, is remarkably magnanimous in the way in which he acts and speaks with Abraham and Sarah. His generosity is evident in the way in which he responds to this family with gifts, though he is the one who has been wronged. His compassion is shown by the way in which he understands what Sarah has been through, and the issues of honor and shame that needed to be addressed.[25] These are human characteristics that insiders deeply prize, and Abimelech exemplifies them as a human being of God's good creation. Indeed, he has learned them quite independently from the chosen people and he practices them in ways that are not shown by Abraham. The overall portrayal of Abimelech suggests a person of character. Even though he is not the root cause of this problem, he seeks to bring healing to the situation far beyond the level of his own involvement.

7. God uses this outsider to be a teacher of the community of faith. Abimelech is a visionary spirit, with insight into the nature of this problematic, indeed potentially devastating situation. God works in and through this outsider to further God's work in the world. And this takes place independently of the chosen people and, given Abraham's all-too-typical response, in spite of them.

One may wonder whether the narrator believed Abimelech had such an accurate and powerful sense of sin or whether an Israelite understanding was incorporated into his words. It may well be that Abimelech's recognition of the divine origin of his dream and his theological understandings are reflective of a rather sophisticated theology that the narrator believed such outsiders could have brought to the occasion. It is clear from ancient Near Eastern texts that that would not at all be out of order. The idea that sinfulness is a universal experience of brokenness at every level of existence, indeed the idea of what has been called "original sin," is not peculiar to the Bible. Such understandings reflect a general theology in the ancient Near East, long before Israel came into being.

This claim can be demonstrated from a sampling of Near Eastern texts from the third and second millennium B.C.E.[26]

A penitential prayer transmitted in Sumerian and Akkadian: "Who is there who has not sinned against his god; who has always obeyed the commandments? Every one who lives is sinful."

A Sumerian wisdom saying: "Never has a sinless child been born to its mother."

An Akkadian confession of sin: "My god, though my transgressions are many—free me of my guilt! Though my misdeeds are innumerable—let your heart be still! Though my sins be countless—show mercy and heal me!"

An invocation to Ishtar: "Forgive my sin, my iniquity, my wickedness and my offence. Loose my fetters, secure my deliverance. Let my prayers and my supplications come to you and may all your grace be with me; then those who see me in the street will glorify your name."

A song of thanksgiving to the Egyptian god Amun-Re: "If it is the nature of the servant to commit sin, it is the nature of the Lord to be gracious."

Such texts witness to a profound understanding of sin and grace across the ancient Near East, and it may well be that Abimelech was understood to reflect such perspectives. These theological perspectives are nothing peculiarly biblical, though indebtedness to these ancient theologians is seldom acknowledged.

The text functions with a sense of natural law, law as a part of the created order of things that can be discerned and observed by human beings apart from faith. The community of faith does not have a corner on ability to discern right and wrong.

8. God raises up such outsiders to be the confessors of the insiders. Once again, an outsider is used by God to convict the chosen ones of their sinful deeds (12:18–19), to call them to account on moral issues. God commonly makes this kind of move, as here, because of problems let loose on the world by the sins of righteous persons such as Abraham. Before the insider ever speaks a prophetic word, the outsider does. The outsider's critical word to Abraham calls him to account for his

behavior. The unattractive face of the chosen people, here exemplified in Abraham's behavior that endangers an entire community, may mean that God will have to go outside of the chosen people to find persons who can be the medium of a word from God.

9. Instead of being an agent of blessing, Abraham had been an agent of curse; but by praying he can begin to turn what he has done around, enabling blessing for the one who has blessed him (Gen. 12:3). Abraham, once again, has brought trouble rather than blessing to outsiders (verse 9); the deeds of the chosen one have led to the suffering of many other people. Such a story no doubt reflects the life of the people of God in later generations, who often mistreated the strangers and aliens in their midst (a concern deeply rooted in Israel's law, for example, Exod. 22:21–27).

10. But Abraham, in spite of his behaviors, is also an agent of blessing on outsiders. God acts in saving ways on behalf of the outsiders, evident here in the healing of Abimelech and the women in his household. Order and well-being, that is, salvation in the broad sense of the term, is thereby brought to this community of outsiders. God enters into this difficult situation and blessings flow in two directions: blessings to Abimelech through Abraham's prayer and blessings to Abraham through Abimelech's generosity. God is shown to be one who works for life and goodness, both within and without the community of faith, and often in spite of the words and deeds of the chosen ones. Abraham's call to be a blessing to all families is a mixed bag. Though the chosen may complicate and frustrate the
– divine activity, they cannot finally stymie it; God will find a way to work toward the divine purposes. The next narrative speaks of other ways in which God continues to be about that task.

11. That Abraham enters into a mutually agreed upon covenant with outsiders (21:22–34) is important quite apart from the religious sphere. God's purposes in
– the world are for the good order of the creation, which includes relationships with all regardless of their faith commitments. It is also notable that Abraham is viewed as one who is not somehow inevitably trustworthy; specific agreements will be needed by the outsider, because loyalty on the part of chosen ones all too often fails.

12. It is striking that the narrator gives Abimelech a voice (21:23) in which he claims loyalty (ḥesed) in his relationships with Abraham (and expects the same from him). From what the reader recalls regarding their prior interactions (chapter 20), this appears to be an accurate self-assessment, and is again testimony to the character of an outsider.

13. In spite of the way Abimelech was treated by Abraham in chapter 20, he discerns that God's presence has been decisive in Abraham's life (21:22). Isaac will also meet up with Abimelech later and, even more expansively, Abimelech confirms that the

divine promises have been fulfilled (26:28–29). That an outsider like Abimelech makes such confessions and treats Abraham (and Isaac) well in spite of his negative experience with him is narrative testimony to God's work as Creator in his life. Such confessions also confirm that Abraham's initial assessment of Abimelech was wrong (20:11); once again, Abimelech gives evidence of his fear of God.

14. Abimelech's reference to his posterity (21:23) brings the problematic relationships between Israelites and Canaanites over the years into view. Abraham's relationship with Abimelech may serve as a mirror in which later generations of Israelites can test their relationships with such outsiders.

CHAPTER 5

ABRAHAM AND OUTSIDERS II
GIFT, THREAT, AND CHALLENGE

Genesis 13:1–14:24; 18:16–19:38

T here are several Abrahamic texts that, among other things, consider the promise of land (12:7), the place of Lot, and the role of outsiders (13–14; 18:16–19:38) These chapters especially relate Abraham and his family to the larger world scene.

ABRAHAM, LOT, AND THE THREAT OF OUTSIDERS, GENESIS 13:1–18

Following his encounter with Pharaoh (12:10–20), Abraham returns from Egypt a rich man, with silver and gold, fields and flocks (13:1–4).[1] Readers are given to wonder how anything can go wrong. But the blessings of God create problems as well as possibilities. These blessings provide the occasion for strife and separation (13:5): "Their possessions were so great that they could not live together" (13:6). A situation of material well-being has not meant that Abrahamic family life would go well; it has raised its own set of problems. Abraham and his nephew Lot begin life in the land from essentially the same point; both are recipients of the blessings of God in great bounty. What will the two individuals now make of the blessing they have received?

Abraham takes the initiative to settle the intrafamilial squabble. Appealing to their kinship, he voices an interest in peace: "let there be no strife between you and me" (13:8).[2] Abraham's action probably also entails an enlightened self-interest in view of his need for "support" (verse 6) for his flocks and herds. That this separation would lead to greater prosperity on the part of all concerned is certainly not far from anyone's mind. The text does not blame either person or regard either of them as especially quarrelsome; it seems to be a responsible way of responding to crowded conditions and maintaining peace and well-being. At the same time, God's promise to Abraham specified that he would be given the land for his "offspring" (12:7; 13:15); that would seem to mean that Lot would not be included in the land promise. Moreover, Abraham's resolution is family separation (the verb occurs in verses 9, 11, 14), with each group occupying different territories.

Abraham gives Lot the option of two lands from which to choose.[3] This gesture by Abraham appears magnanimous, though it is difficult to be certain. Too many unresolved questions remain. Did Abraham have a sense for the choice Lot might make, given its bounty (13:10)? He may not have wanted the land that Lot was apt to choose; indeed, he probably associated the land promised (12:5–7) with the land that Lot did not choose. Or was he tired of strife and willing to take anything for the sake of peace? Did Abraham know what the implications of Lot's choice might be? Does he know about Sodom (verse 13)? Abraham's motivations remain ambiguous.

Some interpreters think that Abraham, in giving Lot the choice, puts the promise in jeopardy. Perhaps so. The promise of 12:7 had specified "this land" (that is, "the land of Canaan," 12:5). Lot does not choose "the land of Canaan"; this is the land in which Abraham settles (13:12). Yet, what becomes the Promised Land (13:14–18) seems not to be confined to "the land of Canaan." What Abraham sees in 13:14–15 seems to include what Lot saw (cf. "the whole land," verse 9); "all the land" in verse 15 seems to be more than the "land of Canaan" in verse 12. Yet, the narrator may understand them to be co-extensive, so that Lot's choice was not included within the land promised (at least at this point in time).[4]

Lot does not respond verbally (why?). Verse 13:10 relates only his thoughts regarding the choice Abraham has put before him. Why does he make the choice he does? On the one hand, he is drawn by what he "saw"; the beauty of the land is a prominent factor. On the other hand, his decision is shaped by what he knows about "the garden of the Lord" (Eden; 2:8; Isa. 51:3) and "the land of Egypt."

These reasons are problematic, or at least insufficient. A significant disjunction exists between Lot's perception and the reality of things. His "seeing" and his knowing are too limited. The narrator makes clear that Sodom is no Eden (verses 10, 13); and Lot's reflections are linked to the comments about Sodom. One cannot go "back to Eden," in any case. As for the land of Egypt, from which Lot has recently returned (13:1; cf. Deut. 11:10), he focuses on its gardenlike quality. It may be that the narrator intends to recall Israel's wandering in the wilderness, begging to return to Egyptian fleshpots (Exod. 16:1–4). Egypt represents a desire for a preredemption state of affairs. Likeness to Egypt also connects with the later language of "outcry" about Sodom (18:21; 19:13; cf. Exod. 3:7–9). These links to Sodom and Egypt suggest that Lot's ethical-theological perspective is questionable. While this perspective does not determine how Lot will respond within his new locale, his conduct in chapter 19 suggests he has begun to take on the character of this environment.

The narrator's announcement that Sodom and Gomorrah had been destroyed (13:10) prepares readers to expect that they would soon hear about their destruction. But, it is important to note that no indication is given as to when this might occur.[5] Chapter 14 probably functions as the portrayal of an initial possibility for such an event, for it suggests that Sodom and Gomorrah are about to be destroyed by the alliance of eastern kings. But they are delivered because of Abraham's intervention for the sake of Lot. God's inquiry in 18:16–19:29 will constitute another time and place when the future of Sodom and Gomorrah is considered. Will Abraham's intervention on behalf of these cities be as effective then as it is in chapter 14?

The story of Abraham and Lot concludes with a repeated promise of a land, enclosing a promise of posterity (13:14–18)—dust is a traditional image for an unimaginably large number (15:5; 28:14). The promise to Abraham is a direct, unconditional proclamation. It is an extension of the promise that appears in 12:7, with a new word about perpetuity (13:15; 17:8; 48:4). God's promise is "forever," but, as we have seen in earlier chapters, disloyal recipients can remove themselves from the sphere of fulfillment.

We have noted that God's promises are repeated throughout the story of Abraham. They are reiterated here because this decision about land constitutes a key transition in Abraham's journey, not least in view of Lot's decision about land. Legal language for the transfer of property is used.[6] Abraham is to lift up his eyes, look around, and walk through the land, concretely laying claim to an actual piece of real estate (cf. Lot in verses 10–12; Josh. 1:3; 24:3). The land is thereby transferred from God to Abraham; it is actually given to him, not simply promised as a future gift (NIV, "I am giving"; 13:17). The narrator reports only his journey to Hebron, however (13:18). Abraham "moves his tent" (as did Lot, 13:12) and settles near a stand of trees, where he (unlike Lot) builds his fourth altar. This will be the area of Abraham's later purchase of land for Sarah's burial place (chapter 23).

THE ROLE OF THE OUTSIDER

The cumulative effect of the narrative is that, while Lot may be an "insider" to begin the Abrahamic journey ("kindred," 13:8), he becomes an "outsider" over the course of the story.[7] Already in 13:14–17 (reinforcing 12:7), he is excluded from the promise, which is directed only to Abraham's "offspring." In his final appearance in the narrative, he is the progenitor of "outsiders," the Moabites and the Ammonites (19:37–38), peoples often at odds with Israel (Deut. 2:9–19; 23:3–4). Lot's "separation" from Abraham in chapter 13 anticipates that of Ishmael and other sons of Abraham (25:1–18) and Jacob (Esau, 36:6–8).

As Lot moves from the "inner circle" to greater identification with an outsider community, he is increasingly associated with a circle of peoples outside of the people of promise. Sodom and Gomorrah are filled with people who are "wicked, great sinners against the Lord" (13:13; 18:20). They are the only people so identified in Genesis and could be viewed as a lively threat to the chosen family. Indeed, as Lot is swallowed up into that alien culture, he becomes an illustration of what could happen to the chosen people more generally. Abraham's land is also potentially within reach of a Sodom and Gomorrah experience. In fact, generations later, Israel will become like Sodom and Gomorrah (Isa. 1:10; Jer. 23:14) and visited with judgments that are described in such terms (Deut. 29:22–25; cf. Lam. 4:6; Amos 4:11).

Outsiders may present a threat to the chosen people, but those threats are not unrelated to choices that the "insiders" make. Choices can jeopardize blessings. Blessings are not some inevitable consequence of being members of the chosen people. What people do with their blessings will determine whether they remain — blessings; in fact, blessings can become a threat to life and well-being. Lot here makes choices and the effects are disastrous; the blessings of the Edenlike setting that he chooses will become a wasteland. Blessings, of course, may only look like blessings; they may not be blessings at all. They may be inappropriately gained through wealth and stealth, built up on the backs of other people (cf. the "outcry" in Sodom, 18:20–21), accrued in and through unwise and wicked choices. The references to Sodom and Gomorrah in 13:10, 13 anticipate issues relating to Lot and these cities in both 14:1–24 and 18:16–19:38. The presence of these chapters in the Abraham story seems to be related in a fundamental way to the decisions that Lot makes and how those choices can indeed become a lively threat to the future of the people of God.

OUTSIDERS: THREAT AND BLESSING, 14:1–24

Readers of the story of Abraham must be alert to making distinctions among outsiders. Not all outsiders are a threat to the people of God. Sodom is; Melchizedek is not. Key features illumine the person and role of Abraham.[8]

The opening verses of this chapter report a gathering of forces, not always identifiable, that endangers Lot and, potentially, Israel's future in the land (14:1–12). In their sweep through the area, a coalition of four Eastern kings, apparently from the Mesopotamian region, capture people and possessions, including Lot, and leave the area. When this is reported to Abraham, he takes his 318 trained men, joins forces with other "allies," pursues the kings to the vicinity of Damascus and brings back all that had been captured, including Lot (14:13–16). The fate of Lot moves Abraham and his small retinue to act, Gideon-like, against the armies of four major nations. In effect, Abraham thereby assumes control over the Promised Land.

When Abraham returns from battle, he is met by the king of Sodom (verses 17, 21–24), who is joined by the king of Salem (verses 18–20) in the King's Valley, of uncertain location but probably near Jerusalem. The king of Salem, Melchizedek, is also a priest of God Most High (El Elyon).[9] He brings Abraham food and drink, blesses him in the name of God Most High, the Creator, and blesses Abraham's God for delivering Abraham, thereby giving a theological interpretation of the prior events. This encounter with Melchizedek is what enables Abraham to respond appropriately to the king of Sodom and not take the spoils.

This seemingly interruptive chapter plays an important role in linking the story of Abraham with Genesis 1–11, for here we have to do with the larger world of families and nations (see especially Genesis 10:1–11:9).[10] Genesis 14 gives particular testimony to the growth and spread of the nations in that part of the world. Moreover, the chosen family is shown not to be isolated from that world, but caught up in this movement of peoples and nations, a movement that often entails conflict and warfare. This family is a part of that larger world and will have to make key decisions about the nature of its involvement in that world. This text demonstrates that the chosen family chooses to become engaged with such "outsiders." As Janzen puts it, this chapter reminds readers "that the human story has many centers—and as many particular stories—as there are peoples." Moreover, in Genesis 14:1, the peoples "are introduced in their own right," without specific reference to the chosen family.[11] Indeed, reference to the chosen people does not occur until 14:12 and then, at least initially, they seem to be but one people among many in that part of the world. In fact, rather than dominating that world as the divine promises of land, great nation, and great name (and later, kings) might suggest, the chosen family seems to be at the mercy of these other families. The recently stated promises of 13:14–18 seem to be but a mirage in such a world.

In addition, this chapter is testimony to the fact that the chosen family has more than a spiritual agenda among the nations. They are not just called to be "church," and to sit back while the rest of the world pursues its contentious and oppressive ways. As Janzen points out, the identification of Abraham as a "Hebrew" (14:13) presents him as the leader of a social group, not the bearer of a divine promise or religious vocation.[12] Here the chosen people get caught up in international conflict with all the social, political, and even economic realities that such engagements entail. Indeed, Abraham chooses to enter into alliance with local Amorites (14:13) and uses force against warring nations in order to rescue Lot from their oppressive actions and to retrieve stolen property—on behalf of Sodom and Gomorrah (14:11, 16). Abraham and his retinue are represented as the key factor in the "defeat" of warring kings, indeed an empire, an empire that had for fourteen years stymied attempts at overthrow by local armies (14:4–12). This move by Abraham contrasts with that which he took in the previous chapter (13), where conflict is resolved peacefully. It is clear from this venture that Abraham is no pacifist. Later we will find Abraham entering into the question of the future of the wicked cities of Sodom and Gomorrah (18:16–19:38) and negotiating with foreign peoples about property (23:1–20). This chosen family has a role among all the families of the earth (12:3) that moves beyond the specifically religious and includes all aspects of their life.

As noted, the strangely detailed coverage of battles in which Abraham engages in defense of Lot contains several important references to Sodom and Gomorrah. The move from Sodom and Gomorrah to just Sodom in 14:10–17 (as in 13:10, 13) shows that Lot's new home is clearly in view. That only the plight of the kings of Sodom and Gomorrah is mentioned in 14:10–11 no doubt anticipates chapters 18–19; their fleeing to the hills (14:10) anticipates what will happen to Lot (19:17–20, 30). The reference to the geology of the valley of Siddim (14:10, bitumen pits) anticipates the means by which Sodom and Gomorrah are destroyed (sulfur and fire, 19:24; Deut. 29:23). Just as Abraham would later intercede for these cities for the sake of the righteous in them (18:22–33), so here in chapter 14 he risks his life in ways that will accrue to their benefit. Lot's freedom centers Abraham's efforts, but in the process he liberates "great sinners" (13:13). These battles may constitute an effort on the part of Abraham to prevent the integration of Lot into the evil cultures of that world, an effort that finally fails. In any case, his concern for his nephew reaches beyond simple common sense or a careful calculation of possible gains and losses. Abraham's actions in the wake of his victory (14:17–24) show this to be the case in a special way, as he separates himself from the politically and economically motivated moves that victors commonly make. In a postvictory encounter, the king of Sodom represents the cities liberated by Abraham (14:17). In 14:21, the king seems to be generous in his offer that Abraham should keep the recaptured goods (the persons, such as Lot, are to be returned). The king focuses on the disposition of the booty, a portion of which was Lot's (verses 11–12, 16). Why does Abraham refuse the offer? The reasons seem to be quite complex. Some interpreters look to Abraham's generosity of spirit, or a refusal to enrich himself, or recognition that Sodom's goods were not his to do with as he will, for Sodom was not the defeated one. But the issue here is not simply whether Abraham will take the spoils offered by the king of Sodom, but whether he will take Lot's goods and use them for gaining hegemony in Lot's land, a matter that they had just settled between themselves (13:6–12). Abraham refusal to do so, then, centers on an issue of justice, namely, his own prior agreement with Lot. Abraham's decision also relates, perhaps even more centrally, to the fact that he is dealing with the city of Sodom. If he took the spoils, he would then be obligated to the king of Sodom, a potentially treacherous relationship given the wicked character of the city (13:13). To have allied himself with this king would have entailed a compromise of basic moral principles. He chooses instead to distance himself from Sodom by rejecting any economic linkage. The fact that Abraham did let his Amorite allies take their share (14:21, 24) makes clear that it is not the issue of spoils generally that motivates him, but his particular relationship with the principals involved: an issue of justice with Lot and an issue of alliance with the wicked cities of Sodom and Gomorrah. Such moves will give Abraham's later intercession on behalf of Sodom a higher level of credibility.

But, finally, there are even more basic religious and theological factors that motivate Abraham's decision, and his engagement with Melchizedek is the decisive factor that enables these realities to become evident to him in this situation (14:18–20).

A few words about the mysterious Melchizedek are important at this point. He is mentioned elsewhere only in Psalms 110:4 (a royal psalm) and Hebrews 5–7 (cf. also Qumran texts), where he is interpreted in messianic terms. His name, similar to the Canaanite king, Adonizedek (Josh. 10:1), probably means "my king is salvation/righteousness." His priest-king status may mean that the Canaanite kingship is understood as a sacral-political office, an understanding not foreign to Davidic kings (cf. Ps. 110:4). These verses may have originated among Davidic-Solomonic apologists, when relationships with the pre-Israelite leaders of Jerusalem (Salem, cf. Ps. 76:2) were important. They sought to anchor new forms of royal-temple practice in Abrahamic times in order to legitimate them, perhaps in view of questions raised about "new" practices associated with the Davidic regime. The priestly name Zadok (2 Sam. 8:17; 15:24–35) is also derived from this root; he was a pre-Israelite Jerusalem priest who became associated with David. His descendants, the Zadokite priestly line, were linked with the Davidic dynasty through the centuries. This encounter of Abraham with Melchizedek may have been understood, at least at one level, as grounding the Zadokite priesthood in ancient times (perhaps in view of claims of illegitimacy). In light of these links, Melchizedek may be viewed as a precursor of both the royal and priestly lines in the Davidic kingship.

Melchizedek's bringing of bread and wine is intended to refresh Abraham after his battles, but because he is a priest, such actions have a religious import and cannot be separated from the blessing by Melchizedek that follows. His act of blessing includes a blessing on Abraham by God the Creator. Melchizedek thus exercises a truly mediatorial function. Abraham is blessed by an outsider (cf. Balaam, Num. 24:1); he does not do the blessing. Melchizedek would thus be a potential recipient of the action of a God who blesses "those who bless you" (12:3). His act also includes a blessing of God (in direct address), which is an act of praise and thanksgiving for delivering them from their common enemy (see the blessing of God in the wake of an experience of salvation by Jethro, also a nonchosen individual, Exod. 18:10). In both cases, the blessing increases power and renown: it bestows strength on Abraham from God and it increases God's renown in the world. Both dimensions of blessing in Israel's later worship are thus set in the time of Abraham.

Abraham's encounter with Melchizedek is literarily inserted between the announcement of the meeting of Abraham and the king of Sodom (14:17) and their actual exchange (14:21–24). Hence, it is presented as crucial to the nature of that interaction. Abraham's refusal to take the spoils is grounded in an oath that he swore to God Most High, the Creator, that he would not take even the smallest of items (14:22–23). The tithe Abraham gives to Melchizedek refers to the spoils; Abraham leaves the other 90 percent with the king of Sodom. Apparently his reception of Melchizedek's blessing and his tithe to Melchizedek entailed such an oath. Abraham's oath was sworn in the name of Yahweh, whom Abraham identifies with the El Elyon of Melchizedek's blessing. Abraham thereby implicitly recognizes the legitimacy of Melchizedek's priesthood of the same God whom he worships. Melchizedek's blessing included specific testimony to El Elyon as both creator and deliverer. This witness enabled Abraham to see that it was not finally his own strength that accomplished these deeds. It was God's deliverance.

At the same time, while the victory is ascribed to God, no specific mention has been made of divine words and deeds up to this point in the narrative. The report of the battle recalls only Abraham's abilities as a military strategist and leader. This focus implies that Abraham as God's agent in this conflict is genuine agency and that his activity is important and effective. The image of kings and armies tumbling all over themselves to get away from Abraham is designed to impress the reader with the boldness and cleverness of Abraham in defeating a much larger, though of uncertain size, force and saving the kidnapped persons and their possessions. Abraham is a Gideon-like figure (Judg. 6) portrayed in larger-than-life proportions, whose talents and skills are not to be downplayed. But it is God who is finally confessed as the one who makes the victory possible. And it is the outsider's testimony that, finally, enables a theological breakthrough for Abraham and thereby helps him see the heart of the issue at stake in this decision. The witness to the faith of Abraham in the following chapter (15:6) is at least in part an effect of the witness of the faith of Melchizedek.

One dimension of this theological breakthrough for Abraham could well be his recognition that it would be improper for the liberator to enrich himself at the expense of the liberated. It is notable that Abraham does not pursue a strategy of rescuing only Lot from among those captured. He acts in such a way as to liberate all captives from Sodom and Gomorrah, quite apart from an assessment of whether they deserved it, or whether their behaviors up to this point would justify the risk. This action is parallel with Abraham's later intercession on behalf of these cities (18:16–33). The effect of Abraham's action is that all Sodomites experienced deliverance, and to take away from that experience by keeping their goods would be to intrude upon the salvific experience itself. It would make salvation something less than the gracious experience it is. It might even appear to make the liberation conditional upon reception of the gift.

It might be further noted that the description of Abraham's group is almost entirely in the language of the family. It is family against nation. When combined with the focus on Lot, family interests take priority over those of nations and kings. For the sake of the family, it may be necessary to counter efforts made by national forces. Peace and war are matters that affect nations because they deeply affect families. It is for the sake of the family that Abraham finally makes his decisions regarding war and peace.

Finally, this text makes clear that issues of war and peace are not a matter for chosen people only. Others who oppose the subjugation of others (14:13, 24) get involved, though they are not people of God. This participation on the part of outsiders, so important for the ongoing life of insiders, witnesses to the work of God the Creator having an impact on their lives so that they work toward the peace and well-being of a human community. The "goodness" of the creation as stated by God in Genesis 1 here is shown to be evident in the lives of communities outside of those who have been specifically called and chosen.

SODOM AND GOMORRAH AS "OUTSIDER" THREAT TO THE CREATION AND THE CHOSEN FAMILY: GENESIS 18:16–19:38

How shall we speak of divine judgment in the world today?[13] Some interpreters of the present world scene are not hesitant in responding. They will point to the depletion of the ozone layer and global warming; "unnatural" developments in the animal world (for example, deformed frogs); the spread of deadly viruses; and weather patterns that seem uncommonly violent. Aside from the heightened rhetoric and undisciplined certainty that often accompany such claims, is there a kernel of truth in the linkage of such phenomena with the judgmental activity of God?

Even those who choose not to draw such conclusions and who recognize our inadequate knowledge of the history of nature, the difficulties of comparative measures, and the "wildness" and randomness integral to God's good creation, have often been given to a nagging bewilderment. What is the import of these environmental events for the future of the earth and its inhabitants? Many would claim that such "unnatural" events are at least significant in part due to human activities that have disrupted the earth's delicate ecology. The truth of such a claim is commonly accepted, both within and without religious communities. But is such an "explanation" sufficient?

For readers of the Sodom and Gomorrah texts in Genesis 18–19, further questions are often asked: What are we to make of textual claims that God is somehow involved in this environmental disaster? If God is in some sense responsible then, how might God be related to contemporary environmental developments and to what end? Even for those who are properly reticent in making theological claims about natural events, these questions are important, not least because they are raised by many biblical texts that link divine judgment with environmental catastrophe.[14]

The story of the destruction of Sodom and Gomorrah in Genesis 18–19 does not stand alone; indeed, the list is long, including the flood (Genesis 6–8) and the plagues in Egypt (Exod. 7–12). While each of these stories indicts sinful human behavior for what happens to the ecosystem, the text certainly portrays God as deeply involved. Indeed, does not God make matters worse? For all the talk today about God being committed to the stewardship of the earth, in these stories we find God contributing to the degradation of the environment. In addition, each of these environmentally related texts raises issues of justice. Could not Abraham's question in Genesis 18:25 be addressed to God in each case: What of the innocent that will be destroyed along with the guilty? What about all the children? If readers were to move beyond these stories to other types of biblical texts, this impression would be vividly reinforced. Take Jeremiah 4:22–26, certainly one of the most vivid biblical portrayals of environmental catastrophe. Again, while human behaviors are cited (verse 22), the climactic point in the text links these environmental disasters to the "fierce anger" of God (verse 26). Again, the question is pertinent: What about the children?

More broadly, this theological narrative may well juxtapose an ancient tradition about an environmental disaster and a religious crisis in the narrator's own community, perhaps the fall of Jerusalem (see chapter 2). Such a narrative strategy grounds later theological reflection regarding sin and judgment deeply within Israel's ancestral heritage. Such crises prompt the question again and again: will the righteous fare as the wicked? In, say, the fall of Jerusalem, why would God sweep away the faithful with the wicked; why not save all Israel for the sake of the righteous few? At least the children.

The story of Sodom and Gomorrah explicitly links human sin, divine judgment, and environmental disaster. At the same time, it also raises the question of justice and how will the chosen family relate to this complicated set of issues? What do Abraham and his family have to do with the future of such cities, wicked as they may be (13:13)?

This question returns us to the issue of the outsider. Sodom and Gomorrah are "outsider cities" into which kindred of the chosen family have moved. Given their declared character as "wicked" (13:13), the Sodomites constitute a threat to the life and well-being of the ancestral family. But the relationship of the chosen family to this reality is complex and ambiguous. On the one hand, Lot and his family live in these cities and both their character and their relationship to God are threatened. Do the texts contain an implicit counsel for Abraham and his family to avoid such cities at all costs? On the other hand, Abraham intercedes on behalf of these cities for the sake of the innocent people in them (Lot may be especially in mind, given his rescue in chapter 14, but Abraham never mentions him). For Abraham this is an issue of justice (Gen. 18:25). Readers are thus faced in these chapters with issues relating both to the threat of the outsider and related threats that catch up issues of justice and the environment.

In this story, God and Abraham concern themselves with the future of cities filled with nonchosen peoples, outside of the community of faith, almost all of them strangers, a few of them righteous, or at least innocent. Moreover, God and Abraham focus here, not on matters such as idolatry, but on the outcry of the oppressed (18:20–21). The Sodomites are "wicked" and condemned because of the way they treat their brothers and sisters. This "outcry" is the same word as that used in Exodus 3:7–9 for the cry of oppressed Israel in Egypt; the plagues are the environmental effect. This theme correlates well with Ezekiel's view that the sins of Sodom were "pride, excess of food, prosperous ease, but did not aid the poor and needy" (16:49). For both Egypt and Sodom, the effect of their wickedness is comparable, namely, the devastation of the environment.

This argument assumes an understanding of natural law, wherein God's intentions regarding the less fortunate are made sufficiently clear in the creational order for all to be held accountable (cf. the prophets' oracles against the nations, for example, Amos 1–2). That God enters into the lives of such persons on the issue of justice sets a pattern for those who are chosen, who are "to keep the way of the Lord," explicitly stated in 18:19 (for God's way as setting such a pattern for Israel, see Deut. 10:17–19). The chosen are to be actively related to such peoples regarding comparable issues, and not simply matters spiritual. The chosen also know that God will hold them comparably accountable; in fact, such divine concerns are built into the heart of Israel's own law (for example, Exod. 22:21–27). In the words of Robert Alter, "The biblical writers will rarely lose sight of the ghastly possibility that Israel can turn itself into Sodom."[15] The fact that God treats Israel and Sodom in the same way with respect to justice and judgment is remarkably inclusive. This text is testimony to an interpretation of 12:1–3 that involves the chosen in an active role in every sphere of life in their relationship to "all the families of the earth."

THE ECOLOGICAL CHARACTER OF THE REGION

The location of Sodom and Gomorrah is not certainly known, but they are usually situated to the southeast of the Dead Sea. These cities lie in a major geological rift, extending from eastern Turkey to Mozambique. The Dead Sea, with its high levels of salinity, is the lowest point in the rift, some 1,300 feet below sea level; earthquakes and volcanic eruptions have occurred in the region. The text lifts up the geological character of the area in 14:3, 10 (cf. 19:24, 26); it has extensive deposits of bitumen and sulfur (brimstone, which ignites at relatively low temperatures) and petrochemical springs. It may be that an earthquake or volcano with associated fires ignited these deposits, producing a major explosion that "overthrew" these cities. Lot's wife being engulfed in the fallout is probably not a far-fetched image (19:26).

The area around the Dead Sea had not always been desolate; Genesis 13:10 sets up the contrast between what this region was once like and what it later became. When Lot chose to settle in the area, it was a veritable paradise, "like the garden of the Lord" (Eden) and like "the land of Egypt," where, ironically, Israel's "outcry" will be heard by God (Exod. 2–3). In contrast, Deuteronomy 29:23 speaks of the area in terms of "soil burned out by sulphur and salt, nothing planted, nothing sprouting, unable to support any vegetation." In modern terms, the area suffered an environmental catastrophe. Then, Genesis 13:13 makes the claim that the residents of the city were "wicked, great sinners against the Lord." Readers of Genesis 13:10 and 13:13 together are thus preliminarily invited to think about the relationship between that Edenlike natural order and the moral character of its human population. The conclusion to be drawn: its present state of environmental degradation was due to human wickedness. When readers of Genesis 13–14 get to the story of Sodom and Gomorrah in Genesis 18–19, they are informed again of the wickedness of the cities and God's consultation with Abraham regarding "whether they have done altogether according to the outcry that has come to me" (18:20–21).

Scholars typically claim that this story is an interpretation of such an event after the fact, that is, it is an etiology that seeks to explain how that region came to have its moonscape character. This explanation may well be accurate, but we must seek to come to terms with the theological interpretation that the text gives. This perspective suggests an understanding of the close relationship between moral order and cosmic order. That is, human behaviors have cosmic effects; as noted, the text itself links human sin and environmental disaster. Given the moral order and the interconnectedness of life, human wickedness triggers environmental disruption (this needs no argument in our ecologically sensitive age). The creational form of the disaster is not fortuitous, but is correspondent to the anti-life, anticreational form of their wickedness. Like begets like. This point of view is reflected in many Old Testament texts, for example, the thorns and thistles of Genesis 3:16, the flood story (Gen. 6:11–13),[16] and many prophetic texts (cf. Hosea 4:1–3).

And how is one to understand God's relationship to the disaster? God is the one who is believed to mediate the linkage between moral order and cosmic order. However one speaks of divine agency in what happened to the cities, the region was of such a character geologically that God had available the requisite raw materials for this type of judgmental event. One might complain that God could have sent in foreign armies to exact the judgment without messing up the environment so. But, typically, God uses the means that are available; God doesn't create the combustible mix of geological realities in this region just for this occasion. Given this particular creaturely reality with which God works, one could say that God's action is restrained by the nature of the means available (not unlike God's use of, say, Babylon). From the sparse details the text gives us regarding the nature of the catastrophe (19:24–28; 14:10), there is no reason to think the event is "unnatural"; these sorts of occurrences actually do take place out and about in God's good creation or have the potential to do so.

In the segment on Genesis 18–19 that follows, two levels of God's engagement in the human situation are woven together, namely, God's consultation with Abraham and God's judgment on Sodom and Gomorrah, and the relation between the two. God takes the initiative and engages in a genuine dialogue with Abraham about the fate of the cities, in which the human partner is given a key role (18:16–33). But the story ends with the fiery devastation of the cities (19:24–29). These are hard themes to keep together.

Readers should note three transitional phrases that mark developments regarding the fate of Sodom: the three men/angels (then two) "looked toward Sodom" (18:16); "went toward Sodom" (18:22); and "came to Sodom" (19:1). This progression correlates with key developments in the story.[17]

A JUDICIAL INQUIRY

The intercessory dialogue between God and Abraham regarding the fate of Sodom and Gomorrah is introduced by divine reflections on the role of Abraham as God's chosen one (18:17–21). The text as a whole constitutes a judicial inquiry. That is, Abraham's intercessory activity functions as a judicial act rather than a prayer, for prayer formulae are absent.[18] James Bruckner understands Genesis 18:16–33 as pretrial, while 19:1–23 is the actual trial, with 19:13–14 the declaration of the judgment.[19] Macdonald similarly understands 18:16–33 as a stage prior to a decision about the guilt or innocence of the cities.[20]

Verses 17–21 are a divine soliloquy (though verse 23 assumes that Abraham has knowledge of verses 20–21; might God be speaking out loud?). Strikingly, readers are made privy to an inner divine reflection about Sodom and Abraham's relationship to it. God raises the issue of "righteousness and justice" (18:19). Abraham's vocation is to charge his family "to keep the way of the Lord by doing righteousness (tsedeqah) and justice (mispat)." These closely related words— uncommon in Genesis—are picked up in the dialog that follows (18:22–33). These words, which describe God's creational purposes for the world (and all creatures therein), also characterize individuals and communities that exemplify and promote life and well-being for all in every relational sphere, human and non-human. The link between the practice of justice and righteousness in a society and the shape of its future—whether negative or positive—is very close.[21] This is the nature of the moral order of things.

Now, having charged Abraham with seeing to such matters, it is fitting that God should bring to his attention an instance where these divine purposes for the creation are being subverted. Having been charged to address issues of justice, then Abraham needs to know what justice means for God. It will not do for God to keep Abraham ignorant regarding what God is about in the world (Amos 3:6; Jer. 33:3). If Abraham is to be a blessing to all the nations, then the people of God must become involved in situations of injustice; this is the case with Sodom and Gomorrah, where the cries of oppression have come up to God (18:20–21; Ezek. 16:49 and Jer. 23:14).[22] That God raises the issue of justice before Abraham does is important, and in turn prompts Abraham's lively concern for such issues.

God proceeds to report the cries of unidentified persons regarding the gravity of the sins of Sodom and Gomorrah (18:20–21) and determines formally to investigate the situation. God will seek to discern whether the situation in the cities is in fact so grave that it warrants the judgment that God has preliminarily drawn. The dialogue that follows thus flows naturally from this divine intent. Abraham understands that he has been invited into a conversation about the future of the city.

That this inquiry is genuine is shown by God's words in verse 21, "and if not, I will know (acknowledge, recognize)." In other words, this divine knowing depends upon the results of the inquiry. God explicitly admits the possibility of an "if not." For God to use "if" language means the future remains open, at least to some extent. God holds out the prospect that the inquiry may issue in a verdict other than that preliminarily drawn. One might claim that God is playing with Abraham, for God knows the number of righteous in Sodom. But the integrity of the inquiry assumes that this is not a charade for God, that what Abraham has to say will be taken seriously by God. Something may emerge out of this consultative interaction between God and Abraham that calls for a different divine direction with respect to these cities. Moreover, given the divine "if," God admits to being less than fully certain exactly how Abraham might push and pull the discussion and the effect it may have on the divine decision.

Many interpreters have thought that God's decision about Sodom is final from the beginning of the conversation. One wonders if this interpretation is informed by a view of God that does not allow for consultation. But here and elsewhere —one thinks particularly of Moses (for example, Exod. 32:7–14), God considers what human beings think and say and understands those matters to be a serious contribution to the shaping of the future. While God would have thought of all the options, to have them articulated by an Abraham gives them a new level of significance for God. Abraham brings new ingredients into the decision-making situation—energies, will, insight—that give God new possibilities with which to work. This divine-human synergy has the potential of influencing God, who might then adjust the preliminary divine decision. If that were to happen, it would not mean that God's preliminary decision was not the best decision, but that God takes the relationship with Abraham seriously into account so that a new "best decision" comes into play.

GOD CONSULTS WITH ABRAHAM

The departure of two of the men for Sodom in 18:22 marks the transition to the dialogue. Abraham now stands before God alone.[23] God here seeks to communicate with Abraham, not the other way around. Even more, God consults with Abraham because he and his descendants have been chosen to have a role among the "nations" (18:18), which includes Sodom. From another perspective, Abraham is here made a coparticipant with God in matters of divine judgment, not unlike the role of the pre-exilic prophets. Nathan Macdonald rightly counters Brueggemann's claim that Abraham is "a theological teacher to God so that God may think more clearly and responsibly about his own vocation."[24]

At the same time, God genuinely invites Abraham's counsel on the matter. Who knows where Abraham's knowledge might lead. There is a sense in which God does learn where Abraham takes the conversation. Macdonald's suggestion that Abraham learns from God in this episode is not made clear in the text; Abraham certainly learns, but the text seems not concerned to specify what he learns and his behavior in the narrative that follows (20:1–18) diminishes those learnings.

Abraham immediately raises very specific questions regarding God's decision (18:23–25). He is blunt, persistent, and nontraditional. His questions pull no punches and they get to the point without preliminary niceties. He understands his relationship with God to be of such a nature that direct questions are not only in order but welcome. And God fields them in a way that does not close off the conversation. Abraham becomes more deferential as the dialogue proceeds, but we do not know enough about ancient methods of argumentation to assess the import of this shift in forcefulness. It may be nothing more than Abraham's recognition that each of God's positive responses makes additional inquiries on his part more on the order of harassment. It is commonly thought that this exchange constitutes "bargaining." Macdonald rightly questions this language.[25] He lifts up some similarities with traditional Near Eastern bargaining, but notes that there is no corresponding bidding by Yahweh (say, specifying a counteroffer); God simply accepts Abraham's offer and moves on.[26] And so, while it may not be bargaining from God's side, it is genuine participation in an ongoing conversation that honors Abraham's concerns.[27]

Macdonald goes on to claim that Abraham's question in verse 23b mistakenly assumes that God has announced that the destruction is certain and hence pursues the conversation on a false premise.[28] That is, Abraham thinks that God "has made an unjust decision to destroy the city."[29] But that interpretation reads too much into Abraham's question. All Abraham needs from God to raise the issue he does is the announcement of a preliminary destruction of the cities. His word to God, "Far be it from you!" makes sense as a response to a preliminary divine decision.

Abraham's initial argument moves in stages to its climactic question in verse 25: "shall not the Judge of all the earth do what is just?"[30] The question does not accuse; rather, it provides a debating point, which Abraham believes has been warranted by God's initiative with him, namely, that doing justice is keeping the way of the Lord (18:19).[31] If God expects Abraham and his family to "do justice" (18:17), then certainly God should do so.[32] Abraham's question also links up with God's concern for the blessing of "all the nations of the earth" (18:18) in his reference to God as the judge of "all the earth"; this universal divine concern would include Sodom.[33] Does Abraham's question imply that he thinks he has a more equitable standard of justice than God does? Not necessarily, especially if the conversation revolves around a preliminary decision. Biblical characters often call upon God to be true to the divine character and the divine commitments (for example, Exod. 32:11–14).

But Abraham's question is still unsettling in the sense that it considers God to be subject to an existing moral order. That is, it claims that God cannot ignore doing justice to established relationships and still be righteous. While God has freely created that order, God has freely bound the divine self to be faithful to it. In effect, God holds God's own self to certain standards regarding issues of justice, and Abraham knows that God has made such a commitment. Hence, in Abraham's eyes, God cannot ignore differences between the righteous and the wicked in acts of judgment. God may be said to accept Abraham's argument in view of the dialogue that follows. In fact, Abraham's argument that, in effect, a strict retribution system should be set aside for the sake of the righteous finds a ready ear with God, for, as Abraham discovers, God does not work within any such system.

Abraham, who asks eight questions in this text, voices concern that God will "sweep away" the righteous-innocent. The identification of the righteous-innocent is uncertain. This language is not a reference to sinless individuals, but to those who abide by creational norms in doing justice to established relationships (as in 18:19, see above) and/or those who are voicing the "outcry" that God has heard (verses 20–21).[34] Abraham's concerns extend beyond Lot, evident in the number of righteous with which he begins (fifty) and his nonmention of Lot. Abraham's key question would seem to be: Should God destroy those voicing the outcry along with those who are perpetrating the injustice? Is it right that those who are experiencing injustice perish in God's judgment upon those perpetrating the injustice? Should not God be engaged in delivering those who are experiencing injustice? It may be that the outcry "against" the cities is coming from people who are not residents of the cities themselves (there are fewer than ten), but from those nonresidents who are experiencing the people of Sodom and Gomorrah as predators. They could include visitors to the cities (as in the story in Genesis 19), resident aliens, and people in neighboring villages. If the number ten is not to be taken literally (as seems to be the case), but is, rather, indicative of a relatively small percentage of the population, then other victims could come into view. Given the low social standing of children in Israelite culture, and their usual non-inclusion in a category such as "righteous/innocent," it is likely that they are not incorporated in Abraham's reckoning. Yet, readers, ancient and modern, would know of the effects of such disasters on children (see, for example, Lam. 2:19–20; 4:4, 10) and they would no doubt come to mind in reflecting on such events.

Abraham's question has to do with issues of both mercy and justice. It is important to state the issue of justice correctly. A surface sense of justice would tend to be individualistic, that is, a separation of righteous individuals from those who are wicked, resulting in two different futures: the righteous delivered and the wicked suffering their just desserts. But Abraham's concern for justice does not take this approach. He argues that the divine attention ought to be given to the salvation of the righteous, even if the wicked are spared in the process. Even more, he argues not only for the saving of the righteous, but also for the sparing of the entire city because of the presence of the righteous; God's response understands this to be the case, for it speaks of sparing "the whole place for their sake" (18:26).[35] In effect, then, the presence of the righteous would lead to the extension of the divine mercy upon all the people involved. This action would, of course, mean that the wicked would not receive their just desserts. But at least the righteous would be delivered, and that is most important for Abraham (and God). But the preserving of the wicked is also important for the ongoing life of the righteous. Bruckner's formulation is helpful: Abraham is concerned to "secure a reprieve for the guilty majority in order to preserve the community in which the innocent may be established."[36] This approach may help to explain why Abraham does not suggest that the righteous few simply be removed from the city. Abraham must be concerned with more than the fate of the righteous; he is concerned with the city as a whole, indeed the entire environment.[37] So also is God: God will not destroy the many for the sake of saving the lives of the few. The righteous do not exercise an atoning function for the others, yet the effect is comparable. The result would be an exercise in divine mercy. To speak more generally, God's mercy (of which both wicked and righteous are in need) grounds this future possibility for even the wicked in Sodom.

Macdonald makes much of the fact that Abraham does not appeal directly to the mercy of God. He even suggests that if Abraham had asked for mercy the cities might have been saved; but, this is to claim that God's merciful action is dependent upon the use of certain vocabulary.[38] But is not Abraham's language of forgiveness-sparing (18:24) by its very nature an appeal to the mercy of God? God, in using the same forgiveness-sparing language in 18:26, must consider it appropriate. It is worthwhile considering whether "forgive" is the proper translation here ("spare" is common, RSV, New American Bible [NAB]), a translation that Macdonald assumes. Usually the verb *nāsā'* in this sense is followed by "sin" or its equivalent. Westermann claims that the verb "means nothing more than to annul the decision to destroy. This, therefore, is not a matter of the turning and repenting of a city"[39] The verb probably refers to "pardon" in the judicial sense (Gen. 40:13; 2 Kings 25:27).[40] But, it could have the more general sense of showing favor, or cutting off the consequences of sins. In any case, divine mercy is integral to the conversation that Abraham pursues.

At the same time, Abraham introduces a qualification in his approach to the matter. He raises the issue of the number of righteous people that ought to be present for this approach to be taken. How many righteous must be present for God to save them, and the cities for their sake? But why introduce numbers at all? Is not the issue clear without the numbers? As we have noted, the numbers should not be taken literally, not least because that would establish a kind of quota to which divine judgment would be bound or, if one knew the population of the city, the percentage of righteous that would be needed in order to save the city. Yet, the numbers are important, not least because of the attention they are given in the text and they help provide direction for consideration of the issues that Abraham raises. It is not the case that Abraham assumes that Yahweh's justice is quantifiable.[41] Yet the issue of quantity is important; if it were not pertinent, would God continue the conversation so long in these very terms? It is not helpful to say that "Yhwh refuses to participate in his game."[42] God does in fact participate at some length with regard to matters of quantity, and it is not a game. Numbers are of real importance—for God as well as for Abraham.

Why does Abraham stop at ten and not take the dialogue with God all the way down to one? Or why does Abraham not begin with the number ten (or one)?[43] If he wanted to focus on the issue of justice in a strict sense, the presence of one righteous person would be sufficient to make his case. That is to say, for even one righteous person to die in the course of the judgment on the wicked would be unjust. Because Abraham does not begin with the lowest numbers, he must want to make another point than one of strict divine justice.

Why, then, are fifty or ten righteous persons enough to spare the city, but, apparently, one to nine persons is not? It may be that the number ten represents the smallest group (some think of a minyan) and that a smaller number would be dealt with as individuals, who could be (and were) led out of the city. Nahum Sarna suggests an appropriate direction for reflection.[44] Ten represents the limit of the number of righteous individuals who could outweigh the cumulative evil of the community. Ten constitutes the "minimum effective social entity." I prefer the language of "critical mass."[45]

It is a truism to say that the wickedness of a few can adversely affect the larger group of which they are a part. Here the point is reversed: the righteousness of a few can so permeate a wicked society that they can save it from the destructive effects of its own evil ways. At the same time, a buildup of wickedness can become so deep and broad that too few righteous may be present and available to have any appreciable positive effect on the situation to keep it from snowballing out of control. For Sodom this is fewer than ten persons; the critical mass effect of the righteous in Sodom is so diminished as to be unable positively to affect the shape of its future. For Jerusalem in a later time, not even one righteous person can be found (Jer. 5:1; Jerusalem is likened to Sodom and Gomorrah in Jer. 23:14).

As Abraham continues to lower the numbers, God responds in a consistently positive way. After God's response regarding ten, it would have been Abraham's "turn" to continue the conversation, but he does not do so. Abraham's "just once more" indicates that Abraham is the one who decides to cut off the conversation at a point of his own choosing. God simply takes leave when they are finished speaking; Abraham and God are in apparent agreement. God's concern for the righteous in the cities has matched Abraham's concerns point for point, marking the extent to which God will go to save life. Readers should not move too quickly past this observation, for it helps elucidate why Abraham cut the questioning off at ten (again, a number not to be taken literally). It may be that Abraham is, finally, convinced that God is more than "just" (and certainly nonretributive in approach) by the willingness to recognize the potentially positive effect of a comparatively small number of righteous persons on a recognizably wicked city. The number ten may then represent the point at which Abraham saw that God's justice had been established beyond the shadow of a doubt; he could now leave the fate of the few righteous up to God. In so doing, he tacitly admits that a few righteous may indeed "fare as the wicked." That judgment may not be "just" in some ideal sense, but it will need to be asked whether the values of the created moral order and its inevitable interconnectedness outweigh even such "injustice" (see below). Eschatological thinking will in time seek to deal with this issue by speaking of a distinction in the world to come, where the wheat and the chaff will be finally and justly sorted out.

And so, contrary to what readers might think, the Sodom and Gomorrah story reveals neither a vindictive God nor a moral order that functions in mechanistic, precise ways. So predominant is God's will to save over God's will to judge that God is open to working in and through a minority of righteous ones so that many wicked can be saved from the consequences of their own sin. At the same time, there may come a point where even God cannot turn the situation around; judgment must fall.[46]

And so this text witnesses to the importance of the presence of the righteous in any situation: they may be able to subvert the effects of wickedness from within the community so that it can be reclaimed for life rather than death. And, the more righteous there are the more of a positive difference they can make, for the world and for God. In effect, this is an argument against any defeatism or fatalism that seeks to downplay the potential impact of human activity for the good of a community. This is an argument against those who would claim that nothing can be done about the environment or poverty or other societal ills. In and through the activity of the righteous, communal or cosmic disaster (divine judgment) may be averted and even the wicked may participate in the good that results. The activity of the righteous can in fact make a difference. There is, hence, no retributionary schema that will explain why sins do not lead to certain communal disasters. The wicked may not suffer the consequences of their own wickedness because of the presence and activity of the righteous among them.[47]

While the presence of the righteous within the city may ameliorate the effects of sin, the text makes an additional point: the intercessory advocacy of those outside the community (in this case, Abraham) may have a comparably positive effect. This recognition of the (potential) efficacy of intercession is also evident in the following story, where Abraham's prayers result in the healing of Abimelech and his community (Gen. 20:17). A note on intercessory prayer more generally may be helpful at this point. God establishes relationships with persons such as Abraham that are of such a nature that God is not the only one who has something important to say. What human beings think and say is important to God, and can contribute in a genuine way to the shaping of the future. While God would certainly have thought about all the options available for action in a given situation, to have those options actually articulated by persons with whom God is in relationship gives them a level of significance that was not present for God before. Human beings may bring some new ingredients into the situation—energies, words, insights—that enable God to have more possibilities with which to work; God's possibilities for that moment are thereby made more extensive. Because God honors the relationship with human beings, who bring their gifts into such moments, that changes the nature of the decision-making situation. Prayers do have the potential of shaping the future in ways different from what would have been the case had no prayers been uttered. The moral order is not a tight causal weave, with no room for chance or randomness, for the serendipitous or the extraordinary event. Enough looseness is present in the moral order for prayers to make a difference and for God to act.

And so, because of the nature of the relationship between God and Abraham, God takes his thinking into account in deciding what the divine action will finally be regarding Sodom. Because of God's commitment to the relationship that has been established (18:17–18), what Abraham thinks and says (including his intercessions) count with God. God will take his energy and insights into account in shaping the divine action. With regard to Sodom, finally, the wickedness in the situation was too pervasive for Abraham's intercessions to be effective. Yet, it may be said that, because of prayers offered, one of the cities (Zoar, 19:21) as well as Lot and his daughters were not destroyed, for God "remembered Abraham" (19:29).

– Generally speaking, intercessory prayers (and other forms of advocacy) have the capacity to shape the future and may turn a seemingly certain divine judgment into a new lease on life. Yet, it may be too late for such prayers to "save the city" and only a remnant will escape the conflagration.[48]

In sum, at least one word to readers of this text, ancient and modern, is that the actions of the righteous within the communities of which they are a part and intercessory advocacy for those of which they are not a part may make a difference— to both community and to God. In a given situation, it may be too late to save the city or the environment. But, as with Abraham, the righteous are called to act and pray as if it were not too late.

COMMUNAL JUDGMENT AND THE PLIGHT OF THE INNOCENT

The issue deserves further consideration: Is it "just" that "the righteous fare as the wicked" (18:25)? The answer, finally, is that it may be just. These issues are raised so sharply because of crisis contexts in which this material functioned. The fate of the righteous, not least the children (Lam. 2:20; 4:10), in the judgment of Samaria (Amos 7:1–6) or Jerusalem (Ezek. 14:12–20) was a lively issue, as was the saving role of the few for the many (Jer. 5:1; Isa. 53:1–12). In such events the innocent (many more than ten) often have perished with the guilty. Would it be Abraham's view that the judge of all the earth has often not done what is right?

In thinking through this question more fully, it is important to remember that this text centers on the future of individuals, but not in isolation from the corporate entity of which they are a part. Finally, it is both individual and community.[49] We have seen that Abraham's concern has significant corporate dimensions, and this consideration leads to further issues. The text does not deny that individuals are to be held accountable, but it focuses on communal responsibility, on what happens when sin and its effects become systemic, that is, so pervasive that an entire community is caught up in them. More specifically, the text links corporate responsibility and the future of a city's natural environment. Human behavior is understood to affect not only the human community, but the entire cosmos (though the link may at times be difficult to discern). Historical evil can cause creational havoc, as moderns know all too well. Many such events are just part of the normal workings of the natural order (the rain falls, or does not fall, on the just and the unjust, Matt. 5:45). Yet, both Israelites and moderns know that human behaviors have led and will lead to cosmic disaster (flood story; plagues). The devastation of Sodom and Gomorrah and their environs offers a major instance; the depletion of the ozone layer may be another.

Usually we conceive of the relationship between act and consequence in individual terms, relying on our judicial system to "take care of" such individuals. Issues of corporate sin and judgment are less often addressed. Issues of war and peace are commonly rooted in such understandings, wherein corporate action is taken against another corporate entity. The environmental crisis is another such instance, where the cumulative effect of the community's neglect has the potential of issuing in an environmental disaster. In the usual functioning of the moral order at such corporate levels, the righteous-innocent will inevitably get caught up in the judgment of the wicked and suffer with them.[50] One thinks of the children in Europe or Japan in World War II or those who are sensitive to ecological issues being caught up in environmental degradation. In ancient Israel, God is believed to be about the business of seeing to the moral order, and this often means judgment upon corporate entities, including entire societies. In executing such judgments, it is recognized that innocent individuals will often suffer adverse consequences. That is to say, in the exercise of such corporate judgments, a precise sorting out of the innocent and the righteous is not often (ever?) possible. Because of the moral order, of which the interconnectedness of life is an integral element, the acts of some will often have dire consequences for the entire society of which they are a part. Innocent individuals will often suffer undeservedly in the wake of such consequences of the unjust acts committed by the wicked.

Does God engage Abraham with respect to this issue precisely because actions that do not distinguish righteous from wicked are a "glitch" in the "system" that God has created? Is this a divine recognition that such an "anomaly" is indeed an inherent problem with the way that God has created the moral order, but that there is apparently no better way in which it could have been done?

Does not God, then, cause all the damage? God is indeed linked with this environmental catastrophe, but how one delineates that relationship is important.[51] The language commonly used in the Old Testament to speak of this reality is "judgment." The issue becomes, then, how one might speak of God's involvement in judgment. We might speak of three ways:

(1) God created the moral order, so that sins do have consequences and this most fundamentally so that sin and evil not go unchecked in the life of the world.

God does indeed care about evil and its effect on the life of the world. What are misdemeanors to us may be disasters to God, not least because God sees the evil effects on the creation in a way that we do not.[52] A basic definition of judgment is the effects or consequences of sin. One way of seeing this is to note the use of ʿāwôn, a common word for sin. While often translated as "punishment" (as in the NRSV, 19:15), it is best translated as calamity or the like (that is, consequence). Sin and its consequences are on a continuum, wherein the effects of sin flow out of the sin itself. Such effects are not introduced from outside the situation by God, but are already at work in a situation as the effect of human sin (the moral order).

So, the environmental devastation is not an arbitrarily chosen divine move, as if foreign armies could have done the job without messing up the environment so. This is not a forensic divine move; rather, it is a matter of God midwifing or seeing to the moral order, through already existing human or nonhuman agents. Some of our everyday proverbs capture the point: what goes around, comes around; chickens come home to roost; sow your wild oats, you will reap them.

(2) But, unlike a deistic understanding, God is not absent in the move from act to consequence. God midwifes or sees to the moral order, working through already existing human or nonhuman agents, from Babylonian armies to the moral order itself.[53] This means that God's judgment is not normally individual divine decisions, lightning bolts from heaven. At the same time, the Old Testament is not completely consistent in the way in which it speaks of judgment; God seems more directly involved in judgment in some texts. Another way of saying this is that the moral order is not a tight causal weave, it does not function mechanically or inevitably, as if every sin would have a precise consequence, or would even always have a negative consequence.

(3) God uses such consequences for God's own purposes, for example, for discipline or testing or deliverance. This story clearly shows that God is not eager that judgment fall. God consults with Abraham about the possibility of another future; God moves with Abraham's every step; God is open to alternatives. The God who speaks Ezekiel 18:32, "I have no pleasure in the death of anyone," also characterizes the God of this text. This cuts against the grain of any notion that Israel's God is punitive, focused on judgment for its own sake. God is "slow to anger" even with such nonchosen folk.

These reflections may profitably be related to Genesis 15:16, "And they shall come back here in the fourth generation; for the iniquity of the Amorites is not yet complete." That is to say, the descendants of Abraham will receive the land, not because of their own qualities of being or life, but because the sins of its present inhabitants will reach such depths that they will be engulfed in their effects (Deut. 9:4–5; 1 Kings 21:26). The relationship between sin and judgment is understood to be of such a nature that sins do not necessarily have immediate disastrous effects. The judgment of God is thus viewed in an accumulative way, as a buildup of the negative effects of sins over time so that a society finally implodes or explodes, and not as the result of a forensic divine act. This kind of reflection is particularly applicable in thinking about communities (though not totally inapplicable to individuals); it may take time for the effects of sin to build up and to overwhelm the social order. The story of Sodom and Gomorrah may be considered the beginning of the fulfillment of Genesis 15:16.

We return to our question about the link between God and all the ecological damage. God does not introduce the consequences into the situation; the consequences are intrinsic to the deed. The creational form taken by the disaster is correspondent to the anticreational form of the human wickedness, focused in the language of outcry and the deprivation of life and well-being (18:20–21; 19:13).

In the course of his conversation with God, Abraham comes to recognize that the answer to his initial question about justice is that God will indeed do what is just with respect to the fate of Sodom (and indeed any corporate entity). But Abraham also comes to recognize that there is a point that, when justice must be done, some righteous people will get caught up in the judgment. The other options are not finally tolerable, especially an option wherein the Sodomites would not be brought to account for all the terrible injustice they are visiting upon people. Evil cannot go unchecked in the world, even if some righteous get swept away.

It might be noted in passing that the prophets were not hesitant to apply the very same principle to Israel itself, particularly in relationship to the fall of Jerusalem to the Babylonians. The destruction of Sodom and Gomorrah may have served as a warning to Israel of what could become of its own future, including its own land. The task God gives to the prophets is sharply corporate in nature, pronouncing a word of judgment on the entire people. And they make clear that the practice of justice and the future of the land are closely linked. The prophets will voice a hope regarding the regardening of the land, but usually only on the far side of environmental and historical disaster. Such texts invite reflection by readers on the various communal contexts of which they are a part and how close they might be to experiencing the "completion" of their iniquities. Environmental disaster is one subject that this Genesis text prompts readers to consider.

AN ILLUSTRATION OF GOD'S PROBLEM WITH SODOM

Chapter 19 brings readers into the city of Sodom. For all they know, ten righteous have been found in Sodom and the city will be saved. The narrator now gives an inside view of the city, enabling readers to judge for ourselves what should be done regarding Sodom. So this chapter develops an illustration of Sodom's character; in view of this, the Sodomites, including Lot, should generate little sympathy among readers (19:1–11). God's "I must go down and see" (18:20) is what

God (represented by the two messengers) in fact does in 19:1–11; on the basis of this "evidence" the judgment is announced in 19:13.[54]

This illustration is developed in dialogue with 18:1–15, the story of Abraham's hospitality toward the three strangers. This dialogue focuses on the issue of hospitality, that is, welcoming relationships that are essential for the well-being of individuals and society.[55] Abraham has shown exemplary hospitality; Lot follows suit to some extent, but finally fails, as his treatment of his betrothed daughters reveals. The Sodomites show no hospitality at all, as every man in the city, young and old (19:4), is caught up in a threat of violence that, if successful, would result in gang rape.[56] That every man is involved would indicate that heterosexuals would be among those who engaged in the threat. This violent activity might be compared to situations in prison or wartime, where same-sex activity is used to exercise domination and control (ancient Near Eastern parallels exist).[57] The text presents the sins of Sodom more as social than individual, revealing the character of the entire city. Inasmuch as Sodom serves as the evil counterpart to Abraham's hospitality, we trivialize the narrative if we focus only on the threat of same-sex activity.[58] Interestingly, reference to Sodom's sins elsewhere in the Old Testament never clearly specifies homosexual behavior (condemned for males in Lev. 18:22; 20:13). The listing in Ezekiel 16:49–50 includes pride, excess of food, prosperous ease, not aiding the poor and needy, and unspecified abominable behavior; Jeremiah 23:14 specifies adultery and deception.[59]

Lot's offer of his two daughters to all the men of Sodom is reprehensible (19:8), though it has often been excused as a parade example of the priorities of ancient Near Eastern hospitality. Interestingly, he thinks that the men of Sodom would be satisfied with heterosexual abuse (cf. Judg. 19). The offer of his daughters to be abused "as you please" is but another example of the depravity of Sodom. In response to those who think that Lot's offer is not an actual offer, but an effort to shock the Sodomites with the offensiveness of his offer,[60] Goldingay remarks: "even risking such an offer raises the question whether he has come to share the sexual oppressiveness of his culture."[61] That this offer, even if not serious (which it is), can be described as a vile act is evident in that his daughters were betrothed (19:14); in Israel, those who rape betrothed women are condemned to death (Deut. 22:23–24). The story of Lot's drunken incest with his daughters (19:30–38) could be understood as a demonstration of the reprehensibility of his offer: he experiences what he had proposed his daughters should experience (what goes around, comes around).

That Lot has become like those among whom he dwells may be evident in his appeal to the men of Sodom as his "brothers" (19:7). In response the Sodomites raise the issue of justice that had been raised by God and Abraham (verse 9). Lot is a resident alien—they alone can judge the rightness of their own action; they are subject to no external standard.[62] The men of Sodom respond by threatening to treat Lot even more violently than the strangers (19:9). In the face of their threatened violence, the two strangers save Lot—who sought to save them—from their violence. The Sodomites are struck with a temporary blindness, perhaps a sudden flash of light (see 2 Kings 6:18; Acts 9:3–9). The men of Sodom are heard from no more; they are left still blindly groping for the door to complete their objective. But God (and the reader) who came to "see" them has seen enough for the judgment to fall. Threatened sexual abuse and violence is sufficient evidence for God to move forward with judgment. What is seen is deemed sufficient to move forward with the judgment ("because," 19:13). Ten righteous have not been found.

And the women and children are caught up in the devastating effects (as in other corporate judgments, as we have noted).

The angelic figures mediate God's destruction of the city (19:13, 24–25) and rescue Lot and his family. Interestingly, the rescue is seen to be dependent upon human action to take up the opportunity of escape; Lot's sons-in-law, for example, refuse the offer of escape (19:14)[63] and Lot's delaying tactics are nearly fatal for him.[64] Lot's wife mirrors his dawdling, only she lingers to the point of death (19:26; see Wisd. of Sol. 10:7).[65] The calamitous effects are only briefly described, from the cities to people and vegetation (19:24–25). The nature of the cataclysm could explain the salt pillar—Lot's wife was engulfed in the fallout of fire and chemicals; the story is probably an etiology of human-shaped pillars of salt found — in the area.

Abraham retraces his steps and freezes at the horror of the sight (19:27–28). He has not a word to say, but his silence speaks volumes. The nations of the earth are to find blessing through him, but not inevitably so. The situation had deteriorated too much for his intercession to turn it around. Lot is rescued (indeed, must be rescued, 19:22) by the messengers because of God's graciousness and kindness (ḥesed; 19:16, 19). Both judgment and escape are witness to the universal work of God the creator. At the same time, such judgmental activity cannot be separated from the kind of delayed response to the warnings one sees in Lot and his family. If such alarms are deemed jesting (19:14), the potential effect of intercession may be cut off. Lot illustrates how the journey of faith may end on a very tragic note. Choices people make can adversely affect the power of intercession and the divine engagement in their lives. Remarkably, no indication is given that Abraham knows what has happened to Lot and his family.

At least two points suggest that Abraham's advocacy had some effect on the situation. One of the cities, Zoar, whose smallness is emphasized, is saved because of Lot's presence, as are the wicked that live there (19:20–23). Moreover, in 19:29, Lot's rescue seems to be the effect of Abraham's expressed intercession—God remembered Abraham.

Does God then here make arbitrary exceptions? At the least, it can be said that the moral order is not a tight causal weave, with no room for randomness, the serendipitous, or the miracle. Intercessory prayer enters the picture at precisely this point. Abraham's intercessory advocacy is what is said to make at least this much of a difference in this situation fraught with danger. Abraham's intercession saves Lot in view of enough looseness in the moral order to enable such events to occur.

The community of faith tends to intercede for those whom it approves or the causes it endorses. The Lots and Sodoms of this world, persons who have disappointed us by the direction they have taken with their lives, are not often the subject of our intercessions.

God is here shown to be one who is not out to distribute punishments according to some calculating scheme. God works to find a way to bring life rather than death in order to save as many as possible. And his incredible patience is such that the move from fifty to ten opens up the future for positive possibilities. At the same time, how people respond to warnings given will have deep and broad implications.

CHAPTER 6

HAGAR AND ISHMAEL AS OUTSIDERS

A SPECIAL CASE

Genesis 16:1–16; 17:18–25; 21:8–21; 25:9, 12–18.

I t is striking, perhaps even disconcerting, that Hagar and Ishmael are given so much textual space in a tale so attentive to persons outside the chosen family (Gen. 16:1–16; 21:8–21, with attention given to 17:15–25; 25:9, 12–18)— almost as much as Isaac. Why would this be so?

The story of Hagar and Ishmael appears in no lectionary series of which I am aware. I cannot recall having heard a sermon on these texts. One wonders why this story has been so neglected or considered a story only with a negative purpose. Is it because Abraham, that exemplar of faith, does not come off so well? Is it because the main characters are women? Is it because Hagar and Ishmael stand outside the community of faith? Indeed, Hagar has several strikes against her: she is a foreigner, a slave, a woman, and probably black (at least African). Is it because in the usual recounting of the salvation history, this story is a dead end? Is it because Muslims track their roots back into these stories, and understand themselves to be heirs of Abraham as much as do Jews and Christians? Is it possible that the story of Hagar and Ishmael is neglected because God makes promises to them, indeed a string of promises worded in language similar to the promises given to Isaac? Listen to God's words to Abraham in 17:20, "As for Ishmael, I have heard you: I will bless him and make him fruitful and exceedingly numerous; he shall be the father of twelve princes, and I will make him a great nation." Does God keep promises only for Isaac, or does God keep promises made to Ishmael, too? Or is God a selective promise-keeper? But, if God does keep promises to Ishmael, where might we look for their fulfillment? Walter Brueggemann has stated the issue sharply: "God has not exclusively committed himself to Abraham and Sarah."[1]

The story of Hagar and Ishmael in Genesis 16 is embraced by chapters devoted to God's exclusive covenant with Abraham (15; 17); in fact, the story of the outsider seems to center these stories of the insider. Does not this placement suggest that the covenant with Abraham find its essential import in the story of such outsiders? And the story of Hagar and Ishmael is not quickly forgotten by the narrator; it punctuates or "interrupts" the chapters that follow (17:18–25; 21:8–21; 25:9–18). That the text does not simply leave their story behind while it moves on with the "mainline" story of Isaac is a witness to their continuing importance. In

the midst of the human and divine decisions and actions relative to Isaac, the line
of the family associated with Hagar and Ishmael is not left behind. Indeed, they are
showered by promises from God at regular intervals (16:10–11; 17:20; 21:13, 18).

Genesis 16, anticipated by Genesis 15:1–6, shifts the focus of the text from God's
promise of land to that of a son and this theme is now carried through Genesis 22.
At the same time, references to Egypt in these narratives relate Hagar to preceding
texts (12:10–20; 13:1, 10; 15:18) and to the larger ancestral storyline (especially
the Joseph story and events in Exodus).[2] While Genesis 16:1–16 and 21:8–21 have
been often considered a doublet, the stories fulfill different functions in the present
redaction.[3] One effect of this "doubling" is that Hagar and Ishmael become more
prominent figures in the story of Abraham; therefore, readers are not well served by
considering their story a minor diversion. However one analyzes this redactional
history, these narratives are given a surprisingly prominent place within the story
of Abraham and have been decisively shaped by theological interests.

More recent studies of these narratives have been forged by two primary interests. On the one hand, feminist analysis has given special attention to Sarah and
her slave-girl Hagar, providing much insight into heretofore neglected depths in
the portrayal of these characters.[4] On the other hand, current interest in the
Islamic tradition, which traces its religious heritage to Abraham through Ishmael,
has prompted special studies of these texts.[5]

These stories have been formally designated as conflict narratives.[6] While the
conflict may be said to center on the interaction of the two women, Sarah and
Hagar, their interrelationships are part and parcel of the dysfunctionality of the
entire family of Abraham. Certainly Abraham contributes his share to the intensification of this discord, and, given the patriarchal system, could be said to deserve
special blame. God, too, plays no small role in these quarrelsome developments;
without God's choices along the way (for example, 16:9; 21:12) life for this family may well have progressed more smoothly (if not, finally, as purposefully). As
such, all of the characters in these stories seem to be caught up in swirls of dis-
sension beyond their own making, though Hagar and Ishmael are especially subject to circumstances beyond their control.

In terms of structure and plot, these narratives begin with a statement of the
problem, articulated by Sarah: she is childless and is desirous of having children
(16:2). In a highly compact way, the story moves through various difficulties
toward an ambiguous resolution—the final departure of Hagar and Ishmael from
the family of Abraham (21:20–21). The story of Hagar and Ishmael has been
divided in the present form of the text by developments related to the birth of
Isaac (21:1–7). While Genesis 16:15–16 (and the thirteen-year time lapse implied
by 17:1) gives readers the impression that Ishmael is the promised son, God's
promise is refined to specify that Sarah is to be the mother of this son (17:15–20).

Yet, the larger narrative does not get so caught up in her son Isaac that it leaves the "fate" of Hagar and Ishmael dangling, but finally returns to their story in 21:8–21. Their story is thereby "rounded off" and by that interest the text witnesses to their continued importance for the life of this chosen family. Janzen wisely notes that this is a story that "Israel tells against itself. . . . To the degree that Israel's story can become an idol—a narrative way of converting Israel's God into a mere projection of its own wishes and powers over against other people—episodes such as this one serve to shatter the idol, and to set the biblical story free to testify to a God who is not possessed by nor captive to any partisan community."[7]

GENESIS 16:1–16

God had promised Abraham a child, but, to this point, Sarai has not been named as the mother. In responding to this situation, Sarai does not raise issues of shame or morality, as if she were being judged by God for something she did. She interprets her situation theologically, understanding that God has kept her from having children. This is, of course, her point of view; readers are not told whether that is actually the case (for related texts, see 20:18; 25:21; 29:31; 30:2, 22). At the same time, she recognizes that God does not act alone, that human agency is important in carrying out divine purposes ("by her"; cf. 4:1; 17:16; 30:3–4; 19:32). Human beings can thwart the will of God with respect to progeny by their sexual practices (38:9–10). It is notable that she does not raise the question of God with respect to the possibility of Hagar's child-bearing. In a matter-of-fact way, she assumes that Abraham will obtain a child through her.

And so Sarai, wanting a child of her own, makes a move common in that world, she offers Abraham her slave-girl, Hagar, as a surrogate mother. She no doubt thought that this approach, being traditional, would meet with God's approval, as do comparable moves by Leah and Rachel at a later point in the ancestral story (Gen. 30:1–13). Ancient Near Eastern parallels show that this was practiced elsewhere in the world.[8] And so Genesis 16:3 proceeds to describe a formal act on Sarai's part. It is important to recognize the na' in Sarai's word to Abraham, as that particle makes her words in verse 2 an entreaty ("please") rather than a command (Abraham also used this particle in his word to Sarai in 12:13).

Without a word, Abraham accedes to Sarai's plan. But when Hagar becomes pregnant, she seeks to diminish Sarai's status in Abraham's eyes in view of her new standing in the family as mother-to-be of Abraham's child (cf. Prov. 30:23). The verb describing her action is qalal, a word used in 12:3 (commonly translated "curse") for contempt shown to the family of Abraham. Through the repeated use of this verb of contempt in 16:4–5, the narrative indicates that Hagar's action would bring her under the divine curse. The precise nature of Hagar's action is uncertain, but readers are invited to think of both verbal and nonverbal activity.

In justifiable response to Hagar's contempt, Sarai insists that Abraham resolve the issue. Abraham is now the husband of both of them and presumably has authority in such matters (and 12:3 was spoken to him). In language from the legal sphere (16:5), she accuses Abraham: "You are responsible for the wrong I am suffering" (NIV). It was within his power to stop this kind of treatment of Sarai and it is his problem to settle now, and God will be the judge of how he handles the issue. Abraham's only speaking in these episodes comes at this point (16:6). He admits no responsibility and tosses the problem back to Sarai, giving her authority to do as she wills. He has no apparent regard for the possible effect of his action on Hagar, though his own child is in her womb. Sarah, seeking no reconciliation with Hagar, responds by treating Hagar harshly. Her action against the Egyptian is strong ('ānāh, 16:6, 9, 11) and invites comparison with Exodus texts, for this language is used for Israel's oppression by Egypt (Gen. 15:13; Exod. 1:11–12; Deut. 26:6–7). Readers may wonder whether the narrator understands oppression in "what goes around comes around" terms.

Hagar runs away toward the land of Egypt (Shur is near the border), with the future of Abraham's child in her hands. She prefers the dangers of the wilderness to continuing life in the community of faith. Ironically, she thinks she can find more freedom in Egypt.

Surprisingly, the attention of the narrative does not return to issues faced by Abraham and Sarah, but remains with Hagar. Indeed, God's attention is focused on Hagar. Sarai and Abraham have sent Hagar away, not God. Having been exploited and excluded by the community of faith, Hagar the "outsider" is encountered by God. Out in the same wilderness where liberated Israel would later wander, Hagar is engaged by the "angel of the Lord" (repeatedly introduced, verses 7, 9–11). This messenger is not to be confused with later angelic beings, but is God in human form (cf. 21:17–19; 22:11–12, 15–16; 31:11, 13), as the narrator's report in 16:13 shows. Hagar appropriately testifies that she has seen God.[9] God has come on the scene on behalf of this oppressed one, as one day God would act on behalf of oppressed Israel.

God, the first to address Hagar by name, engages her in conversation and focuses on her future. Hagar's reply to God's inquiries suggests that she envisions no future for herself, for she only speaks of a past (16:8). God's response, however, tends to both the past and the future, though focusing on the future. Regarding the past, God directs Hagar to return to Sarai and to submit to her (interestingly, her return is not reported). This divine directive has sometimes been interpreted as insensitive, indeed continuing the oppressiveness of Abraham and Sarai.[10] To the contrary, given her contempt of Sarai (16:4–5) her future stands in danger (in view of 12:3), so she must get this matter resolved before true freedom for her becomes possible. At the same time, she will not return defenseless and she will not return with the same dependent status as before. She will go back to Abraham and Sarai with strong promises received directly and personally from God. With these promises in hand, Hagar will no longer be dependent upon God's promises to Abraham and Sarai as she stands on her own in her relationship with God. While readers might wish for a freer future for Hagar herself at this point, she (and God) moves with what is possible in the situation. She trusts in the word of God that the future will contain a new form of freedom. Salvation must take the form — of waiting for Hagar, but she knows that God sees and hears the afflicted, and so she can rest back in the knowledge that God keeps promises.[11]

One remarkable feature of God's response to Hagar is that God does not "curse" Hagar in the terms of Genesis 12:3. Instead of following through on the curse, as a mechanical view of the moral order would ordain, God responds positively to her affliction and makes promises to her (verses 10–12). In fact, God names Hagar's affliction in Exodus-like terms (*'ānāh,* verse 11). Unlike Abraham and Sarai, God addresses her by name, and for the first time she speaks. God presents the divine self to her in such a way that she is drawn out rather than reduced to self-effacement and silence (in both verses 8 and 13).

God's promises to Hagar focus on her offspring (16:10–12), as they had with Abraham (13:16; 15:5) and would with Sarai (17:15–16); indeed, in 16:11 readers can hear the familiar cadences of the annunciation in Isaiah 7:14. The oracle of 16:12 is more difficult to evaluate and it has occasioned both negative and positive outlooks with respect to Ishmael's future. Given Hagar's welcoming response and the narrator's point of view, the positive perspective is most likely. Ishmael will be free, roaming without restraint in the wilderness (21:20–21; God celebrates the "wild ass" in Job 39:5–8) and no longer submissive to oppressive people such as Sarai and Abraham. In von Rad's language: "there is undoubtedly undisguised sympathy and admiration for the roving Bedouin who bends his neck to no yoke. The man here pictured is highly qualified in the opinion" of people from that part of the world.[12]

Ishmael will also be at odds with other peoples, but such antagonisms are common among sedentary and nomadic groups in that world, and that kind of future is projected for the other side of Abraham's family as well (cf. 25:23; 27:28–29, 39–40).[13] No subsequent text will speak of a fulfillment of these projections regarding conflict, and, in any case, such oracles are not to be interpreted as a precise shaping of the future (as is also the case regarding 25:23 and the future of Jacob and Esau). In the report that these two sons came back to bury their father (25:9), there is no indication that they are in conflict.[14]

In response, Hagar publicly confesses that it is God who has seen her and is the one responsible for her rescue. The last phrase in 16:13 is difficult to interpret, but at the least it speaks of a mutual seeing on the part of God and Hagar ("I have now

seen the one who sees me," NIV), and may include the idea of still living after having seen God ("Have I really seen God and remained alive after seeing him?"
NRSV; cf. Exod. 33:20). Her confession focuses on a God who sees rather than a
God who speaks; this formulation lifts up God's attentiveness to her in her affliction. A parallel theme has been sounded about a God who hears (16:11). The
name Ishmael ("God hears") witnesses to God's hearing a person in distress
(17:20; 21:17; 29:33; 30:6, 17, 22).

Hagar responds to God's promises by giving God a new name that reflects her
experience (16:13; "you are El-roi," that is, "a God of seeing" or "a God who sees
me"). This naming of God and the theological reflection that was necessary to do
this makes Hagar unique among biblical characters. Hagar's new name for God is
a metaphor born of her experience of having been given a future and a hope. This
is not a "new" God who needs a name; the word to her uses the name Yahweh
(16:11), as does the narrator (16:13). Hagar may also give a name to the well
(NRSV fn.; 16:14); that name also centers on God as one who "sees" me. By these
namings Hagar's experience is pressed into the memory of succeeding generations
in terms of a seeing God. And so Hagar's experience will also become that of Leah
and Jacob (Gen. 29:32; 31:42), as well as Israel in Egypt, whom God "sees" and
delivers (Exod. 2:25; 3:7; 4:31).

At times the community of faith can so center on the speaking God that the
theme of the seeing God is left aside. Not so with Hagar, and not so with Israel
either. Central to Israel's confession is that its God sees the human situation and
responds to it (29:31–32; 31:12, 42; Exod. 2:25; 3:7; 4:31). God's seeing (and
hearing) is crucial, because it means that God's speaking will be directed to the
human need in a precise way. The reason why God's word can bring a future and
a hope is that it is grounded in God's having seen the situation for what it is and
hence being able to address actual needs in a specific way. God's saving acts
directly respond to creaturely need (cf. also how God's promises to Abraham in
Genesis 15:3–5 correspond to his expressed need).

Hagar returns to the chosen community and gives birth to Ishmael. Abraham
now has a son. The strong and repetitive declarations of the narrator in 16:15–16
in the wake of the promise of 16:10, the repetitiveness (the verb *yālad*, "bear,"
occurs five times), and the inclusio with the theme of 16:1–2, demonstrate that,
whatever happens later, Ishmael is a genuine fulfillment of God's promises to
Abraham of a son and descendants (detailed in 25:12–18). Hagar bears "Abraham
a son," and Abraham gives "his son" the name that God had given him (verse 11).
This assumes that Abraham was told of the encounter between Hagar and God,
and Abraham knows the significance of the name. It is notable that Sarai is not in
view; her intent to have children (16:2) is not specifically stated as having been
realized.

Thirteen years will pass before the story is picked up again, and the promise is spoken to both Sarah and Abraham (17:15–16) and the fulfillment of God's promise comes again with the birth of Isaac. Ishmael is indeed a fulfillment of the divine promise to Abraham. The passing of thirteen years between 16:16 and 17:1 reinforces this conviction. At this stage of the narrative (16:15–16), only a new word from God will move the issue further along (17:15–21).

That new word from God treats the two sons somewhat differently, as God speaks of establishing the covenant with Isaac, but not with Ishmael (17:20–21). God is responsive to Abraham's concerns about Ishmael, however. He speaks promises regarding Ishmael similar to those given Isaac, which include nationhood and royalty (21:13, 18; 25:12–16 lists the twelve princes). The heart of the difference that the language of covenant entails would seem to be 12:3b, the role of being a mediator of blessing to the nations.[15]

Ishmael, the one who stands outside the chosen line, remains closely linked to the chosen family because he is circumcised. Generally, a democratizing tendency is evident in this rite, at least among the males in the community: slaves as well as sons, foreigners as well as family, chosen as well as unchosen, are included within its scope. For all the exclusive tendencies in the rite, there is a genuine openness to the outsider. Both individual and community are in view.

GENESIS 21:8–21 AND BEYOND

The fulfillment of the divine promise in Isaac's birth (21:1–7) occasions problems as well as possibilities for Abraham and Sarah. The immediate problem that the text presents has to do with the relationship between Abraham's two sons. Ishmael and Isaac are both children of promise to whom God has made commitments. Yet, God has made a distinction between the sons (17:19–21). God has promised to make a covenant with Sarah's son, the yet-to-born Isaac, but not with Ishmael. At the same time, God has not overlooked Ishmael, as, indeed, God has made promises to him as well (16:10; 17:20; 21:13, 18).

Dynamics associated with this divinely determined distinction are played out in 21:8–14. Three years have passed since Isaac's birth (the common time for weaning, 21:8). At this time of rejoicing because he has survived the difficult first years, his relationship with Ishmael becomes a more pressing issue, especially for Sarah. Apparently, the conflicted relationship between Sarah and Hagar (16:3–6) was either not resolved amicably or has deteriorated in the three years since Isaac's birth. Sarah's repeated reference to Hagar as the "slave woman" (21:10; cf. 16:2, 5) and her concern about inheritance rights (legally, both sons would inherit) indicate that she is concerned about her maturing son's future. These factors seem to be sufficient explanation for Sarah's action.

Yet the difficulty in translating verse 9 (Gal. 4:29, where Ishmael "persecutes" Isaac) prompts a closer look. The root *tṣāḥaq,* "mocking" (NIV) or "playing" (NRSV, adding "with her son Isaac," see footnote), can have a negative sense (as in 19:14, "jesting"; cf. 17:17; 18:12–15). Some commentators through the years have interpreted Ishmael's action in abusive terms, even abusive sexual terms. Alter says: "Some medieval Jewish exegetes, trying to find a justification for Sarah's harsh response, construe the verb as a reference to homosexual advances."[16] The issue of Sarah's motivation has also prompted much discussion. Does she view this as a time to take revenge on Hagar's earlier action against her (16:5)? The positive sense of laughter seems more likely here, as in the divinely chosen name Isaac, "he laughs" (17:19) and Sarah's exclamation at his birth (21:6, "God has brought laughter for me; everyone who hears will laugh with me"). Perhaps Ishmael's activity reminded Sarah of the divine choice of Isaac. In any case, Sarah decides it is time to act—Abraham must choose between his sons. Sarah's strategy seems unnecessarily harsh, however. She does not speak with Hagar and demands that Abraham send Hagar and Ishmael away, using language that recalls Pharaoh's action in Exodus 12:39 ("drive out") that led to Israel's freedom. Yet, inasmuch as God supports her objective (21:12), the narrator views the action by Sarah in essentially positive terms.

Sarah's decision to choose between the two sons distresses Abraham (verse 11). The narrator's use of "his son," a reference to Ishmael, serves to intensify his anguish. His concern seems to center only on Ishmael (cf. 17:18), but God's reply shows that Abraham is concerned about Hagar as well (verse 12). Abraham is genuinely torn. This characteristic of Abraham has been recurrent in the narrative (cf. 16:6; 17:18). He has difficulty taking decisive action; yet, he shows deep levels of concern for the plight of the human beings involved, and he does not finally stand in the way of God's directive. Schneider thinks that God's reply to Abraham's distress over Ishmael reveals his less than fully trusting response to God's choice of Isaac with respect to the covenant line.[17] God needs to remind Abraham that it is through Isaac that descendants shall be named for him (21:12), and also repeats the promises regarding Ishmael (cf. 17:20; 21:13). This scene may be at least part of the background for God's "need to test Abraham in the next chapter (22) since Abraham's actions do not indicate complete acceptance of the plan the Deity lays out in Genesis 17."[18]

God responds to Abraham, sides with Sarah, adopts some of her language, and tells him to do as she says. God supports her objective and lets her strategy stand and Abraham's own feelings about Ishmael and Hagar must be set aside. God's rationale basically repeats earlier statements about Isaac (17:19–21) and makes it doubly clear that Abraham must make a choice. Both sons are recognized as Abraham's offspring (verses 12–13), but God's particular future in and through this family is to be worked out through Isaac, however difficult or unpleasant that may be. God's word to Abraham that descendants shall be "named for you" through Isaac (NRSV) or "reckoned" (NIV) is difficult, because both Ishmael and Isaac would qualify (25:12, 19).[19] At the same time, God makes clear that the future of Ishmael is secure; God repeatedly states—to both Abraham and Hagar—that Ishmael will be made a great nation (verses 13, 18). It has commonly been pointed out that God specifies (again) a future for Ishmael, but expresses no specific concern for Hagar's future (though in 21:17, God does voice a concern for her present distressed situation).

Abraham does as God tells him and sends Hagar (and Ishmael) away (*šālaḥ*, "send away" again is language for Israel's freedom in Exodus, for example, 5:1–2). The picture drawn in verse 14—not a single word is spoken—is a poignant one and is parallel to Abraham's action regarding Isaac in 22:3 (as are other elements in this text, see below). The parallels with Israel in the book of Exodus continue. Hagar and Ishmael "wander in the wilderness," in the area between Israel and Egypt, again mirroring Israel's later experience (as does the provision of water). With water supplies depleted, Hagar puts Ishmael under a bush and moves away, voicing a deep lament to God: do not let the child die. She refuses simply to accept such a fate for her son. God hears "the voice of the boy" (her lament and Ishmael's are telescoped, but why is only the cry of Ishmael reported?) and responds to "her" (by name; no "slave-girl," recognizing that this is no longer her status) with a salvation oracle: God quells her fear and assures her of Ishmael's future in words that had been used with Abraham (verse 13). This time (cf. 16:7–10), only God's voice is heard ("from heaven"), though it is also made clear again that the voice of the "angel of the Lord" is in fact the voice of God (for only God can make the promise of verse 18; cf. verse 13). God opens Hagar's eyes and she sees (cf. the seeing in 16:13; 22:13) the source of water needed to save Ishmael's life. The claim made is that Hagar was enabled to see water that was in fact in the vicinity, not that God miraculously produced the water at that moment.

The story closes with three claims that bode well for the future of both mother and child: (1) The continuing divine presence: "God was with the lad" (as with Abraham in verse 22); (2) Hagar's continuing strength to care for Ishmael's needs (she finds a wife for him among her own people, the only time a mother does this in the Old Testament); and (3) Ishmael thrives in his new home, becoming an expert hunter.

Two further references to Ishmael in the text testify to God's continued activity in his life. One, the return of Ishmael (but not the sons by Keturah) to participate with Isaac in Abraham's funeral is striking (25:9). This reference, with its witness to cooperation between the two "sons" of Abraham, has often been cited in contemporary discussions of the conflicts between their descendants. Perhaps the collaborative efforts of the two sons at the conclusion of Abraham's life could serve as a model of more positive ongoing relationships among those who call Abraham their father.

Two, the special place of Ishmael as a child of promise is seen in the detailed genealogy of Ishmael (25:12–18). This genealogy, which immediately precedes the brief genealogy of Isaac (25:19), bears witness to God's continuing presence in the life of his family, specifying in detail that God's numerous promises to him are being fulfilled (16:10; 17:20; 21:13, 18). While the language of promise is not specifically recalled, it goes without saying that these descendants are a fulfillment of key divine promises. God has been faithful; Ishmael has a future, too. Especially to be noted is the fact that Ishmael (verse 12) is described in terms identical to Isaac (verse 19) because both are "sons of Abraham." The reference to his life span is unique outside of the chosen line (verse 17). Moreover, the twelve princes that are descended from Ishmael (verse 16) mirror the twelve tribes of Israel. Indeed, his twelve sons parallel Jacob's progeny.[20] The translation of the last sentence of verse 18 is uncertain (cf. the footnotes). Did the descendants of Ishmael "live in hostility toward all their brothers" (NIV) or did he "settle down alongside of all his people" (NRSV)?[21] Genesis 25:9 would seem to support the latter translation (16:12b). In any case, the witness of the text is clear: God has been faithful to promises made to those both within and without the chosen family.

SARAH AND HAGAR

It may be helpful to look at these narratives again from the perspective of the two key characters, Sarah and Hagar (Abraham plays a minor role throughout). This angle of vision may help readers see the issues more clearly. The story in 16:1–16 begins by introducing two female characters, either for the first time (Hagar, though probably implied in 12:16) or for the first time as a character in her own right (Sarah, 11:29–31; 12:10–20).

SARAH

Interpretations of Sarah as a character are remarkably wide-ranging in view of the relatively small number of texts in which her activity is described. The telling of her story has probably been especially affected by the fact that she is active in situations that are highly conflicted. Schneider summarizes these options well: For some scholars Sarah "appears as petty, indulgent, self-absorbed, and the oppressor of Hagar. Others treat her as passive or in league with Abraham at his worst moments. There are those who do not even consider her a good mother and describe her as overprotective. Some also depict her as having no faith in the Israelite Deity . . . According to some rabbinic texts, she is a symbol of hope and even a prophetess. Teubal goes so far as to claim that Sarah was a Mesopotamian priestess and the powerful one in the family."[22] Schneider proceeds to draw an entirely positive view of Sarah. How to sort these options out is not an easy task.

Sarai takes the initiative with Abraham regarding her barrenness and, through- — out these texts, she remains "in charge" regarding issues that she believes need to be addressed (16:2, 5–6; 21:10), receiving support even from God (21:12). To address the issue of her childlessness, she makes a self-sacrificing move, even if customary. She not only shares her husband sexually, but Hagar is to be a "wife" to Abraham (16:3). Scholars are often critical of Sarai's approach to her barren- ness, claiming that she seeks to fulfill God's promise by her own efforts. A typical interpretation: Sarai's is "a fainthearted faith that cannot leave things with God and believes it necessary to help things along. A child so conceived in defiance or in little faith cannot be the heir of promise."[23] But, aside from the fact that such a — perspective speaks of Ishmael's (non)election as grounded in human behaviors, this is a docetic view of God's ways of working in the world. God often works in and through human beings to carry out the divine purposes in the Old Testament. Theologically, it should be stated strongly: Sarai should not in any way be faulted — for taking the initiative, and the means she uses was typical for that culture. Divine promise, appropriated by faith, does not entail human passivity in working — toward God's goals for the creation. Sarah's actions are true to this divine way of working in the world.

At the same time, Sarai does treat Hagar harshly (16:6), though this response is prompted by the pregnant Hagar's treatment of her. Sarai's dealing harshly with Hagar could be said to be her execution of justice at being wronged. At the same time, the language of oppression (cf. 15:13) suggests that it is an expression of justice taken too far. That God gives heed to Hagar's "affliction" (16:11; the same Hebrew root) means that God expresses judgment on Sarai's treatment of Hagar. While Sarai's action should not be excused, it may also be informed by her knowl- edge of God's promise in Genesis 12:3 ("the one who curses you, I will curse"). As human beings may be the mediator of divine blessing, so also may that be the case with respect to the curse. In her charge to Abraham to resolve the issue, she appeals to God (16:5); Sarai thereby gives evidence of her own relationship with God and claims that that relationship entails a divine obligation with respect to her; it is not simply Abraham to whom God has made commitments (formally stated in 17:15–16). It could be said that Abraham's response (16:6) is not "an abdication of his responsibility," but "a recognition of Sarai's claim and of her own power of action."[24] At the same time, Abraham provides no helpful counsel in this situation and hence tacitly participates in this oppressive treatment of Hagar.

Subsequent to the narrative events of chapter 16, God takes a new initiative with Sarah, extending the Abrahamic promises specifically to her (17:15–16). As an integral part of the revised covenant with Abraham, Sarah is, for the first time, named as the mother of the promised child. While Abraham and Sarah each receive the promise of a child with incredulity in view of their advanced age (17:17; 18:12–15), they both finally rest back in trust that God will be able to see to the promises. This trust is evident particularly in the wake of the birth of Isaac, when Abraham responds with action in the circumcision of Isaac (21:4) and Sarah with words, testifying with joy regarding the God who has fulfilled the promise of a son (21:6–7).

Sarah's directive to Abraham in 21:10 to "cast out this slave woman with her son" has often been questioned. This word is "distressing" to Abraham, and the reader might expect him to intervene on behalf of his son, Ishmael. The modern reader may tend to side with Abraham rather than Sarah on sending Hagar and Ishmael away. Yet, some such move is in order if the sons are to shape their separate futures in view of God's choice (17:19–20), a historical and theological reality for the narrator. Her objective seems to be on target, even if the means are unnecessarily harsh. It may be more troubling that God lets Sarah set the strategy for the separation. Yet, this is another instance in which God chooses to work through complex situations and imperfect human beings on behalf of the divine purposes. God works with what is available; God doesn't perfect people before deciding to work through them. God may see Sarah's strategy, however inadequate, as the best possible way into the future for this particular moment in the life of this family.

HAGAR

The text stresses that she is an Egyptian (16:1, 3; 21:9; 21:21) and that she is a slave of the chosen family (16:1–3, 5–6, 8; 21:10, 12–13). She is thus an "outsider."[25] Given her status, she has no voice when Sarai decides that Abraham should bear a child through her; she is simply taken and given to Abraham as a "wife" (16:2–3). She may have accepted the customs of surrogate motherhood current in that culture, but her vulnerability should not be downplayed. She has no legal rights in this situation, and when Abraham, having voicelessly accepted Sarah's proposal, shows up at her tent door to fulfill his "obligation," she has no choice but to acquiesce. When she is treated "harshly" by those in authority over her (16:6), she runs away. That Abraham and Sarai never call her by name (she is by God, 16:8; 21:17), and only refer to her as a slave-girl, suggests that we are to be mindful of her precarious situation (the narrator never calls her a slave-girl; God does in 21:12–13). The chosen become the oppressors of Egyptians. The elect have shown the "outsiders" how to oppress. Perhaps their words and deeds towards the "outsiders" are so oppressive that God must work around them as well as through them.

Hagar is the first person in Genesis to be encountered by the angel of God, that is, God in human form (16:7–12). God engages her in conversation and focuses on her future and that of her child. In response to God's query, Hagar does not hide the fact that she is Sarai's slave-girl, a status that God acknowledges (verse 9), but implicitly claims that she is fleeing for good cause, naming it as "affliction" (verse 11). At the same time, God commands that she return to Sarai. Hagar must get the conflict with Sarah resolved in order to ensure her future (in view of 12:3, "the one who curses you, I will curse"); hence, this divine command should be interpreted, finally, as a gracious divine move.

To accompany Hagar on her return, God showers her with promises (verses 10–12). Hagar is the first woman to receive promises from God (cf. 25:23). Indeed, directly and indirectly, she is given a series of promises that specify God's commitment to her future and that of her son. The language that God uses is surprisingly reminiscent of the promises to Abraham and Sarah (16:10–11; 17:20; 21:13, 18). God's promise in 16:10 picks up on the promise in 1:28 ("be fruitful and multiply"); God's designs for the creation are being realized in and through her. While an explicit promise of land is not present, it is assumed in the promise of nationhood (17:20). The only promissory language used with Isaac that is not used with respect to Ishmael is that of covenant (17:20–21). Obviously this difference is important, but it should not minimize or set aside the vigorous promises given to Hagar and Ishmael.

Given the divine word of promise, Hagar is not destined to eternal slave status in the household of the chosen family. God has heard her in her affliction and promises that her offspring will enjoy the freedom she has not been able to experience (16:11–12). While Hagar resubmits herself to Sarah and Abraham, it proves not to be for a lifetime (21:8–21), and the promise of God about her son is that he will not have to submit. In other words, the act of submission on the part of Hagar is for the sake of the freedom of her descendants. "Her child, born in her servitude, will be free: He will be a wild ass of the wilderness, not a domestic; he will not be under anyone's power (hand), but will enjoy parity with those who act against him; and he will dwell alongside his own kin."[26]

This move from servitude to freedom for Hagar's descendants parallels the move that God has announced for Abraham's descendants in 15:13–16. In effect, it is the announcement of an Exodus for Hagar and her offspring, from a God who "does Exodus" for peoples throughout the world (Amos 9:7). That Hagar, repeatedly mentioned by the narrator in 16:15–16, is not there identified as a slave-girl indicates the character of her future status. Though she initially returns to the oppression of the household of Abraham and Sarai, God has made clear that she is not characterized by her present situation but by God's promised future of freedom. That God would make such promises to those who stand outside the line of Isaac is remarkable; moreover, God's promises to her are not dependent on the promises to members of the chosen line. In other words, she submits to God in her external status—and that is only temporary; but in terms of her faith, and in terms of God's promises, she stands free from them. With these promises, Hagar has been given independence in her relationship with God, which will significantly qualify any continuing dependence she has on Abraham and Sarai. By having Abraham name Ishmael with the same name that Hagar does (16:15–16), the narrator has Abraham unwittingly affirm the relationship with God that Hagar has independently established.

The response of Hagar to the God who appears to her and gives her promises is one of faith and trust. She recognizes the voice of the messenger as the voice of God, even though God has not spoken a word of self-identification (cf. 31:11–13). She recognizes that the God of Sarah and Abraham is the one who speaks to her, and she gives God a new name. In deciding on this name, she utilizes her own experience with God and the knowledge of God gained thereby to shape new language for God—an ever-contemporary responsibility. Hagar thereby shows the chosen people the way in the need to develop new language for God in view of that ongoing experience. In this naming of God, Hagar herself understands that she has a relationship with God that stands on its own. Indeed, Hagar becomes the only person in the Bible to give God a name (16:13); in all other instances, God reveals God's own name.

This remarkably wide-ranging story leads Phyllis Trible to speak eloquently of Hagar becoming many things to many people: "Most especially, all sorts of rejected women find their stories in her. She is the faithful maid exploited, the black woman used by the male and abused by the female of the ruling class, the surrogate mother, the resident alien without legal recourse, the other woman, the runaway youth, the religious fleeing from affliction, the pregnant young woman alone, the expelled wife, the divorced mother with child, the shopping bag lady carrying bread and water, the homeless woman, the indigent relying upon handouts from the power structures, the welfare mother, and the self-effacing female whose own identity shrinks in service to others."[27] How does the community of faith relate to the Hagars of this world?

CONTEMPORARY QUESTIONS

For Israel to tell and retell the stories of Hagar and Ishmael serves to remind the chosen people again and again that Israel's God plays an important role in the life of "unchosen" persons. Such "outsiders" have experienced God, even if they have not realized that it was God. The text specifically witnesses that Hagar does realize the reality of her experience. She knows that God is active in her life in both word and deed and the text witnesses that this activity takes place outside the boundaries of the community of faith. The testimony is clearly stated: God appears to Hagar, converses with her, and makes promises to her—independently of the chosen family.

In these stories, God is portrayed as a Creator who makes promises to those who do not belong to the "people of God" (which should include their descendants, both physical and spiritual, in Islam). While the contact with the family of Abraham is important, and indeed enables Hagar to interpret her experience in the way she does, God's attentiveness to Hagar and Ishmael comes more in spite of what that family has done than because of their concern for outsiders and their welfare. Indeed, God enters her life at precisely that point when her exclusion from the chosen family has taken place (16:7; cf. 21:17). God's action on behalf of Hagar and others often takes place more in spite of the chosen than because of them. The chosen people cannot confine God's works and ways—even words of gospel and promise (verses 10–11)—within their often oppressive and narrowly conceived structures.

Hagar's laments (in both 16:8 and 21:16) are followed by the assurance of salvation from God. This is a typical rhythm for Israel's communal and individual life, so evident in the Psalms. In this story the people of God should recognize and rejoice that God's saving acts are not confined to their own community. God's acts of deliverance occur out and about in the seemingly godforsaken corners of the world, even among those who may be explicitly excluded from the "people of God." Here we see God at work among the outcasts, the refugees of the world— who fill our world as much as they did then. Persons of faith are to participate in their lives, to lift them up and hold them fast until the wells become available. They are also to seek to discern where God's delivering activity may have occurred out and about in the world, to name these events for what they are, and to publicly confess them as such. Once again, we see how Genesis witnesses to the workings of the creator God. Telling and retelling stories like this one keeps that testimony alive, and serves to remind the chosen that their God is the God of all the world, including the outsiders.

The story of Abraham does not culminate with reference only to Isaac. This is a significant theological claim with important implications for contemporary reflection and practice. Given the variety of negative and positive relationships that the people of God have had with some of these families over the years, it is striking that at the beginning of their history stands this word about the various lines of the family of Abraham. This genealogical reference suggests that relationships among people in that part of the world ought to be conceived most fundamentally in familial language rather than in national or political or religious terms. Of course, differences among these families have emerged over the years that cannot be lightly set aside. But significant commonalities continue in place as well, to which these very deep roots in the family of Abraham testify. These familial links should provide some continuing basis for working with the inevitable, but not insurmountable differences among these peoples in a creative and peaceful way.

The promises that God makes to Hagar and Ishmael need focused attention in this connection. They should occasion especially sharp questions for those who are the descendants of Isaac. For Abraham, the promises chart a vocation: through him shall all the families of the earth be blessed, including the families of Hagar and Ishmael. At the same time, these descendants are a special "case"; God has made promises to Hagar's family that are unique among outsiders, and their fulfillment is not said to be dependent on her descendants' relationship to the elect.

Those who are descendants of Isaac need to ask what God's promises to Hagar and Ishmael mean for the shape that their mission takes with this particular family. Indeed, what does it mean for insiders that Hagar and Ishmael are recipients of the continuing promises of God? This is a contemporary theological question. What might the fulfillment of such promises mean for the people of God, not least for their continuing relationships to the descendants of Ishmael in Islam? What might it mean to continue to confess in and through the retelling of this story that the Ishmaelites are who they are because God has kept promises? A key question for the modern interpreter thus becomes: Is it possible that the descendants of Hagar and Ishmael, both physical and spiritual descendants,[28] now more than one billion Muslims strong across the world,[29] are who they are because God has kept promises? Has God indeed been faithful to these promises made to Sarah and Ishmael? In search of the answer, it is well to remember that Ishmael does not receive negative treatment in the rest of the Old Testament.[30]

How is the other half of Abraham's family going to relate to these brothers and sisters in ways that acknowledges this ongoing work of God? Readers must remember that God has made a "covenant" with the line of Isaac and not with the line of Ishmael. This strong claim should not be minimized. Indeed, God has sworn by God's own self in chapter 15 that God would be true to God's own promises to Abraham. Indeed, God passed through the fire as a sign of self-imprecation should God ever be proved unfaithful. As strange as it may sound, God puts God's own life on the line for the sake of the promises. Christians count themselves the spiritual descendants of Abraham; they have been made the recipients of God's promises to him. But that occasions a sharper question for Isaac's descendants than if the treatment of Ishmael and Isaac had been more "even-handed." What one does with the Ishmaels of this world in the face of the claims for Isaac comes front and center. Abraham was chosen so that all of the families of the earth might be blessed through him. This means that the children of Abraham, who are also the children of Isaac, are to so comport themselves that blessing rather than curse comes upon the nations. Our words and actions may be so counter to God's activity, that the divine will for this people, embodied in the promises, is frustrated thereby and hence less effective than it might otherwise be.

CHAPTER 7

ISAAC—BIRTH, ENDANGERMENT, AND SIGN OF THE FUTURE

THE TURNING OF THE GENERATIONS

Genesis 17:15–21; 18:1–15; 21:1–7; 22:1–19; 24:1–67; 23:1–20; 25:1–11

One of the more interesting features of the Genesis ancestral narrative is the lack of a sustained story relating to Isaac. While subsequent texts often refer to the ancestors with the trio of names (Abraham, Isaac, and Jacob), the story of Isaac is remarkably sparse. Genesis 26–27 contains important snapshots of his life, but they are enfolded within the framework of the story of Jacob. Isaac is indeed the fulfillment of God's promise of a son to Abraham and Sarah, but the narrative quickly moves beyond him to the next generation.

Isaac specifically comes into view in the narrative in association with God's promise of a son to Abraham through Sarah (17:19, 21).[1] Yet, given the birth and early life of Ishmael, Abraham seems to be satisfied that he is the fulfillment of God's promise of a son (17:17–18); Isaac is almost an unwelcome afterthought. It is as if Ishmael did not work out, so God will try again. At the same time, Sarah as the mother of the promised son sharply comes into view, and in spite of the incredulity of both Abraham and Sarah (17:17; 18:13–15), Isaac becomes the son with whom God's covenant will now be continued (17:21). It is striking that Abraham never explicitly agrees with God's plans in 17:20–21, though his move to circumcise his household (17:23–27) would be a general sign of trust and obedience.

SARAH FINALLY GETS THE WORD, GENESIS 18:1–15

This story is centered on an appearance of God to Abraham and Sarah, with whom God has just made commitments regarding their future (17:1–21). While God conveys no self-identification, this text is similar to other theophanic narratives (cf. 16:7–14; 26:24). Scholars make much of the fact that verses 1–8 center on issues of hospitality extended to strangers. Both biblical and nonbiblical parallels to this narrative combine the themes of hospitality and birth announcement.[2]

While this concern is certainly not absent, as we shall see, another angle on the text, focused on Sarah, seems more prominent. The divine commitment in 17:1–21 had included the promise of a son to Abraham, with Sarah specifically mentioned as the mother for the first time. God's promise had also been made very specific with respect to the male gender of their child, whom God had given the name Isaac (17:19). At first glance, the crux of the story in 18:1–15 seems simply to repeat that point. But this divine appearance at the familial tent—where Sarah is most likely to be present—seems especially designed to reinforce the promise of a son by conveying the word directly to Sarah herself—she is referred to by name nine times in verses 9–15 (plus pronominal references)—and the promise itself, repeated twice, mentions only Sarah as the parent (verses 10, 14). That the visitors begin the conversation with reference to Sarah reinforces this point (verse 9).

At the same time, issues of hospitality are indeed present. Because God does not leave the conversation until 18:33, the purpose of the visit seems also to anticipate the interchange with Abraham regarding the future of Sodom and Gomorrah. The issue of hospitality may provide the link across this span of texts. Abraham and Sarah (verse 6) are ideal hosts to the strangers, which include God. Verses 9–15 retain some interest in hospitality, with their focus on Sarah's reception of the announcement: how hospitable will Sarah be to this word? Will her response be similar to Abraham's (17:17)? Issues of hospitality relate both to receiving others and receiving the words they may speak. This theme plays a key role in 19:1–3 (Lot) and 24:18–20 (Rebekah). Moreover, in 18:16–33, issues of divine hospitality are raised, especially regarding God's reception of the human word. God receives the "outcry" from those affected by the conduct of the people of Sodom and Gomorrah and moves to deal with it. Moreover, God is highly receptive of the words of Abraham and takes them into account in moving into the future. Another link with verses 16–33 has to do with the prominence of questions, from Abraham and God. In all cases, the questions raised are serious and posed for the purpose of continuing the conversation. The divine conveyance to Abraham of matters that pertain to the future also provide a link between verses 10–14 and verses 17–19.

We sketch the flow of thought in this section. The visitors who appear at the home of Abraham and Sarah are initially presented in enigmatic terms. From the narrator's point of view, it is Yahweh who appears to Abraham at his home (verse 1). From Abraham's point of view, however, three men stand near him (verse 2). The reader knows more at this early point in the narrative than does Abraham. Yahweh has assumed human form (16:7–13; 17:1, 22) and is included among the three men.[3] The other two are angelic attendants, who continue on to the city of Sodom (19:1). The separation between Yahweh and two of the messengers in 18:22 and 19:1, 13 supports this interpretation, as does the shift between singular (18:3, 10–15) and plural (18:9) references to the visitors (19:17–19, cf. NIV footnotes). It is not certain at what point either Abraham or Sarah come to recognize that this is indeed a divine appearance. But it is clear that Abraham's hospitality is not prompted by a desire to please a divine visitor. Sarah's response in verses 9–15 also must be interpreted with this uncertainty in mind.

Seeking to identify which persons are involved in the conversation is difficult. Initially all seem to be involved (18:9, "they"), then "one" takes the lead (NIV's use of "LORD" in verse 10 is an inference drawn from the words that follow). In verse 13 the narrator identifies the speaker as Yahweh, but the speaker does not so identify himself to Abraham and Sarah. Verse 14 speaks about Yahweh in the third person, so that the "I" reference could be understood by Sarah as someone other than Yahweh. Perhaps angelic mediation is in view, though in the Old Testament God often uses the third person when speaking of divine action. All three visitors are eventually involved in destruction of the city, as the angels mediate God's action (19:13 with 19:14, 24). The fear shown by Sarah (verse 15) probably stems primarily from the uncertainty regarding who is speaking and from knowing that this person has said what he has about her (including her laughing to herself where she could not be seen). These features introduce an element of mystery into the moment; it is little wonder why she is puzzled as to how this individual could speak for God so specifically.

It is helpful to see the detailed way in which the characteristics of Abraham's hospitality are portrayed:[4] it is extended to strangers and to those who appear unexpectedly. It follows a certain protocol: seeing, running to meet, honoring, inviting, refreshing, preparing, and serving. Bowing is an everyday gesture, not only extended to important people. Haste language appears five times (verses 2, 6–7; cf. 24:18–20). He takes his best animal to provide food for them (a calf), makes and serves the food, is available to the visitors, is concerned about their welfare, and accompanies them on their way (verse 16). The phrase, "find favor in your eyes" (verse 3; 19:19; 32:5; 33:8–15) is a matter of courtesy; it gives the visitors a higher status (whether or not this is the case) and they then have greater freedom to respond without embarrassment. Abraham depicts what the visitors may expect from his hospitality (verses 4–5), in view of which they accept the invitation. When he provides meat as well, he goes beyond their expectations and what he had promised them. These heavenly beings, one of whom is God, eat (God apparently also eats in Exod. 24:11).[5] As the visitors stand near Abraham (verse 2) so he stands near them (verse 8); reciprocating their attentiveness, he understands himself to be their servant (verses 3, 5).

The visitors take the initiative in the conversation, focusing on Sarah (see above). Their question (verse 9) seems designed to make sure Sarah is within earshot of what is about to be said; the narrator states (verse 10) that she is in fact listening "off camera." When the visitors are assured by Abraham that she is listening, one of them (presumably God) makes the planned declaration: in due season (or at this time next year) she will experience a divine visitation and will give birth to a son. The relation between the twice-stated temporal—but general— reference to the divine visitation (verses 10, 14; 17:21) and Sarah having a son finds its resolution in 21:1. God is there said to visit Sarah "as he had said," and it is made clear that it is an explicit divine action that enables Sarah to become pregnant; at the same time, the normal time for the child to develop in the womb is not set aside (see also the "due time" reference in 2 Kings 4:16). The mother is not somehow made irrelevant.

Upon overhearing this conversation, Sarah laughs "to herself." The reader will recall that God had spoken such a promise to Abraham and that he had also laughed (out loud?) and spoken "to himself" (17:15–17). He asked essentially the same questions (17:16–17), though his "falling on his face" seems to be a more incredulous response than that of Sarah. The narrator inserts a word about their age (verse 11; cf. Abraham's comment about Sarah in 17:17) and that Sarah no longer menstruates (verse 11), as if to provide an objective view on Sarah's own comments (verse 12). These comments by the narrator soften Sarah's response, making it more understandable, as does her observation about the end of sexual pleasure (note that Abraham fathers other children, 25:1–4). The issue for Sarah is no longer barrenness, but age (cf. 11:30; 16:2).

The visitor's next question inquires of Sarah's laughter at hearing of a child they say she will bear (verse 13). If the visitor's question is accusatory (the narrator has God speaking at this point), then it claims that Sarah should know better than to laugh, for nothing is too wonderful for God. Yet, the visitor would not likely be critical of Sarah's incredulity if God had not been critical of the more incredulous response by Abraham (17:17). That Abraham's response is made knowing that God is the speaker, while Sarah makes her response without such knowledge, is also a significant matter to consider in making judgments. It should also be remembered that Sarah's incredulous response is part of a literary convention for such announcements; see, for example, the response of the Shunammite woman to a "man of God" (2 Kings 4:16) and Mary to an angel (Luke 1:34). Many Old Testament texts report such questioning responses. They are considered to be a natural part of a genuine conversation, even a God-human conversation, and Abraham will shortly engage God in a sustained way (18:23–33; cf. Moses in Exod. 3–6; Gideon in Judg. 6:13). Commentators have often been unfair to Sarah here, evident especially in the way in which Abraham's laughter (17:17) is excused and Sarah's judged severely.[6]

It is probable, then, that God's "why" question regarding Sarah's laughter (verse 13) is not accusatory, but is a genuine question designed to continue the conversation (whether or not Sarah realizes that the speaker of verse 10 is God). This interpretation is also suggested by the way in which God paraphrases Sarah's question, omitting references to the end of sexual relations and Abraham's age. And so God's response aims to continue the conversation, and God makes no judgment on Sarah, even when Sarah denies that she laughed. At the least, God reminds

Sarah that she has laughed and impresses her response of laughter on the occasion, a theme that will return later (21:6–7).

That the questions of verses 13–14 are directed to Abraham means that God seeks a reaction from him regarding Sarah's laughter. He is the one who is called to explain her response. This may be due to Abraham's not informing Sarah of what he had learned from the events of chapter 17; if someone is to be blamed (and it seems unlikely that this is what is going on), then Abraham is the one who is called to account. It is notable that Abraham makes no response to God's questions—a strange silence, especially in view of 18:23–33. At the same time, verses 13–14 are also intended to be heard by Sarah; inasmuch as she responds, she so understands this to be the case (verse 15). She does not step forward to speak, however, so hers is a voice from "off stage." Her denial of laughter (verse 15) could be a lie, or, more likely, an attempt to withdraw her laughter, having been made more aware of the nature of the moment and the identity of the one who has spoken.[7] But the visitor (God) says her laughter remains a fact. This exchange keeps both Sarah and Abraham on the same level regarding the reception of the promise and will link up with her response to the naming of Isaac ("he laughs").

A scholarly effort to claim that Sarah's laughter is only one of joyfulness (and Abraham's laughter is not so interpreted) seems to be wishful thinking.[8] The question about why Sarah laughed and her own denial that she had laughed pushes in another direction. That Sarah's laughter is initially a sign of incredulity at the possibility of having a child is suggested by God's response precisely at the point of possibility/impossibility (18:14). In the face of such incredulity, God reiterates the promise that she will bear a child. Inasmuch as God knows she is listening, this reiteration of the promise should be understood as spoken to her, even if indirectly.[9]

The narrator's phrase, "for she was afraid," deserves more comment. Of what was she fearful? Perhaps it has to do with her realization that this "other" has "overheard" her speak and laugh to herself. Who must this "other" be to have engaged in such overhearing? And, if this other has overheard, and still repeats the claim that she will have a child, then something strange indeed is going on. Or was she fearful because, at the end of this conversation, she realizes that what this "other" was saying just might be true. And life would be turned upside down. Or having lived for so many years with an unrealized dream, might Sarah now want to believe that it is true and she is fearful that it might not become a reality? And she is afraid that her laughter will somehow be offensive to this creator of possibilities and he will take back the word. Generally, if Sarah realizes that the speaker is God, fear can be a natural response in the midst of the experience of such divine words.[10]

God's reply countering Sarah's denial of laughter can then be interpreted positively. Her laughter, however incredulous she is, provides an opening into this new possibility and constitutes a signal that her laughter may turn from incredulity to joy (21:6–7). So, in effect, God is saying: do not deny the laughter, but continue to laugh and in time it will be transformed. In effect, the denial means that her laughter does not stand in the way of her becoming a mother and she need not fear that it will.

The question God asks in verse 14 ("Is anything too wonderful for the Lord?") seems designed to move Abraham and Sarah beyond their limited view of the future based on their age to a consideration of God's possibilities. The specific mention of the Lord in this question is meant to make it clear to them that God is the subject of the promised activity. The meaning of the question, however, is difficult to discern. The difficulty is in part due to uncertainties regarding the precise meaning of the word pele', translated "wonderful" or "hard/difficult" (verse 14).[11] Does the word push in the direction of competence (Deut. 17:8) or the ability to accomplish something (Jer. 32:17, 27) or that which is extraordinary or marvelous (Ps. 118:23; 139:14)? The plural form of the word commonly refers to God's wonderful deeds of redemption and judgment (Exod. 3:20; 34:10). Is the question designed to link this moment in the life of Sarah and Abraham with those later salvific deeds? The latter would not have been possible without God's activity in this ancestral moment.

The nature of the question is also uncertain. Is it a genuine question designed to continue the conversation by engaging the question, or, as often interpreted, is it a rhetorical question designed to declare that nothing is too hard for God? Brueggemann's comments are helpful in showing that the divine question has no simple yes or no answer. If the answer is "yes," then that would be to delimit in a specific way what is or is not possible for God. No human construct can finally define God's possibilities in a given situation. If the answer is no, "that is an answer which so accepts God's freedom that the self and the world are fully entrusted to God and to no other."[12] Such a clear negative answer would fail to recognize that God has given genuine power into the hands of the creation (Gen. 1:28) and that what is possible for God must be consistent with who God is.[13] For example, God cannot act in such a way as to compromise or negate divine promises that have been made. Issues of divine self-limitation are thereby raised.

The point of this question seems to be that no obstacles are available that can stop God from finding a way into the future of this promised son. Not the seemingly insurmountable hurdles of human bodily limits (postmenopausal births have been documented in modern times) or the uncertain and incredulous responses of both Abraham and Sarah. Nothing in the present circumstances can stymie the carrying forth of the divine purposes. The question is not designed to make a claim that God is the only one with power or that the divine power is irresistible in every situation. The point made is that God's promise of a son will not fail, that God will be able to find a way into this particular future.

A text such as this calls for sentences in which God is the subject. God is the one who makes the promised future possible. God is the source of hope in a situation where the way into the future seems entirely blocked off. God gives shape to possibilities when everything seems impossible. The active engagement of God in the midst of a remarkably common problem of daily life opens up the future rather than closes it down. Yet, God, as always, acts in and through means, indeed through less than obvious means. And God will not perfect the means before determining to act in and through them.

The end of this textual segment seems incomplete, ending as it does with the exchange about Sarah's laughter. Yet, the narrator's intent may well be to leave the reader (and Sarah and Abraham) in a state of some uncertainty as to how God's future will work itself out.[14]

AND SARAH LAUGHED, GENESIS 21:1–7

The narrative of the birth of Isaac, the chosen one of God, is surrounded by texts that are associated with nonchosen people. The story is immediately preceded by the exchange with Abimelech (20:1–18), who will return at the end of this chapter (21:22–34) and is directly followed by the story of the banishment of Hagar and Ishmael (21:8–21). This literary embrace suggests that Israel's relationship to outsiders is once again a central issue (12:3). Another common feature in these juxtaposed texts has to do with women who have difficulty bearing or raising children, from the women in Abimelech's land (20:17–18) to Sarah and Hagar. The water and wells that resolve the life and death issue for Hagar and Ishmael also play a role in the peace-making between Abraham and Abimelech (21:22–34).

The story of the birth of Isaac brings a key aspect of the Abraham narrative to a climax. Twenty-five years have passed since Abraham's call at age seventy-five (12:4) and the promised son is finally born. Considering all the problems and possibilities that have led up to this moment, the depiction of his birth is brief and to the point. No special miracle language is used, though it is made doubly clear that God is the one who is, finally, responsible for what has happened (21:1–2; cf. Luke 1:68). The first verb (*pāqad*, various translations are possible) links this act of God with Exodus events (50:24–25; Exod. 3:16; 4:31), showing the import of Isaac's birth for the larger divine purpose. The several references to the age of Sarah and Abraham (also in 24:36) helps lift up the wonder of the occasion. Four citations of earlier narratives (verses 1, 2, 4) stress that God has made good on the promises (17:15–21). At the same time, Abraham's actions are especially noted; he has been obedient in naming and circumcising Isaac (17:12, 19; cf. 17:23). The theme of laughter associated with Isaac's name continues.

Only Sarah speaks in response to Isaac's birth (verses 6–7). Abraham is silent here and through much of the chapter.[15] He names him and circumcises him, but he has nothing to say and his feelings are hidden from view. The reader cannot help but wonder why this is so. It is not so with Sarah. Indeed, the focus of this text is on Sarah—she is mentioned by name six times. Her response to the birth of Isaac is sketched in terms that evidence deep feelings of joy and delight. She also testifies to her faith in the God who has made this possible in spite of seemingly impossible odds (21:6–7). It has been suggested that Sarah thinks that people will laugh at her having a baby at her age. But it is more likely that Sarah's exclamations in verses 6–7 are understood only in positive terms, as a joy-filled occasion not a matter of shame. Verse 6 refers to Sarah's joy at the birth of Isaac; others who hear about the birth will rejoice with her. Isaac's name is thus related to the joy at his birth, with only an indirect reference to the earlier laughter of Abraham and Sarah at God's promise of a son. Indeed, the former incredulity on their part is implicitly softened: no one would have dreamed that they would become parents. The final line in verse 7 (an inclusio with verse 2) is best understood as a cry of joy: I have borne Abraham a son in his old age.

The story of the birth of Isaac (and the announcements related thereto) raises several issues for the modern reader. In what sense, if at all, can we (do we) still speak of God's involvement in bringing new life into being? Other Old Testament texts speak of such divine involvement in even more graphic terms (Job 10:8–12; Ps. 139:13). These texts suggest that God, for special purposes, can set aside natural processes (for example, age, barrenness) in the conception and birthing of children. The issue is especially poignant for those couples who have had difficulty having their own children or could not bear them at all. The question often arises: If God could "intervene" on behalf of aged and barren women in biblical times, why not with me? A closer look at the text may shed some light on issues of this sort. At the same time, one of the difficulties in working through such questions is that the text itself seems not to be mindful of them.

At least one thing is clear: God, in working with Sarah, does not act in independence from her; God works with her (16:2, "by her"). God's power, as typically in the Old Testament, is not understood as all-determinative. The narrator uses the verb *yālad* (bear, beget) five times in this segment (twice in verse 3, see New Jerusalem Bible [NJB]) to describe the roles of both Abraham and Sarah in the birthing of Isaac. At the same time, the birth occurs only because God has been involved in some way, when seemingly impossible hurdles present themselves (age is stressed). One might, therefore, speak of multiple agency; both God and parents are involved in the creating of this new life. That is typically the way in which God works in the biblical world. God acts in and through human beings (and other creatures) to carry out the divine purposes in the world, with all the potential complications and difficulties related thereto. The promise language in 17:16, in speaking of a son for Sarah as due to God's blessing, invites readers to think of a divine creative activity that makes Sarah's pregnancy possible. The repeated reference in 21:1–2 to earlier narratives, wherein God announced this birth (17:15–16; 18:9–15), stresses the fulfillment of God's word. At the same time, the text's reiteration of promises being fulfilled testify indirectly that Isaac's birth was not the only future that could have been realized.

The faith of Abraham and Sarah remain relevant in considering God's possibilities in this situation (Rom. 4:16–21 and Heb. 11:11–2 so understand the matter). These New Testament texts indicate that this divine action is not unrelated to human response (in this case, faith in a specific promise). A possible reason for the long delay in the fulfillment of the promise relates to the developing response of Abraham and Sarah (including their lack of trust). The texts would thus be a witness to divine perseverance in the face of human mistrust and resistance. Generally speaking, God's resolve within a human situation may find openings into the future that seem impossible for human beings; at the same time, God's will is able to be frustrated in view of human response. We do not normally understand conception and birthing as determined only by divine activity: parental actions can profoundly affect matters (for example, fetal alcohol syndrome). The randomness of the gene pool and other unknown factors make any analysis of these kinds of situations even more complicated. In terms of God's use of agents in a modern situation, one might think of God's creative involvements in and through the medical community seeking to overcome these realities, resulting in (potential) breakthroughs for many parents.

THE BINDING OF ISAAC, GENESIS 22:1–19

Genesis 22 has long captivated the imaginations of interpreters, drawn by its literary artistry, its religious depths, and its sheer horror.[16] Along with other aspects of the Abrahamic tradition, it has played a significant role in three major religious traditions. At the same time, Genesis 22 is a deeply troubling text, perhaps even a hurtful text, and one that must be used with great care.[17] Religious interpretations, especially since Kierkegaard's *Fear and Trembling*,[18] seem often to intensify the contradictoriness of the story, perhaps in the interests of heightening the mystery of God's ways. While the reader should not discount the unusual, even frightening character of God's command, it must not be exaggerated either, not least because the narrator gives Abraham no explicit emotional reaction.

While this text has long occasioned theological and pastoral problems for interpreters, readers' anxieties have been more sharply intensified over the course of the last century or so, not least because of the increasing attention given to the abuse of children. Interrelated issues have been raised with respect to each of the three main characters: God, Abraham, and Isaac.

God

What kind of God would command the sacrifice of a child? What does this command say about God's character? Even if God does not intend Abraham to follow through and slaughter his child, what kind of God would test Abraham in just this way? We shrink back at the severity of the test. We question God's use of violence, especially violence against a child, as a means to test faithfulness. Can this God be trusted? This God promises a son, proceeds to fulfill that promise, and then seems to take it back. Is this like trusting abusive parents? Can we trust this God only because we know this is a test and that God does not intend to kill Isaac? Abraham trusted without this knowledge, but how many can claim such a level of trust? Or God commends the father for not withholding "your only son from me." What does the "from me" entail? That God wanted Isaac more than Abraham did? Sounds like an all too common "explanation" at the funeral of a child.

Readers may be set to wondering whether we still have to deal with this kind of God and what testings God might put faithful followers through today. Should every parent wonder: Might my child be endangered by God? Is the God whom we worship a God who might force us to choose between love of our children and love of God? If God asks me to sacrifice myself, that is one thing, and a case could be made that a person of faith should stand ready to do so. But it is another matter altogether to be asked to sacrifice someone else, not least a child, especially when I, the parent, escape with my own life. Or why the praise for God's providing? If God set up the test in the first place, why should God be praised for providing a resolution? Or why should God be praised when Abraham is the one who passes the test? Does God go to such ends in order to receive applause? From another angle, the lives of both mother and son are endangered by Abraham in this story (12:10–20; 20:1–18). Might it be that the endangerment of the son is understood to be a consequence of the endangerment of his mother? And if so, what kind of retribution is that—children suffering for parental behaviors?

Various responses to such questions have been suggested over the years. Sometimes it is thought that, if we object to such severities and consider the text offensive, then the problem is with us, and with our relationship with God, and not with the text. Faith should be blind to possible consequences; a faithful one follows where God leads, especially what God commands, come what may. Or it is sometimes thought that in order to be responsible before God at times we may have to be irresponsible before others, at least in terms of any known rationale or ethical standard. And one thinks of Tamar's prostituting herself in order to produce an heir for her husband, and Judah's recognition of this as a righteous act (Gen. 38:26). Or from another angle, there is a sense in which I make choices that endanger children every day. I choose to spend my time and energy doing certain things because of my faith in God, and that will inevitably mean that I will choose not to do other things, and that nonaction may be hurtful to others; it might even mean that somewhere a child will die. But it does seem to be a matter of a different order to be commanded by God to thrust an actual knife into that child's heart. Such a perspective seems to grant to faith in God a blank check so that the ethical can be suspended whenever one thinks that that faith is being served. Jonestown and Waco, to name but two examples, seem not too far away. We continue with responses to the God of this text later in the chapter.

Abraham

What kind of faith does Abraham have? He seems to have a blind faith; no questions are asked, no objections are raised. In fact, he shows no emotion whatsoever, though many retellings of the story have portrayed an agonized Abraham. Earlier in the narrative (chapter 18), Abraham could raise sharp questions with God about the fate of the righteous in Sodom and Gomorrah (and in 15:2, 8), but he is strangely passive and acquiescent when it comes to his own son. This Abrahamic behavior raises a further question: what kind of father is this? The narrator assures us that Abraham loves his son (22:2). Yet Abraham not only considers sacrificing his son, but apparently thinks nothing of putting him through the severe trauma that must have been involved. Is this not child abuse? Or is Abraham (and the culture of which he is a part) oblivious to such a reality? Still another question arises, what kind of husband is this? Abraham gives Sarah no clue as to what God has told him to do with their son and decides on his own to sacrifice him. Is this not spousal abuse?[19]

A suggestion might be made as to why Abraham raises no objection. By this rhetorical feature, the narrator has succeeded in raising these "why" questions in generations of readers. It may be that Abraham responds as he does because he learned from his encounter with God over the fate of Sodom that God is indeed just, and that he need only trust on this occasion. It may be that the narrator intends that the reader, having learned from Abraham in chapter 18 how to question God, is the one who is to ask the questions on this occasion. Initially, one might suggest that verse 8 is a delayed clue: Abraham obeyed because he trusted that, given his prior experience, God would provide a way through this moment that would not entail giving up on the promise.

From another perspective, interpreters can get into a kind of quantitative game; does Abraham love God more than he loves his son Isaac (recognized in 22:2).[20] But this story should not be reduced to a matter of how much love Abraham has for one or the other. God commands Abraham to "sacrifice" Isaac, not murder him (God would, of course, not be pleased if Abraham succeeded). To be a genuine sacrifice, it must be an act of faith and love of God, a giving back to God what is

truly dear and costly to one, and not simply the loss of a child or an animal. And
so for the sacrifice to be genuine, at the end of the day must not Abraham's love for
Isaac and Abraham's love for God be comparably great? Would not, then, issues of
the degree of Abraham's love of God compared to the child be beside the point?

Isaac

What kind of son is this who asks only one question and exhibits no struggle—
right up to the point of staring at a knife about to be plunged into him? What kind
of child would be so passive in the face of such danger? Does this behavior reveal
a child who is completely cowed by an authoritarian, if loving father? Or is this
a son who trusts his father as his father trusts God? And, if so, is that real for a
child?

IS THIS CHILD ABUSE?

This story has occasioned deep reader concern about Isaac, especially in this time
when the abuse of children has screamed its way into the modern consciousness.[21]
A 1990 book by Alice Miller, a Swiss psychoanalyst, has put the question sharply
before us.[22] Miller suggests that this text has contributed in subtle ways to an
atmosphere in church and society that makes it possible to justify the abuse of
children. She grounds her reflections on some thirty artistic representations of this
story over the centuries. This includes two of Rembrandt's paintings, in which
Abraham is faced toward the heavens rather than toward Isaac, as if in blind obedience to God and oblivious to what he is about to do to Isaac. Abraham has his
hands over Isaac's face, seemingly preventing him from seeing or raising a cry. Not
only is Isaac silenced, only his torso is visible, so that his personal features are
obscured. Miller says Isaac, "has been turned into an object. He has been dehu-
manized by being made a sacrifice; he no longer has a right to ask questions and
will scarcely even be able to articulate them to himself, for there is no room in him
for anything besides fear."[23] Even if she is wrong about Isaac asking no questions,
does she not raise an important issue?

I have often heard students testify to this point. They recall their fear as children upon hearing this story, wondering whether their father or mother might be
asked by God to do the same with them. And we have the testimony of a few parents who have in fact killed their children and ascribed the act to obedience to a
divine command.[24] It will not do for us simply to dismiss this negative impact of
Genesis 22 and it would not be the first time that the Bible has been used know-
ingly or unknowingly in such distorted ways. Traditional understandings of this
text may in fact have contributed to this more recent reading of the text: the place
of the child has been sorely neglected in an overwhelming focus on the trusting
response of Abraham to God's testing.

Caravaggio, *The Sacrifice of Isaac*, ca. 1603–1604. Uffizi, Florence, Italy. Courtesy of Scala / Art Resource, N.Y.

Rembrandt, *Sacrifice of Isaac*, 1635.
Courtesy of Hermitage, St. Petersburg, Russia. Scala / Art Resource, N.Y.

It seems clear that more recent problems with Genesis 22 have been sparked by the increasing attention given to the vulnerability of children, whether at the hands of family members within the home or the larger society in its lack of attention to the needs and problems children face.[25] Such realities of our own context and experience have sharpened and intensified our reading experience of Genesis 22. Meanings of texts are always, of course, the product of the interaction of the text and the reader and his/her experience. At the same time, the issue cannot simply be laid at the feet of readers; at the least, the text does not provide safeguards against negative interpretations. Even if child abuse was not in the mind of the narrator or those who heard this text in ancient Israel, what modern readers hear is not totally irrelevant. Indeed, the language of the text itself can contribute to such an understanding, for God asks and then twice commends Abraham for not withholding his son, his only son "from me" (verses 2, 12, 16). It is as if the child is simply a pawn in the hands of an issue between God and Abraham. Of course, modern adults have little room for criticism of either God or Abraham, given the extent to which we remain silent about child abuse among us.[26] But there appears to be some room for an evaluative stance on the basis of the Bible's larger perspective regarding children. If the child in the text is carefully and concernedly remembered, can we ignore this direction of reflection?

HISTORY AND METAPHOR

Seeing this text in view of the issue of child abuse has not been common among interpreters until quite recently.[27] In response, several scholars have claimed that this approach is a misuse, even gross misuse of the text.[28] Two directions of responding to the "charge" of child abuse might be especially noted. One such way is to lift up the historical context of the text; the other is to interpret the text as metaphor. Neither approach, in my opinion, finally succeeds in setting aside the issue that has been raised.

Jon Levenson has been particularly concerned to draw out the religio-historical dimensions of the text. His discussion is often helpful. Initially, the text speaks of Isaac as a "burnt offering" (22:2; Exod. 29:38–46; Lev. 1:3–17), and a "substitute" sacrifice is finally given by Abraham (22:13).[29] These references at the beginning and end of the basic story place the entire episode within the context of the sacrificial system. This reality should be placed alongside the fact (known from other texts) that child sacrifice was an important part of the context within which Genesis 22 was written. More specifically, "the first-born son was long and widely believed to belong to God and must be offered to him, either through literal sacrifice (rarely, as in Genesis 22) or through one or another of the rituals by which a substitution was made" (for example, Exod. 22:28–29; cf. Ezek. 20:25–26). The first-born son was to be thereby "redeemed" (Exod. 13:11–16; 34:20; Num.

3:40–51); in Genesis 22 God does just this in a narrative equivalent of the ritual, that is, God commands that Isaac be sacrificed and then provides an animal "instead of" Isaac.[30] To the father about to make the offering "the prospect was doubtless painful in the extreme, perhaps too painful for words, but it was not unconnected to the larger culture and its ethical and theological norms, nor was it incomprehensible or incommunicable to others in the same cultural universe." An important matter for Levenson is that, "*in the biblical text, sacrifice is not deemed unethical or irrational*" and so it requires no more an act of faith to adhere to such demands than to ethical demands."[31] The texts generally recognize the difference between murder and sacrifice.[32]

For Levenson, that Abraham's response would not have been offensive back then does not in any way imply that a contemporary person of faith should do likewise; in our culture it would rightly be considered murder. Between the Akedah and today lies the Torah, which includes the redemption of the firstborn and the prophetic condemnation of child sacrifice (for example, Jer. 9:3–6),[33] and hence one cannot read a validation of child abuse off of the text. Levenson goes to great lengths in seeking to demonstrate that Abraham is not a child abuser. In fact, "it is a symptom of acute myopia and mind-numbing parochialism to think that this must also have been the case in a society that practiced sacrifice (even, on occasion and for a while, child-sacrifice) and did not confuse it with murder."[34]

Perhaps so, but I wonder if the factors cited are sufficient to shut down the conversation about abuse. First, three details might be more closely considered. (1) The text bears no explicit mark of being a polemic against child sacrifice (unlike the prophets, for example, Jer. 19:3–6). Abraham, finally, is commanded not to sacrifice his son, but the text does not generalize the point. (2) The text makes no explicit reference to its being an etiology of the redemption of the firstborn.[35] Is it because Isaac is not a firstborn son? Is it because the ram is not clearly a "substitute" for Isaac?[36] (3) From another angle, while the factors relating to the emergence of laws prohibiting child sacrifice in Israel are unclear, might it have had to do, at least in part, with observed negative effects on the lives of children and their families?[37]

Second, to speak more generally, to say that the divine command would not have been offensive in Israel's world begs the question as to whether it should have been deemed so. Can evaluative judgments not be made of Israelite thought and practice? For example, patriarchy was characteristic of Israel's life, but does this mean that no evaluative words can be directed at those who exercised patriarchal practices?[38] Levenson and others are on target when they criticize those who speak of Abraham being mentally unbalanced or cruel. But if Abraham should not be criticized at those points, given the realities of sacrifice in that world, what of the practice itself? Perhaps even more important, the issue should not simply revolve around the issue of the behaviors of the "adults" involved (God and Abraham). Whatever the evaluation of their actions (on either side of the issue), the negative effects on the child (emotional and otherwise) should be placed front and center. Whatever Abraham's (and God's) intent, is it not likely that Isaac was traumatized by the threat of imminent and violent death at the hands of his father?[39]

Moving beyond simple historical issues, Levenson promotes a metaphorical (he uses "symbolic") interpretation of the text. That the sacrificial death "is only symbolic, that the son, *mirabile dictu,* returns alive, is the narrative equivalent of the ritual substitutions that prevent the gory offering from being made."[40] Early in its history, Israel had prohibited child sacrifice as an abomination hateful to God, yet they could see in Abraham's deed "a paradigmatic disclosure of deeper truths." Among the truths he sees in the text: "all we have, even our lives and those of our dearest, belong ultimately to God; His claim must be honored; God's promises are often painfully at odds with empirical reality."[41]

Walter Moberly also speaks of a metaphorical understanding of the chapter and notes that such a way of interpreting the text has long been present in the life of the church. He admits that the metaphor is a "dangerous" one, open to abuse on the part of the unscrupulous and misguided. But all metaphors are "in some way 'dangerous.'"[42] He summarizes the metaphorical value of this story in these terms:[43]

- relinquishing to God that which is most precious (sacrifice Isaac, the beloved son);[44]
- self-dispossession of that on which one's identity and hopes are most deeply based (sacrifice Isaac, the bearer of promise, as hope for the future);
- response to God may be costly, or even more costly, at the end of one's life as it was earlier on (relinquish future as well as past);
- the outcome of obedience is unknown and cannot be predicted in advance (a real test);
- the religious community to which one belongs cannot become complacent.

In these terms, the story is "a paradigm of life with God." To that end, the "purpose of YHWH's testing is to promote such a way of living."[45] Though the "literal" practice had been set aside, the story retained its power as a paradigm of religious life.

Moberly sees the metaphorical value of Isaac at two levels:[46] He is one whom Abraham loves (22:2), implicitly more than any other, and is "supremely valued by Abraham"—he is the one offered. Also, Isaac is the bearer of God's promise of descendants—they, too, would be sacrificed. Yet, it must be said, these points of significance retain a focus on Abraham, the adult, and tend to move past the child. If one is to interpret the text as a metaphor for Israel's life with God, it seems necessary to understand that Israel is both Abraham and Isaac. And so Israel is not simply one who makes a sacrifice (Abraham), Israel is also the one who is the sacrifice (Isaac). Various issues related to the fall of Jerusalem and Babylonian exile would come into play at this point, including the Suffering Servant in Isaiah 53.[47]

In any interpretation of the text as metaphor, it would be important not to deplete the story of its sheer horror (remembering that metaphor does include a literal dimension). To identify the story as metaphor should not set readers' minds to looking for the "real" meaning of the text and away from the sacrifice of a child.[48] The potential sacrifice of an actual child is certainly intended to come to the mind of the reader, to confront the reader with the difficult nature of the divine command and the complexity of the journey with God. Readers may disagree with the narrator's strategy of doing so, and appropriately so, but the point remains.

LITERARY AND CONTEXTUAL ISSUES

Modern readings of the text have been particularly interested in delineating its literary artistry.[49] Erich Auerbach's 1965 treatment set the initial pace. His insights into the text remain influential, for example: "thoughts and feelings remain unexpressed, are only suggested by the silence and the fragmentary speeches; the whole, permeated with the most unrelieved suspense and directed toward a single goal . . . remains mysterious and fraught with background."[50] Significant gains have resulted from this approach, while at the same time, this angle of vision may have overplayed its hand at times by overdramatizing the story and reading too much between the lines, especially the feelings of Abraham and Isaac. We take a closer look at some literary features of this text.

The opening words of Genesis 22 ("After these things") invite the reader to look closely at the story of Abraham's life up to this point. Such a probe may help readers discern the reason for God's testing of Abraham: What has Abraham done or not done that might occasion the "need" for God to test him? Three key features of the nature of their relationship up to this point may be noted.

First, there are the parallels with Abraham's call in 12:1–4. The two texts use the same vocabulary ("take, go" to a "place that I shall show you") to speak of a divine command to Abraham to embark on a journey to an uncertain destination. In each case Abraham silently responds. Both journeys are ventures in faith. As he once responded in trust of the God who called him, so he responds again. Abraham's first journey mirrors this, his last journey. The former cuts Abraham off from his past, the latter threatens to cut him off from his future.

Second, there is the shape of Abraham's life. Over the course of the narrative, the relationship between God and Abraham has been shown to be a relationship in progress. It has had its ups and downs, in which each has been affected by the other. God has engaged Abraham's questions in a welcoming way (15:1–9;

18:23–32), even in the face of incredulity (17:15–21), and has responded in a way that is open to a future in which Abraham's participation counts. For his part, Abraham has responded with a deep faith (for example, 15:6) and has engaged God in theological dialogue regarding the fate of Sodom and Gomorrah (18:23–32). Abraham has discerned that the God who issues commands is also the one who has filled his life with promises; God does have his best interests at heart. He has been given no reason to mistrust the God from whom his call has come.

At the same time, Abraham at times has responded within the relationship in mistrustful ways. He has endangered Sarah's life and well-being twice, placing the mother of the promised son in jeopardy (12:10–20; 20:1–18).[51] He has distrusted the God who has promised him a son (17:17). Though the relationship between God and Abraham has exhibited "familiar mutual trust," built up over considerable experience together, these negative elements in Abraham's life to this point have raised an issue for God: will Abraham now trust God in all circumstances (verse 12)? His self-seeking and self-preservation at the expense of others may prompt God to seek to discern whether Abraham is willing to sacrifice himself rather than others.

Third, there are the parallels and contrasts with the story of Ishmael.[52] Genesis 22 has gotten all the attention, but the story of Ishmael is certainly just as difficult and heart-rending (21:8–21). This reality should occasion reflection as to why the threat to the life of the "outsider" is so widely neglected by interpreters compared to the life of the chosen one. The narrator thinks otherwise. The narrative holds us to "the tension between the one elected and the not-elected one who is *treasured*" by God.[53] The testing of Abraham comes almost immediately after the loss of his firstborn son, Ishmael, to the wilderness (21:8–21). This may explain the repeated reference to Isaac as "only son" (22:2, 12, 16). The use of such language at this juncture means that Ishmael hangs like a specter over the narrative. Abraham has just lost one son, and now he is asked to sacrifice the one son remaining. The character of God's "test" of Abraham in chapter 22 is intensified by following in the wake of his loss of Ishmael.

This carefully drawn relationship between the two sons is supported by the remarkable number of parallels between the stories of Ishmael and Isaac—the stories are mirror images, focusing on the loss of sons. Perhaps most centrally, God's promises are placed in jeopardy in both cases, promises to Ishmael (21:13, 18) and promises regarding Isaac (17:19–21). Also to be noted: in 21:14; 22:3 Abraham rises "early in the morning" and wordlessly proceeds to put a son's future in jeopardy; both sons seem to move relentlessly toward death. In both cases, Abraham is obedient to God's behest and trusts in the divine promise, leaving the future of his sons in the hands of God. The angel of the Lord calls from heaven to both Hagar and Abraham (21:17; 22:11–12) and speaks of a role for their "hands" (holding Ishmael; not touching Isaac). Each parent is assured that the son would live. The eyes of both are used to see a source of life that saves their sons. Abraham sees (verses 4, 13) and Hagar sees (21:19; cf. 16:13). It is seeing that saves the son. As Hagar's seeing saves Ishmael, so also Abraham's seeing saves Isaac. At the same time, there are contrasts between the two texts. For example, Abraham's "distress" over the loss of Ishmael (21:12) seems to be contrasted with his apparent lack of distress regarding the potential loss of Isaac. Or both sons give voice to laments/questions, though only Isaac is given words (21:17; 22:7). Or Hagar voices her lament over what is happening to Ishmael (21:16), while Abraham does not lament, voicing only confidence that God would provide for Isaac's future.

Repetition is a key rhetorical feature of the story that can assist the reading process. Five such instances are important to note here.

First, there is "The mountain that I will show you" (verse 2; cf. 12:1). This destination is stressed early on (verses 3, 4, 9; cf. verse 5) and returned to in verse 14, where it is named: God will provide. It is a place that God shows Abraham (verse 3), though it is not reported in the narrative. Perhaps God has prepared the scene ahead of time, ram and all, and hence Abraham must be precisely directed to it. How would Abraham have understood this kind of precision in the command? Why not just sacrifice Isaac in any place suitable for such activity? The answers may be hidden in the word "Moriah," the "mount of the Lord" (verse 14), an unknown place to us but not to Abraham, perhaps Jerusalem (2 Chron. 2:1; cf. "the mount of Yahweh" in Ps. 24:3; Isa. 2:3).[54] This detail gives the command a special character: Abraham is to sacrifice in a God-chosen place, not just in any place. Might this special arrangement—repeatedly lifted up by the narrator—have given Abraham some clue as to what God was about?

Second, there is "Your son, your only son" (22:2, 12, 16). The readers' sympathies are initially directed by the narrator toward Isaac as a child: "Take your son, your only son, Isaac." That Isaac is the child of promise is not mentioned. From the narrator's point of view, Isaac is a child whom, in God's judgment, Abraham loves (verse 2); readers are thereby informed that this is not an abusive relationship.[55] Yet, the inevitable adverse effects of such an action on the child seem not to be recognized by God, Abraham, or narrator.

Third is the use of the term "seeing." The repeated use of the language of "seeing" suggests that readers should give it special attention. Twice, Abraham lifts up his eyes (verses 4, 13), and five times the verb $rā^{\jmath}āh$ is used, both of Abraham (verses 4, 13) and of God (verses 8, 14, 14).[56] Abraham sees the place where God told him to sacrifice Isaac from a distance and then, after the angel of the Lord has stopped the sacrificial act, he sees the ram provided at that very place. These references are a witness to a progressively clearer seeing. It is God's seeing in which Abraham places his trust (verse 8) and that trust finally enables Abraham to see the sacrifice that God has seen to. Abraham's faith that God will provide centers the text (verse 8). The seeing of both God and Abraham saves the son. A comparable progression may be seen in the movement from the more distancing language of "boy" in verse 5 to the repeated "my son" in verses 7–8, testifying to an increase in the confidence that the son will be saved.

Fourth is "Here I am." This thrice-repeated response of Abraham, to God (verses 1, 11) and to his son Isaac (verse 7), seems especially important. Abraham's statement of faith that God will provide in verse 8 is at the center of his three "Here am I" responses; this is the only point where Abraham responds more fully. Moreover, only here does Isaac speak.

And fifth is the verse "The two of them walked on together." The only interchange between Abraham and Isaac in verses 7–8 is enclosed by the repeated statement: "the two of them walked on together." From another angle, both of these references follow expressions of trust on the part of Abraham (verses 5, 8). This phrase suggests that Abraham's trusting departure in and of itself does not settle the issue for God, or God could have ended the journey much earlier. That God does not convey all the necessary information to Abraham immediately (upon which mountain?) also lifts up the importance of the journey itself. Even more, the journey continues even after Abraham exhibits his trust that both of them would return and that God would provide (verses 5, 8). The question becomes: Will Abraham stay with the journey? Perhaps the reason for its length is to give Abraham time to have second thoughts. The tension continues even when the journey itself comes to an end; Abraham is shown to attend to all the details for the sacrifice without hesitation (verses 9–10). Abraham shows his continuing trust by staying on course, though given several opportunities to cut it short. Only at the end of the journey can God say, "Now I know." These rhetorical features (especially the last three) give to verses 7–8 a place of special import.

Though Isaac is not told the purpose of the journey, that he is not entirely passive over the course of the journey is important. He breaks the silence of the journey with a question of his father (verse 7) and it is the only recorded exchange between them. He senses that something is not right (his lack of reference to the knife no more suggests this than does the absence of fire in verses 9–10). Yet, Isaac does not focus on himself as the matter of concern and displays no special emotion. Isaac addresses Abraham as a loving father, mirroring Abraham's trusting relationship to God. Abraham responds in like manner.

Structurally, Isaac's question occurs at the center of the story, signaled by Abraham's response, "Here I am." In the other two uses of "Here I am," Abraham responds to God but here he centers on what his child has to say. He attends to Isaac as he has attended to God; he is at his child's disposal. He does not dismiss Isaac's question or consider it inappropriate. Isaac's question is important also in that it elicits a public statement of trust in God from Abraham, enabling Abraham's trusting action to now be joined with trusting words.

Abraham's response to Isaac does not tell him everything (what God has commanded)—in any case, he does not know everything. But he does answer Isaac's question directly and conveys what he believes is the truth about Isaac's future: God will provide. Abraham testifies to exactly this form of divine action in verse 14. This response of straightforward, unhesitating trust in God is precisely what is being tested here. As God himself puts it in verse 12, it has to do with Abraham's fear of God: that is, a trust or confidence in God's purposes without concrete evidence on which to rely, and which works itself out in daily life as truth and justice.[57] Abraham obeys because he trusts God; it is the trust which is most basic, out of which the obedience flows. Disobedience would be symptomatic of a lack of trust. Abraham could have obeyed because he was commanded to do so; God is God. He could have said: God can command whatever God wants, and if God commands, I had better jump through whatever hoops he puts before me. But, at least by verse 8, Abraham's obedience is shown to be informed and undergirded by a trust that God will find another way through this situation that is in the best interests of the promise, short of obeying the command.

This trust that God will provide may already be present in verse 5. Abraham specifies that both will return and the servants function as witnesses of this conviction. What had been implicit in his report to the servants that both of them would return (verse 5), becomes explicit in verse 8. The reference to worship in verse 5 anticipates the word about worship in verse 8. While some have suggested that Abraham is being deceptive in these verses, the reader knows from knowledge of the story that, in both cases, Abraham tells the truth. Indeed, it would be unusual for a narrative designed to demonstrate Abraham's faith and obedience to be punctuated with acts of deception on his part. Moreover, given the utter lack of interest in the motives of Abraham on the part of the narrator, readers should accept the force of his statements unless and until the narrative gives a clue to the contrary.

Isaac's reply to his father's response is conveyed indirectly in the narrator's repetition of the report that "the two of them walked on together" (verses 6, 8). That the interchange between father and son is enclosed by this report emphasizes continuity, and that Isaac is satisfied with his father's reply to his question. Isaac exhibits no resistance to what is happening and the journey continues unabated. Isaac's nonresistance continues even later when his father prepares him for the sacrificial moment (some descriptions of the knife poised to fall go beyond the text). In effect, Isaac trusts that his father's trust is well placed. Abraham's trust in God has become Isaac's trust: God will provide. God intends this provision from the beginning, of course, and father and child are now both attuned to that intention and trust it.

While moderns might appropriately wonder about the psychological abuse Isaac endures in all of this, it is important to note that he is given a questioning voice and his father does attentively respond to him. This leads Isaac to place himself trustingly in the arms of his father and his God. The text offers no evidence that trust in God ever wavers for either father or child. Readers must be very careful to stress these elements for the sake of children's proper hearing of the text, perhaps even more for a parental hearing of this text.

Yet, the text does not finally enable one to sit comfortably with the obvious abuse that Isaac undergoes. Readers have wondered whether this is evident in the fact that the return of Isaac with his father is not reported in verse 19 (though Abraham had so assured his servants in verse 5).[58] Abraham and Isaac never again converse in the narrative that follows, not even in connection with the search for a wife for Isaac (chapter 24). While Isaac attends Abraham's funeral (25:9), he does not attend Sarah's or even return to her deathbed (chapter 23). And why would God, but not Abraham, bless Isaac (25:11)? Might this distancing between father and son have anything to do with his horrific experience on Mt. Moriah?

THE TEST—OF ABRAHAM AND OF GOD

The usual way into this story is through the eyes of Abraham and the test he is asked to undergo at God's behest. I would suggest that the text has at least as much to do with God, not least because God set up the test in the first place. Hence, this question seems especially pertinent: What is at stake in this for God and how might God be responding to Abraham's journey and the way in which he handles it?[59]

The narrator places the issue of testing up front (22:1), thereby indicating that this theme is central to understanding all that follows. A few general words about testing may be a helpful way to begin this discussion. Testing must be understood relationally rather than legalistically; it is characteristic of all relationships of consequence. For all persons, life in relationship with God or with other human beings will inevitably bring tests over the course of their journey with each other; that is, they will often find themselves in various situations where their loyalty to the one with whom they are in relationship is tested. What constitutes testing in one situation or another will be determined by the nature of the relationship and the expectations the parties have for it. As a relationship matures and trust levels are built up, faithful responses to the testing of the relational bond will tend to become second nature. And yet, there may be moments, even in a mature relationship, where sharp, even absurd moments of testing present themselves. This may be the kind of moment with which Abraham is faced. Abraham, and readers, might learn from such experiences that receiving promises from God does not entail being protected from times where those promises are called into question.

Will God still be trusted in such moments? Even if God, as here, is the one who speaks or acts in such a way that calls those promises into question? It is wise to remember that the confession that God will provide pertains as much to times of resisting and challenging as to moments of "blind" trust.

Walter Moberly is correct in emphasizing with many scholars that, as with all genuine tests, this is "a *real* test in which the future is unknown." At the same time, he goes too far in adding, "in which there is no reason to suppose that the test will have a benign outcome."[60] If Abraham responds to the command, trusting that God will find a way to be true to the promises, then he at least trusts that there will be an outcome that is "benign." Yes, there is a certain "unknown" character to the future, an unpredictability, into which Abraham walks, but that future is not fully unknown, because he assumes a certain kind of God with whom he has to do.

From another angle, given the narrator's opening line, God and reader know that this is a test; Abraham does not. Readers are thus immediately informed that God's intention is not to kill Isaac, but to test Abraham. It is not "only" a test, but it is a test. That knowledge removes some of the "edge" for readers. Does Abraham also understand that this is a test, given his prior history with God, especially God's involvement in the birth of Isaac? Commentators commonly observe that Abraham was probably alert to the contradictory character of the command: God, having just fulfilled the promise of a son, now asks him to sacrifice that son and presumably the promised future that goes with him. That God's promise was explicitly related to a son named Isaac (17:19, 21) makes the contradictoriness even sharper. That Abraham goes anyway, shows, it seems, that his response was grounded in a trust that God would find a way of being true to that explicit promise. Abraham has had a history with this God dealing with seemingly impossible futures. For example, when faced with the issue of Sarah's barrenness, an earlier situation that also seemed contradictory to the promise, God had found a way to be true to the promise of a son named Isaac. God's earlier witness to Abraham regarding that event was that nothing is too wonderful or impossible for God (18:14).[61]

Given that earlier experience of God, a not unnatural conclusion for Abraham to draw at this moment is that, once again, a seemingly impossible situation would not be beyond God's ability to resolve satisfactorily. As we have seen, by the stage of the journey reported in verse 8 (and anticipated in verse 5), Abraham places trust in God that God will in fact find a way through this dilemma: God will provide a lamb for the burnt offering in place of Isaac as a way to remain true to the promise.

This response of Abraham creates a new situation for God. Abraham's public confession of trust voiced to his son Isaac constitutes a new situation with which

God must now work. Such a confession means that Abraham trusts that God's promise and command are not finally contradictory, but it is up to God to resolve it. This response ups the ante for God, indeed it puts God on the spot. The test of Abraham has now become a test for God. The test no longer involves simply Abraham's trust in God, it has become a test of God's faithfulness in providing. As Westermann puts it, Abraham's trusting response to God "throws the ball back into God's court."[62] What ensues now constitutes a test of God's faithfulness. Will God provide, as Abraham trusts God will? Will Abraham's trust in God be in vain? Is God free to ignore Abraham's trust? If God does not provide, and Isaac is sacrificed, then Abraham's trust that God will provide is placed in severe jeopardy. Such an eventuality would constitute another kind of test for Abraham, a test at a much deeper level than the one that initiated this journey. And so, Abraham, by silently setting out to obey the command and expressing trust in God, places the entire matter in God's hands.

More can be said on this point that the test is as real for God as it is for Abraham. God has as much at stake in Abraham's response as does Abraham. Some read this story as if God were a detached observer, a heavenly homeroom teacher watching from afar to see if Abraham passes the test. But given Abraham's somewhat mixed responses to God up to this point in the story, God takes something of a risk to put so much on the line with this man. This means that the test is a witness to God's vulnerability, not just Abraham's. God has chosen Isaac to continue the line of promise. Though God does not intend that Isaac be killed, the test places God's own promised future at risk, at least in the form of Isaac. Isaac could be killed. The command has the potential of taking back what God has taken so many pains to put in place. To put it more sharply: Does God in effect make the promise, or at least this shape of the promise, dependent on what Abraham does (see below on verses 15–18)? Is this not only a test of Abraham's faith in God, but also of God's faith in Abraham—after all, God does not want Isaac killed. Indeed, God places the shape of God's own future in Abraham's hands, in the sense that Abraham's response will affect the nature of the moves that God makes next. One cannot project what God might have done had Abraham failed, or if Abraham had actually killed Isaac, but God would have had to find another way into the future, perhaps another way with Abraham. Something is at stake for God in this matter.[63] Might Abraham realize what is at stake for God and might this account for his silent response, that God is taking a risk and is deeply and vulnerably engaged in this test? Eugene Roop puts the issue this way: "God took the risk that Abraham would respond. Abraham took the risk that God would provide."[64]

At the same time, if Abraham had known for sure that this was only a test, it would have been no real test, for he (or anyone) would respond differently to a test as test. Moreover, the test would not have worked simply at the verbal level, as if

God could have just asked Abraham whether he would obey such a command. The move from verbal commitment to action is not inevitable; words might not lead to deeds. May Abraham recognize this by responding in deed rather than word? Generally in the Old Testament, the purpose of God's testing is to discern whether people will do justice to a relationship in which they stand. In Deuteronomy 8:2–3, for example, God tests Israel in the wilderness in order that God might know whether they will be true to the relationship. Discerning a response to a divine command is another such way to put the test: Is Abraham's loyalty to God of such a character that he will rest back in the arms of the one who has made the command? God initiates the test in order to gain divine certainty about the genuineness of Abraham's faithfulness.

Readers are challenged to take the test at its face value. That is to say, the command is not a ploy on God's part, it is a genuine command. The command ("take"), however, is qualified by *nā*', a particle of entreaty or urgency that is often used "to soften a command, or to make a request in a more courteous form."[65] It is commonly translated, "please, I pray," or the like, but is rarely so conveyed in translations of Genesis 22:2. It is rarely used with a divine command (cf. Isa. 1:18; 7:3; Judg. 13:4). But, by using this particle, does God thereby signal to Abraham the highly unusual character of the moment and the special relationship of mutual trust with Abraham? Does the use of the particle help Abraham to see that God has as much stake in this matter as he does?

At the same time, that this is a test qualifies the nature of the command. That is to say, from God's perspective this command is not of the same type as, say, one of the Ten Commandments—the command does not have universal validity.[66] This is so in at least two respects. First, this is a command for a particular moment, a one-time event; it is not intended to be applicable in an ongoing way or to persons other than Abraham. Second, the genuineness of Abraham's trust will not be discerned only when he has fully obeyed the command, that is, actually sacrificed Isaac. God does not desire that the commandment be fully obeyed; as noted, God's intention is to test Abraham, not to kill Isaac. Hence, God revokes the command when the results of the test become clear. More precisely, God comes with a second command that overrides the first (verse 12). Abraham's trust may be said to be evident not only in his initial obedience to God's command but in his second obedience, staying his hand. He trusts that God's initial command is no longer relevant to the situation.

Contrary to many commentators, the test is not designed to teach Abraham something: that Isaac is "pure gift" (von Rad) or that he is too attached to Isaac or that Abraham must cling more to God than to the fulfillment of the promise. Experience always teaches, of course, and Abraham certainly learns. But the text does not say that Abraham now trusts in God in a more intense way, or that Abraham has learned a lesson of some sort (unlike Deut. 8:2–3).[67] Rather, the test confirms a fact: Abraham trusts that God has his best interests at heart and, given that reality, he will follow where God's command leads (a point repeated in verses 12 and 16).

The only one said to learn anything from the test is God. The climactic verse 12 states this clearly: "Now I know." That the "angel of the Lord" speaks these words does not suggest that that it is the angel that learns rather than God. The use of the first person ("from me") in these words can only have reference to God. The issue here is not what God teaches Abraham, but what God learns about Abraham. The issue, for the sake of the future, was God's knowledge of Abraham's faithfulness in relationship. Brueggemann notes correctly that this test "is not a game with God; God genuinely does not know. The flow of the narrative accomplishes something in the awareness of God. He did not know. Now he knows."[68] Comparably, James Crenshaw: "The fundamental assumption lying behind divine testing is that God lacks a certain kind of knowledge, that is, precisely how men and women will act in trying circumstances. Of course, such ignorance arises from human freedom, which is itself a gift from the transcendent one. Therefore, the divine act of self-limitation has created the necessity for such testing."[69] If God knew absolutely or precisely how Abraham would respond to the test, then God was just playing with Abraham.[70] At the same time, the question is in order: Would not there be other, less destructive ways for God to learn about Abraham?

While God no doubt knew what was likely to happen given the intimate knowledge of Abraham, God in fact gains new knowledge with respect to Abraham (as does the reader). This is a hard, even offensive word about God for many, and readers are advised not to follow their instincts and seek to interpret their way out of it. The point seems to be that God does not have absolute certainty with respect to a future matter, that is, how Abraham would respond to the command (God's knowledge of the past and present are not in question).[71] The test constitutes the means by which God works out an issue that God has with Abraham. At the same time, it is important to keep the larger divine purpose in mind. Hence, the test is not a matter of the divine curiosity, or some internal divine need that must be satisfied; at issue is a future toward which God is moving that encompasses all the families of the earth. This global purpose is why God needs to know about Abraham. Hence the question for God is: Is Abraham the faithful one who can in fact carry that purpose along? Or does God need to take some other course of action, perhaps even look for someone who would be more faithful? The faithfulness of Abraham is not an option for God and for God's purposes in the world.

The text to this point, however, makes one wonder why Abraham is the one who is commanded to undergo the test. Isaac, the child of promise, has been born. The promised line has been assured of continuity into the next generation, so why test Abraham? Why does God not just get on with it, or wait to put Isaac to the test? Could not Abraham now just pass out of the picture, as he now does for all practical purposes? But it is not enough for the sake of the history of the promise that Isaac be born. Other promises remain to be fulfilled. God waits upon Abraham before getting on with other dimensions of the promised future. Having seen — Abraham's faithfulness, God "swears" by the divine self for the first time in the narrative with respect to those promises (verse 16).

If God tests within relationship to determine loyalty, then can God disdain the expression of such loyalty and remain faithful? Given God's previous commitments (especially in chapter 15), God has bound himself to stay with a trusting Abraham. Now, in swearing by himself, God in effect lays the divine life on the line, putting the very divine self behind the promise. Before taking a further look at verses 15–18, more comments are in order.

Why the stress on God's providing, if this is a test? Why should God be praised as a provider for following through on God's own test? It would appear that God is deemed worthy of praise because God has passed the test; God has responded to Abraham's trust and kept the divine commitment to Abraham. May the praise also be due to what God has put the divine self through? For the sake of the future of the divine purposes, God has had to pass through this valley of endangered promises.

After discerning Abraham's faithfulness, God stopped him before the ram was spotted (verses 12–13). So the provision of the ram was not necessary to save Isaac. Indeed, Isaac's sacrifice was stopped independent of the role of the ram, so that "instead of" does not have a "substitution" sense.[72] Why would the ram, then, be sacrificed? Is it because of the way in which Abraham states the trust in verse 8? Abraham has faith that God will provide an animal for the offering instead of his son, and so that's what God provides. Is it because God requires a sacrifice of some kind, even if not expressly commanded? If not Isaac, then it must be another. Or is it that Abraham uses the ram as an occasion to offer a sacrifice of thanksgiving, out of gratitude to God for not having to follow through on the sacrifice of Isaac?

GOD'S PROMISES AND HUMAN FAITHFULNESS, GENESIS 22:15–19

We turn to verses 15–19 and the difficult but repeated word from God: because you have obeyed my voice and have not withheld your son, I reiterate the promises. Is this reiteration a consequence of Abraham's proving himself trustworthy? Is Abraham's trustworthiness the occasion or the cause of the promises? Certainly, the promises are not new as they originally came to Abraham independently of his response. Indeed, God's word of promise created his faith (15:3–6) and continued to make trust possible over the course of his journey. Indeed, the trust that Abraham exhibits in response to this test has been created by God's prior promises.

This reality is not reversed somehow here so that now his faith creates the promises. The promises are not causally related to Abraham's trustworthiness. One way to state it could be: as a faithful one he continues to be the focus of the promises. Yet, there is more: the promises are reiterated in an emphatic way to a trusting Abraham. Having seen Abraham's faithfulness, God swears by the divine self for the first time in the narrative, though it recalls the self-binding ritual of God in Genesis 15. In effect it lays the divine life on the line, puts the very divine self behind the promise. This divine action does not mean that the promises are given a new shape, but they receive a new emphasis in view of Abraham's response.[73]

Walter Moberly's reflections are helpful at this point: "The will and purpose of YHWH is transformed so that it is now *grounded* both in the will of YHWH and in the obedience of Abraham. It is not that the divine promise has become contingent upon Abraham's obedience, but that Abraham's obedience has been incorporated into the divine promise. Henceforth Israel owes its existence not just to YHWH but also to Abraham. Theologically this constitutes a profound understanding of the value of human obedience—it can be taken up by God and become a motivating factor in his purposes toward humanity."[74] But is it "grounded" in both? I would say that it is grounded in the divine will and purpose only. But God does take up Abraham's faithfulness (Moberly says "obedience")[75] and incorporates that into the already existent divine purposes. That is to say, that Abraham's faithfulness is not an option if God is going to work out God's purposes in and through him, but God's promises and purposes for the world would not finally be stymied by Abraham's resistance.

This raises the question: if Abraham had said no to God, would he have forfeited the promise? In responding to such a question, the placement of the text is important to observe. This text is virtually the last exchange between Abraham and God; it follows closely on the heels of the birth of Isaac and precedes Sarah's death (23:2). This suggests a concern about an unprecedented turning of the generations; Isaac will now move out into the world as the inheritor of the promises. A precedent seems in need of being established. One promise has been fulfilled. Yet, promises of land, numerous descendants, being a blessing to the nations remain. What status do these other divine promises have now? Are they a matter of course, to be fulfilled for Abraham and his family irrespective of Abraham's (or Isaac's) faithfulness? Are God's promises now to be carried by genetics, by a natural succession, by dynastic control—even if Abraham (Isaac) is unfaithful?

Another way of putting the issue is this: What happens to faithfulness when the promise is fulfilled? To have the promised son could have tempted Abraham to push other promises onto the sidelines: I've now got what I want. How do promises already fulfilled affect the relationship with God? Will Abraham still ground his life in the divine promises rather than bask in the sunshine of fulfillment? In order to discern this, the test is focused precisely on the point of fulfillment, namely, Isaac. Abraham does not claim ownership of the promise here, as if it were his possession, to do with as he pleased: God, you have promised, hence you cannot do this.

At times we speak of the unconditionality of the promises to Abraham in such a way that Abraham's (or anyone else's) faithfulness becomes irrelevant. God created Abraham's faith, yes, but not in such a way that God's word was irresistible. If it were not resistible, then God's command to sacrifice Isaac would have been no test at all, for the outcome would have been settled in advance. God, however, does not coerce or program Abraham's response. God is not so in control of the situation that it ceases to be a test. While the promise will never be made null and void as far as God is concerned, people do not participate in the sphere of the promise independent of a faithful response. Abraham's trust in the God who makes promises is not an optional matter. Abraham could have said no to God, and complicated God's moves into the future, though not finally stymied them. The promise will be reiterated by God to Isaac because of the way in which Abraham responded in faith and obedience to God (26:3–5). Hence, the promise is not automatically or naturally carried on into the next generation of the family, it cannot be secured by having children.

This understanding also shows that we are not simply speaking of a spiritual linkage across the centuries. The promise takes shape in the actual lives of people, whose own words and deeds are centrally involved in its transmission. This means that, not only is genetic transmission impossible, it is also insufficient to say that the word of God provides the continuity across the generations. The continuing transmission of the promise is placed in the hands of those who are faithful, and the importance of their witness ought not be discounted.

ISAAC AND REBEKAH: THE NEXT GENERATION (GENESIS 24:1–67)

We treat this Josephlike story briefly, for Abraham is a character only at the beginning of the chapter (12:1–9).[76] Abraham's final days are an occasion to note how God has filled his life with blessings (24:1; verses 31, 35, 36, 60) and granted him success (verses 12, 21, 40, 56). Blessing and success have here to do largely with quite tangible realities, from wealth and property to posterity. God has indeed kept his promise to him (12:1–3).[77]

Such blessings testify to God's work as creator in Abraham's life. This is consonant with the universal claims made for Yahweh as "the God of heaven and (the God of) earth" (verse 3) and more briefly as "the God of heaven" (verse 7; cf. 14:19, 22). While these divine epithets are often considered late because of their use in postexilic literature (for example, Ezra 5:12; 1:2), such universal understandings of God were necessary in order to speak properly of the servant's task of reaching out into the wider world of Mesopotamia (verses 4, 7).

Abraham's activity is now focused on Isaac's future, namely, finding him a proper wife among family members back in the old country (the Nahor of verse 10 is near Haran), not from among the resident Canaanites (24:3). The twice-expressed concern that Isaac not be brought back to Haran (24:6, 8) is explained in 24:7: for Isaac to settle in the place from which Abraham migrated would be untrue to God's call and the promise relative to the land.

Functioning without divine directive, Abraham commissions the most senior of his servants for the task—God's leading will actually be in response to Abraham's initiative. After that commissioning, with an appropriate oath (24:2, 9), Abraham is no longer a character in this narrative. At the same time, his background presence is evident, not least in the ongoing reference of the servant to "the God of my master Abraham" (24:12, 27, 42, 48).

It is noteworthy that Abraham, in these, his last words, is quite uncertain what will come of this venture; he makes no easy recourse to a divine guarantee of success. He makes his servant swear (not) to do certain things (24:3–4, 6, 8); therefore, his conduct and that of others are not determined in advance. In fact, Abraham considers it possible that this venture might fail because "the woman" might refuse to cooperate (24:8; in 24:41, it is the woman's family). This could happen even though God would "send his angel before you" (32:1; Exod. 23:20; 32:34). The servant takes human behaviors into account in carrying out the task—what people customarily do counts (24:11) and the numerous gifts (24:10) are certainly an effort to persuade. These factors suggest that it is much too easy to say that "the success or failure of the commission depends on whether God grants success or not."[78] While the success may well depend finally on God, the activity of human beings may occasion failure even though God intends otherwise. We do not have here a divine "all-pervasive management" of events,[79] human activity can shape the future, though it cannot finally stymie God's purposes. One may speak of God's highly effective work behind the scenes without resorting to such deterministic descriptions.

Abraham has no personal contact with either Isaac or Rebekah in this story, though he does spend considerable energy and financial resources in bringing them together. Moreover, Abraham has no communication with God (not since 22:15–18), though God clearly is working behind the scenes with respect to the finding of Rebekah. Over the course of the story the focus passes from "master" Abraham to "master" Isaac (24:65) and Rebekah succeeds Sarah as the matriarch of the family (24:67). Notably, it is Rebekah who will follow exactly in Abraham's footsteps (24:38 with 12:1) and will receive the same blessing (cf. 24:60 with 22:17).

It is not enough to say that a new generation is in the process of being born, or even that God's promises of posterity through Isaac can now be realized. It is also important to say that Isaac loves Rebekah (24:67). Life in God's good creation is more than divine promises and religious practice. It includes such creational gifts as the love between husband and wife. While "faithfulness and steadfast love" depict God's relation to this family (24:12, 14, 27), they also characterize inter-human relationships (24:49), which are integral to the furtherance of God's purposes. God's work as creator is evident in and through the ordinary, everyday workings of this family rather than in miraculous or extraordinary events.

THE DEATH AND BURIAL OF SARAH (GENESIS 23:1–20)

The death and burial of Sarah and Abraham (23:1–20; 25:1–18) are embraced by the search for a wife for Isaac (24:1–67). In the midst of death and discontinuity the future is assured.

Genesis 23–24 transfers the reader's attention from Sarah to Rebekah. These chapters constitute a move from death to life, from burial to marriage, or, symbolically speaking, from Sarah's burial site to the well at which Rebekah is found (24:11, 20).[80] While Abraham and Isaac are characters in these two chapters, the focus, remarkably, is on the matriarch. The burial site purchase is framed by references to Sarah (verses 1–2, 19–20), and both chapters are so framed (23:1–2; 24:67). Sarah is the only woman whose lifespan is indicated in the Old Testament. She is the first member of this family who comes to rest in the new land, and in time Abraham will join Sarah (25:10).

Within the inclusio provided by the death and burial of Sarah, Genesis 23 is a report of negotiations between Abraham and the Hittites for purchase of a family burial place.[81] Machpelah was located in the southern part of Canaan near Mamre.[82] The report of the land purchase begins with the Abraham of chapter 14 very much in evidence; he identifies himself as a lowly outsider, but his reputation is immediately recognized and acknowledged by the Hittites ("mighty prince," verse 6; cf. 24:35). Abraham, who will not be obligated to strangers (cf. 14:23–24), and is alert to the need to remain free with respect to the use of the land, insists on paying for it (it is not known if 400 shekels is a fair price).

The land is transferred to Abraham in a legal and a public manner—in contrast to some of his other relationships with outsiders.[83] Abraham seems to act entirely within legal and moral bounds here, and hence the deed should be honored by future generations. The end of the matter (23:20) is that this particular space within the Promised Land is legally transferred to Abraham. The purchase of land may be considered a symbol of hope, a concrete anticipation of what God has in store for those who trust in the promises.

No explicit theological language is used in this chapter; any such understandings must be developed in relation to promises in the larger context (for example, Gen. 15:18–20; 17:8). That God is not mentioned witnesses to human ingenuity and activity in the initial fulfillment of God's promise of land. Again and again, God works through human beings on behalf of the divine purposes. How are we to understand this land as an "everlasting possession" (17:8; cf. 23:18–20)? Janzen makes two helpful points: It is "God's intent (1) that the descendants of Abraham and Sarah are to have a bona fide place to live among the other peoples and nations of the earth and, (2) that, likewise, all communities and peoples are entitled to such a place, so that no community is doomed to endless landlessness."[84] Strategies with regard to how best to accomplish these good ends remain very much in debate; but the objective should be clear to all who take these texts seriously.

THE DEATH AND BURIAL OF ABRAHAM (GENESIS 25:1–11)

Abraham outlives Sarah by thirty-eight years. He dies at the age of 175, exactly one hundred years after his call (12:4). In fact, Abraham lives for fifteen years after Isaac's sons are born (21:5 and 25:26). For reasons unknown, the text betrays a remarkable lack of interest in the many years of Abraham's later life. What we have is probably all that the narrator had available.

The story of Abraham ends as it began, with genealogies (11:27–32 and 25:12–18). Indeed, the death and burial of Abraham (25:7–11) is placed between genealogies (25:1–6, 12–18), as if to suggest that Abraham's life continues on in many children (cf. 17:5). Abraham is indeed the father of a multitude of nations. While the narrative does not recall the language of promise at this point, it goes without saying that these descendants are a fulfillment of key divine promises to Abraham. That the promises to Abraham continue with his son Isaac is made clear in 25:11: "After the death of Abraham God blessed his son Isaac." The genealogy of Isaac is picked up in 25:19–20.

Special care is taken to include two additional families among Abraham's descendants, those born of Hagar and Keturah. First, Genesis 25:1–6 introduces us to a side of Abraham's life completely unknown up to this point. He takes a wife named Keturah, about whom we know nothing except that she bore Abraham six children. Presumably it occurred at some point after Sarah's death. Given all the divine and human activity necessary in order for Abraham to have Isaac, and the various reports of his advanced years (17:17; 18:12; 24:1), this is a somewhat surprising development. Notably, Abraham is buried with Sarah (25:10), and no mention is made of Keturah's death and burial.

The names of Abraham's children by Keturah are not all certainly known. They are generally associated with the Syro-Arabian desert, but the historical relationship between them is not clear and they do not seem to be sharply distinguished geographically. These sons are progenitors of peoples with whom Israel as a nation had to do over the years.[85] A point for later Israel may be that such peoples are ultimately a part of their family.

The apparent reference in 25:6 to the sons of both Hagar and Keturah draws Ishmael and the sons of Keturah together as those whom Abraham "sent away" (cf. 21:14).[86] This action serves to settle Isaac's standing and any issues of inheritance (cf. 21:10 with 25:5). Yet that these sons are recipients of Abraham's wealth specifies a relationship of concern and generosity.

Second, the families of Hagar and Ishmael are presented in an extended genealogy (25:12–18). These descendants of Abraham are witness to the fulfillment of God's promises to both Abraham and Ishmael (16:10–12; 17:20; 21:13, 18). Theologically, this is not an insignificant matter. God has been faithful to promises made to those both within and without the chosen family.

Abraham's death is described in quite matter-of-fact ways. Death is not described as the enemy, but simply as the end of a good and full life (cf. 15:15; contrast 47:9).[87] Isaac and Ishmael, with no sign of disharmony between them, see to his burial with Sarah in the cave he had purchased (chapter 23). The return of Ishmael but not the sons by Keturah is striking; it testifies to the special place of Ishmael as a child of promise (17:18; 21:11). Interestingly, Isaac may settle near Ishmael (16:14; 24:62; 25:11, 18).

Given the relationships Israel has had with some of the peoples in this region over the years, both negative and positive, it is striking that at the beginning of the history of Jacob/Israel stands this word about their belonging to the family of Abraham. These connections suggest that relationships among people in that part of the world should be conceived most fundamentally in familial rather than national or political or religious terms. There are of course differences among these families that have emerged over the years that cannot be lightly set aside. But there are significant commonalities as well, to which very deep roots in the family of Abraham testify. These links should provide some continuing basis for working with continuing differences among these peoples in a creative and peaceful way.

CHAPTER 8

ABRAHAM IN MEMORY AND TRADITION

A survey follows. The study of the role that Abraham played in the rest of the Old Testament and the New Testament, with reference to other ancient literature, has intensified in recent years, at least in part because of the importance of Abraham in interreligious conversations.[1]

THE OLD TESTAMENT OF THE OLD TESTAMENT?

R. W. L. Moberly has written an influential book on the relationship of Genesis 12–50 to the rest of the Old Testament.[2] Beginning with an analysis of the early chapters in Exodus and the revelation of the name Yahweh in Exodus 6:2–3, Moberly considers how the God who makes promises to Israel's ancestors constitutes the foundation for that development. In his language, "the relationship of patriarchal religion in Genesis 12–50 to Mosaic Yahwism in Exodus onward is analogous to the relationship of the Old Testament as a whole to the New Testament. Or to put the same point differently, the position of the adherent of Mosaic Yahwism with regard to the patriarchal traditions in Genesis 12–50 is analogous to the position of the Christian with regard to the Old Testament."[3]

While finding Moberly's study to be important and insightful, I concur with J. G. Janzen's disagreement with a key point in this study.[4] Moberly claims that just as the coming of Jesus Christ in the New Testament witness has "in some ways superseded" the religion of the Old Testament, so also the faith of Israel (Mosaic Yahwism) has "in some ways superseded patriarchal religion."[5] Janzen's response is apt: by "the logic of supersession, this should mean that Christians are twice removed from the religion of Israel's ancestors, and that that religion should be even more relativized for Christians than it was for adherents of the Mosaic Torah."[6] But he goes on to note the Apostle Paul actually leaps back over the Mosaic expression of Israel's religion and lifts up the promises of God to the ancestors, giving them a special place for the Christian that the Mosaic Torah does not have.[7] Appealing to Galatians 3:15–18, Janzen concludes: "So far as Paul is concerned, the theological core of the ancestral religion remains foundational, and the theological core of Mosaic religion, however great in importance, does not annul or supersede it. The difference between Paul and his fellow Jews who do not follow Jesus is precisely that, in Paul's view, they have allowed the Mosaic dispensation to supplant the Abrahamic."[8] For Paul (Rom. 4:13–14; 9:6–16, 28–32), the Mosaic Torah fulfills an important function in revealing sin, but Paul's appeal, finally, rests back on God's pre-Mosaic promises (Rom. 9:6–8): "It is not as though the word of God had failed. For not all Israelites truly belong to Israel, and not all of Abraham's children are his true descendants; but 'It is through Isaac that descendants shall be named for you.' This means that it is not the children of the flesh who are the children of God, but the children of the promise are counted as descendants."⁹

It can be claimed that the Apostle Paul has learned of the Abraham-Moses relationship from Moses himself. At a key juncture in the story of Israel in the book of Exodus, Moses appeals to the ancestral promises. The people of Israel have worshiped the golden calf and God has responded by threatening to consume them. But Moses, in various intercessory arguments on behalf of Israel, states clearly (Exod. 32:13): "Remember Abraham, Isaac, and Israel, your servants, how you swore to them by your own self, saying to them, 'I will multiply your descendants like the stars of heaven, and all this land that I have promised I will give to your descendants, and they shall inherit it forever.'" Israel's future is thus grounded by Moses, not in their keeping the law or maintaining loyalty to the Sinaitic covenant, but in the promises of God to the ancestors. In other words, Moses gives the promises of God to the ancestors a higher priority for the future of the people of God than obedience to the law.¹⁰ The merciful character of God is lifted up in the verses that follow the golden calf debacle (Exod. 33:19; 34:6–7) and, as Janzen notes, this understanding of God's steadfast love and faithfulness is grounded in claims about God in the ancestral narratives (cf. Gen. 24:27).

This appeal by Moses to God's promises to the ancestors reflects the leitmotif in the treatment of Abraham in the rest of the Old Testament.

ABRAHAM BEYOND GENESIS 12–25

Old Testament

Beyond Genesis 12–25 the name Abraham occurs forty-three times in the Old Testament, in fifteen books, though not often in association with specific Genesis stories (cf. Josh. 24:2–3; Neh. 9:7–8; Ps. 105:8–11; Isa. 41:8–10; 51:1–3).¹¹ The one story that is referenced repeatedly (Sodom and Gomorrah, for example, Jer. 23:14) is never linked to Abraham. Genesis 12:1–3 (and related texts) is also echoed in books beyond Genesis without reference to Abraham. These verses are caught up in the kingship of David and the associated promises (cf. 2 Sam. 7:9; Ps. 47:9; 72:17).¹² The prophets also draw on these Abrahamic texts in their articulation of promises to the exiles (for example, Isa. 44:3), as well in the theme of blessing on the nations (Isa. 19:24–25; Jer. 3:17; 4:2; Zech. 8:13).

The Abraham of Genesis 12–25 stands in basic continuity with the Abraham presented in the rest of the Old Testament. Later generations reflecting on this material did not produce a "new" Abraham.¹³ At the same time, there are some exceptions, or at least partial exceptions, to this claim. For example, the negative features in the Genesis depiction of Abraham never appear elsewhere in the Old Testament (or New).[14] All subsequent biblical texts interpret him in a solely positive way. The reason for making Abraham so immaculate is not clear. The options include: purposeful neglect, a kind of myopia, a rationalized assessment of his behaviors, conviction that, finally, it is faithfulness that truly counts. Interpreters through the centuries, perhaps taking their cue from the biblical witness, have not uncommonly made a comparably positive assessment. This one-sided portrayal of Abraham means that contemporary interpreters must take special pains to introduce the negative side of Abraham that clearly is present in the text. Most modern interpreters seem to be truer to this dimension of the text's portrayal of Abraham than their predecessors through the centuries.

Another exception, at least in part, is Abraham's faith and faithfulness. An initial testimony to Abraham's faithfulness is presented in Genesis 26:3–5, 24: Abraham "obeyed my voice and kept my charge, my commandments, my statutes, and my laws" (and this before Mt. Sinai).[15] Beyond Genesis, Abraham's faith (as distinct from faithfulness) is specifically referenced only in Nehemiah 9:8 ("found his heart faithful"); this is likely a reference to Genesis 15:6, though this text never surfaces in the rest of the Old Testament (in contrast to the New). One might also say that Abraham's faith is implicit in the continuing designation of Abraham as God's "servant" (Gen. 26:24; Exod. 32:13; Deut. 9:27; 1 Chron. 16:13; Ps. 105:6, 42) and as God's "friend" (Isa. 41:8; 2 Chron. 20:7; cf. James. 2:23).[16] Yet, when one thinks of the New Testament focus on the faith (distinguished from faithfulness?) of Abraham, the Old Testament witness is remarkably minimal. At the same time, this focus is not new in the New Testament, as Deuterocanonical and Pseudepigraphical literature already give attention to this dimension of the Abraham story (see below).

Most basically, Abraham is remembered in the rest of the Old Testament because he was the recipient of God's promises. In view of that divine commitment, God's mercy is extended to Israel in every generation. We have shown that the history of Israel, in considerable detail, is anticipated in the narratives regarding Abraham.[17] In effect, this means that the history of Israel, indeed the very identity of Israel, is the fulfillment of God's promises to Abraham. It is because of God's fulfillment of these promises that Israel is known as "the people of the God of Abraham" (Ps. 47:9; cf. 2 Chron. 20:7); Abraham was Israel's "father" (Josh. 24:3; Isa. 51:2; cf. Luke 1:73; 16:24; Acts 7:2; Rom. 4:12; Jas 2:21).[18]

It should be noted, especially, that the book of Exodus grounds God's deliverance of Israel from Egypt in the promises given to the ancestors (2:24; 3:6, 15–16; 4:5). God's promises lead to Israel's redemption from slavery and, later, to Israel's deliverance from exile (Isa. 41:8–10). God's deliverance and Israel's future in the land are assured because God keeps promises, specifically promises to the ancestors. It is God's promising, not Abraham's faith/faithfulness or his character, that is the decisive theological move made throughout these texts. God's promises remain even in the face of heinous Israelite sin (Exod. 32:13; Lev. 26:39–42; Isa. 41:8–14; 51:1–3; Neh. 9:7–8).

Pentateuch

Within Genesis, God's promises to Abraham are repeated to Isaac (26:3–4, 24) and to Jacob (28:4, 13–14; 35:11–12) and through Joseph to the sons of Jacob (50:24). The book of Exodus explicitly links the certainty of the land promise to God's covenant with the ancestors (6:3–5, 8; 13:5, 11; 33:1). As noted above, Moses understands that God's promises to (covenant with) Abraham take precedence over the covenant with Israel at Sinai (Exod. 32:13; cf. Num. 14:13–19; which also cites Exod. 34:6–7) and remain in place in spite of Israel's apostasy.[19]

The subsequent Pentateuchal references to Abraham are associated primarily with the promises of land and descendants. The references in Leviticus to Abraham and to the ancestral covenant anticipate a future loss of the land in the face of which the promises still hold true (Lev. 26:9, 42–45). This context also includes God's continuing promise that "I will be your God, and you shall be my people" (26:12, 45; Gen. 17:1–8). Comparably, the book of Numbers lifts up the promise of land that God has sworn to the ancestors (Num. 11:12; 14:16); even if the present generation will not live to see that promise fulfilled, the promise remains (Num. 14:23, 30; 32:11; 20:12, 24; 27:12; 33:53).

The book of Deuteronomy is especially marked by references to the ancestral covenant (for example, 4:31; 8:18; 29:12–14). God's promise of land occurs at the beginning and end of the book (Deut. 1:8; 34:4). Indeed, God's "swearing" the promises to Abraham, Isaac, and Jacob (or simply "ancestors") occurs over thirty times in the book (for example, Deut. 1:8; 6:10; 9:5; 34:4). These promises were put in place because God had "set his heart" "in love on your ancestors alone and chose you" (Deut. 10:15). It was because God "kept the oath that he swore to your ancestors" that God has delivered them (Deut. 7:7). Emphasis is thereby placed on God's choosing of Abraham—Israel's creation is not an accident, Israel has come to be because God specifically willed that it be so. In other terms, it is because of God's love and God's gracious activity that Israel exists.

Moses' intercessory prayer in Deuteronomy 9:25–29 on behalf of a recalcitrant Israel resembles his prayer in Exodus 32:13; he appeals to the ancestral promises as grounds for an amelioration of the consequences of their sin. Deuteronomy also envisages a future loss of land in view of Israel's unfaithfulness (28:63–64; 29:28). At the same time, beyond judgment, God promises that Israel will be restored to the land (30:1–5). So, for Deuteronomy, the promise of land has a double horizon:

a near future (see Joshua) and a distant future. Both horizons are possible because God keeps promises. The land is pure gift from a promising God.

The combination of references in Deuteronomy 4:31 and 30:1–5, where the ancestral promise seems unconditional, and 7:7–12, where the promise seems to be conditional, raise issues of consistency. The passages might be brought together in the following way. These divine promises to the ancestors will not fail; they will never be made null and void as far as God is concerned. While a rebellious generation might not live to see the fulfillment of the promise because they have rejected God, the promise can be relied on. God's promises are everlasting, though participation in their fulfillment is not guaranteed to every person or generation. The call to repentance can be resisted and rejected (2 Kings 17:13). The promises are always there for the believing to cling to, however, and they can be confident that God will ever be at work to fulfill them. Only within such a promissory context is repentance possible.[20]

Chronicles and Ezra/Nehemiah

God's covenant with Abraham is cited in 1 Chronicles 16:15–17 (see also Ps. 105:8–10) and Abraham is referred to as the "friend" of God in 2 Chronicles 20:7 (see also Isa. 41:8), whose descendants have been gifted by God with the land.[21] Ezra's prayer in Nehemiah 9:6–38 is especially to be noted.[22] The era of Ezra is commonly noted for giving special attention to Mosaic law, and yet Ezra's prayer begins and ends (9:7–8, 38), and is punctuated throughout (9:15, 17, 19, 27–28, 31), with an appeal to God's promises and God's mercy. Indeed, Nehemiah 9:7 may be said to summarize Israel's basic understandings of Abraham—chosen, led into Canaan, given a new identity (renamed), found faithful, with whom God made a covenant. Fredrick Holmgren concludes: "it is the covenant with Abraham that determines the basic movement of the text."[23] However much the law shaped the postexilic community, the ancestral promises give decisive shape to Israel's identity and its ongoing relationship with God.

Psalms

Reference to Abraham in the Psalms is surprisingly rare. Psalm 105 focuses on the covenant promise with Abraham (Ps. 105:6, 8–11, 42; cf. 106:45). This is an "everlasting covenant" of which God is ever mindful; the promise of land is given special attention (Ps. 105:11). Abraham is twice recognized as a servant of God, indicating his trusting relationship with God, while functioning as God's agent (see below for further comment). The only other passage in the Psalms is 47:9, a remarkably inclusive reference. Nations, their kings and subjects, are identified as "the people of the God of Abraham." One cannot help but wonder if Genesis 12:3 stands in the background: "through you shall all the families of the earth be blessed."

Prophets

In the former prophets, Abraham is specifically mentioned only in three contexts (Josh. 24:2–3; I Kings 18:36; 2 Kings 13:23).[24] In Joshua 24:2–3, a brief reprise of the story of Abraham is given as part of a rehearsal of God's actions on behalf of Israel (also in Neh. 9:7; cf. 9:15). Abraham is uniquely referenced as belonging to an idolatrous family (and contemporaries of Joshua are commanded to put away those gods, 24:14).[25] The implication is that Abraham becomes the exemplar; as Abraham had put away such gods, so it shall be with you. Judges 2:1 is an especially strong reference to the ancestral promise, where God says: "I will never break my covenant with you"; this promise, importantly, is stated in Judges in introduction to repeated references to Israel's unfaithfulness. 2 Kings 13:23 is noteworthy in that, with reference to events ca. 800 B.C.E., it grounds God's ongoing gracious activity on behalf of an oppressed Israel in God's covenant with Abraham (Isaac and Jacob). Because of that promise Israel would not be destroyed.[26]

Abraham is specifically mentioned seven times in the latter prophets (Isa. 29:22; 41:8; 51:2; 63:16; Jer. 33:26; Ezek. 33:24; Mic. 7:20).[27] Because the historical setting is clearer with the prophetic texts, a few more contextual comments are in order.

The pre-exilic prophets make surprisingly little mention of Abraham (Isa. 29:22; Mic. 7:20); if, as many say, these are actually exilic/post-exilic texts, there would be no such reference. It has been plausibly suggested that, if and when appeal was made to God's promissory commitment to Israel, it was the Davidic covenant that prevailed.[28] The failure of the Davidic monarchy and the (imminent and actual) fall of Jerusalem and the exile prompted renewed reflection on Abraham. The loss of land, in turn, served to focus attention on God's ancestral promise of land, perhaps especially in the midst of conflict regarding the identity of the people who are to possess it. Questions such as these arose: were those divine promises still in place, and to whom are they now addressed?

Attention to several texts helps fill out this picture. In Ezekiel 33:24, persons remaining in the land after the fall of Jerusalem claim that they are the inheritors of the Abrahamic promises of land, not the exiles. But Ezekiel denies this claim (33:25–29; cf. 11:14–21; Jeremiah 24; the theme of "remnant"); he, in effect, revises the range of the promises the other way round. He claims that not all who are genealogically related to Abraham will be the recipient of the promises; among the people of Israel, the exiles are the recipients. This distinction among the people of Israel (and also the theme of "remnant") connects well with the distinction the Apostle Paul makes in Romans and Galatians.[29]

Numerous echoes of the ancestral traditions are found in Jeremiah (see listing above).[30] The one specific reference to Abraham (33:26) stands at the end of the Book of Consolation (probably Jer. 30–33) and may provide an inclusio with

Jeremiah 30:3, where God's promise of land to the ancestors may provide a lens for the interpretation of these four chapters. The essential point may be similar to that which is formulated in Jeremiah 31:35–37 and 33:14–26 regarding God's commitment to the creation and to the Davidic promises. In spite of Israel's apostasy that has led to the destruction of Jerusalem and dispersion, the exiles can rely on God's ancient promises to see to their future in the land.

It is possible that Micah 7:20 belongs to this same context; this verse concludes a psalm full of hope (7:8–20). The basic theme is a return to the land with its repopulation, with important echoes of the Exodus and wilderness wanderings (7:12, 14–15). The concluding references to forgiveness (7:18–20) specifically recall Exodus 34:6–7, with its confession of the Lord as gracious, merciful, slow to anger, abounding in steadfast love and faithfulness, and forgiving iniquity, transgression, and sin. Abraham (and Jacob) in 7:20 becomes a shorthand way of referring to the people, who have decisive continuities with the ancestors. Abraham is Israel.

In words articulated by God himself, Second Isaiah links Abraham in a specific way to the exiles in order to assure them that the ancient promises of God still stand for them. In Isaiah 41:8–10, God specifically refers to Abraham as "my friend." Given the fact that the exiles are "the offspring of Abraham" means that they, too, are the friends of God. God chose Abraham (and Jacob/Israel) and hence, for the exiles, that means that God has chosen them. Just as God had taken Abraham from "the ends of the earth," so, too, God will take the exiles from the ends of the earth where they have been scattered and return them to the land God had promised Abraham as "a perpetual holding" (Gen. 17:8; cf. 13:15). God had assured Abraham to "fear not" (Gen. 15:1; cf. 26:24), so also are the exiles so assured (Isa. 41:10). God had promised Abraham, "I will . . . be God to you, and to your offspring after you" (Gen. 17:7), and so God promises the exiles, "I am with you . . . I am your God" (Isa. 41:10).

Both Abraham and Sarah are recalled in Isaiah 51:1–3.[31] Sarah and Abraham are "the rock from which you were hewn . . . the quarry from which you were dug." It is as if Abraham and Sarah were the bedrock of Israel. In other words, to use more personal images, they are the mother and father of Israel (Isa. 51:2). Just as God blessed them and multiplied their offspring, so the exiles, though barren as was Sarah, would be blessed and have many offspring (see the barrenness theme in Isa. 49:14–21; 54:1; cf. 29:22–23). The argument, though similar to the one rejected in Ezekiel 33:24 for those who remained in the land, rings true: that Abraham got the land, even though he was only one man, surely they will possess the land, for they are many. The insignificant become significant once again. In Isaiah 63:16, the people complain that God is not attending to them, even though God is their father (Isa. 64:8). Moreover, Abraham and Jacob/Israel are long dead and do not know or acknowledge them. This claim does not stand in contradiction to the claim about the fatherhood of Abraham in Isaiah 51:2, not least because that was God's point of view (63:16 is the people's point of view). Somehow, both God and Abraham are fathers of Israel; it is not a contradiction to say that God is Creator and a human being such as Abraham is father.

It is striking that the near-sacrifice of Isaac (Gen. 22:1–14) is nowhere explicitly cited in the Old Testament (though it is in several Deuterocanonical works, for example, Judith; Wisdom; 4 Maccabees; see below). It has been suggested that the image of the suffering servant as a lamb (*śeh*) in Isaiah 53:7 may allude to Isaac's and Abraham's references to a lamb (*śeh*) in Genesis 22:7–8 (cf. Jer. 11:19). If this Abrahamic story becomes a metaphor for Israel in exile, it participates in a perspective that bespeaks Israel's redemption from final destruction, but not without cost to God, who groans like a mother in labor in bringing forth a newborn Israel (Isa. 42:14).

The theme of remembrance is associated with Abraham (and Sarah) in several texts, especially the memory of God.[32] The prophet calls upon the exiles to "consider Abraham your father and Sarah who bore you" (Isa. 51:2). Such a consideration on the part of the exiles would bring to memory the promises of God, that God would remain faithful to them in such times of crisis; such a remembrance would enable them to renew their hopes in their continuance as a people and their restoration to the land. In Psalm 105, commonly thought to be exilic or postexilic, God's memory is twice recalled: God "is mindful of his covenant forever" and "remembered his holy promise, and Abraham, his servant" (Ps. 105:8, 42; quoted in Luke 1:72–73). Just as God remembered Israel during their wilderness journey (Ps 105:37–42), so God would remember the exiles in their desert experience. And they would return to their land in joy (105:43–44; cf. Isa. 55:12–13). "This promise of future memory intimates a future restoration of Israel, providing solace for the exiles, both past and present."[33]

These remembrance passages may have their roots in the Abrahamic narrative itself. At the end of the story of Sodom and Gomorrah, "God remembered Abraham" (Gen. 19:29) and Lot's family is delivered from the devastation of the cities (cf. Luke 17:32, "remember Lot's wife"). In post-Genesis uses, these memories of Abraham are linked with times of crisis in Israel's journey. When enslaved Israel cries out to God in Egypt, God remembers Abraham and the covenant with him (Exod. 2:24). And Exodus 6:5 states the matter succinctly: "I have remembered my covenant." This is not to be understood as a jogging of the divine memory, as if God had forgotten promises made. It is for God an active attentiveness to that which is remembered, a divine sense of obligation to a prior commitment.[34] Later in the book of Exodus, when Israel's future is imperiled in the wake of the golden calf debacle, Moses pleads with God to "remember Abraham" (and Isaac and

Israel; Exod. 32:13).[35] And God does remember, and turns from the decision to destroy the people and begin again with Moses. In Deuteronomy 9:7, in the face of the stubbornness of the people of Israel, Moses calls upon God to "remember Abraham" (and Isaac, Jacob). In Leviticus 26:42, when times of destruction and exile in Israel's future are envisaged, God promises to remember the covenant with Abraham (and Isaac and Jacob). They can be assured by such memories that God will be faithful to them, come what may in their historical experience, even in the direst of circumstances (1 Macc. 4:10).[36] "In each of these dangerous times, the memory of Abraham induces a turn of mind and opens a possibility for overcoming a dire crisis."[37]

A note on the most frequently cited Abrahamic text beyond Genesis (though Abraham is not mentioned in any of them).[38] Twelve contexts refer to Sodom (and Gomorrah).[39] Seven of them function in much the same way (Deut. 29:23; Jer. 49:18; 50:40; Isa. 13:19; Amos 4:11; Lam. 4:6); they cite no sin, but focus on the disaster experienced by the cities. The cities have become a conventional image for the disastrous consequences of human sin. Apparently the fate of Sodom and Gomorrah is the worst that can be imagined. The other five texts make explicit reference to Sodom's sins and their comparable fate (Jer. 23:14; Ezek. 16:46–56; less directly, Deut. 32:32–33; Isa. 1:9–10; Zeph. 2:9–10). The sins mentioned include: lack of social justice; adultery, lying, strengthening the hands of evildoers, pride, excess of food, prosperous ease, haughtiness, not aiding the poor and needy, and "abominable things."[40] Sodom had already become a byword in Ezekiel's time (16:52). Jerusalem's sins are much greater than those of Sodom. The nature of Sodom's sins may vary, but the mistreatment of other human beings seems to top the list; this may be developed from the language of "outcry" in Genesis 18:20–21 (with its links to Exod. 2:23–24; 3:7). In other terms, inhospitality lends itself to diverse development.

APOCRYPHAL/DEUTEROCANONICAL LITERATURE

Abraham continues to be an important figure in Deuterocanonical Jewish literature.[41] Yet Abraham is explicitly mentioned only thirty-one times in the Apocryphal/Deuterocanonical books, and nearly half of these references are in 4 Maccabees.[42]

The historical experience of the Jewish community in the last two centuries B.C.E. certainly affects how Abraham is interpreted for their often conflicted life. One thinks of their experience at the destructive hands of the Seleucid overlords, the Maccabean revolt, and diverse commitments regarding the Hellenization of Jewish life. As in any age, contemporary experience will affect a community's ways of interpreting biblical texts and imaging characters such as Abraham.

A brief survey of the Apocryphal/Deuterocanonical literature is revealing of key emphases regarding Abraham. It is surprising that the theme of Abraham's rejection of idolatry and his worship of the one God, present in other works from this period, is so infrequent (Jdt. 5:6–10, though Abraham is not specifically mentioned). Continuity with the canonical literature is strong, though a greater emphasis upon the faithfulness of Abraham begins to emerge, perhaps influencing New Testament emphases. At the same time, specific attention to Abraham's Torah observance is infrequent and minimal (Sirach; 4 Maccabees). It is thus much too simple to suggest that Jewish tradition tends to focus on Abraham's rejection of idolatrous practices.[43]

Two themes may be lifted up.[44] First, the divine covenant/promises to Abraham are a prominent feature. In Baruch 2:34–35 (200–60 B.C.E.), the land promise is sworn by God to Abraham, Isaac, and Jacob, with associated promises relating to increase of offspring and "an everlasting covenant with them to be their God and they shall be my people" (Gen. 17:1–8).[45] In the Prayer of Azariah 11–13 (ca. 100 B.C.E.), God is petitioned not to annul the covenant with the ancestors or withdraw mercy. Abraham is referred to as the "beloved" of God who, with Isaac and Israel, was promised numerous descendants, like stars of the sky and the sands of the sea (Gen. 15:5; 22:17). In 2 Esdras 3:13–15 (70–100 C.E.), Abraham is one whom God loved, to whom God revealed himself secretly by night regarding the end times (cf. Gen. 15:17; Apocalypse of Abraham), and with whom God made "an everlasting covenant," promising never to forsake his descendants (cf. Gen. 17:1–8), and giving him Isaac.[46] Sirach 44:21 (200–180 B.C.E.) reflects God's promises to Abraham in Genesis 22:15–18; because he "proved faithful" the nations will be blessed through his offspring, who will be as "numerous as the dust of the earth" and exalted like the stars, and a land "from the Euphrates to the ends of the earth" will be their inheritance. In 2 Maccabees 1:2 (ca. 100 B.C.E.), God is called upon to remember his covenant with Abraham, Isaac, and Jacob, his "faithful servants."[47]

A second theme is Abraham's faith and faithfulness. This portrayal is at times related, directly or indirectly, to the test of Abraham in Genesis 22, viewed in terms of Abraham's obedience to the command of God. 1 Maccabees (ca. 100 B.C.E.) reflects an extraordinarily difficult time for the Jewish community, as a dying Mattathias appeals to his sons to be loyal to God in their faith and life. Recalling the deeds of the ancestors, Abraham was "found faithful (*pistós*) when tested, and it was reckoned to him as righteousness" (2:51–52).[48] In 4 Maccabees 16:20–22, it is the "faith" (*pístis*) of Abraham that is in evidence in the Akedah. It is noteworthy that 1 Maccabees 2:52 cites Genesis 15:6 in connection with the Akedah (rather than with Gen. 15:1–5),[49] and so links Abraham's response to God's command as a matter of being "found faithful (*pistós*) when tested, not as obedience of law." Abraham is declared righteous in view of this faith/faithfulness. In 2 Maccabees 1:2, Abraham is referred to as a "faithful (*pistós*) servant." In Wisdom of Solomon

10:5 (ca. 100–50 B.C.E.), Abraham is recognized as "a righteous man" who was preserved "blameless before God" and was kept strong "in the face of his compassion for his child." In Judith (ca. 100 B.C.E.), in a reference to God's testing his people, Abraham, Isaac, and Jacob are mentioned as examples.[50] The faithfulness of Abraham is also implied in Judith 5:6–10, with its specific reference to his family being called out of Chaldea because they would not serve other gods and they worshiped "the God of heaven." In the Prayer of Manasseh 1:8 (ca. 100 B.C.E.), Abraham, mentioned along with Isaac and Jacob, is considered "righteous," as one who "did not sin against you."[51]

Sirach's reference to Abraham in a hymn to honor the ancestors is more complex (44:19–22). This is especially evident in the way it combines the themes of God's promise and Abraham's faithfulness. It is the only apocryphal book (besides 4 Maccabees) that mentions that Abraham obeyed the law. Abraham was the "father of a multitude of nations, and no one has been found like him in glory (fame)." He kept the law of the Most High (reflecting Gen. 26:4–5?), entered into covenant with God, certified by circumcision (Gen. 17:1–14), and "when he was tested he proved faithful" (Gen. 22:1–14). Therefore (Gen. 22:15–18), God promised him with an oath that the nations would be blessed through his offspring, who would be as numerous as the dust of the earth, be exalted like the stars, and receive a worldwide inheritance. It seems unnecessary to conclude that God's entering into covenant is understood to be conditioned by his keeping the law (44:20; see the similar order in Neh. 9:7–8),[52] not least because the various Abraham stories tend to be collapsed into one another here and elsewhere. Also, the relation between Abraham's being tested and the articulation of the promises ("therefore") simply follows the pattern in Genesis (22:15–18; "because"). The strong reference to Abraham's observance of the law already in Genesis 26:4–5 makes it clear that this portrayal of Abraham is not a new development in postexilic Judaism.[53]

4 Maccabees (ca. 50–100 C.E.) is a philosophical treatise defending key Jewish teachings. It speaks of Abraham's faithfulness and obedience to the law and, indirectly, assumes the promises to Abraham. It mentions the "children of Abraham" (6:17, 22) with reference to Torah observance and food laws. Like the ancestors Abraham, Isaac, and Jacob, they are called to trust God and control their emotions with reason. Abraham's "faith" (*pistis*) was exhibited in his openness to sacrifice Isaac (16:20–22). In 16:25 (cf. 7:19), "those who die for the sake of God, live to God," as do Abraham and all the patriarchs. An example is given of a faithful youth who, tortured to death, did not groan; he is "worthy of Abraham" (9:21). The martyrs, who are the "true descendants of father Abraham" (17:6), will be welcomed by Abraham, Isaac, and Jacob into immortality (13:17). Abraham was "god-fearing" (15:28) and "zealous to sacrifice his son Isaac, the ancestor of our

nation." When "Isaac saw his father's hand wielding a knife and descending upon him, he did not cower" (16:20). Isaac, therefore, was not a victim, but cooperated in the sacrificial act. There is common allusion in 4 Maccabees to the near-sacrifice of Isaac, wherein Abraham serves as an example for those who are tested with their lives (7:14; 13:12, 14:20; 14:20; 15:28; 16:20; 17:6; 18:11). Israelite children, "offspring of the seed of Abraham," are called to "obey this law and exercise piety in every way" (18:1); these "sons of Abraham" will receive immortality" (18:23). The overriding concern is to urge Torah observance even in the midst of the most horrible of circumstances.

SOME GATHERED COMMENTS

Some gathered comments regarding the traditions about Abraham in the Old Testament (with Deuterocanonical books) may be helpful. These often theologically charged texts in the several contexts reflect an internal hermeneutic for the interpretation of Abraham centered in God's promise. God's promises are decisive for the future of Abraham and his family and, through them, all the world's families. Were it not for the promises there would be no faithful Abraham. Even more, God's promises shape the future of God, for God will always act in faithfulness to the promises.

God's commitment to the relationship with Abraham that promising entails, makes for a new identity for the one who responds in trust and obedience. Abraham now takes into his life the character of the promises made, he is now one whose future looks like this. The future is not yet, but because it is promised by one who is faithful to promises, Abraham's very being takes on the character of that future, though not apart from his own faithful response to the word of God which created his faith in the first place. Even more, it is promise as promise that is a key point here. In the ongoing use of the Abrahamic tradition, it is not only important that Israel be able to point to particular ancient moments when these promises were fulfilled (for example, the land). What counts, finally, is their continuing status as promise, which can then be appropriated by the community of faith in later generations as still applicable to them and their future. For example, it is striking that God's promises to Abraham—land, nationhood, name, descendants, to be their God—are so attuned to the needs of the exiles. In essence, this is a time when Israel's future as a people is at stake. That descendants are explicitly referred to thirteen times in Genesis 17, for example, would not be missed by these dispersed and depleted people. They would be living short of fulfillment; but promises generate hope in God's possibilities. The key would be their trust in the God who keeps promises.

The paucity of reference to the faithfulness of Abraham, especially in the Old Testament, limits such a discussion. The following claims may be made. While

God's promise generates Abraham's faith, his future is understood to be shaped not simply by the God who promises, but also by the way in which Abraham responds. Abraham is not passive, as if the drama were shaped solely by God's will and word. Human beings can neither preserve nor annul God's promises, for God will keep promises, but their words and deeds will have much to say in how that promise moves toward fulfillment. Human beings make a difference to God and to the shape the future takes. One factor that lifts up the human role is the general way in which God states promises (for example, nation, blessing, descendants). Such indefiniteness leaves room for human freedom in response, so that the track from promise to fulfillment is not precisely determined in advance. God uses human beings as instruments in and through whom to carry out the divine creational intentions. God gives them responsibilities within this intention, choosing to trust human beings such as Abraham and Sarah with a significant role, while continuing to see to the promises in an attentively personal way.

The theme of Abraham as a "friend" of God cuts across this literature (and reappears in the New Testament and other literature). What it means for Abraham (also true of Moses) to be the friend of God entails at least the following: a close relationship, a relationship of mutuality and genuinely interactive communication, a relationship of give and take, a relationship of some dependence on the other. That Jesus calls his disciples friends (John 15:14–15) may be dependent on this tradition.[54]

God's promising affects God as well. Having given promises, God is committed to a certain future for Abraham and his descendants, and so the future changes for God as well: God must always act in such a way as to be faithful to these particular promises. Because God will always be faithful to promises, God's options for acting in the future, indeed God's freedom, will be limited thereby. Moreover, the covenant ritual of Genesis 15 means that God commits the divine self to the promise at such a depth that God considers for the divine self an experience of suffering and even death. This reveals the depth of the divine faithfulness to Abraham and the divine willingness to become vulnerable for the sake of the promise. The promises that God makes to Abraham are as firm and good as God is.

PSEUDEPIGRAPHICAL LITERATURE

Abraham is prominently featured in several Pseudepigraphical works. As representative works, I here consider Jubilees, Pseudo-Philo, the Testament of Abraham, and the Apocalypse of Abraham. A full treatment of Abraham in these texts is not possible, but basic directions may be noted.[55] As with the (Deutero) canonical literature, the themes of God's promise and Abraham's faith/faithfulness will be especially lifted up.

One of the concerns addressed in these early interpretations was ambiguities presented by the texts, including gaps, syntactical difficulties, and (apparent) contradictions. Moreover, several Abrahamic texts were at times viewed as problematic, for example, Abraham's endangerment of Sarah and the near-sacrifice of Isaac. These authors sought to resolve such issues with interpretations sensitive to the integrity of the ancestors. These interpretive concerns were pursued in several ways, not least through retelling biblical stories, especially evident in Jubilees and Pseudo-Philo (cf. also the Genesis Apocryphon from Qumran). In the process of retelling, gaps were filled out, and appropriate omissions, additions, and other adjustments were made. An ever-present issue was to extend the authority of ancient figures (and related texts) to speak more directly into their contemporary situations.

JUBILEES

Jubilees (ca. 160–100 B.C.E.), a narrative retelling of Genesis 1–Exodus 14, is especially important.[56] It is presented as an inspired divine revelation, having been transmitted to Moses by an angel at Mt. Sinai. Probably written in Hebrew, and anti-Hellenistic in perspective, it gives important evidence regarding early Jewish biblical interpretation. Generally, Jubilees may be said to be an effort to ground the Jewish community of the second century B.C.E. in the ancestral traditions, promoting their authority for the continuing life and faith of the author's community.

Jubilees 11.14–23.10 is the section devoted to Abraham, interpreting the Genesis texts with certain emphases, and overlaying the story with chronological details. The storyline of Genesis is essentially followed, with additions, omissions, and some reordering of materials. For example, considerable information is given in Jubilees regarding Abraham's younger years (Jub. 11.14–12.8). There are even references to his being revealed a knowledge of Hebrew and reading/copying books (Jub. 12.25–27; cf. 11.16; 21.10). This expansiveness is also evident in the presentation of Abraham's older years, as he continues to be active into the lives of Jacob and Esau.[57]

The theme of God's promises is prominent in Jubilees, as prominent as in Genesis. Israel was chosen to be an elect people from the beginning of creation, and God entered into an "eternal" covenant with Abraham and his descendants, like the covenant with Noah (Jub. 14.20; 15.30–31). The promises of Genesis 12:1–3, 7 and 17:7 are presented in Jubilees 12.22–24; 13.3; those of Genesis 13:15–17 in Jubilees 13:20–21; the promises of Genesis 15, with the accompanying ritual, are retold in Jubilees 14.1–20;[58] and the covenant with its promises in Genesis 17 is retold in Jubilees 15:1–32, including the promises regarding Ishmael (Jub. 15.17–21). A divine appearance to Abraham in Jubilees 16.15–19 (with no parallel in Genesis) reflects themes from Exodus 19:5–6 and announces promises relating to

Isaac's descendants. The promises following the near-sacrifice of Isaac in Genesis 22:15–18 are expressed in revised form in *Jubilees* 18.14–16. Promissory language is especially present in Abraham's testament to Jacob (*Jub.* 19.16–29; 22:10–30).[59]

A second strong theme is Abraham's faithfulness. Abraham is consistently presented as the exemplary pious man whose character is unassailable. As with most other literature regarding the ancestral figures, *Jubilees* ignores or explains away any negative or questionable behaviors on Abraham's part.[60] In response to God's promises, *Jubilees* 14.6 directly quotes Genesis 15:6: "And he believed the Lord and it was counted for him as righteousness." Several *Jubilees* texts draw out the theme of Abraham as the faithful lover of God who conformed his own will to the divine (17.15–18; 18.14–16; 19.9; 23.10). In the words of *Jubilees* 23.10, "Abraham was perfect in all of his actions with the Lord and was pleasing through righteousness all of the days of his life." Abraham says of himself (to Isaac), "throughout all of the days of my life I have been remembering the Lord and sought with all my heart to do his will and walk uprightly in all his ways. I hated idols, and those who serve them I have rejected. And I have offered my heart and spirit so that I might be careful to do the will of the one who created me because he is the living God" (*Jub.* 21.2–4). In effect, readers of *Jubilees* are encouraged to "be like Abraham" and to remain faithful to the one God to the point of death.

Abraham rejected idolatry and was devoted to the one God. *Jubilees* illustrates this point by expanding upon the somewhat enigmatic Joshua 24:2–3, where it is not clear whether or not Abraham "served other gods." *Jubilees* makes sure that Abraham is not understood to be an idolater; indeed, he is a believer and rejects idols from an early age (*Jub.* 11.16–17; 12.1–8, 12–20). To illustrate the point, *Jubilees* 12.1–8 contains a scene in which Abraham reproaches his father Terah for his belief in empty images and attempts to convince him to worship the one God: "There is not any spirit in them, for they are mute, and they are a misleading of the heart. Do not worship them. Worship the God of heaven, who sends down rain and dew upon the earth, and who makes everything upon the earth, and created everything by his word, and all life is in his presence" (12.3–4). When Abraham is sixty years old he sets fire to the house of idols (which prompts his leaving Ur), and prays to "my God, the Most High God, you alone are God to me" (cf. James 2:19). This story is at least in part an attempt to fill out issues presented by the abruptness of the revelation of God to Abraham in Genesis 12:1–3.[61] For *Jubilees*, God chooses to call Abraham for a reason—because of his rejection of idolatry and his recognition of the authority of the one God.

While *Jubilees* lifts up obedience of the law in a general way, Abraham is not commonly commended for observing the law. The summary statements regarding Abraham's faithfulness do not commend him for Torah observance (17.15–18; 18.16; 19.9; 23.10); one exception is *Jubilees* 24.11, and that is a reflection of

Genesis 26:4–5. This is a striking reality. While Abraham decisively rejects idolatry in his early years, and confesses worship of the one God (12.4, 19–21), the issue of idolatry and the related issue of the worship of one God do not surface in most of the chapters devoted to the broad sweep of the story of Abraham. Certainly Abraham initiates the celebration of key ritual practices, often moving beyond Genesis,[62] but these actions are not generalized regarding his observance of the law. More generally, Abraham's blessings of his (grand)children (*Jub.* 19.15–22.24) contain the clearest conveyance of the importance of keeping the commandments and rejecting idols. Abraham obeyed the law which he "found written in the book of my forefathers and the words of Enoch and in the words of Noah" (*Jub.* 21:10). *Jubilees* 22.10–30, unparalleled in Genesis, contains an intriguing combination of promises-blessings and relatively limited charges to "keep the commandments" (*Jub.* 22.16, 20). Separation from the Gentile world is also an important theme in these texts (for example, 21.21–24; 22.16–19).

Abraham's faithfulness is especially evident in the retelling of the near-sacrifice of Isaac (*Jub.* 18.1–19).[63] The Akedah, being such a difficult text, is the subject of much reflection in this literature. God commends Abraham for his faithfulness in *Jubilees* 18.16, which suggests that the purpose of the Akedah is to stress Abraham's faithfulness. Abraham is presented with a series of tests, including the famine, the wealth of kings, "his wife, when she was taken from him," circumcision, and the sacrifice of Isaac (*Jub.* 17:17–18). In all of these "works" Abraham is faithful and fears God (*Jub.* 18:9). As the last of the tests that Abraham undergoes, the Akedah is the most severe, and hence is the supreme example of his faithfulness (*Jub.* 17.17–18; 19.8).[64] In *Jubilees,* that Abraham was commanded to sacrifice Isaac is not due to God but to the temptation of Mastema, the prince of evil (*Jub.* 17:15–18; 18:9, 12), a text that may be modeled on Job 1–2. Not unlike Job, God and Mastema disagree on the depth of Abraham's faithfulness (*Jub.* 17.16). *Jubilees* is clearly reluctant to consider God as one who tempts human beings, but it is not made clear why God goes along with this test or any other test. Moreover, the difficulty presented by Genesis 22:12 that God "now" knows that Abraham fears God is revised. It is Mastema, not God who needs to be convinced that Abraham feared the Lord (*Jub.* 17.15–18.16). God already knows from a series of tests that Abraham fears God (*Jub.* 17.17; cf. Gen. 22:12).

PSEUDO-PHILO'S BIBLICAL ANTIQUITIES

This work[65] is basically a retelling of biblical stories from Adam to David, interweaving legendary elements. Probably written originally in Hebrew in Palestine (100 B.C.E.–70 C.E.), its concern is to place current Jewish teachings in the mouths of ancient figures. The story of Abraham is sharply compressed compared to the biblical narrative and somewhat scattered.[66]

The emphasis in *LAB* regarding Abraham lies clearly on the two themes we have observed up to this point: God's promises and their fulfillment, and Abraham's trust in God.

Regarding the promises, "At the basis of Pseudo-Philo's views on God and humanity is the biblical notion of covenant."[67] God says: "I will choose my servant Abraham, and I will bring him out from their land and will bring him into the land upon which my eye has looked from of old . . . there I will have my servant Abraham dwell and will establish my covenant with him and will bless his seed and be lord for him as God forever" (*LAB* 7.4; cf. 9.3–4; 18.5). The covenant in Genesis 15 is specifically recalled in *LAB* 23.5–8, with emphasis upon promises of land and descendants. Compare also 23.11–13, "I fulfilled my covenant that I promised your fathers"; other people will take note of this people and say, "Behold a faithful people! Because they believed in the Lord, therefore the Lord freed them and planted them." In the turmoil of the time of Deborah, she states, "the Lord will take pity on you today, not because of you but because of his covenant that he established with your fathers and the oath he has sworn not to abandon you forever" (*LAB* 30.7). In spite of continuing sinfulness, God will be faithful to the covenant made with Abraham and the ancestors. This tradition of the unbroken covenant is a key to Pseudo-Philo.

Pseudo-Philo also lifts up the faith/faithfulness of Abraham. Indeed, Abraham's trust in God is the most distinctive characteristic of Abraham in this account—Abraham knows the one Lord and worships only him (*LAB* 6.4). God's promises and Abraham's faithfulness are brought together in *LAB* 4.11, and it is prophesied that Abraham "will be called perfect and blameless; and he will be the father of nations, and his covenant will not be broken, and his seed will be multiplied forever." Joshua 24:2–3 is paraphrased so as to make it clear that Abraham "believed in me" (23.5), though no specific statement is made that Abraham rejected idolatry.[68]

Unlike Genesis, Pseudo-Philo (*LAB* 6.1–18; 32.1) connects the Tower of Babel story (Gen. 11:1–9) and the call of Abraham from Ur. This linkage is a means by which the author can give strong evidence of Abraham's piety, which in turn prompts the divine calling (Gen. 12:1–3).[69] Genesis 11:3 speaks of the perpetrators making bricks and burning them thoroughly. Connecting this with their interest in making a name for themselves (11:4), *LAB* suggests that they were interested in burning their names (and perhaps the names of their gods) into the bricks. Because of his opposition to this name burning, Abraham was thrown into a fiery furnace (links with the fiery furnace in Daniel 3 have been noted). But Abraham trusted in God (*LAB* 6.11) and did not fear death, and God delivered him unharmed, destroying the perpetrators.[70] Abraham thus repudiates Gentile practices and is faithful to the one God.[71] His descendants are to follow in his steps. It is notable that Abraham is not said to obey the law.

The near-sacrifice of Isaac is retold in *LAB* 32:1–4 (cf. 40.2). The reason for God's command to sacrifice his son is not prompted by God, but by the envy (source unknown) of angels and the "worshiping host." It could be that these divine beings thought that Abraham's faithfulness might be compromised. This reflection is perhaps prompted by the open-ended "after these things" (Gen. 22:1), which could be translated as "after these words," prompting speculation regarding a heavenly dispute. When God does stop Abraham, he explains that this has been done to "shut the mouths of those who are always speaking evil against you" (32.4).

Abraham responded positively and immediately to God's call to sacrifice his son; Abraham then proceeded to tell Isaac what was happening: "I am offering you as a holocaust and am delivering you into the hands that gave you to me" (*LAB* 32.2). Isaac questions his father, yet he becomes a willing victim, thereby playing a significant role in the testing (cf. Jdt. 8:26, God "tested Isaac"; see also 4 Macc. 14.20). Isaac even exclaims that he was born to be offered as a sacrifice to God and that "there will be nothing like this; and about me future generations will be instructed and through me the peoples will understand that the Lord has made the soul of a man worthy to be a sacrifice" (*LAB* 32.3–4). Isaac's offering of himself freely has salutary effects upon subsequent generations. In effect, Isaac is an exemplary martyr. The "one being offered was ready, and the one who was offered was rejoicing" (*LAB* 40.2).[72] The faithfulness of Isaac joins that of his father Abraham.

The test of Abraham occurs as an example to others (*LAB* 32.4). Abraham will be made known "to those who do not know you," presumably, not only Israel but all people. Even more, Abraham's faithful act will benefit Israel, "in return for his blood I chose them" (*LAB* 18.5). In some sense, Israel was chosen by God because of Abraham's faithful response to God's command.

TESTAMENT OF ABRAHAM

The *Testament of Abraham* (100 B.C.E.–200 C.E., with later Christian additions)[73] is not a testament as usually defined and has some characteristics of apocalyptic literature. It can be said to be a mixed genre, which uses humor and irony in getting its message across.[74] It is likely that its present form may be characterized as a Christian revision of a Jewish original, set in Egypt.[75]

The narrative, probably originally written in Greek, is set in the final days of Abraham's life. At this point, God sends the angel Michael to prepare him for death. But Abraham refuses to accept his death, demanding to see the entire inhabited world before he will acquiesce. In his journey across the face of the earth, Abraham sees several wicked deeds and immediately has the perpetrators liquidated. God is concerned that the overzealous Abraham will continue to act without mercy and destroy everyone on earth. Abraham is turned around when he is taken to watch the divine judgment; he observes the mercy of God at work in the judgment of sinners, desiring that all would come to the knowledge of the truth. Abraham repents of his self-righteous sinfulness and is forgiven by God, giving evidence of God's approach to all sinners. At the end of the *Testament*, Abraham dies and is cared for by the angels. Such a vision of the time of passing through death, with its emphasis on divine mercy, was intended to bring comfort and lessen the fear of death. A key point of the *Testament* seems to be: The righteousness and hospitality of Abraham, so emphasized throughout, pales in the recognition of the mercy and hospitality of God to sinners.

The purpose of the *Testament of Abraham* is unclear. On the one hand, it may simply be a story designed to present the final days of a righteous patriarch, friend of God. Others have thought it to be an essay on the crises associated with the final days of the life of anyone approaching death. Allison refers to Death as "the central issue." The "focus on Abraham is ultimately incidental. The patriarch is not, so to speak, his biblical self but rather everyman, the human being faced with death, who is, no matter how pious, anxious about quitting this life."[76] In the end, Abraham "never comes to terms with the fact that death is at hand." But the Testament "copes with death-related anxiety by teaching that death is not the end but instead the beginning of a better existence."[77] Other commentators have thought the work to be an essay on the dangers of self-righteousness.

The *Testament of Abraham* is "one of the few witnesses . . . to the existence in Egypt of a form of Judaism that stressed neither the philosophical interpretation, as did Philo, nor the need to retain the commandments that set Jews apart from gentiles . . . Judaism is depicted here as a religion of commonplace moral values, which nevertheless insists both on the strictness of God's judgment and on his mercy and compassion."[78] The Testament "does not make Scripture the last word but creatively exploits it for novel ends."[79]

Except for basic references to Abraham, little of the material in the *Testament* is correspondent to the Abraham of the Genesis narrative and little is said about Israel or the Jewish people. Regarding God's promises, God's fulfillment of the promise of Isaac is mentioned (6.5) and a review of divine promises and fulfillments occurs in 8.5–7 (cf. 4.11), including the land and the opening of Sarah's womb. Integrated elements reflecting Genesis 12:1 and 17:5 regarding the call and the covenant with Abraham are present (Recension B [hereafter "B"] 2:8–10). God's blessing continues to be in force. God says, "I will give you whatever you ask of me; for I am the Lord your God and besides me there is no other" (8.7).

Regarding Abraham's faith/faithfulness, the language used to speak of him in the *Testament* is remarkably positive.[80] An example of the strong emphasis on the faithfulness of Abraham: "All the years of his life he lived in quietness, gentleness, and righteousness, and the righteous man was very hospitable"; "on equal terms did the entirely holy, righteous, and hospitable Abraham welcome" everyone (*Test. Abr.* 1.1–2; 2.2; 4.6). Genesis 18:1–8 is at least indirectly referenced in illustrating his hospitality (*Test. Abr.* 1–2, 6 and B 6.10–13). At the same time, unlike other biblical images of Abraham (and other contemporary literature), negative features of Abraham are present, including self-centeredness and defiance.[81]

Because of who he was, God calls Abraham "my beloved friend" and is said to "have blessed him as the stars of heaven and as the sand by the seashore" (1.4–6; 4.11). He is called "true friend of the Heavenly One" (2.3), "my true friend" (16.5).[82] "There is no man like him (Abraham) on earth, not even Job" (15.15). Abraham is routinely called "righteous" and "most righteous." In Recension B, a shorter version of *The Testament of Abraham,* this language for Abraham is almost entirely missing (cf. 13.1), for reasons unknown.

APOCALYPSE OF ABRAHAM

This is probably a Jewish work, post 70 C.E., with some Christian interpolations, originally written in Hebrew or Aramaic. The destruction of Jerusalem in 70 C.E. lies in the background. Its theme is "Israel's election and its covenant with God."[83] Israel is the elect of God, a remnant of true believers.

The promises of God to Abraham are not especially featured, but are clearly present, especially in the revelation of *Apocalypse of Abraham* 10:1–17. God reveals God's mysteries to Abraham in the context of his sleep and the darkness related thereto. Abraham's trembling response leads to key revelations about God designed to quell his fear, including: "Abraham friend of God who has loved you . . . I am sent to you to strengthen you and to bless you in the name of God, creator of heavenly and earthly things, who has loved . . . I am sent to you now to bless you and the land . . . prepared for you . . . with me Michael blesses you forever" (*Apoc. Abr.* 10.5–17; 16.3–4). While covenant language is not used, the language clearly reflects God's promises of blessing and land in Genesis 12; 13; 15. These promises are also evident in Abraham's prayer: "Receive me favorably, teach me, show me, and make known to your servant what you have promised me" (*Apoc. Abr.* 17.21). Familiar promises are then extended (20.3–4; cf. 29.17–21).

Regarding the faith/faithfulness of Abraham, chapters 1–8 tell the story of Abraham as a model of the person of faith in the one true God. Abraham is not explicitly associated with obedience of the law (32.4), though he rejects idols and believes in the one true God (primarily imaged as a Creator God). These materials are minimally dependent on the Abrahamic narrative in Genesis (some influence of Ezekiel and 1 Enoch is present). Presented in narrative form, Abraham struggles against idolatrous practices and other evils, strongly promoting worship of the one God and resisting assimilation into the larger (Hellenistic) culture. Not unlike other literature we have noted, the *Apocalypse* develops Joshua 24:2–3, giving details regarding Abraham's struggle against the gods of his father and brother.[84] Terah is an idol maker and worshiper who cannot fathom Abraham's aversion to idolatry. Abraham, who understands that the idols are nothing, seeks to show his father the error of his ways, saying to him: "The gods are blessed in you, because you are a god for them, because you made them" (*Apoc Abr.* 4:3). Drawing inferences from the creation, he witnesses to his father regarding the creator God (*Apoc. Abr.* 7.1–12; cf. *Jub.* 12.4–5, 16–20; *LAB* 6.1–18). The author concludes that Abraham discerns that the idols of Terah are not gods because some of them have been destroyed. As Abraham says, the idols "did not help themselves; how then can they help you or bless me?" (*Apoc. Abr.* 4.3).

Imploring that God be revealed, Abraham receives the word that he is to leave his home (8.1–6; 9.1). It is then that the encounter of Genesis 12:1–3 occurs (*Apoc. Abr.* 8:4). This direction of thought is prompted by God showing Abraham all the stars (Gen. 15:5), an implicit suggestion that the astral deities are to be rejected in favor of the one God. Reflections on the ritual of Genesis 15 attend to the ritual itself, rather than to God's promises (*Apoc. Abr.* 9.1–10; 12–15).

Chapters 9–32 are typical apocalyptic literature, reporting revelatory visions about the future of Israel that Abraham receives on a heavenly journey. Notably, Azazel cannot seduce Abraham or the righteous (*Apoc. Abr.* 13.10–14). Those who are true to the faith of Abraham will be vindicated by God.

SOME GATHERED COMMENTS

First of all, our study of Abraham in Genesis has commonly stressed the significance of the divine promises. It is important to note that this prominent theme has not been neglected in this Jewish literature.[85] In fact, "the promises to Abraham did provide significant common ground for diverse expressions of Jewish faith, and they were a unifying bond for the Jewish people."[86] Jewish theological concerns from this era did not collapse everything of importance into Torah observance, a claim that is at times suggested by the emphasis given to it.

Moreover, consideration of the theme of the faith/faithfulness of Abraham, relatively infrequent in the Old Testament, was not reduced to obedience of the law, as important as the latter was in several texts. Abraham's faith was a gift of God and found its basis in God's action alone, in view of which Abraham's faithfulness worked itself out in his daily life. The points of Abraham's faithfulness that are mentioned include: his love of the Lord, his confession/worship of one God and God the Creator, his enduring trials, including his willingness to offer up his son Isaac, his rejection of idol worship, his repudiation of Gentile practices, his hospitality, and his law observance.[87] As an exemplary man of faith, Abraham became a model for the Jewish community, not least in view of the often difficult times and testings through which it was living in the last two centuries B.C.E.

NEW TESTAMENT

Abraham is explicitly mentioned more times in the New Testament (seventy-two) than any other Old Testament character. The New Testament attends primarily to the twin foci of the Abrahamic tradition we have observed in the Jewish literature, namely, the divine promises and Abraham's faith/faithfulness.[88] In this respect the New Testament is continuous with the depiction of Abraham in the Old Testament and post-exilic Judaism, recognizing that different texts will emphasize one dimension or another of the Abrahamic tradition. This variety of emphases is true of the New Testament itself, as comparisons of, say, Paul, James, and Hebrews demonstrate. But, generally speaking, the promises of God to Abraham are never revoked and Abraham's faith becomes a pillar for the New Testament (especially Pauline) argument that Christians are to be included among the people of God. Islam, in turn, will stress Abraham's rejection of idolatrous practices and stake a claim with respect to his foundational witness to monotheism.

In some cases, as in the Synoptic Gospels, Abraham is referenced in individual texts, but not in sustained argument. At the same time, such a use of the figure of Abraham assumes already existing arguments.[89]

THE GOSPELS

In Matthew the New Testament begins with a claim about the relationship between Jesus and Abraham (Matt. 1:1–2, 17). A genealogical linkage is drawn from "Jesus the Messiah" back through David to Abraham (cf. Luke 3:23–38, where Abraham has a less prominent position). This genealogy seeks to demonstrate that no break exists in the long line from Abraham to Jesus; indeed, Jesus' own identity is marked by this long history of God with the people of Abraham. By this genealogy, Jesus is shown to stand in the line of Abraham, not against Abraham or in place of him. Jesus' Jewishness is thus made clear and stands against any perspective that would reject the literal descendants of Abraham. Matthew 3:7–10, in turn, will claim that being genealogically related to Abraham is not a guarantee of being identified with the people of the God of Abraham (cf. Paul). The "children of Abraham" includes those whom God may choose to raise up, including Gentiles.

Other texts will more explicitly extend the "offspring" of Abraham to include all those who "belong to Christ" (cf. Gal 3:29; 6:16). In the language of Matthew 8:11–12, "Many will come from the east and the west (exemplified in, of all people, a Roman centurion, that is, Gentiles) and will sit at table with Abraham, Isaac, and Jacob in the kingdom of heaven" (Matt. 8:11–12; cf. Luke 13:28–29; Isa. 25:6). It sounds like Abraham is being claimed exclusively for Gentiles. More likely, it is a warning to the Jewish community (they are called "heirs of the kingdom," that is, the elect ones), perhaps especially to the Pharisees (Matt 23:29–36).

The story of Sodom and Gomorrah is referenced in Matthew 10:5; 11:23–24 (cf. Luke 10:12). Jesus, in commissioning the twelve disciples, uses Sodom as a paradigm for disrespect and inhospitality.[90] The disciples are made analogous to the two angels in Genesis 19.

In Mark God's reference to Jesus as "Beloved Son" at his baptism in 1:11 (cf. Matt. 3:17; Luke 3:22) and at the Transfiguration in 9:7 (cf. Matt. 17:5) may be intended to reference the story of the Akedah in Genesis 22:2 (cf. Ps. 2:7; Isa. 42:1). As Isaac was the beloved son of Abraham, so Jesus was the beloved son of God. An Isaac/Christ typology may lie in the background.

In Luke-Acts[91] there are numerous echoes of the Abraham story present in the birth story of Jesus (cf. also the parallels between Sarah and Elizabeth, and the announcement they received in a theophany). Mary's Magnificat (Luke 1:54–55) ends on an Abrahamic note of promise and Zechariah's Benedictus (1:67–79) incorporates Abrahamic motifs (especially the covenantal promises, 1:72–73). These key opening poems, drawn heavily from Old Testament texts, show that God's new thing in Jesus Christ stands in fundamental continuity with God's promises to Israel. At the same time, Jesus addresses common Israelite men and women with language that identifies them as belonging to the family of Abraham: daughter of Abraham, son of Abraham (13:15–16; 19:9–10). Such a perspective stands over against any idea of divine rejection of the Israelites per se.

In the parable of Lazarus and the rich man, Abraham plays a significant role (16:19–31). After his death Lazarus, a poor Israelite, rests in the "bosom of Abraham," while the rich man is in a place of torment. The rich man tries to get Abraham to intercede for him, but Abraham refuses him, even to warn those still alive. Abraham here becomes an authoritative voice on behalf of the eminently available word of God in Jesus.

In the book of Acts, Abraham is mentioned exclusively in sermons. In Peter's sermon (Acts 3:11–26) the God who is present and active in Jesus is initially identified as "The God of Abraham and of Isaac and of Jacob, the God of our fathers" (3:13; cf. Luke 20:37). It is this same God who raised Jesus from the dead. Peter claims that his hearers stand in the tradition of God's covenant with Abraham, but, potentially, the entire human race are potential participants in the benefits of this covenant. Genesis 12:3 is used to ground the point regarding the inclusion of Gentiles in the community of faith, since God said that "in your posterity shall all the families of the earth be blessed" (3:25; cf. Gal 3:8). God has sent his messengers to the literal descendants of Abraham first of all (3:26). Jesus is the basis upon which their participation in God's purpose is to be determined.

Stephen's speech recounting Israel's history (Acts 7:1–53) stresses the role of Abraham and God's promises to him. God's call of Abraham (Gen. 12:1) occurred while he was still in Mesopotamia (Gen. 15:7) and Abraham left and settled in

Haran. God promised Abraham a land, but it would be fully possessed only by his descendants (Acts 7:5). There would be significant delays in fulfillment, including a time of slavery, but the oppressor would be judged by God and Israel would worship God in the land of Canaan (Acts 7:6–7; reflecting Gen. 15:13–16). The promise was reaffirmed to Abraham, and his response to the covenant was given concrete expression in circumcision (Acts 7:8). It is stressed not only that Abraham became the father of Isaac, but also circumcised him (Acts 7:9). Details regarding Abraham's purchase of a burial place from the sons of Hamor in Shechem reflect a different tradition from that in Genesis 23:1–20.

In Acts 13:13–52 Paul addresses his audience as "descendants of Abraham's family"(13:26). God has in Christ brought about the promises given to the ancestors (13:23–32). Paul declares that God's people have not comprehended the full range of what God promised to the ancestors, but that God has fulfilled those promises in Jesus. The extension of the promises to the Gentiles is not a change in God's promises, but the culmination of those very promises.

John 8 is the only text in which Abraham appears in this gospel (John 8:33–58). Jews claim that they are descendants of Abraham (8:31–37), which Jesus acknowledges. But Jesus disputes that they are children of Abraham (8:39–40), for Abraham would never have done what they are seeking to do: kill Jesus. Hence the sharp reference to them being the children of the devil (8:42–44). In their challenge to Jesus with regard to his claim that he is greater than Abraham, Jesus responds that before Abraham was, he was. Jesus' pre-existence with God seems to relativize the place of Abraham. At the same time, Abraham rejoiced in that he would see the day of Christ (John 8:56; perhaps a positive interpretation of Abraham's laughter in Gen. 17:17). It is unlikely that John's argument reduces the stature of Abraham or Israel, especially in view of the claim that salvation does "come from the Jews" (John 4:22). At the same time, the harsh language has problematized ongoing relationships between Christians and Jews.[92]

PAULINE LITERATURE

Central to Paul's consideration[93] of Abraham is the way in which he uses Scripture, particularly Genesis texts, and especially Genesis 15:6 ("Abraham believed God, and it was reckoned to him as righteousness"; in Rom 4:3, 9, 22–24; Gal 3:6).[94] Paul uses the Scriptures as paradigm. And so, the word of Genesis 15:6 was not written for Abraham's sake alone, but for ours as well (Rom. 4:23–24; cf. 1 Cor. 9:10); "whatever was written in former days was written for our instruction," not just theirs (Rom. 15:4; cf. 1 Cor. 10:11).[95] Just as the Scriptures described the essentials of the relationship with God then, so that is also the case now. Just as God reckoned Abraham's faith to him as righteousness then (Gen. 15:6), so is that also the case with Christians who live by faith now. Just as God's promises to Abraham included Gentiles then, so also do they include Gentiles in the present. We look briefly at how Paul works this out.

Except for a word identifying himself as one who belongs to Israel, in terms of both genealogical and religious heritage (1 Cor. 11:22; cf. Rom. 11:1), Paul's references to Abraham occur only in Romans and Galatians (especially Rom. 4; Gal. 3–4). In these texts, Paul makes a theologically significant distinction between (the time of) Abraham and Moses. That is to say, Paul links Christian faith to the faith of Abraham and especially to the promises of God extended to Abraham, which occurred prior to his circumcision and the giving of the law to Moses at Mt. Sinai (Gal. 3:17). Ironically, Paul may have learned this move from Moses himself, who moved in time back over the broken covenant of Sinai to make an appeal to God's promises to Abraham (Exod. 32:13). Even in the wake of the idolatry of the golden calf, Moses understood that God's promises to the ancestors were still in place. As Abraham was the key to Moses' argument, so was Abraham also the key to Paul's argument.

When Paul introduces Abraham in both Romans 4 and Galatians 3–4, he immediately refers to Genesis 15:6 (Gal. 3:6 and Rom. 4:3; cf. James 2:23). Paul thereby seeks to make his case directly from Scripture, indeed the Torah itself. Even more, he uses the pre-Moses/Sinai law Abrahamic tradition to make a key point: God makes Abraham righteous (and by implication, all persons) on the basis of faith apart from circumcision (and prior to it, Rom. 4:10–12) and other works of law. As is evident immediately in the story of Abraham (Gen. 12:2–4), God's gracious promises generate Abraham's response to God's command, though not irresistibly so; Genesis 15:4–6 also makes it clear that the prior word of promise creates Abraham's faith. God observes Abraham's faith and declares that Abraham is righteous. Reflecting the language of Galatians 3:6–7, Paul "wants to argue that Judaism itself, rightly understood, claims its relation to Abraham not by virtue of physical descent from him" ("according to the flesh"), but "by virtue of sharing [Abraham's] trust in the God who made the promises."[96] Hence, the point: God, who acts consistently, will also justify Gentiles who have faith. Abraham, who was also a Gentile, is the father of all who have faith (cf. Eph. 2:8–10).

Key concerns of Paul are not only to ground the inclusion of Gentiles within the fulfillment of the Abrahamic promise (long a Jewish practice), but more basically, how they can be so included. Do they need to be circumcised first or not? And so Paul argues that the Torah itself claims in its repeated articulation of God's promises that Abraham is to be the "ancestor of a multitude of nations" (citing Gen. 17:5 and 15:5 in Rom. 4:17–18). Citing also Genesis 12:3; 18:18; 22:18 in Galatians 3:8, "all the Gentiles shall be blessed in you," Paul argues that Gentiles are included among the recipients of the divine promises. In sum, from the beginning of the history of God's people in the person of Abraham, God's promises

included Gentiles. And what God has promised will come to pass. Such a maxi-
malist sense of inclusion in the people of God has been God's intent all along,
throughout the history of Israel (and that point necessitates no particular Christological reading). As such, Paul stresses the long articulated universal dimension
of the faith of Abraham. Whenever the families of the earth are blessed, Genesis
12:3 (and parallels) is fulfilled, becoming a powerful reality in the life of the
world.

In view of these promises, Abraham is the forefather of more than the physical
descendants of Abraham. The promises of God cannot be reduced to genetics
(Rom. 4:16–25; Gal. 3:6–9).[97] Those who have faith in the God of Abraham are
recipients of the promises irrespective of biological succession. Like faithful Jews,
the Gentiles receive the promises by faith alone. "Those who believe are the children of Abraham" (Gal. 3:6–7), whether Jew or Gentile (Gal. 3:28; Rom. 3:29;
4:10–12). Paul does not stake a claim for a "new faith" for Christians, it is the
same faith that Abraham had, and like him, Christians can entrust their life to God
with confidence that their faith will be reckoned as righteousness. To be a child of
Abraham was not now made exclusive to Christians. All who have faith in Abraham's God are (still) children of Abraham (Rom. 4:12). God's promises to Abraham are Paul's way of linking those who have faith in Christ with the long history
of the faith of the people Israel.

Paul addresses himself further to the continuing place of the Jews in the divine
economy in Romans 9–11.[98] Paul asks the direct question: "Has God rejected his
people? By no means!" (Rom. 11:1). Paul uses his own standing as a "descendant
of Abraham" to conclude that "God has not rejected his people whom he
foreknew" (11:2). Indeed, to Israel belongs "the adoption, the glory, the covenants,
the giving of the law, the worship, and the promises; to them belong the patriarchs,
and from them, according to the flesh, comes the Messiah who is over all" (Rom.
9:4–5). As "regards election they are beloved, for the sake of their ancestors; for
the gifts and the calling of God are irrevocable" (11:28–29; see also the "call" language in 9:11–12). These claims make it clear that the ancestral promises have not
been revoked, and persons of faith in the Jewish community continue to be identified in terms of Abraham, Isaac, and Jacob.

At the same time, "not all of Abraham's descendants are his true descendants"
(Rom. 9:7); some have rejected the God of promise, so Paul speaks of a "remnant"
of the people of God (Rom. 11:5; cf. 9:27).[99] Citing Genesis 21:12 ("It is through
Isaac that descendants shall be named [called] for you"), and linking the point to
God's promise of Isaac in Genesis 18:10, 14 (God "will return, and Sarah shall
have a son"), Isaac (rather than Ishmael) is seen to be God's specific and free
choice of the son who will bear the promise.[100] Isaac thus becomes a key figure for
Paul to argue that God is free (9:15–18) to extend the "call" to those who are not

literally descended from Abraham, those who are "not from the Jews only but also from the Gentiles" (9:24, citing the "call" of Hosea 11:1; 2:23 in support).[101] The story of God's choice of Abraham's son Isaac is a prefigurement of God's choice of the children of God in every generation.[102] Those who believe are children of Abraham and "children of the promise, like Isaac" (Gal. 4:28).

The Pauline argument we have sketched to this point has been intentionally free of explicit Christological references. In this we have followed the argument in Romans 4; the only such reference comes in 4:24–25 (and even then the focus is on faith in God). Romans 11 is also without such reference and Romans 9 as well (after the introduction). The basic Pauline argument, using Old Testament texts, has not necessitated explicit Christological reference. But such a reference does, finally, have a crucial place. The Pauline word in Romans 3:21–26 brings to the discussion an explicit and central Christological focus, "the righteousness of God through faith in Jesus Christ for all who believe . . . they are now justified by his grace as a gift, through the redemption that is in Jesus Christ." Only in Christ has the universal promise of God to Abraham been made available to all (Gal. 3:13–14). Galatians 3:26–29 states the matter succinctly: "And if you belong to Christ, then you are Abraham's offspring, heirs according to the promise." To be in Christ is to be a child of Abraham. To be a descendant of Abraham is now interpreted in a new way, not in denying a place for faithful Jews, but through an expansion of an already existing trajectory of understanding, that is, through faith in the promising God in view of the work of Jesus Christ (see the tree and branches image in Rom. 11:17–24).

Yet, it might be argued that Galatians 3:16 makes Christ the only offspring of Abraham and that that disinherits Israel (unless they become Christians). Galatians 3:16 quotes Genesis 17:7, appealing to "seed" as singular rather than plural, understanding that the promise looked forward specifically to the Christ (probably linked to the singular "seed" of David in 2 Sam. 7:12–14). In view of Galatians 3:17, Paul's argument seems to be a way of countering his opponents who use literal descendance from Abraham in their arguments about the priority of the law— most basically, circumcision—over the promise (could not Paul have translated "seed" as a collective noun to make the same point?). For the promise came long before the law and the promise remains in effect quite apart from the obedience or disobedience of the law (see above). Abraham's faith and the promise are the decisive matters, not the law, though the latter remains important (Gal. 3:19–22; Rom. 4:13). Again, Galatians 3:26–29 completes the argument: If you are Christ's, then you are Abraham's "seed" (because Christ was), heirs according to promise. This usage of "seed" in 3:29 makes clear that the "seed" of 3:16 is not meant by Paul to be interpreted in the sense of a singular descendant, but in a representative sense (this would also be shown by the use of the plural "sons" in Gal. 3:7, "those who believe are the descendants of Abraham").[103] Because Gentile Christians have put on Christ in baptism (Gal. 3:27), they have become united with him and hence they participate in his inheritance and his destiny.[104]

Yet, difficulties remain in the nature of the argument regarding a singular "seed" (commonly associated with rabbinical exegesis). The phrase "throughout their generations" in Genesis 17:7 makes it clear that "seed" is the collective "progeny," a reference to the entire people of Israel (and, hence, has at least a literal sense).[105] Paul would certainly have understood that Jews are the literal descendants of Abraham, and while a fulfillment of God's promise cannot be understood simply in genetic terms, in other texts we have noted above, Paul does not exclude faithful Jews from participating in the promises.

Paul's theological moves would not have been surprising in view of the texts we have observed from the Deuterocanonical and Pseudepigraphical literature.[106] While Paul sharpens and intensifies the argument, he does not differ from (at least many of) his Jewish forebears regarding the priority of Abraham's faithfulness and God's promises (and not obedience of the law). We have seen that Paul takes pains to ground his understanding in the Genesis text. That Genesis text itself speaks of Abraham's obedience of the law (Gen. 26:4–5, which is a summary statement) without compromising the claims of promise and faith in Genesis 15:4–6. To affirm the former text about obedience does not stand in contradiction to the latter text, which, in turn, does not set faith over against "works." "Works" do not become irrelevant for Paul (Rom. 2:7–8, 13; 3:31; 13:8–10;15:27; Gal. 3:19–22). Rather, Paul claims in 1 Corinthians 7:19 that, "obeying the commandment of God is everything," and in Galatians 5:6, "the only thing that counts is faith working through love" (cf. Rom. 7:14). "Works" are essential to the Christian life, but they must be properly related to the centrality of God's promises and the faith in view of which God makes righteous.

Paul's particular context seems important here (as well as the contexts of the Jewish literature, as far as they are known). In his argumentation, Paul likely has Jewish Christians primarily in mind, not Jews per se.[107] Paul may seek to counter the claims of his opponents in Galatia and the "weak" in Romans, whose scrupulosity regarding Torah observance exhibited a misunderstanding regarding the relationship of law and gospel in the life of the Christian (Rom 14:1–15:6). The issue is not that these opponents of Paul attend to the law per se, but the relationship they see between law and gospel. Paul's rivals had appealed to Abraham's obedience of the law in their claim that obedience to the law, especially circumcision, was essential for incorporation into the people of God. But, as we have seen, for Paul Abraham's faith was decisive for inclusion in the community before he was circumcised (Rom. 4:9–12) and before the law was given.[108] Obedience of the law, important as it is, did not have saving power for Abraham nor was it a necessary "add-on" to faith; righteousness came to him and comes to all (whether circum-cised or uncircumcised) only through faith, which has been generated by the pro-mises of God, not the laws of God (Rom. 4:13–16; Gal. 5:2–12; 6:12–15).

Finally, we touch on Paul's complex argument in Galatians 4:21–5:1.[109] In call-ing this interpretation "allegory" (Gal. 4:24), Paul proposes a meaning of the text that is more than a surface reading suggests. More specifically, this interpretive move is designed to show a correspondence between the "then" of the text and the "now" of Paul's audience. On the one hand, Hagar gave birth to Ishmael in natu-ral, humanly conceived ways, that is, the way of law (Gen. 16:1–4); on the other hand, Sarah gave birth to Isaac only as an "impossible" gift of God's promise (Gen. 17:19, 21; 18:14; 21:1–7). As such, Hagar and Sarah symbolize "two covenants," two different ways of conceiving the life of faith.[110] That is, Hagar (the slave-girl) is the way of slavery and law (that is, the bilateral Sinai covenant, in which obe-dience of the law was an obligatory dimension). She corresponds to the present Jerusalem, that is, those among Paul's contemporaries who consider obedience of the law necessary for God's making righteous.[111] On the other hand, Sarah is the way of promise and the freedom of the Spirit (the unilateral Abrahamic covenant in which God's promises create faith). She corresponds to the Jerusalem above, that is, the new age, wherein the understanding of faith as God oriented and God generated will be made manifest.[112] Christians, then, are "children of promise, like Isaac" (4:28) who live by faith, while Paul's opponents are enslaved to the neces-sity of law observance.[113]

From another angle, Hagar could have been used by Paul as the embodiment of his argument, with her combination of necessity (her return to Sarah at God's behest, Gen. 16:9) and her freedom from the oppressive household of Sarah and Abraham (Hagar's affliction is recognized by God in Genesis 16:11 and, while she returns as slave, she is eventually freed and graciously cared for by God (Gen. 21:15–21).[114] Even more, Paul's word in Galatians 3:28–29 that there is neither slave nor free, but that all are one in Christ Jesus, could provide another perspec-tive on Hagar, who bears public witness to the God of Abraham and Sarah, and uniquely in the Bible provides a new name for God (Gen. 16:13).

JAMES

The discussion of Abraham in the Letter of James (2:14–26) may have been writ-ten to oppose an antinomianism that would diminish, or discount altogether, the importance of works on the part of those who have faith.[115] In response, James seeks to show that faith is inseparable from works; indeed, works are the indis-pensable fruit of true faith. Most scholars understand that James was not directly reacting to Paul, for James does not speak of obedience to Jewish law (such as cir-cumcision, Sabbath, and food laws).[116] Rather, he speaks of acts of mercy (James

2:13–16). This difference makes it difficult to compare Paul and James. James grounds this call to mercy in the commandment "You shall love your neighbor as yourself" (2:8; cf. Lev. 19:18); to do acts of mercy is what love of neighbor looks like (1 John 3:17–18). This text is used also by Paul in Romans 13:8–10 to indicate what love of neighbor does not look like, while Romans 12:9–21 gives some positive examples. There seems not to be much space, if any, between James and Paul on this point.

Paul and James can also be compared at another point, if only indirectly. James 1:22 states: "But be doers of the word and not merely hearers who deceive themselves." This verse echoes Paul in Romans 2:13, "For it is not the hearers of the law who are righteous in God's sight, but the doers of the law [if they could do so] who will be justified." Romans 3:20 makes it clear that human beings, sinful as they are, cannot be justified by works of law (cf. 3:28; Gal. 2:16). Does James 2:21, 24–25, then, in effect, contest this point? "Was not our ancestor Abraham [and Rahab] justified by works when he offered his son Isaac on the altar?" It seems unlikely in view of James 2:22–24, where Abraham's faith clearly precedes, and therefore is "active along with," this "work"; Abraham's already existent faith was "brought to completion" by his "work" of offering up Isaac (a text not referenced by Paul). The assumption is that this key "work" of Abraham was possible (only) because Abraham was a person of faith.[117]

It is likely that James, by giving the example of the near-sacrifice of Isaac, has Genesis 22:15–18 particularly in mind (as does 1 Macc. 2:52; Sir 44:19). Therein God twice states that "because" Abraham has not withheld his only son, the promises, earlier given, continue to be applicable. The promises were originally given independently of Abraham's response (Gen. 12:1–3; 15:4–5); this ordering of God's promises and Abraham's faith is not being reversed in Genesis 22:15–18.[118] But it is not unimportant that Abraham could have rejected the divine command (if not, the test was irrelevant) and perhaps removed himself from the sphere of promise (we don't know what would have happened, but it is conceivable that God would have had to begin again). One claim that seems to be made is that the passing on of the faith to the next generation is not a matter of genetics (an important point for Paul as well). James seems to acknowledge this point by quoting Genesis 15:6 and by making reference to the tradition of Abraham as "friend" of God (James 2:23; Isa. 41:8; 2 Chron. 20:7; also common in Jewish literature as noted above). Abraham could have rejected God's promises in 15:4–5; the fact that he didn't (Gen. 15:6) makes that situation parallel to that in Genesis 22.

One other possible angle on the use of the Abrahamic tradition by James relates to the use of "righteousness (tṣedeqah)" in Genesis 18:19. Abraham is to "keep the way of the Lord by doing righteousness and justice; so that the Lord may bring about for Abraham what he has promised him." The word "righteousness" in Genesis (and the Old Testament) can mean either "being in a right relationship with God" (Gen. 15:6) or "doing righteousness" (Gen. 18:19). And so Abraham, by doing justice to an already existing righteous relationship in which he stands, and not rejecting that, demonstrates that he is righteous. James may have the latter text in mind in quoting the former. In any case, James focuses not on faith per se but on doing justice in daily life on the part of one who has faith. Faith is to issue in a shape for life that is correspondent to the relationship with God in which one stands.[119]

HEBREWS

Hebrews is a letter of exhortation, addressed to second generation Christians where a diminished commitment to the Christian faith is perceived to be threatening the community. One strategy that Hebrews uses to address this situation is to link the Christian community with the long history of Israel, which similarly and often faced such times. Jesus Christ is understood to be the culmination of this long history, indeed the history of creation, which is now to be interpreted through a Christological lens (Heb. 1:1–2). At the same time, Israel's history is not to be set aside; its Scriptures are to be made newly available to the Christian community for reflection and insight.[120]

Abraham is mentioned by Hebrews in several contexts (2:16; 6:13–15; 7:1–10; 11:8–19). The primary ways in which the Abrahamic texts are appropriated relate to the priestly order of Melchizedek, God's promises to Abraham, and the exemplary faith of Abraham.

Hebrews 6:13–15 and 7:1–10 speak of the figure of Abraham in connection with the Melchizedek of Genesis 14:18–20 and Psalm 110:4 and the divine promises to Abraham. He is a mysterious figure whose origin is not recorded; his standing for Abraham is as a priest-king of Salem who blesses him and to whom Abraham gives a tithe of the spoils of war. Basically, the argument of Hebrews runs like this: Abraham (and, by implication, his descendant Aaron, father of the Levitical priesthood) acknowledged the primacy of Melchizedek and his priesthood through the giving of a tithe. Hence, Jesus Christ, who belongs to the priestly order of Melchizedek, reaches back beyond Aaron's priesthood and, in effect, relativizes it. This establishes Abrahamic, pre-Israelite priesthood roots for Christ's priesthood, thereby exhibiting its preeminence. Hebrews uses Melchizedek (and Abraham) with respect to Jesus in ways not unlike Psalm 110 does for the United Monarchy.

Hebrews 6:12 encourages readers to be "imitators of those who through faith and patience inherit the promises." This verse prompts, among other things, the references to Abraham that follow. First, Hebrews 6:13–20 emphasizes God's promises to Abraham, which the readers (and the persons of faith in Heb. 11) inherit. The divine promises noted in Hebrews 6:13 ("I will surely bless you and multiply you") specifically recall Genesis 22:16–18, where, notably, the promises are "sworn" to Abraham for the first time. Hebrews 6:17–18 picks up on both the promises and the oath and repeatedly speaks of both as "unchangeable," concerning which "it is impossible that God would prove false."

These unchangeable promises to Abraham must be related to Hebrews 8:13, where the "first" (that is, Sinai) covenant is called "obsolete" (after a lengthy quotation of the new covenant text from Jer. 31:31–34). This reference to obsolescence is often called supersessionist, but mistakenly so.[121] The quotation of Genesis 22:16–18 cited in Hebrews 6:13–20 makes clear that the promises of God to Abraham are not changeable, and hence the word to readers of Hebrews is similar to the word of Paul in Romans 11:29 (see above for discussion): those who have been recipients of this Abrahamic promise remain the people of God. No negative conclusions regarding the relationship of the Jewish people to God should be drawn. The relationship between these promises to Abraham and the "obsolete" Sinai covenant could be understood in terms not unlike that stated above regarding Exodus 32:13. That is, even though the Sinai covenant is broken or obsolete, God's promises to Abraham remain, and to those promises the faithful (Heb. 11) could cling. In this light, the formulation in Hebrews regarding the new covenant could well mean that Christians are now drawn into the new relationship with God of which Jeremiah 31 speaks, not unlike the manner in which Paul speaks of being grafted into the vine (Rom. 11).

The second anticipation of Abraham in Hebrews 6:12 ("imitators of those who through faith and patience inherit the promises") is picked up in Hebrews 11:8–19 (see the summary statement in 11:39–40). In Hebrew 11, the entire history of Israel is read as a history of faith, which is understood as basic to Israel's long relationship with God. This history of faith has not been set aside as a source of reflection on faith and life for Christians. Jesus, "the pioneer and perfecter of our faith" (12:2), stands at the apex of this tradition of faith. As such, Jesus is not the starting point for what the life of faith entails; rather, he stands in continuity with the faithful ones of Israel and shows decisively what the life of faith truly entails.

Abraham is seen to be a major example of faithfulness, a key figure in a "cloud of witnesses" (12:1). About one-third of Hebrews 11 is devoted to a rehearsal of Abraham's life of faith in view of the promise. Abraham believes in God without having any concrete evidence that God's promise would come to pass (Heb. 11:1, 8–12). Generally, his life is characterized as a journey of faith; he is called a "stranger and a foreigner" wherever he goes (11:13; echoing Gen. 23:4; Acts 7:2–5). Its unfinished character is sharply noted. This journey is such that he does not arrive at its promised destination in this life; in faith he is always "looking forward" (11:10) and not looking back (11:15). He is one who faithfully lived even though he did not experience the fulfillment of God's promises to him ("without having received the promises," Heb. 11:13, 39). God's promises to Abraham constitute a continuing reality for him and are specifically cited in Hebrews 11:12 and 11:18.[122]

The phrase "by faith" occurs four times in the Abrahamic portion of the chapter. All four instances cite particularly difficult situations in his life. In two instances, "by faith" has reference to his long and difficult stay in the land of promise (11:9, 11) and his trusting in God's promise of descendants in a time of old age and the barrenness of Sarah (11:11; Rom. 4:19). In the other two instances, Abraham obeyed God's command because he had faith, both in his initial leaving of home and family and in his willingness to offer up Isaac (11:8, 17). Interestingly, these two texts are made parallel in Genesis (cf. 12:1; 22:2). Faith enabled his obedience; obedience follows from faith. In the second instance, Abraham's faith is connected closely with his "consideration" of God's ability to raise people from the dead (11:19). The theme of resurrection, particularly in view of the fact that Isaac did not return with his father, is a theme available also in Jewish sources.[123] Such "considerations" means that Abraham's faith is not understood to be "blind," pursued in isolation from thoughtful reflection.

The story of the pilgrimage of Abraham has been overlaid with indirect references to other persons of faith, and so has become a metaphor for the Christian life. It is a journey that reaches out toward a promised future, but which comes up short of final fulfillment within one's own lifetime. There are signs of that future along the way—indeed God regularly provides blessings for the journey. But persons of faith will realize that there is no time when hope becomes obsolete, for "here we have no lasting city" (Heb. 13:14). The "better country" (Heb. 11:16) will remain stretched out before readers until their dying day, as it did for Abraham.

ABRAHAM IN ISLAM

The legacy of Abraham includes not only Jews and Christians, but also Muslims, who track their descendance through Abraham, Hagar, and Ishmael. That this reality is basically a spiritual heritage is evident in that over 80 percent of Muslims in the world are not of Arabian descent.[124] That all three religions hold the Abrahamic tradition dear should assist us in our continuing conversations with one another.[125] For this conversation to be maximally helpful, however, greater knowledge of Abrahamic texts on the part of the adherents of all three religions will be necessary.

Abraham has a prominent role in the Qur'an, second only to Moses.[126] The Qur'an contains some 250 references to the Abrahamic tradition in twenty-five (of 114) suras. Unlike Genesis, the storyline is neither sequential nor as detailed. Some Quranic texts regarding Abraham have biblical parallels; others do not.

Some of the latter texts do have parallels in Deuterocanonical/Pseudepigraphical texts (see above).

Abraham is presented throughout the Qur'an as "the first true believer and the prototypical Muslim," who "possessed the quality of submission (islam) to the will of Allah which is essential for true belief."[127] As the Qur'an itself puts it, "Truly, Abraham was a model of virtue, obedient to Allah, upright, and not one of those who associate [with shirk]" (Sura 16:120). Indeed, Abraham was "mild, tender, and repentant" (11:75). Following in the biblical tradition, Abraham is "friend of Allah" (4:125; cf. Isa. 41:8).[128] Abraham is praised by the Qur'an as one who, even under threat, is unalterably opposed to idolatry and to those who practice it, and who introduces reforms related thereto. Abraham is thereby presented as a model for all believers (6:75–84; 14:37; 19:41–50; 21:51–75; 26:69–104).[129] As the exem- ‑ plary practitioner of pure monotheism, Abraham stands prior to Judaism, Christianity, and Islam, and shows the way for the adherents of all three religions. As such, Abraham is universalized as the ideal believer.

Ishmael plays a more prominent role in the Qur'an than in the Old Testament; for example, he is engaged in the establishment of monotheism and the Islamic community, and in building the house of Allah (Ka'ba).[130] At the same time, the ‑ Qur'an does not claim that God prefers one son over the other; generally in the Qur'an, covenant language does not occur nor is the idea of a chosen people present. Indeed, the Qur'an contains no division between the two sons, either as ‑ individuals or as the progenitors of differing religious communities.[131] Several comparative textual notes help us discern key features of the Islamic interpretation of the Abrahamic story.[132]

The Call of Abraham

That Abraham makes a clean break from his idolatrous family roots is evident in both Bible and Qur'an (Josh. 24:2–3). Stories regarding Abraham's rejection of idolatry are also found in the Jewish tradition (for example, Jdt. 5:6–10; Jub. 11–12). Correspondences between Abraham and Muhammad's early life are often cited (for example, destruction of idols), as well as their linkage to several traditional Muslim practices (for example, pilgrimage rituals, building the Ka'ba).[133] Abraham even prays for the coming of Muhammad.

Genesis 18–19

This story of an angelic visitation to Abraham is presented in compressed form, with a number of different details and emphases (Sura 11:69–82).[134] The Qur'an exhibits a strong emphasis upon the sovereignty of Allah. As a result, only passing reference is given to the interchange in Genesis 18:22–33 between Allah and Abraham over the fate of the cities (which are not named), with a focus on positive human response to punctuated divine commands. The human characters "come across as submissive figures who model perfectly the attitude of the ideal believer, and Allah is the omniscient, omnipotent presence who is totally in charge of events and deserves such submission."[135] The sexual relationship between Lot and his daughters (Gen. 19:30–38) is missing, Sarah's laughing response to God in Genesis 18:12–15 is diminished, and Lot is presented as a pious and faithful believer (as is Lot's wife, whose fate is determined by the will of Allah, not her own).

The Akedah

The Quranic treatment of the near sacrifice of Abraham's son (37:100–112) exhibits little narrative detail (for example, lack of reference to a journey, the place of sacrifice, the wielding of the knife). Moreover, the Qur'an does not certainly identify the son of Abraham involved.[136] The son was identified as Isaac early on in Quranic interpretation; now most Muslim thinkers identify him as Ishmael. Most important for the Qur'an is that Abraham was faithful in following God's command. In Sura 37:103, both father and son "submitted" themselves to Allah, but only after Isaac interprets Abraham's dream of a divine command. Upon waking from this dream, Abraham asks the son: "What do you think of that?" (37:102). The son then sets the direction for the story that follows. This theme of the faith of both father and son is also common in Jewish literature (see above).

Jon Levenson responds to recent efforts regarding the place of Abraham in the three religions in a helpful way. Generally, he states that "efforts to refashion Abraham in the image of the religions that claim him have been the norm and not the exception. Thus has the first patriarch of Genesis become a Torah-observant Jew before Moses, a man of Christian faith before Jesus, and a Muslim prophet before Muhammad."[137] Levenson responds particularly to the analysis of Kuschel, who seeks to move beyond common articulations of the significance of Abraham in the three religious traditions and find an underlying unity.[138] For Levenson, the underlying unity is not as evident as Kuschel thinks, for in emphasizing Abraham's "dedicated trust," he still sounds like a "Protestant Christian Abraham" for whom faith is decisive.[139] To claim that "dedicated trust" is the center would not be accepted by either Jew or Muslim. For another example, Kuschel ignores the interpretation of Abraham as one who was Torah observant (Gen. 26:5). For Levenson, "there is no master category in which Abraham can be viewed; there is no vantage point independent of the three religions that call him father that those traditions can adopt. Abraham's particularism is indeed stubborn and persistent, and efforts to ignore or circumvent it cannot succeed." This is the case because "the material about Abraham in the Hebrew Bible is so elusive, so enigmatic, so suggestive, and so nondidactic."[140] Levenson wisely asks that we steer between mutual contempt and cultural relativism, with its attendant leveling of ultimate differences, and recognize that Christian and Jewish (and Muslim?) traditions "have within them notes that develop fully only in the other community, thus providing a basis for empathy without homogenization."[141]

The Genesis text does say that the line of Isaac is chosen by God for "covenant" rather than that of Ishmael (Gen. 17:19, 21). This divine choice is a strong claim, not to be neglected. At the same time, it must be remembered that the descendants of Ishmael are also recipients of God's promises. That occasions a sharper question for Isaac's descendants than if the Genesis treatment had been more "even-handed": does the phenomenal growth of this side of Abraham's family over the centuries mean that God has been faithful to promises made to Hagar/Ishmael? How are the other members of Abraham's family going to relate to these brothers and sisters in ways that acknowledge and honor these divine promises? From another angle, those who honor the Genesis texts must remember that Abraham was chosen so that all families might be blessed through him. At the least, − this means that the children of Abraham, who are also the children of Isaac, are to so comport themselves that blessing rather than curse comes upon the nations, including the descendants of Ishmael.

ABBREVIATIONS

BR	*Bible Review*
BTB	*Biblical Theology Bulletin*
CBQ	*Catholic Biblical Quarterly*
CC	*Christian Century*
CurTM	*Currents in Theology and Mission*
EvQ	*Evangelical Quarterly*
ExpTim	*Expository Times*
FOTL	*Forms of Old Testament Literature*
GKC	*Gesenius' Hebrew Grammar.* Edited and enlarged by E. Kautzsch. Translated by A. E. Cowley. 2nd ed. Oxford / New York: Oxford University Press, 1910; reprinted, Oxford, 1966.
HBT	*Horizons in Biblical Theology*
HTR	*Harvard Theological Review*
IDB	*The Interpreter's Dictionary of the Bible.* 4 vols. and supplementary volume. Nashville: Abingdon, 1962, 1976.
JAAR	*Journal of the American Academy of Religion*
JAOS	*Journal of the American Oriental Society*
JB	Jerusalem Bible
JBL	*Journal of Biblical Literature*
JBQ	Jewish Bible Quarterly
JPS	Jewish Publication Society Hebrew-English Tanakh
JSOT	*Journal for the Study of the Old Testament*
JSOTSup	*Journal for the Study of the Old Testament: Supplement Series*
JSS	*Journal of Semitic Studies*
JTS	*Journal of Theological Studies*
KJV	King James Version
LXX	Septuagint
MT	Masoretic Text
NCB	New Century Bible
NEB	New English Bible
NIB	The New Interpreter's Bible
NICOT	The New International Commentary on the Old Testament
NIV	New International Version
NJB	New Jerusalem Bible
NRSV	New Revised Standard Version

NTS	New Testament Studies
OBT	Overtures to Biblical Theology
OTL	Old Testament Library
RSV	Revised Standard Version
SJOT	*Scandinavian Journal of the Old Testament*
SJT	Scottish Journal of Theology
TDOT	Theological Dictionary of the Old Testament. Edited by G. Johannes Botterweck et al. Grand Rapids, Mich.: Eerdmans, 1974– .
TS	*Theological Studies*
USQR	*Union Seminary Quarterly Review*
Vg.	Vulgate
VT	*Vetus Testamentum*
WBC	Word Biblical Commentary
W&W	*Word and World*
ZAW	*Zeitschrift für die alttestamentliche Wissenschaft*

NOTES

PREFACE

1. Though prior to Gen. 17:1–8, Abraham is spelled Abram, I will use Abraham throughout.

2. Note the number of publications since 1980, and especially since 1990, in the bibliography.

3. Hagar is also mentioned in Gal. 4:24–25 (see below, last chapter).

4. The reference in Gen. 15:7 to God bringing Abraham from Ur of the Chaldeans to Canaan probably does not have reference to his call, but to God's providential guiding of this family in its journeys.

5. See also Deuterocanonical and Pseudepigraphical sources as well as the Qur'an.

6. See discussion below.

7. Though somewhat problematic, I use the language of "outsider" for all those who do not belong to the line of promise through Abraham and Sarah, the "insiders." See especially the discussion in Hemchand Gossai, *Power and Marginality in the Abraham Narrative* (Lanham, Md.: University Press, 1995), passim; Frank A. Spina, *The Faith of the Outsider: Exclusion and Inclusion in the Biblical Story* (Grand Rapids, Mich.: Eerdmans, 2005), 1–13.

8. On blessing, see below.

9. This reading does not strictly follow the sequence of the biblical story in the manner of a commentary. At the same time, the canonical sequencing is recognized throughout the discussion. For my commentary work on the Abraham story, see Fretheim, "The Book of Genesis," *NIB* 1 (Nashville: Abingdon, 1994).

1. THE UNIVERSAL FRAME OF REFERENCE

1. For detail, see Terence Fretheim, "The Reclamation of Creation: Redemption and Law in Exodus," *Interpretation* 45 (1991): 354–65; Fretheim, *The Pentateuch* (Nashville: Abingdon, 1996), 39–53. For a fuller treatment of creation in Genesis 12–50, see Fretheim, *God and World in the Old Testament: A Relational Theology of Creation* (Nashville: Abingdon, 2005), 91–109.

2. J. G. Janzen, *Abraham and All the Families of the Earth: A Commentary on the Book of Genesis 12–50* (Grand Rapids, Mich.: Eerdmans, 1993), 6. His language is that Gen. 1–11 is "the foundation and continuing frame of reference" for the story of Israel that begins with Abraham.

3. The phrase "patriarchal history" has long been used. The word "ancestral" makes it clearer that both the men and the women of this story have a crucial role to play in how the story develops.

4. For discussion of the issue and details on Gen. 11:26–32 in particular, see Tammi J. Schneider, *Sarah: Mother of Nations* (New York: Continuum, 2004), 8–23.

5. Several postbiblical texts will make connections between Abraham and the Tower of Babel story.

6. For further detail on the call of Abraham in 12:1–3, see below.

7. Donald Gowan, *From Eden to Babel: A Commentary on the Book of Genesis 1–11* (Grand Rapids, Mich.: Eerdmans, 1988), along with many other scholars, understands Gen. 1–11 as "the preface to salvation history" (4).

8. See D. J. A. Clines, *The Theme of the Pentateuch,* rev. ed. (Sheffield: JSOT Press, 1997); Brevard Childs, *Introduction to the Old Testament as Scripture* (Philadelphia: Fortress, 1979); B. Dahlberg, "On Recognizing the Unity of Genesis," *TD* 24 (1977): 360–67; Thomas Mann, "All the Families of the Earth: The Theological Unity of Genesis," *Interpretation* 45 (1991): 341–53.

9. The first three texts use *ʾereṣ* for "land, earth," the last uses *ʾadāmāh,* as in Gen. 12:3.

10. Moberly's proposal in *The Old Testament of the Old Testament: Patriarchal Narratives and Mosaic Yahwism* (Minneapolis: Fortress, 1992), which has the effect of "demoting" the stature of Gen. 12–50, also risks diminishing the status of Gen. 1–11. See below, last chapter, for a discussion of Moberly.

11. Janzen, *Genesis 12–50,* 12. Cf. T. Fretheim, "Reclamation of Creation."

12. See William P. Brown, *The Ethos of the Cosmos: The Genesis of Moral Imagination in the Bible* (Grand Rapids, Mich.: Eerdmans, 1999), 65–66.

13. The material content of Genesis 24 may further explain this usage. Abraham's servant is to swear regarding matters that reach out into the wider world of Mesopotamia. While the divine epithets in Genesis 24 may be considered late because of their use in postexilic literature (e.g., Ezra 5:12; 1:2), the narrator apparently thought that such universal understandings of God were necessary in order to speak adequately about God's activity in this ancestral period.

14. For a fuller discussion of the universality of the presence of God, see Fretheim, *God and World,* 22–27.

15. For detail, see Fretheim, *God and World,* 106–8.

16. See Claus Westermann, *Blessing in the Bible and the Life of the Church,* trans. K. R. Crim (Philadelphia: Fortress, 1978). Westermann's understanding of blessing is insufficiently comprehensive, for blessing can also be used with reference to divine acts of salvation.

17. See Westermann, *Blessing in the Bible.* Westermann divides God's activity in the world into categories of saving and blessing. This is a useful distinction, but should not be understood too strictly, for God's saving activity is also described in terms of

blessing. One should not translate these categories into a creation-redemption distinction or, for that matter, into a law-gospel distinction.

18. See Frederick J. Gaiser, "Why Does it Rain? A Biblical Case Study in Divine Causality," *HBT* 25 (2003): 1–18.

19. For detail, see Fretheim, "The Reclamation of Creation."

20. See especially Walter Brueggemann and H. W. Wolff, *The Vitality of Old Testament Traditions,* 2nd ed. (Atlanta: John Knox Press, 1982), 41–66.

21. On the relationship of these various peoples to the chosen family in Genesis, see Robert Cohn, "Negotiating (with) the Natives: Ancestors and Identity in Genesis," *HTR* 96 (2003): 147–66.

22. See Hugh White, *Narration and Discourse in the Book of Genesis* (Cambridge: Cambridge University Press, 1991), 107–12, 169–73.

23. Karl Loning and Erich Zenger, *To Begin With . . . God Created: Biblical Theologies of Creation,* trans. O. Kaste (Collegeville, Minn.: Liturgical Press, 2000), 119.

24. Walter Brueggemann, *Genesis* (Atlanta: John Knox Press, 1982), 153.

25. One might also distinguish between communal promises (e.g., Gen. 28:13–14) and personal promises (28:15). Laurence Turner, *Announcements of Plot in Genesis* (Sheffield: JSOT Press, 1990), 116, is right to criticize the distinction between "religious" promises and "earthly" promises (see Brueggemann, *Genesis,* 206–7). The last two phrases of Gen. 27:29 do refer to Gen. 12:3, but this is the only time these phrases are recalled in Genesis and hence they are not integral to the "blessing of Abraham." They may be a more personal reference (cf. Gen. 28:15).

26. Claus Westermann, *Genesis 12–36: A Commentary,* trans. J. J. Scullion (Minneapolis: Augsburg, 1985), 192. See also Devora Steinmetz, *From Father to Son: Kinship, Conflict, and Continuity in Genesis* (Louisville, Ky.: Westminster / John Knox, 1991), 143–47.

27. Further reflections on Genesis 14 are presented below.

28. On Abraham as prophet, see below.

29. For further detail on Abimelech, see below.

30. See Nahum Sarna, *Understanding Genesis* (New York: Schocken, 1966), 179. See also James Crenshaw, *Defending God: Biblical Responses to the Problem of Evil* (Oxford: Oxford University Press, 2005), 66–67.

2. THE ABRAHAMIC NARRATIVES

1. For a thorough introduction to these issues, see especially Claus Westermann, *Genesis 12–36: A Commentary,* trans. J. J. Scullion (Minneapolis: Augsburg, 1985), 23–121; for my own brief introduction, see Terence E. Fretheim, "The Book of Genesis," NIB 1 (Nashville: Abingdon, 1994) 321–30.

2. See Westermann, *Genesis 12–36,* 35–58.

3. See Gary Rendsburg, *The Redaction of Genesis* (Winona Lake, Ind.: Eisenbrauns, 1986), 27–52; Thomas Brodie, *Genesis as Dialogue: A Literary, Historical, and Theological*

Commentary (Oxford: Oxford University Press, 2001), 11–25; T. D. Alexander, *From Paradise to the Promised Land: An Introduction to the Main Themes in the Pentateuch* (Carlisle: Paternoster Press, 1995), 102–5.

4. See the helpful discussion of Devora Steinmetz, *From Father to Son: Kinship, Conflict, and Continuity in Genesis* (Louisville, Ky.: Westminster / John Knox), 63–85.

5. For a brief survey of the presentation of Abraham on the part of the various sources, see Ronald S. Hendel, *Remembering Abraham: Culture, Memory, and History in the Hebrew Bible* (Oxford: Oxford University Press, 2005), 37–41. Several of the distinctions he observes in these sources, particularly regarding human agency, seem overly subtle to this reader.

6. For efforts to discern the "kerygmatic" interests of the various sources, see the essays by Walter Brueggemann and H. W. Wolff, *The Vitality of Old Testament Traditions*, 2nd ed. (Atlanta: John Knox Press, 1982).

7. For example, Samuel Balentine, *The Torah's Vision of Worship* (Minneapolis: Fortress, 1999).

8. See William McKane, *Studies in the Patriarchal Narratives* (Edinburgh: Handsel, 1979).

9. See Frank M. Cross, *Canaanite Myth and Hebrew Epic* (Cambridge, Mass.: Harvard University Press, 1973), 293–325.

10. We will deal with other biblical references to the content of Gen. 12–25 in chapter 8.

11. On this "world within the text" as compared to the "world behind the text" and "the world in front of the text," see Terence Fretheim, *The Pentateuch* (Nashville: Abingdon, 1996), 23–36. See also W. R. Tate, *Biblical Interpretation: An Integrated Approach* (Peabody, Mass.: Hendrickson, 1991); John Barton, *Reading the Old Testament: Method in Biblical Study* (Philadelphia: Westminster, 1984).

12. For surveys, see R. N. Whybray, *The Making of the Pentateuch* (Sheffield: JSOT, 1987); J. Blenkinsopp, *The Pentateuch: An Introduction to the First Five Books of the Bible* (New York: Doubleday, 1992).

13. See the recent, helpful studies of Ronald Hendel, *Remembering Abraham*, 31–55; G. I. Davies, "Genesis and the Early History of Israel: A Survey of Research," in *Studies in the Book of Genesis: Literature, Redaction, and History*, ed. A. Wenin (Leuven: Leuven University Press, 2001), 104–34. See also the discussion in R. W. L. Moberly, *The Old Testament of the Old Testament: Patriarchal Narratives and Mosaic Yahwism* (Minneapolis: Fortress, 1992), 191–98.

14. See, for example, the work of Thomas Thompson, *The Historicity of the Patriarchal Narratives: The Quest for the Historical Abraham* (Berlin: de Gruyter, 1974); John van Seters, *Abraham in History and Tradition* (New Haven, Conn.: Yale University Press, 1975). For the development of criteria to discern the historical value of narratives, see my *Deuteronomic History* (Nashville: Abingdon, 1983), 27–35.

15. Julius Wellhausen, *Prolegomena to the History of Israel* (Edinburgh: Black, 1885), 319.

16. W. F. Albright, *The Biblical Period from Abraham to Ezra: An Historical Survey* (New York: Harper & Row, 1963), 2.

17. See A. R. Millard, "Abraham," *ABD* (New York: Doubleday, 1992), 1:35–41; A. R. Millard and D. J. Wiseman, *Essays on the Patriarchal Narratives* (Winona Lake, Ind.: Eisenbrauns, 1983); K. A. Kitchen, "The Patriarchal Age: Myth or History?" *BAR* 21/2 (1995): 48–57, 88–95. For a critical response to Kitchen's arguments, see Ronald S. Hendel, "Dating the Patriarchal Age," *BAR* 21/4 (1995): 56–57.

18. Thomas L. Thompson, *The Historicity of the Patriarchal Narratives*; John van Seters, *Abraham in History and Tradition.*

19. Hendel, *Remembering Abraham*, 46. This conclusion is similar to that of Westermann, *Genesis 12–36*, 40; and Moberly, *The Old Testament of the Old Testament*, 191–202.

20. Hendel, *Remembering Abraham*, 46–47. His discussion on pages 46–55 is a balanced assessment of the current situation.

21. That Abraham is specifically mentioned with relative infrequency in Gen. 27–50 (and Sarah only in 49:31) may be important in this connection. The specific references back to the Abraham cycle in these chapters have mostly to do with the land (28:4, 13; 35:12; 49:30; 50:13, 24).

22. Hendel, *Remembering Abraham*, 35, 37.

23. See Brueggemann and Wolff, *The Vitality of Old Testament Traditions.*

24. See articles in the bibliography by Polzin, Exum, Eichler, Clines, and Biddle.

25. For a preliminary effort, see D. M. Carr, "Genesis in Relation to the Moses Story. Diachronic and Synchronic Perspectives," in *Studies in the Book of Genesis: Literature, Redaction, and History*, ed. A. Wenin (Leuven: University Press, 2001), 273–95.

26. Many scholars have pointed out these parallels. See, for example, Moberly, *Old Testament of the Old Testament*, 135–46.

27. Parallels between the covenants between God and Abraham and God and David have long been noted. See, for example, R. Clements, *Abraham and David: Genesis 15 and Its Meaning for Israelite Tradition* (London: SCM, 1967).

28. See my "The Plagues as Historical Signs of Ecological Disaster," *JBL* 110 (1991): 385–96.

29. See Stuart Lasine, "Guest and Host in Judges 19," *JSOT* 29 (1984): 37–59.

30. I have shown this to be the case with respect to virtually every text in the story of Abraham in my commentary on Genesis.

31. The seminal work for studies of the religion of Israel's ancestors, originally published in 1929, is that of Albrecht Alt; see his "The God of the Fathers," in *Essays on Old Testament History and Religion* (Oxford: Blackwell, 1966), 3–77. See also F. M. Cross, *Canaanite Myth and Hebrew Epic* (Cambridge, Mass.: Harvard University Press, 1973), 46–60; Gerhard von Rad, *Old Testament Theology*, vol. 1 (New York: Harper,

1962), 165–87; G. J. Wenham, "The Religion of the Patriarchs," in *Essays on the Patriarchal Narratives*, eds. A. R. Millard and D. J. Wiseman (Leicester: IVP, 1980), 157–88. For a helpful survey, see R. W. L. Moberly, *The Old Testament of the Old Testament*. For an interpretation that the Genesis texts reflect religious practice from a later era, see John van Seters, "The Religion of the Patriarchs in Genesis," *Biblica* 61 (1980): 220–33. For family religion in Israel, see Patrick D. Miller, *The Religion of Ancient Israel* (Louisville, Ky.: Westminster / John Knox, 2000), 62–76; K. van der Toorn, *Family Religion in Babylonia, Syria, and Israel: Continuity and Changes in the Forms of Religious Life* (Leiden: Brill, 1996).

32. For detailed discussion, see Moberly, *The Old Testament of the Old Testament*. For fuller discussion of Moberly's work, see chapter 8.

33. See especially the work of Moberly.

34. Moberly, *The Old Testament of the Old Testament*, 165.

35. See Samuel Balentine's discussion of ancestral worship in Genesis 15–17 in *The Torah's Vision of Worship* (Minneapolis: Fortress, 1999), 102–18.

36. See, for example, the work of Rainer Albertz, *History of Israelite Religion in the Old Testament Period,* trans. John Bowden (Louisville, Ky.: Westminster / John Knox, 1994).

3. ABRAHAM

1. See the discussion in John Goldingay, *Old Testament Theology: Israel's Gospel*, vol. 1 (Downer's Grove, Ill.: InterVarsity Press, 2003), 196–97.

2. See chapter 1.

3. See Goldingay, *Old Testament Theology*, 197–99. I think that it is not helpful, however, to subvert the distinction between faith and obedience (198–99). Yes, faith without works is dead, but the distinction is still important (even for the Old Testament). Faith is a sheer gift from God, generated by God's word of promise; obedience is to act on the faith that one has been given. I'm not certain how Goldingay relates grace and faith; he seems to equate them.

4. See Janzen, *Abraham and All the Families of the Earth: A Commentary on the Book of Genesis 12–50* (Grand Rapids, Mich.: Eerdmans, 1993), 20.

5. See Goldingay, *Old Testament Theology*, 1:195–96.

6. Janzen, *Genesis 12–50*, 21.

7. The presence of Lot would seem to be in violation of the divine command to leave kindred (12:1), but that seems an overly precise interpretation. The explanation that, in view of Sarah's barrenness, it is possible that Abraham considered Lot to be his heir, though the promise of land in 12:7 already specifies Abraham's "seed" (as in 13:15). Abraham recognizes the importance of "seed" to the promise in 15:3–4. It seems more likely that Lot was a character existent in the tradition, not least as the progenitor of Moab and Ammon (19:37–38), and is woven into the stories in several

ways. See Naomi Steinberg, *Kinship and Marriage in Genesis: A Household Economics Perspective* (Minneapolis: Fortress, 1993), 48; Laurence Turner, *Announcements of Plot in Genesis* (Sheffield: JSOT Press, 1990); W. J. Lyons, *Canon and Exegesis: Canonical Praxis and the Sodom Narrative* (London: Sheffield Academic Press, 2002), 131–35.

8. See chapter 1 for further information.

9. See R. W. L. Moberly, *The Old Testament of the Old Testament, Patriarchal Narratives and Mosaic Yahwism* (Minneapolis: Fortress, 1992), 120–27.

10. Claus Westermann, *Genesis 12–36: A Commentary,* trans. J. J. Scullion (Minneapolis: Augsburg, 1985), 152.

11. See chapter 1 for further reflection.

12. The point at which the vision comes to an end is not made clear, but it may continue through 15:11.

13. For ties between the chapters, see Nahum Sarna, *Understanding Genesis* (New York: Schocken, 1966), 112.

14. For God as shield in Davidic contexts, see 2 Sam. 22:3, 31, 36; Ps. 144:2.

15. Notably, Gen. 15:6 is the *narrator's* interpretation, not Abraham's point of view, making sure that readers will not interpret this point as Abraham's opinion.

16. See last chapter.

17. See last chapter. For a contrary view, see the article by Jon Levenson, "Abusing Abraham: Traditions, Religious Histories, and Modern Misinterpretations," *Judaism* 47 (1998): 259–77.

18. See Gerhard von Rad, *Genesis,* rev. ed. (Philadelphia: Westminster, 1972), 184–85.

19. Credit language (see NIV) is less than adequate because it suggests a divine keeping of account books.

20. See Sarna, *Understanding Genesis,* 114–15.

21. An allegorical interpretation, where, for example, the birds of prey are foreign nations, perhaps Egypt, whom Abraham drives away, seems strained in view of Jer. 34:18–20. For example, see Gordon Wenham, *Genesis 1–15* (Waco: Word, 1987), 332. Inasmuch as Abraham brings the animals directly *to God* (v. 10), one should think of the presence of God in human form.

22. Later texts that refer to "God's swearing by his own self" have reference to this promise (see 22:16; 24:7; 26:3; 50:24; cf. 2 Sam. 3:9; Pss. 89; 100:4; 132:11; Isa. 54:9). This phrase is used because God cannot invoke a higher power regarding the penalty.

23. See M. Weinfeld, *"berith," Theological Dictionary of the Old Testament* (Grand Rapids, Mich.: Eerdmans, 1975), 253–79.

24. The relationship between the four hundred years of v. 13 (Acts 7:6; 430 years in Exod. 12:40, cf. Gal. 3:17) and the fourth generation of v. 16 is uncertain, and may reflect different traditions. The "generation" is probably a lifetime (approximately one hundred years, see 6:3; Ps. 90:10; Isa. 65:20). It could, however, refer literally to the fourth generation, namely, Jacob's sons; they come back from a kind of exile (in Haran)

and begin to settle in the land (cf. the "Amorites" in 48:22), a process not completed for centuries. The lack of reference to Egypt in 15:13 evidences less than total concern for speaking about the future with precision. This would enable readers to apply the word to more than one life situation (fourth generation language would work well for the exiles).

25. The boundaries specified are important to Israel at various times (cf. Isa. 27:12; Deut. 11:24; Josh. 1:4). They extend from the Euphrates to the "Brook of Egypt" (not the Nile, but of uncertain location). That God has promised such a land, however, does not necessarily mean that they *must* possess every territory that is specified or do so at all times. Only with Solomon does the land even approach this size, and then not totally (1 Kings 5:1, 4; 8:65). The list of ten peoples in 15:18–21 is unique and contrasts with most Old Testament lists, which have five to seven names enumerated. All the peoples that are listed lived within a territory smaller than that envisaged in v. 18.

26. Westermann, *Genesis 12–36,* 227.

27. See the discussion in Paul Williamson, *Abraham, Israel and the Nations: The Patriarchal Promise and its Covenantal Development in Genesis* (Sheffield: Academic Press, 2000).

28. Williamson's claim that Gen. 17 is an entirely different covenant does not withstand closer scrutiny. The lapse of thirteen years between 16:16 and 17:1 can be interpreted in several ways, as we will suggest. For Williamson, Gen. 17 is only a reference to a future covenant that awaits Abraham's obedience; the covenant is only established in Gen. 22:15–18. If the latter text is the point at which the covenant is established, one would expect explicit reference to covenant at that point. The circumcision, carried out in 17:23–27, would not then function as a sign of this covenant. It is best to see the covenant in Gen. 17 as being established by the word of God's promise, to which circumcision is a response; as 17:4 states, this *is* my covenant.

29. Abraham is literally the father of many nations (through Hagar and Ishmael, Keturah and her sons, and Isaac and Rebekah and their sons). Whether Abraham's fatherhood is *also* metaphorically understood in this text is less than fully clear, though as Sarna claims, the phrase "has a more universal application in that a larger segment of humanity looks upon Abraham as its spiritual father" (*Understanding Genesis,* 124). New Testament texts will also make this claim (Gal. 3–4).

30. Cf. the relationship between the covenants in Exod. 24 and 34, with the intervening sin in Exod. 32

31. See Samuel Balentine on God's new identity, *The Torah's Vision of Worship* (Minneapolis: Fortress, 1999), 111.

32. See Terence E. Fretheim, *God and World in the Old Testament: A Relational Theology of Creation* (Nashville: Abingdon, 2005), 13–22.

33. John Goldingay, *Old Testament Theology: Israel's Gospel,* vol. 1 (Downer's Grove, Ill.: InterVarsity Press, 2003), 200–201. Though it is not clear to me what the word "exactly" entails.

34. Terence E. Fretheim, *Exodus* (Louisville, Ky.: Westminster / John Knox, 1991), 209–11.

35. Because Ishmael is also circumcised, it means that the "covenant" with Isaac but *not* Ishmael (17:19–21) is not a reference to circumcision.

36. Contrary to W. Sibley Towner, *Genesis* (Louisville, Ky.: Westminster / John Knox, 2001), 162.

37. Given this difference regarding covenant, it is unclear to me how Goldingay can claim in *Old Testament Theology* that in circumcision "God confirms that Ishmael belongs to the covenant people" (203). As for the "more" that is entailed in the covenant given to Isaac that is not given to Ishmael, see above on "constitutive" blessing.

38. See Sarna, *Understanding Genesis*, 124.

4. ABRAHAM AND OUTSIDERS, I

1. Among many studies of these texts, see Susan Niditch, *Underdogs and Tricksters: A Prelude to Biblical Folklore* (San Francisco: Harper & Row, 1987), 23–69; Robert Polzin, "The Ancestress of Israel in Danger," *Semeia* 3 (1975): 81–98.

2. Gen. 12:10–20 and 26:1–11 are usually assigned to the Yahwist, 20:1–18 to the Elohist. Gen. 12 may be the more original story; chapters 20 and 26 may be reworkings of that story in view of issues in different locales. Stories of this sort were common in the ancient world, however, and these examples may reflect such a convention (type-scenes; see Robert Alter, *Art of Biblical Narrative* [New York: Basic Books, 1981], 47–62).

3. Suggested by Tammi J. Schneider, *Sarah, Mother of Nations* (New York: Continuum, 2004), 33.

4. Hugh White, *Narration and Discourse in the Book of Genesis* (Cambridge: Cambridge University Press, 1991), 179

5. See Schneider, *Sarah,* 34.

6. See Terence Fretheim, "The Plagues as Historical Signs of Ecological Disaster," *JBL* 110 (1991): 385–96.

7. See Terence Fretheim, *God and World in the Old Testament: A Relational Theology of Creation* (Nashville: Abingdon, 2005), 109–28.

8. See F. V. Greifenhagen, *Egypt on the Pentateuch's Ideological Map: Constructing Biblical Israel's Identity* (Sheffield: Academic Press, 2002), 28–33.

9. J. G. Janzen, *Genesis 12–50,* 25.

10. Such a statement reflects the earlier-noted tension regarding Abraham's wealth and social standing.

11. These texts are mostly assigned to the Elohist.

12. For a close look at the legal referents in this chapter, see James K. Bruckner, *Implied Law in the Abraham Narrative: A Literary and Theological Analysis* (Sheffield: Academic Press, 2001), 171–98.

13. On salvation, see Terence E. Fretheim, "Salvation in the Bible vs. Salvation in the Church," *WW* 13 (1993): 363–72.

14. To use the word "prophet" for Abraham is anachronistic, and may be used here because prophets were commonly associated with intercessory activity (cf. 1 Sam. 12:23; Jer. 11:14).

15. Bruckner, *Implied Law*, 196 (italics his).

16. On this issue, see especially Bruckner, *Implied Law*, 192–204.

17. Bruckner, *Implied Law*, 198.

18. Bruckner, *Implied Law*, 204.

19. This narrative may be an interweaving of two covenant stories (from J and E?) that explain the name Beersheba (cf. 26:33) as the "well of the oath" and the "well of seven (ewe lambs)." This may help explain earlier forms of the narrative, but there is little scholarly consensus.

20. This covenant between two human parties is sometimes called a "parity" covenant and differs from the divine-human covenants, though it provides an analogy for them, and the "yes" and the "no" in the use of the analogy need to be sharply recognized.

21. The "land of the Philistines" (21:32) could be an anachronism (the Philistines settled in that land around 1200 B.C.E.), yet it probably represents the knowledge of the Abrahamic era available to the narrator. The "Philistines" may represent all the pre-Israelite inhabitants of the land.

22. See Robert Cohn, "Negotiating (with) the Natives: Ancestors and Identity in Genesis," *HTR* 96 (2003): 147–66.

23. Westermann, *Genesis 12–36*, 322.

24. Jesus' evaluation of the centurion in Matt. 8:10 could well apply to Abimelech, "in no one in Israel have I found such faith."

25. See the discussion of Hemchand Gossai, *Power and Marginality in the Abraham Narrative* (Lanham, Md.: University Press, 1995), 129–32.

26. For these texts, see W. Beyerlin, ed., *Near Eastern Religious Texts Relating to the Old Testament* (Philadelphia: Westminster, 1978), index under "sin."

5. ABRAHAM AND OUTSIDERS, II

1. Verses 1–4 are ordered in terms of Israel's early history (cf. chapter 2; Gordon Wenham, *Genesis 1–15* [Waco: Word, 1987], 300). This text (mostly J) is bracketed by an itinerary (vv. 1–4, 18), and includes a quarrel narrative (vv. 5–13) and an oracle of promise (vv. 14–17). Abraham's journey from Bethel to Hebron is replicated by Jacob, 35:16–27.

2. Claus Westermann, *Genesis 12–36: A Commentary*, trans. J. J. Scullion (Minneapolis: Augsburg, 1985), suggests that this "narrative of Abraham, who brought a dispute to peaceful solution by personal renunciation, still spoke across the era of Israel's wars; it was a pointer to another way of solving a conflict. The promise of a king of peace had a predecessor" (181).

3. Given Abraham's settlement in Hebron and v. 11 ("all the plain of the Jordan"), the axis seems to be east-west, though it is argued that the "right" and the "left" (13:9) are north and south, and did not include the plain of Jordan that Lot saw (13:10). There is a fine view of the Jordan Valley from elevations near Bethel. See L. Helyer, "The Separation of Abram and Lot: Significance in the Patriarchal Narratives," *JSOT* 26 (1983): 79; William Lyons, *Canon and Exegesis: Canonical Praxis and the Sodom Narrative* (London: Sheffield Academic Press, 2002), 132.

4. See Lyons, *Canon and Exegesis,* 133.

5. Nathan Macdonald, "Listening to Abraham—Listening to Yahweh: Divine Justice and Mercy in Genesis 18:16–33," *CBQ* 66 (2004): 29.

6. For Near Eastern parallels, see Nahum Sarna, *Understanding Genesis* (New York: Schocken, 1966), 99–100.

7. On Lot as "outsider," see Lyons, *Canon and Exegesis,* 222–25; Hemchand Gossai, *Power and Marginality in the Abraham Narrative* (Lanham, Md.: University Press, 1995), 75–101.

8. The chapter is a composite, but the component parts are usually not associated with the Pentateuchal sources (occasionally J, as part of a Lot-Abraham tradition). Vv. 18–20 interrupt reference to the king of Sodom and may have been added to link Abraham with David and Jerusalem. Regarding form, it may be that vv. 12–24 are based on an old hero story about Abraham, similar to stories from the period of the judges. Vv. 1–11 are a report of a military campaign, though with few details. Dialogue occurs only in the aftermath of the entire affair (vv. 21–24). An unusual number of rare words and phrases occur. In spite of much scholarly effort, persons and places are not always identifiable. The historical basis of the story remains difficult to discern (see Sarna, *Understanding Genesis,* 101–11; Wenham, *Genesis 1–15,* 318–20).

9. "El" is the general word for deity in the ancient Near East; Elyon, usually translated "Most High," is probably an epithet rather than a name; it was also used outside of Israel. The two words occur together elsewhere only in Ps. 78:35, but they are used in parallel with El (Num. 24:16; Ps. 73:11), with other divine names (Ps. 18:13; 46:4), and independently (Deut. 32:8; Ps. 82:6).

10. See especially J. G. Janzen, *Genesis 12–50,* 30–31, on these links.

11. Janzen, *Genesis 12–50,* 31.

12. Janzen, *Genesis 12–50,* 32.

13. A case can be made for including 18:1–15 in this story (see Lyons, *Canon and Exegesis,* 124–25), especially the parallels between Abraham's hospitality and Lot's. It is difficult to say whether that means they belong to the same story or that the redactor has provided an important link between stories.

14. I only touch on several dimensions of this story here; for a fuller explication of this text, see Terence Fretheim, "The Book of Genesis," in *The New Interpreter's Bible* 1 (Nashville: Abingdon, 1994), 465–79; Fretheim, "Divine Judgment and the Warming of the World," in *God, Evil, and Suffering: Essays in Honor of Paul R. Sponheim,* eds. Fretheim and Curt Thompson (St. Paul, Minn.: Word and World, 2000), 21–32.

15. Robert Alter, "Sodom as Nexus: The Web of Design in Biblical Narrative," in *The Book and the Text,* ed. R. Schwarz (Oxford: Blackwell, 1990), 157.

16. Parallels with the latter have been noted, from the lack of sexual restraint (6:1–4), to natural disaster (note 19:24, "rained" on Sodom), to the saving of a remnant (and God's remembering, 8:1, 19:29), to the drunken aftermath (cf. 9:20–27 with vv. 30–38).

17. For studies of this text, see Lyons, *Canon and Exegesis;* Nathan Macdonald, "Listening to Abraham—Listening to Yahweh"; Hemchand Gossai, *Power and Marginality.*

18. See Samuel Balentine's discussion of Genesis 18 in the context of other biblical prayers for justice. Balentine, *Prayer in the Hebrew Bible: The Drama of Divine-Human Dialogue* (Minneapolis: Fortress, 1993), 118–45.

19. James Bruckner, *Implied Law in the Abraham Narrative: A Literary and Theological Analysis* (Sheffield: Academic Press, 2001), 127.

20. Macdonald, "Listening to Abraham," 29.

21. See John Goldingay, *Old Testament Theology: Israel's Gospel,* vol. 1 (Downer's Grove, Ill.: InterVarsity Press, 2003), 218; cf. 204, for helpful reflection on the "so that" of 18:19: This is "not so much a condition for the fulfilling of the promise as part of the actual fulfillment. As Abraham does this, the promise comes true." I would also want to speak of the natural consequences of the doing of justice and righteousness.

22. On the significance of the "outcry," see Gossai, *Power and Marginality,* 55–57, 88–94.

23. Though originally the text probably read: "God stood before Abraham" (NRSV footnote). The subjects may have been reversed by scribes who thought it improper for God to stand before a human being, but that is commonly disputed.

24. Walter Brueggemann, *Genesis* (Atlanta: John Knox Press, 1982), 176. See Macdonald, "Listening to Abraham," 25–43.

25. Macdonald, "Listening to Abraham," 30–35.

26. Does Abraham abase himself by referring to himself as "dust and ashes"? Cf., J. G. Janzen, *Abraham and All the Families of the Earth,* "is it precisely when dust and ashes concerns itself in this way over justice that it images God?" (61).

27. Nathan Macdonald's suggestion is that a better analogy is that of child who persistently tests parental boundaries, whether real or imagined ("Listening to Abraham," 35).

28. Macdonald, "Listening to Abraham," 30. This interpretation is key to Macdonald's discussion.

29. Macdonald, "Listening to Abraham," 36.

30. James Bruckner, *Implied Law,* speaks of "what is just" as "make a just decision" (133). On the questions of Abraham as "leaving big questions for the audience to answer," see J. R. Lundbom, "Parataxis, Rhetorical Structure and the Dialogue over

Sodom in Genesis 18," in *The World of Genesis,* eds. P. R. Davies and D. J. A. Clines (Sheffield: Academic Press, 1998), 144.

31. See the helpful comment by H. Gossai, *Power and Marginality:* "the issue in the mind of Abraham is the righteousness of God and not so much the righteousness of the people of Sodom" (60).

32. Macdonald, in "Listening to Abraham," thinks it important that Abraham omitted "righteousness" in 18:25, whereas God in 18:19 included both justice and righteousness. He thinks that God is speaking of social justice in v. 19, whereas Abraham speaks of judicial procedure. Bruckner, *Implied Law,* thinks of justice in the courts in both cases (89–91, 101–2).

33. See Bruckner, *Implied Law,* 150.

34. Notably, righteous behavior is expected of people independent of their relationship to the chosen family.

35. Lyons, *Canon and Exegesis,* 185–93, considers Abraham to be incoherent on this point. I do not understand why he understands this to be the case, though his discussion is extensive. It seems that he *assumes* that Abraham is incoherent; for example, he critiques some interpretations because they do not recognize that Abraham is incoherent. As far as I can tell, he has not considered the argument presented here (and in an earlier form in my "Genesis," 477–79).

36. Bruckner, *Implied Law,* 133. Bruckner helpfully notes: "Abraham negotiates for the innocent (18:23), but also argues for saving the guilty if enough innocent men are found" (125).

37. See the helpful comments of Bruckner, *Implied Law:* "In order to spare the innocent God must also spare the guilty. Abraham's premise of cosmological judgment cuts in two directions. It assumes that the only two possibilities are indiscriminate destruction and indiscriminate sparing. Saving the guilty is not a matter of atonement, but is a matter of the cosmology and physical implications of the sentence" (162).

38. Macdonald, "Listening to Abraham," 41.

39. Westermann, *Genesis 12–36,* 292. God is not the subject of forgiving activity elsewhere in Genesis (not until Exod. 34:6–7).

40. See Bruckner, *Implied Law,* 161–62.

41. Macdonald, "Listening to Abraham," 35.

42. Macdonald, "Listening to Abraham," 35.

43. It is hard to know if Abraham starts with fifty because he thinks this is a number that is "easily attainable" (Macdonald, "Listening to Abraham," 32).

44. Sarna, *Understanding Genesis,* 134. It is not clear to me why neither Lyons nor Macdonald consider this argument.

45. Cf. Bruckner's language (*Implied Law*), "that the judging link may be loosened if enough innocent stand in the gap against the guilty. (Whether this suggests that the virtue of the innocent causes the loosening, or that it frees God to loosen the

connection, or that God is willing to loosen it when [enough] innocent people are present, is not clear in this text.)" (129).

46. See Terence Fretheim, "Is Anything Too Hard for God? (Jeremiah 32:27)," *CBQ* 66 (2004): 231–36.

47. Jeremiah (and others) will speak of this divine turning away from judgment in view of human responsiveness as the repentance of God (see Jer. 18:7–8; 26:3, 13).

48. See Jer. 7:16; 11:14; 14:11; 15:1, where Jeremiah's prayers are forbidden because it is already too late for Jerusalem, as are the prayers of the people (Jer. 14:7–10).

49. Macdonald, "Listening to Abraham": "Abraham seems to be concerned with righteous individuals, but he appeals for corporate forgiveness based on [the presence of] these individuals" (39). Note the language of "forgiveness."

50. See Bruckner's language (*Implied Law*): "Judgment by cosmological consequence is not person-specific" (169).

51. On the "cosmological consequences" and the link between moral order and cosmic order, see also Bruckner, *Implied Law,* 158–69.

52. One of the most helpful discussions of divine wrath is that of Abraham Heschel, *The Prophets* (San Francisco: Harper & Row, 1962), 279–306.

53. See Klaus Koch, "Is There a Doctrine of Retribution in the Old Testament?" in *Theodicy in the Old Testament,* ed. J. Crenshaw (Philadelphia: Fortress, 1983), 57–87. Note the wind and waves in Exod. 14–15, where the nonhuman also is the vehicle for the salvation of the human.

54. See Bruckner, *Implied Law,* 151–52.

55. On issues of hospitality, see V. H. Matthews, "Hospitality and Hostility in Genesis 19 and Judges 19," *BTB* 22 (1992): 3–11; Lyons, *Canon and Exegesis,* 161–65, 216–19. The discussion of Lot as "outsider" and his downward spiral is well developed in Lyons, 222–53, and Gossai, *Power and Marginality,* 75–101.

56. For a helpful discussion of rape and the violence against women in this context, see Gossai, *Power and Marginality,* 82–87; Lyons, *Canon and Exegesis,* 226–31.

57. See Marti Nissinen, *Homoeroticism in the Biblical World: A Historical Perspective,* trans. K. Stjerna (Minneapolis: Fortress, 1998).

58. For a discussion of the sin of Sodom, see Lyons, *Canon and Exegesis,* 234–39. He refers to the sin of Sodom as "a particular wicked way of life" (234).

59. The story of Sodom and Gomorrah is the most frequently referenced Genesis text in the Old Testament and in the New Testament (see also chapter 8). The one possible reference to sexual activity is Jude 7, and the clarity of that reference is disputed.

60. See, for example, Lyn Bechtel, "A Feminist Reading of Genesis 19:1–11," in *A Feminist Companion to Genesis,* 2nd series, ed. A. Brenner (Sheffield: Sheffield Academic Press, 1998), 122–25. See critique of Bechtel in William Lyons, *Canon and Exegesis,* 216–17, n. 2.

61. John Goldingay, *Old Testament Theology: Israel's Gospel,* vol. 1 (Downer's Grove, Ill.: InterVarsity Press, 2003), 218.

62. Bruckner, *Implied Law,* notes that the comment to Lot by the men of Sodom in their use of "worse" (or more wickedly) is "an implied admission of wrongdoing" (154).

63. For a helpful discussion of Lot's sons-in-law, see Gossai, *Power and Marginality,* 95–97.

64. On the importance of human response, see Bruckner, *Implied Law,* 164–67.

65. Bruckner, *Implied Law,* 164–65, correctly notes that it is her foolishness in not heeding the warning that seals her fate, not her guilt at disobeying a command not to look back.

6. HAGAR AND ISHMAEL AS OUTSIDERS

1. Walter Brueggemann, *Genesis* (Atlanta: John Knox Press, 1982), 153.

2. In terms of source-critical analysis, Gen. 16 has been identified with the Yahwist (with Priestly framing elements), Gen. 21:8–21 with the Elohist, and 17:15–25 with the Priestly source. The story of Hagar and Ishmael has thus found a place in all the major Pentateuchal traditions.

3. At the same time, the separate segments of this story have been literarily shaped. For example, the inclusion provided by the repeated word "bear" (*yālad*) in 16:1–2, 15–16 ties the chapter into a unified whole.

4. For example, Phyllis Trible, *Texts of Terror: Literary-Feminist Readings of Biblical Narratives* (Minneapolis: Fortress, 1984); Katheryn P. Darr, *Far More Precious than Jewels: Perspectives on Biblical Women* (Louisville: Westminster / John Knox, 1991), 132–63.

5. For an up-to-date bibliography, see John Reeves, *Bible and Qur'an: Essays in Scriptural Intertextuality* (Atlanta: Society of Biblical Literature, 2003).

6. See Claus Westermann, *Genesis 12–36: A Commentary,* trans. J. J. Scullion (Minneapolis: Augsburg, 1985), 235, for Gen. 16.

7. See J. G. Janzen, *Abraham and All the Families of the Earth: A Commentary on the Book of Genesis 12–50* (Grand Rapids, Mich.: Eerdmans, 1993), 47.

8. See Nahum Sarna, *Understanding Genesis* (New York: Schocken, 1966), 119.

9. For details, see Terence Fretheim, *The Suffering of God* (Minneapolis: Fortress, 1984), 79–107.

10. See Trible, *Texts of Terror,* 216.

11. See J. G. Janzen, "Hagar in Paul's Eyes and in the Eyes of Yahweh (Genesis 16)," *HBT* 13 (1991): 1–22.

12. Gerhard von Rad, *Genesis,* rev. ed (Philadelphia: Westminster, 1972), 194.

13. See also J. G. Janzen, "Hagar in Paul's Eyes," 13

14. None of the ten or so references to the Ishmaelites and Hagrites in the rest of the OT is negative.

15. See above discussion on Gen. 17.

16. Robert Alter, *Genesis: A New Translation with Commentary* (New York: W. W. Norton, 1996), 98.

17. Tammi J. Schneider, *Sarah, Mother of Nation* (New York: Continuum, 2004), 99; Sharon Jeansonne, *The Women of Genesis: From Sarah to Potiphar's Wife* (Minneapolis: Fortress, 1990), 28, also thinks that Sarah understands God's plan better than Abraham does, and hence God's command to Abraham to do what Sarah says.

18. Schneider, *Sarah*, 99. She notes that God never refers to Ishmael as Abraham's "son" and asks whether the stress on Isaac as the "only son" of Abraham in Gen. 22:2 might be pertinent. One unfortunate dimension of Schneider's often helpful discussion is that while Abraham's faults are often on display, no fault of Sarah's is ever thought to be present in the text.

19. This text is quoted in Rom. 9:7 (and Heb. 11:8), where it is interpreted as a reference to "children of the promise" (rather than "children of the flesh"), a probable reference to the covenantal line.

20. Some of the names in Ishmael's genealogy have been identified with Arabian tribal groups to the east and south of Canaan, but other names are unknown.

21. It is not clear why NRSV translates this phrase in the former sense in 16:12b.

22. Schneider, *Sarah*, 1; she refers to Savina Teubal, *Sarah the Priestess: The First Matriarch of Genesis* (Athens, Ohio: Swallow Press, 1984).

23. See von Rad, *Genesis*, 196.

24. See Janzen, *Genesis 12–50*, 43.

25. Among the many studies of Hagar, see especially Trible, *Texts of Terror*, 9–35; Hemchand Gossai, *Power and Marginality in the Abraham Narrative* (Lanham, Md.: University Press, 1995), 1–33. Among other scholars, Gossai uses the language of "outsider" for Hagar and "insider" for Sarah. It is important to recognize that, as a slave, Hagar faces discrimination and oppression in a more intense way than does Sarah. See Renita Weems, *Just a Sister Away: A Womanist Vision of Women's Relationships in the Bible* (San Diego: LuraMedia, 1988), 8.

26. See Janzen, *Genesis 12–50*, 45. The translation "alongside" in the last phrase of 16:12 (Tanakh; cf. KJV) is to be preferred to NRSV/NIV, yet see fn. 21.

27. Trible, *Texts of Terror*, 28

28. It is wise to remember at this point that Christians also speak of physical and spiritual descendants of Abraham.

29. Approximately 85 percent of Muslims live outside the Middle East.

30. Among the rare mentioning of the Ishmaelites: one of David's sisters married an Ishmaelite (1 Chron. 2:17) and an Ishmaelite and a Hagrite were administrators for David (1 Chron. 27:30–31).

7. ISAAC—BIRTH, ENDANGERMENT, AND SIGN OF THE FUTURE

1. See discussion of Gen. 17 above.

2. One example is 2 Kings 4:8–17, a story of a "man of God" and a Shunammite woman. Parallels in Greek literature—perhaps late developments of Near Eastern prototypes—include a story in which three gods in human form are received hospitably

and give the childless host a son. It is unlikely, however, that the promise of a son, to which God is already committed (17:15–20), is understood as a "reward" for Abraham's hospitality or a "gift" from the guests. Generally speaking, stories about visits from strangers are found in many cultures. See Claus Westermann, *Genesis 12–36: A Commentary*, trans. J. J. Scullion (Minneapolis: Augsburg, 1985), 275–76.

3. For the idea that "Yahweh appeared in all three" men, see Gerhard von Rad, *Genesis*, rev. ed. (Philadelphia: Westminster, 1972), 204; see also Terence Fretheim, *The Suffering of God* (Minneapolis: Fortress, 1984), 79–106.

4. See the details in Sharon Jeansonne, *The Women of Genesis, From Sarah to Potiphar's Wife* (Minneapolis: Fortress, 1990), 22–24.

5. Through the centuries (e.g., Josephus), it has often been thought that angels could not eat and so, in this text, they only appear to eat!

6. See examples in Jeansonne, *The Women of Genesis*, 121, n. 28.

7. Westermann, *Genesis 12–36*, 282.

8. Tammi J. Schneider, *Sarah, Mother of Nations* (New York: Continuum, 2004), 72.

9. God speaks throughout vv. 13–14; that v. 15b is also spoken by God is likely. It seems clear that Sarah's speaking in v. 15 is still taking place "off stage," and that God's speaking to "you" is not face-to-face. God's speaking to Sarah in v. 15 is, finally, no less direct than v. 13, which is clearly intended for Sarah's hearing.

10. Schneider, *Sarah*, 73, suggests that "it is hard to imagine that Sarah would fear the Deity" in view of God's providential work in her life. It is not clear why this would be so. Schneider also thinks that Abraham is the speaker in v. 15, but that is highly unlikely in view of the progress of the conversation to this point. She also claims that v. 14 is spoken by a speaker different from v. 13, but there is no marker to indicate a change in speaker. Schneider's effort to "excuse" Sarah's response seems too strong; indeed, Sarah does not need to be tested for she has been constantly faithful throughout (106).

11. See Fretheim, "Is Anything Too Hard for God? (Jeremiah 32:27)," *CBQ* 66 (2004): 231–36. See Walter Brueggemann. "'Impossibility' and Epistemology in the Faith Tradition of Abraham and Sarah (Gen. 18:1–15)," *ZAW* 94 (1982): 615–34.

12. Walter Brueggemann, *Genesis* (Atlanta: John Knox Press, 1982), 159.

13. See Fretheim, *Suffering of God*, 71–78.

14. On New Testament texts that use this material, see chapter 8.

15. See Jeansonne, *Women of Genesis*, 27; Schneider, *Sarah*, 92–93, notes the differences between Abraham and Sarah.

16. The literature on this passage is immense. See the up-to-date bibliography in Edward Noort and Eibert Tigchelaar, eds., *The Sacrifice of Isaac: The Aqedah (Genesis 22) and its Interpretations* (Leiden: Brill, 2002). For commentary and artistic representations, see Gerhard von Rad, *Das Opfer des Abraham* (Munich: Kaiser, 1971); Robin Jensen, "The Offering of Isaac in Jewish and Christian Tradition: Image and Text," *Biblical Illustrator* 2 (1994): 86–220. See also Jurgen Ebach, *Gott im Wort: Drei Studien zur biblische Exegese und Hermeneutik* (Neukirchen-Vluyn: Newkirchender, 1997), 1–25;

Georg Steins, Die "Bindung Isaaks im Kanon" *(Gen. 22): Grundlagen und Programm einer kanonisch-intertextuellen Lekture* (Freiburg, Germany: Herder, 1999).

17. The disturbing content may be the reason the decision was made not to read this text in the common lectionary; in the Jewish community, however, it is annually read on Rosh Hashanah.

18. Sören Kierkegaard, *Fear and Trembling: A Dialectical Lyric,* trans. Walter Lowrie (Princeton: Princeton University Press, 1941). For a critical analysis of Kierkegaard, see Jon Levenson, "Abusing Abraham: Traditions, Religious Histories, and Modern Misinterpretations," *Judaism* 47 (1998): 259–77. The "teleological suspension of the ethical" says too much. Because God's commands in the Bible are not grounded in some universal morality, so Abraham is not suspending the ethical foundations or "relying on a faith that transcends and diminishes ethical action" (270).

19. See Phyllis Trible, "Genesis 22: The Sacrifice of Sarah," in *'Not in Heaven': Coherence and Complexity in Biblical Narrative,* eds. J. Rosenblatt and J. Sitterson (Bloomington: Indiana University Press, 1991).

20. See the argument of Trible, "The Sacrifice of Sarah," who thinks that the issue is idolatry, becoming more attached to Isaac than to God. On her questionable analysis of "love" in v. 2, see R. W. L. Moberly, *The Bible, Theology, and Faith: A Study of Abraham and Jesus* (Cambridge: Cambridge University Press, 2000), 163–68; see also fn. 41.

21. This story has, of course, long raised troubling issues, but they have largely been focused on the dilemma faced by the parent in the face of the divine command.

22. Alice Miller, *The Untouched Key: Tracing Childhood Trauma in Creativity and Destructiveness* (New York: Doubleday, 1990). She has been joined by many others.

23. Miller, *The Untouched Key,* 139.

24. See Carol Delaney, *Abraham on Trial: The Social Legacy of Biblical Myth* (Princeton, N.J.: Princeton University Press, 1998), regarding related trials; Wayne Oates, *The Bible in Pastoral Care* (Philadelphia: Westminster, 1953), tells the story about a mother's response to hearing a sermon on this text. R. W. L. Moberly's claims, "There is *no* recorded example of Jews or Christians using the text to justify their own abusing or killing of a child," but his statement is insufficiently researched (*The Bible, Theology, and Faith: A Study of Abraham and Jesus,* 129).

25. More broadly, one might cite twentieth century experiences of poverty, homelessness, and violence that have so often caught up the young. Or one thinks of the sending of young men and women into battle to settle conflicts that adults have failed to resolve. Or the saturation bombings of cities that wipe out large numbers of children. Or the death camps and gas chambers that snuff out the lives of children. Or the virtual ignoring of genocidal activities in far-off lands (e.g., Rwanda, Darfur). Sadly, one could go on.

26. A related theme is present in twentieth-century war literature, for example, the poem of Wilfrid Owen who died fighting for England in 1917, "The Parable of the Old Man and the Young." Appended to a posthumous edition was this line: "The willingness

of the older generation to sacrifice the younger." See also Danny Siegel's 1969 look at this text in poetic form: "Father Abraham Genesis 22—Slightly Changed." These poems are gathered in Jo Milgrom, *The Binding of Isaac: The Akedah—A Primary Symbol in Jewish Thought and Art* (Berkeley: BIBAL Press, 1988), 276–78.

27. See the survey in R. W. L. Moberly, *The Bible, Theology, and Faith: A Study of Abraham and Isaac* (Cambridge: Cambridge University Press, 2000).

28. Especially to be noted are Levenson, "Abusing Abraham," 259–77; Jon Levenson, *The Death and Resurrection of the Beloved Son: The Transformation of Child Sacrifice in Judaism and Christianity* (New Haven, Conn.: Yale University Press, 1993); R. W. L. Moberly, *The Bible, Theology, and Faith,* 127–31, 162–83, who follows Levenson. Levenson describes this approach in these terms: Abraham's action has been "increasingly and loudly developed into an interpretation of the last trial as an act of unspeakable cruelty, a paradigm not of love, faith, and submission to God, as in Judaism, Christianity, and Islam, in their traditional formulations, but of hatred, mental illness, and even idolatry" (262).

29. On whether it is appropriate to use the language of substitution, see below.

30. Levenson, "Abusing Abraham," 270–71. He notes parallels in the ancient world (*Death and Resurrection,* 3–24, 43–52). Child sacrifice in general is different and is prohibited in Lev. 20:2–5 and denounced by several of the prophets (e.g., Jer. 19:3–6).

31. Levenson, "Abusing Abraham," 271 (emphasis his). These comments occur in a context of a critique brought against Kierkegaard's *Fear and Trembling,* who, Levenson claims, failed to recognize this historical reality and hence "opens a door to those who judge Abraham to be an unbalanced person."

32. Levenson ("Abusing Abraham," 271–72) suggests that this is a difference between Gen. 18:16–33, against which Abraham protests, and Gen. 22; the former is a "forensic" context (where the death of an innocent person is an outrage, and hence Abraham's intervention), while the latter is a sacrificial context.

33. It should be noted that child sacrifice was a sometime problem for Israel (cf. Lev. 20:2–5; 2 Kings 3:27; Jer. 7:31; 32:35), even if finally abhorrent.

34. Levenson, "Abusing Abraham," 271. R. W. L. Moberly's comments are comparably sharp: "To disregard the context which enabled the meaningful preservation of a story about child sacrifice, and then proclaim the story a problem for contemporary readers, is to create a more or less artificial problem. It exemplifies the truism that context is crucial for meaning" (*Bible, Theology, and Faith,* 129).

35. The etiological reference in 22:14b is unclear (see Westermann, *Genesis 12–36,* 362–63), but has no known reference to the redemption of the firstborn.

36. See discussion below.

37. Levenson ("Abusing Abraham") in considering the question of the emergence of the prohibition (277, fn. 50) considers basically cultic factors, with a mention of Gen. 9:6 and not shedding the blood of human beings made in the image of God. Given what we are told about the suffering of children in the fall of Jerusalem (e.g., Lamentations),

and our knowledge of children more generally, might the suffering of children have been a key factor? It should at least be considered.

38. Generally on the issue of the evaluation of biblical texts, see my essays in *The Bible as Word of God in a Postmodern Age* (Eugene, Ore.: Wipf & Stock, 1998), with Karlfried Froehlich.

39. That Isaac did not return with his father, though that was promised (v. 5), is sometimes cited as a sign of this, but that remains uncertain. For further reflections on the role of Isaac in the text, see below.

40. Levenson, *Death and Resurrection*, 59. The force of the word "only" needs discussion.

41. Levenson, "Abusing Abraham," 272–73.

42. Moberly, *Bible, Theology, and Faith*, 130. I wonder whether this claim slides over much too quickly the vast difference among metaphors regarding their "danger."

43. Moberly, *Bible, Theology, and Faith*, 182. The extent to which the language of self-sacrifice permeates his discussion deserves closer attention on his part. For example, Abraham is "required to sacrifice to God not only the centre of his affections but that which he has lived for and is the content of his hope and his trust in God" (131). Or "the whole burnt offering is symbolic of Abraham's self-sacrifice as a person who unreservedly fears God" (118). He seems not to recognize the dangers of this kind of sacrificial language on the shape and character of the life of faith.

44. See the theme of mourning over an only son. The question may be asked: Has Isaac been sacrificed? Certainly in some respects. And, as Janzen states (*Genesis 12–50*), "Isaac has truly been sacrificed—truly given up and given over the God. The life he will go on to live is now wholly God's, and Abraham no longer has any claim to it" (80–81).

45. Moberly, *Bible, Theology, and Faith*, 101. Moberly emphasizes *Abraham's* learning.

46. Moberly, *Bible, Theology, and Faith*, 130–31.

47. For Israel as the firstborn of God, see Exod. 4:22, an issue faced by the exiles (Jer. 31:9, 20; cf. 2:3). I have spoken of Gen. 22 as metaphor with reference to Israel as firstborn in, "The Book of Genesis," *NIB* 1 (Nashville: Abingdon, 1994), 494, 499. See also Fretheim, "Christology and the Old Testament," in *Who Do You Say That I Am? Essays on Christology*, eds. Mark A. Powell and David R. Bauer (Louisville, Ky.: Westminster / John Knox, 1999), 201–15. The New Testament connections are explicit only in James and Hebrews (see below). For the parallels of Jesus and Abraham, see Ellen Davis, *Getting Involved with God: Rediscovering the Old Testament* (Cambridge, Mass.: Cowley Publications, 2001), 63.

48. I wonder whether Moberly understands metaphor in such a way that the actual sacrifice of the child is not to come to the mind of the reader.

49. This story is commonly assigned to the Elohist (E), with supplements. Because it remains firmly within the circle of the family, it likely has an original pre-Israel setting. At the same time, the theological force of the story takes on new contours as it is

transmitted through the generations, especially vv. 15–19. On this point, see R. W. L. Moberly, "The Earliest Commentary on the Akedah," *VT* 38 (1988): 302–23.

50. Erich Auerbach, "Odysseus' Scar," in *Mimesis: The Representation of Reality in Western Literature* (Princeton, N.J.: Princeton University Press, 1953), 11–12.

51. See the formulation of David Gunn and Danna Nolan Fewell, *Narrative in the Hebrew Bible* (Oxford: Oxford University Press, 1993): "Abraham is a man who has shown that he has no problem sacrificing members of his family" (98). For their reading against the grain, see pp. 98–100; see also David Gunn and Danna Nolan Fewell, *Gender, Power, and Promise: The Subject of the Bible's First Story* (Nashville: Abingdon, 1993), 52–55.

52. For detail, see Scott Nikaido, "Hagar and Ishmael as Literary Figures: An Intertextual Study," *VT* 51 (2001): 219–42.

53. Brueggemann, *Genesis*, 183.

54. Too much can be made of the identification of the place with Jerusalem (e.g., Moberly, *Bible, Theology, and Faith*, 108–18), not least because the explicit connections are so tenuous in the text itself (readers may have seen more clues than we can, but we have to go with what is given). That the linkage to Jerusalem has not been claimed by many modern scholars is probably due to their careful attention to the text itself.

55. Phyllis Trible ("Genesis 22: The Sacrifice of Sarah") considers v. 2 to portray a defective relationship between parent and child. Moberly's critique of this perspective (*The Bible, Theology, and Faith*, 163–68) is based particularly on a study of the words of v. 2, which denote only positive dimensions of a relationship. Moberly may not sufficiently take into account that the prior narratives do not portray a particularly close relationship between Abraham and Isaac (see especially 21:1–14). Tammi Schneider (*Sarah*, 104) even suggests that the "only" son "whom you love" of 22:2 may be ironic because it is not fully true in that Ishmael is still alive; hence the question becomes: "Is *Isaac* the son whom Abraham loves?" She notes that Abraham's distress over the loss of Ishmael (21:12) is not replicated with the potential loss of Isaac. The scene in 21:8–21 "may be the background for the Deity's need to test Abraham in the next chapter (22) since Abraham's actions do not indicate complete acceptance of the plan the Deity lays out in Gen. 17" (99).

56. For a study of divine seeing, see Moberly, *The Bible, Theology, and Faith*, 107–18.

57. Cf. the lengthy discussion of "fear of God" in Moberly, *The Bible, Theology and Faith*, 80–97. It is not entirely clear to me how Moberly understands this phrase (see 96–97). He is certainly correct in eliminating the sense of "fear of unpleasant consequences," but his use of "obedience," "human integrity, rooted in responsive recognition of God," and "fundamental trust in God" seems to need further nuance. Trust seems to be a secondary meaning of the word for him. For Levenson ("Abusing Abraham"): "what is tested in Genesis 22 is not Abraham's *faith* but his *fear* of God (v. 12)—that is, his responsiveness to the divine imperative." He stresses the sense of obedience and reverence. The essence of the test: "That Abraham is required to

choose his fear of God over his love of Isaac may seem unfair or unnecessary, but it is precisely the agony of the choice that makes the act a 'sacrifice' in the larger sense of the word" (270).

58. For detail, see the discussion in Hemchand Gossai, *Power and Marginality in the Abraham Narrative* (Lanham, Md.: University Press, 1995), 158–60. Cf. also M. J. Kohn, "The Trauma of Isaac," *JBQ* (1991–1992): 100. Is this experience at all related to Isaac's ineptness in Gen. 26–27?

59. See my study of this text and its implications for reflections on the God of the text in "The Book of Genesis," 494–501.

60. Moberly, *The Bible, Theology, and Faith*, 97 (emphasis his). See his full discussion, 97–107.

61. See the discussion in Brueggemann, "'Impossibility' and Epistemology."

62. Westermann, *Genesis 12–36*, 359; see also John Goldingay, *Old Testament Theology: Israel's Gospel*, vol. 1 (Downer's Grove, Ill.: InterVarsity Press, 2003), 237.

63. Ellen Davis (*Getting Involved with God*, 60–63) also speaks of the vulnerability of God in this story. She speaks of "God's supreme vulnerability to human unfaithfulness" (63); see also James Crenshaw, *Whirlpool of Torment* (Philadelphia: Fortress, 1984), 29.

64. Eugene Roop, *Genesis* (Scottsdale, Pa.: Herald Press, 1987), 151.

65. Wilhelm Gesenius, Emil Kautzsch, and A. E. Cowley, *Gesenius' Hebrew Grammar* (Oxford: Oxford University Press, 1910), 324.

66. Moberly calls attention to Exod. 20:20, with its linkage of testing and the fear of God in connection with the giving of the Ten Commandments (*The Bible, Theology, and Faith*, 81–84). He thinks that this text shows that "Abraham is a type or model of Israel"; he gives "narrative embodiment" to obedience of commandments; "this is what the shape of Israel's obedient life should look like" (83–84). While he recognizes that the Ten Commandments are ongoing in a way that the command to Abraham is not, his discussion of the point is insufficient. Generally, it seems to me unlikely that Abraham is considered a model for Israel, not least because the specific command to Abraham would never be asked of Israel in any circumstance of life. For my treatment of Exod. 20:20, see Fretheim, *Exodus* (Louisville, Ky.: Westminster / John Knox, 1991), 214–20.

67. As Trible ("Sacrifice of Sarah") suggests, a "lesson of nonattachment" to Isaac.

68. Brueggemann, *Genesis*, 187.

69. Crenshaw, *Whirlpool of Torment*, 2.

70. For detail on this issue, see Fretheim, *Suffering of God*, 45–59. Moberly's claim that testing in the Bible has to do with "human growth to moral and spiritual maturity" (*The Bible, Theology, and Faith*, 175) insufficiently recognizes that testing also has to do with divine knowledge. He does claim that it is a matter of divine "concern"; "the test and its outcome *matters* to God. . . . The logic of God's 'need to know' is that of

relationship and response. . . . God is engaged within the encounter in such a way that the outcome is a genuine divine concern" (105, 107; emphasis his). Can it be such a concern for God if God has full knowledge of what Abraham will do?

71. Divine omniscience is also not placed in question, for God knows all there is to know, but there is a future which is not yet fully available for knowing.

72. See Westermann, *Genesis 12–36*, 362. Westermann does not use "substitute" language, but it is common for scholars to do so.

73. One new theme is the possession of the "gate of their enemies" (as in 24:60). This raises a question as to whether the blessing of God will always be good for the world (12:3); it may be a note of realism that the promise of kings and nations (17:16) will at times entail warfare against enemies, perhaps even the dispossession of nations (e.g., the Canaanites; see 15:16).

74. Moberly, "The Earliest Commentary on the Akedah," 321 (emphasis mine). He draws a helpful analogy with intercessory prayer, where "faithful human response to God is taken up and incorporated within the purposes and activity of God." My theological reflections on Gen. 45:5–9 and 50:21 take a similar approach to God's use of human activity, in this case, evil (Fretheim, "The Book of Genesis," 646).

75. It is important to distinguish faithfulness and obedience. Faithfulness may, at times, entail disobedience of particular laws. See, for example, Tamar's action in Gen. 38, Jesus' disobedience of Sabbath law, the parable of the Good Samaritan, etc.

76. It is commonly assigned to the Yahwist (J).

77. No claim is being made that wealth and success are always due to the blessing work of God. People can come by possessions and prosperity through evil means. It is always a matter of interpretation as to whether one can ascribe such realities to divine blessing.

78. Westermann, *Genesis 12–36*, 382.

79. Gerhard von Rad, *Genesis,* 260.

80. In Gen. 21:25–32, the interaction between Abraham and Abimelech over a well, issuing in a covenant, may constitute some claim to the land, especially with the symbolic value of the water and the well. See also the emphasis on wells in the stories of Isaac in 26:15–32.

81. The chapter is usually assigned to Priestly writer. The Hittites, a people infrequently encountered in the Old Testament, may have been an enclave of non-Semitic peoples in Canaan or a variant name for Canaanites.

82. This is also the burial place of Isaac and Rebekah, Jacob and Leah.

83. Ancient Near Eastern documents provide parallels to aspects of this transaction. See Nahum Sarna, *Understanding Genesis* (New York: Schocken, 1970), 156–60.

84. Janzen, *Genesis 12–50,* 85.

85. For details, see Sarna, *Understanding Genesis,* 170–77. The Midianites are one known family, see Gen. 37:28, 36.

86. Gen. 25:6 refers to both wives (so 16:3; 25:1) as "concubines," perhaps to set them off from Sarah.

87. Being "gathered to his people" (Gen. 25:8, 17; 35:29; 49:33), a phrase unique to the Pentateuch, does not refer to death or burial; Sheol or some other form of afterlife may be in mind.

8. ABRAHAM IN MEMORY AND TRADITION

1. For a very helpful collection of early (approx 200 B.C.E. to 150 C.E.) interpretations of the Abraham stories, Jewish and Christian, see James L. Kugel, *Traditions of the Bible: A Guide to the Bible As It Was at the Start of the Common Era* (Cambridge, Mass: Harvard University Press, 1998), 244–340.

2. R. W. L. Moberly, *The Old Testament of the Old Testament: Patriarchal Narratives and Mosaic Yahwism* (Minneapolis: Fortress, 1992).

3. Moberly, *The Old Testament of the Old Testament,* 126.

4. J. G. Janzen, *Abraham and All the Families of the Earth: A Commentary on the Book of Genesis 12–50* (Grand Rapids, Mich.: Eerdmans, 1993), 7–12. See also Jon Levenson, "The Conversion of Abraham," in *The Idea of Biblical Interpretation: Essays in Honor of James L. Kugel,* eds. H. Najman and J. Newman (Leiden: Brill, 2004), 7–18.

5. Moberly, *The Old Testament of the Old Testament,* 156, 161.

6. Janzen, *Genesis 12–50,* 8. See also Jon Levenson's critique of Moberly's supersessionism in "Abusing Abraham: Traditions, Religious Histories, and Modern Misinterpretations," *Judasim* 47 (1998): 14–18.

7. It is striking that Moberly, in developing his thesis, does not consider in any detail the use of Abrahamic texts in the New Testament; especially pertinent would be Gal. 3–4 and Rom. 4.

8. Janzen, *Genesis 12–50,* 8.

9. For further discussion of the Pauline argument, see below.

10. Moberly does not discuss this verse.

11. For a traditional view of the history of the Abraham tradition, see Ronald Clements, *Abraham and David: Genesis 15 and Its Meaning for Israelite Religion* (London: SCM, 1967). This perspective takes seriously a relatively early date for the Yahwist, perhaps the United Monarchy, while recognizing a renewed interest in Abraham in the exilic and postexilic periods. Others would date most or all of the Abrahamic materials from this later era; see, for example, John Van Seters, *Abraham in History and Tradition* (New Haven, Conn.: Yale University Press, 1975). I believe that our knowledge, particularly regarding the dating of texts, is insufficient to sort this matter out in any thoroughgoing way. It seems to me that the traditional view still has much to commend it. Our concern here is more thematic in its basic orientation. For historical issues more generally, see above, chapter 2.

12. For detail, see Clements, *Abraham and David,* 47–60.

13. Ample opportunity must have existed for later editors to have the Abrahamic texts speak to issues in their own time, such as idolatry (see Josh. 24:2–3). Yet, Genesis presents a remarkably peaceful religious atmosphere; it has not been shaped by later religious conflicts in Israel in any significant way.

14. This is also the case with David.

15. For detail, see Terence Fretheim, "The Book of Genesis," *NIB* 1 (Nashville: Abingdon, 1994), 529. Karl-Josef Kuschel, *Abraham: Sign of Hope for Jews, Christians and Muslims* (New York: Continuum, 1995), says its well: Abraham's faith is quite complex, "there is a touch of doubt and a touch of cunning, a touch of anxiety and a touch of risk-taking with his God; a touch of wordless obedience and a touch of canny haggling" (26).

16. Also to be noted in this connection are the ongoing references to Israel's God as the "God of Abraham" (Exod. 3:6, 15–16; 4:5; 1 Kings 18:36; 1 Chron. 29:18; 2 Chron. 30:6; Ps. 47:9; cf. Mark 12:26; Luke 20:37; Acts 3:13; 7:32).

17. For discussion, see above, chapter 2.

18. For a survey of later usage of the Abrahamic tradition, see Clements, *Abraham and David*, 61–78. He treats the Yahwist and Priestly accounts of Abraham separately; the Priestly account makes certain advances over the older accounts (e.g., circumcision), though the theme of divine promise remains prominent; indeed, it is even more decisively emphasized (Gen. 17). As such, the Priestly treatment of the Abrahamic covenant participates in the postexilic renewal of the importance of Abraham for the community of faith. On the differences between the covenants in Gen. 15 and 17, see above, chapter 3.

19. On the Priestly "subordination of the Sinai event to the Abrahamic covenant," see Clements, *Abraham and David*, 74–77. The "everlasting" promises to David constitute a comparable divine commitment to later Israel; Jer. 33:14–26 explicitly brings these promises together. On the relationship between God's covenants with Abraham and David, see Clements.

20. See T. Fretheim, "Repentance in the Former Prophets," in *Repentance in Christian Theology*, eds. Mark Boda and Gordon Smith (Collegeville, Minn.: Liturgical Press, 2006).

21. Other references to Abraham include the genealogy (1 Chron. 1:27–34) and the identity of Israel's God as the "God of Abraham" (1 Chron. 29:18; 2 Chron. 30:6).

22. Janzen, *Genesis 12–50*, 10. Also helpful here is Fredrick Holmgren, "Faithful Abraham and the 'amana Covenant: Nehemiah 9:6–10:1," *ZAW* 104 (1992): 249–54.

23. Holmgren, "Faithful Abraham," 252.

24. Several references are also made to the ancestors, especially as associated with the promise of the land (e.g., Josh. 1:6; 5:6; 18:3; 21:43–44; Judg. 2:1).

25. Later Jewish writings (see below) will expand upon this theme. See especially the work of James Kugel, *Traditions of the Bible: A Guide to the Bible as It Was at the Start of the Common Era* (Cambridge, Mass.: Harvard University Press, 1998).

26. In these texts, Israel's God is occasionally named the "God of Abraham (Isaac, Israel)" (1 Kings 18:36) or the "God of your fathers" (Josh. 18:3; Judg. 2:12), thus continuing to link Israel's very identity with these ancestors.

27. Several references to the "ancestors" should also be noted, especially regarding the promises of land and posterity (Jer. 7:7, 14, 11:5, 14:21, 30:3, 32:22, 33:22; Ezek. 36:28, 47:14, cf. Ezek. 16:60). Moreover, the repeated use of the "covenant formula" ("you shall be my people, and I will be your God; Jer. 11:4; 24:7; 30:22; 31:1, 33; 32:38) recalls covenant formulations in Gen. 17:7–8.

28. See Clements, *Abraham and David,* 63, 69–70.

29. See below for discussion.

30. See T. Fretheim, *Smith & Helwys Bible Commentary: Jeremiah* (Macon, Ga.: Smith & Helwys, 2002), 414.

31. This is the only reference to Sarah in the Old Testament beyond Genesis.

32. On this theme, see Ronald S. Hendel, *Remembering Abraham: Culture, Memory, and History in the Hebrew Bible* (Oxford: Oxford University Press, 2005), 32.

33. Hendel, *Remembering Abraham,* 32.

34. See Terence E. Fretheim, *Exodus* (Louisville, Ky.: Westminster / John Knox, 1991) 48.

35. See discussion above.

36. Judith. 8:26, with its call to "remember Abraham," refers to the story of the near-sacrifice of Isaac (which is not referenced in the shorter Old Testament).

37. Hendel, 32

38. See the list of texts in William Lyons, *Canon and Exegesis: Canonical Praxis and the Sodom Narrative* (London: Sheffield Academic Press, 2002), 236–39; J. A. Loader, *A Tale of Two Cities: Sodom and Gomorrah in the Old Testament, Early Jewish and Early Christian Traditions* (Kampen: J. H. Kok, 1990).

39. Sodom and Gomorrah occur together in ten of these texts. Sodom alone is mentioned in three contexts (Isa. 3:9; Lam. 4:6; Ezek. 16:46–56); Gomorrah never occurs alone. There are three references in the Apocrypha (2 Esd. 2:8; 5:7; 3 Macc. 2:5); in the last two texts Sodom occurs alone. Eight New Testament contexts refer to these cities (Sodom alone in four of them). The disaster experienced by Sodom and Gomorrah may also be recalled in the images of disaster used in several texts (Ps. 11:6; Ezek. 38:22).

40. None of the sins seem to be referenced in Genesis, unless "abominable things" includes them (cf. Loader, *A Tale of Two Cities,* 65; Walther Eichrodt, *Ezekiel: A Commentary* [London: SCM Press, 1970], 168, speaks of a separate tradition upon which Ezekiel is dependent).

41. I follow the listing in the NRSV (see *The HarperCollins Study Bible* [New York: HarperCollins, 1993], 1435). Generally speaking, these works may be dated in the last two centuries B.C.E., with 3–4 Macc. and 2 Esd. likely originating in the first century C.E. (2 Esd. 1–2, 15–16 are commonly considered Christian additions). For resources,

see commentaries on individual books. For texts, see James Charlesworth, ed., *The Old Testament Pseudepigrapha*, 2 vols. (New York: Doubleday, 1983–1985). For a survey of Abraham in this Jewish literature (and Pseudepigrapha), see G. Walter Hanson, *Abraham in Galatians: Epistolary and Rhetorical Contexts* (Sheffield: JSOT Press, 1989), 175–99; Samuel Sandmel, *Philo's Place in Judaism: A Study of Conceptions of Abraham in Jewish literature* (New York: KTAV, 1971). See also E. P Sanders, *Paul and Palestinian Judaism: A Comparison of Patterns of Religion* (Philadelphia: Fortress, 1977). For an up-to-date introduction to this literature, see George W. E. Nickelsburg, *Jewish Literature between the Bible and the Mishnah*, 2nd ed. (Minneapolis: Fortress, 2005).

42. Sarah and Ishmael are not mentioned at all and Hagar only in passing ("the descendants of Hagar," Bar. 3:23). Lot is mentioned explicitly once (destruction of "the neighbors of Lot," Sir. 16:5) and indirectly in Wis. 10:6–8, where Lot "a righteous man" escaped from the cities; reference is also made to "a pillar of salt," a "monument to an unbelieving soul." The destruction of Sodom and Gomorrah is mentioned rarely (2 Esd. 2:8; cf. 5:7; 7:36/106). God consumed with fire the people of Sodom "who acted arrogantly, who were notorious for their vices" (3 Macc. 2:5; see also Wis. of Sol. 19:13–17). Isaac is mentioned some twenty times, always associated with Abraham, as part of the triad Abraham, Isaac, and Jacob (Tob. 4:12; Bar. 2:34; Azar. 1:12; Man. 1:1, 8; 2 Esd. 1:39; 2 Macc. 1:2; 4 Macc. 13:17; 16:25), as fulfillment of the promise to Abraham and as in turn blessed with children (Sir. 44:22; 2 Esd. 3:15; 6:8), and particularly in association with the testing of Abraham (Jdt. 8:26; 1 Macc. 2:52; 4 Macc. 7:14; 13:12; 16:20; 18:11; cf Wisd. of Sol. 10:5).

43. See Nancy Calvert-Koyzis, *Paul, Monotheism, and the People of God: The Significance of Abraham Traditions for Early Judaism and Christianity* (London: T&T Clark, 2004).

44. See Jeffrey Siker, *Disinheriting the Jews: Abraham in Early Christian Controversy* (Louisville, Ky.: Westminster / John Knox, 1991), 19–24.

45. The fulfillment of the Abrahamic promise is also alluded to in Jth. 5:10.

46. Abraham is also mentioned in passing as the "father" of Isaac and Esau (2 Esd. 6:8) and as one who prayed for Sodom (7:36/106; cf. also 1:39).

47. This promise may be assumed in 3 Macc. 6:3 (ca. 30 B.C.E.–70 C.E.), wherein God is called upon to look favorably upon the "descendants of Abraham," who are perishing.

48. A false claim regarding the "family of Abraham" is mentioned in passing in 1 Macc. 12:21.

49. This quotation from Gen. 15:6 is unique in the Deuterocanonical books. Gen. 15:6 seems to be interpreted as having a force comparable to Gen. 22:15–18, where it is twice stated that "because" Abraham did not withhold his son, the promises of God were now, for the first time, "sworn" to him. See discussion above in chapter 7.

50. The reason for speaking of God testing *Isaac* is probably related to other texts that speak of the full cooperation of Isaac (see 4 Macc. 16:20). God "tested *Isaac* (!)

. . . with fire . . . to search their hearts" (8:26–27). But God "has not tried us with fire, as he did them" (8:12).

51. In the Additions to Esther (ca. 100 B.C.E.), two references to the "God of Abraham" are mentioned in passing (13:15; 14:18).

52. Contrary to Kuschel, *Abraham,* 33.

53. See Levenson, "The Conversion of Abraham." Tobit (ca. 200 B.C.E.) may allude to a comparable relationship of practice and promise. Abraham is mentioned in a list of ancestral figures who practiced endogamy and whose children were blessed, inheriting the land (4:12).

54. See B. W. Anderson, "Abraham, the Friend of God," *Interpretation* 42 (1988): 353–66; Jacqueline E. Lapsley, "Friends with God? Moses and the Possibility of Covenantal Friendship," *Interpretation* 58 (2004): 117–29; Luke Timothy Johnson, *The Letter of James: A New Translation with Introduction and Commentary* (New York: Doubleday, 1995), 243–44.

55. Genesis Apocryphon, Philo, and Josephus are also to be noted; Philo especially gives considerable attention to Abraham. Among the resources for this, see various collections of essays edited by Craig Evans and James Sanders; volumes by James Kugel and Nancy Calvert–Koyzis. For a survey of Abraham in this literature, see Sandmel, *Philo's Place;* Hanson, *Abraham in Galatians.*

56. For recent perspectives on the book, see James Vanderkam, *The Book of Jubilees* (Sheffield: Academic Press, 2001); Betsy Halpern-Amaru, *The Empowerment of Women in the Book of Jubilees* (Leiden: Brill, 1999). See also works by James Kugel, including *Traditions of the Bible.* On Abraham in *Jubilees,* see Sandmel, *Philo's Place,* 38–49.

57. The Genesis chronology is open to this expansion to some degree, for Abraham lives for fifteen years after the births of Jacob and Esau (see Gen. 21:5; 25:7, 26). Moreover, *Jubilees,* perhaps expanding upon "the charge" in Gen. 18:19 (cf. *Jub.* 20.2) and in view of the final testament of Jacob (Gen. 49), has Abraham giving testaments to all his sons (20:6–10), then Isaac alone (21), and then to Jacob (22.10–24, 28–30), drawing on several biblical texts (e.g., Gen. 12:2).

I include some other examples of change from the *Jubilees* presentation of Abraham here. *Jubilees* has a streamlined version of the introduction to the Sodom story (cf. Gen. 18:1–15 with *Jub.* 16:1–4) and the destruction of the cities, with expansions on the sins of Sodom (Gen. 19:24–28, with parallels in *Jub.* 16:5–6; cf. 9.15; 20.3–6; 23.14). *Jub.* 16:5 (cf. 23.14) refers to the sexual sins of the Sodomites, with no apparent reference to same sex behaviors. References to Sodom's sins as sexual are also present in *Testaments of the Twelve Patriarchs,* with possible reference to same sex activity (*Levi.* 14:6–8, "sexual relations" with "loose women" like Sodom and Gomorrah; *Naph.* 3:4, "departed from the order of nature"; *Benj.* 9:1, "promiscuity of the Sodomites"). *Jubilees* omits the dialogue between Abraham and God regarding the fate of Sodom (Gen. 18:23–33), though includes their questioning exchange from Gen. 15:1–8 (*Jub.* 14.1–9). Direct speech is omitted altogether and hence the character of the narrative is shifted (see J. van Ruiten, "Lot Versus Abraham, the Interpretation of Genesis 18:1–19:38 in *Jubilees* 16:1–9," in *Sodom's Sin: Genesis 18–19 and its Interpretations,* eds. E. Noort and E. Tigchelaar (Leiden: Brill, 2004), 29–46. *Jubilees* presents an ambivalent attitude toward Lot. He is given an extensive genealogy and stands in the affection of Abraham (*Jub.* 13.18). Yet, the report of Lot and the visitors and the story of Lot and his daughters are abbreviated, with no mention of births or children's names, and, unlike Gen. 19:30–38, their sinfulness is unambiguous, with the initiative ascribed to Lot rather than to Lot's daughters (*Jub.* 16.7–9).

Whereas in Gen. 18:10–15, God speaks to Abraham about the birth of a child, in *Jubilees* it is the angels speaking to Sarah (whose status is thereby elevated). Sarah has more knowledge of developments in the narrative than in Genesis (*Jub.* 14.21; 16.3, 19). See Halpern-Amaru, *The Empowerment of Women,* for this and other examples. The place of Sarah is rewritten in such a way that "the supportive wife is transformed into a copartner" (47). In response to the announcement, Abraham fell on his face as an expression of joy (not incredulity), pondering in his heart whether a child would be born to him at his age (*Jub.* 15.17; cf. Gen. 17:17). Sarah's laughter is not comparably interpreted (*Jub.* 16.2). See Elaine Phillips, "Incredulity, Faith, and Textual Purposes: Post-Biblical Responses to the Laughter of Abraham and Sarah," in *Function of Scripture in Early Jewish and Christian Tradition,* eds. Craig A. Evans and James A. Sanders (Sheffield: Academic Press, 1998), 22–33. The point of the annunciation story has also been adjusted from God's (remarkable) fulfillment of the promise of offspring to Abraham, to one of the proper lineage of Isaac through Sarah and Abraham. The story of Hagar in Gen. 16 is abbreviated and Sarah's treatment of Hagar is softened (*Jub.* 14.21–24; cf. Gen. 16:1–14).

When Gen. 13:4 states that Abraham called on the name of the Lord, *Jub.* 13:16 states what Abraham said. On the other hand, the long narrative in Gen. 24 regarding a search for a wife for Isaac is reduced to a single verse (*Jub.* 19.10).

58. They occur in a somewhat different order (and, unlike Genesis, Abraham even "told all of these things to Sarah," *Jub.* 14.21).

59. The angelic visitors also announce to Abraham that he will bear six sons by Keturah (*Jub.* 16.16; cf. Gen. 25:1–6).

60. It omits the story of Abraham's endangerment of Sarah in Gen. 20 and recasts it in Gen. 12:10–20, so that Abraham is not to blame; rather, Pharaoh endangers Sarah by "taking" her from Abraham (*Jub.* 13.10–15). Notably, *Jubilees* also omits all references to Sarah's barrenness and Sarah is clearly Abraham's sister (cf. Gen. 20:12). See Paul Borgman, "Abraham and Sarah: Literary Text and the Rhetorics of Reflection," in *The Function of Scripture in Early Jewish and Christian Tradition,* eds. Craig A. Evans and James A. Sanders (Sheffield: Academic Press, 1998), 45–51. See his citation of an Emily Dickinson poem (45). Jon Levenson, "The Conversion of Abraham," agrees with Eichler's more positive reading of Gen. 12:10–20. "Those who think the future patriarch should have told the truth need to explain how Sarah would have been better off

with him dead and herself absorbed indefinitely into the Pharaoh's harem" (5, fn. 11). Yet, this argument would not pertain to Gen. 20. Levenson notes the parallels with the opening chapters of Exodus.

61. See James L. Kugel and Rowan A. Greer, *Early Biblical Interpretation* (Philadelphia: Westminster, 1986), 85–90.

62. For detail, see VanderKam, *The Book of Jubilees,* 50–51, 100–109. Examples include the law of the tithe in association with the story of Abraham's encounter with Melchizedek in Gen. 14:20 (*Jub.* 13.25–27). The law of circumcision is much expanded (*Jub.* 15.11–14, 23–34). Abraham is the first to celebrate the Feasts of Weeks (*Jub.* 14:20; 22.1), Booths (16.20–31), Unleavened Bread (18.17–19), First Fruits (22.1–9), and he transmits sacrificial legislation to Isaac (21.1–26).

63. For the history of interpretation of Gen. 22, see Edward Kessler, *Bound by the Bible: Jews, Christians, and the Sacrifice of Isaac* (Cambridge: Cambridge University Press, 2004); Edward Noort and Eibert Tigschelaar, eds., *The Sacrifice of Isaac: The Aqedah (Genesis 22) and its Interpretations* (Leiden: Brill, 2002).

64. The completion of the story of the near-sacrifice of Isaac becomes the occasion for the origin of the Feast of Unleavened Bread (*Jub.* 18.17–19). It may have been generative of theological reflection that *Jubilees,* with its concern about chronology and the timing of festivals, has Abraham and Isaac arriving at Moriah at the beginning of Passover. See Kessler, *Bound by the Bible,* 140–41. The location of the place of sacrifice is identified with Mount Zion in *Jub.* 18.8, 13 (probably based on 1 Chron. 3:1, where Mt. Moriah is identified with Jerusalem).

65. This work came to be associated with Philo (hence the title), but most agree that is not the case. The work is often referred to by the Latin title *Liber Antiquitatem Biblicarum (LAB).* For a basic introduction, see D. J. Harrington, "Pseudo-Philo: A New Translation and Introduction," in *The Old Testament Pseudepigrapha* 2, ed. James Charlesworth (Garden City, N.Y.: Doubleday, 1983, 1985), 297–303.

66. See *LAB* 4.11; 6.3–8.3; 18.5–6; 23.5–8, 11–13; 30.7; 32.1–4; 40.2.

67. Harrington, "Pseudo-Philo," 301.

68. Howard Jacobson, *A Commentary on Pseudo-Philo's LAB* (Leiden: Brill, 1996), 356–58, shows that the issue of Abraham's loyalty in *LAB* 6 is related to rebellion, not idolatry. Nancy Calvert-Koyzis, *Paul, Monotheism, and the People of God: The Significance of Abraham Traditions for Early Judaism and Christianity* (London: T&T Clark, 2004), 44–48, disagrees but can only draw inferences to that end. That Abraham is never specifically said to reject idolatry seems important, especially in view of the fact that numerous other figures specifically are named as succumbing to idolatry (e.g., 36.3; 44.1–5).

69. For detail on this motif, see Kugel and Greer, *Early Biblical Interpretation,* 85–90. Gen. 12:1–3 is spoken in Ur (not Haran), which jibes with Gen. 15:7 (so 11:31 and 12:1–3 are not in chronological order). That "Ur" has another meaning in Hebrew (fire

or flame) provides a "fire" motif, perhaps a connection to the idea that Abraham set fire to the house of idols.

70. As with *Jubilees*, Abraham is saved from "the fire [cf. Ur] of the Chaldeans" (cf. Gen. 15:7).

71. Terah is not an idolater in *LAB* (unlike *Jubilees*).

72. For Pseudo-Philo, "there is one central virtue, ideal and obligation, aside from the necessity to obey God's Law. That is to have absolute and unyielding faith in God and God alone." Jacobson, *A Commentary on Pseudo-Philo's LAB,* 1:245.

73. The most recent and thorough analysis is that of Dale Allison, *Testament of Abraham* (Berlin: de Gruyter, 2003).

74. Allison, *Testament,* 42, 51, considers it a parody, an "anti-testament."

75. Allison, *Testament,* 28–31. There are two recensions in which the Testament of Abraham appears: a longer form, most likely best representing the contents and ordering of the original (A), and a shorter, less verbose, and less Christianized form (B). Both may go back to a common original.

76. Allison, *Testament,* 50.

77. Allison, *Testament,* 51.

78. E. P. Sanders in Charlesworth, 876–77.

79. Allison, *Testament,* 50.

80. As nearly as I can tell, Allison considers this dimension of the book ironic. At the same time, the pervasiveness of the positive language leaves one wondering whether the point is not ironic, but a recognition that even the righteous, the friends of God, can be stupid and sinful. This would, finally, make the Testament more like the Genesis narrative.

81. Allison, *Testament,* 51.

82. See also 2.6; 4.7; 8.2–4; 9.7; 15.12–14; 16.5, 9; 20.14; B4.10; 8.2; 13.1. For the many references to Abraham as the friend of God, see Allison, *Testament,* 77–78. Abraham does not use it for himself.

83. R. Rubinkiewicz in Charlesworth, 681.

84. Other texts testify that Abraham was an astronomer who taught the Chaldeans (Artapanus; various rabbinic writings, for example, *Genesis Rabbah* 39:1).

85. In addition to the literature cited above, see also Ezekiel the Tragedian, 104–7; 4 Ezra 3:14–17; 9:7–9; 13:48; Genesis Apocryphon (1 QapGen. 21:8–14); 1QS 8:4–7; Pss. Sol. 9:9; 18:3; Ass. Mos. 1:8–9; 2:1; 3:9; 2 Bar. 3:4–5; 9:2; T. Levi 15:4; T. Isaac 2:22.

86. J. Siker, *Disinheriting the Jews,* 21.

87. Cf. the list in J. Siker, *Disinheriting Abraham,* 22. For other texts from this literature, see 2 Bar. 57:1–2.

88. 1 Corinthians, Ephesians, Philippians, Colossians, Thessalonians, the Pastorals, 2 Peter, Jude, and Revelation do not explicitly mention Abraham, and Mark, 2

Corinthians, and 1 Peter do so only in passing. We are not concerned here with the question of the dependence or nondependence of New Testament writers on existing Jewish literature, though it is difficult to imagine that readers of this literature would remain unaffected by it.

89. Jeffrey S. Siker, *Disinheriting the Jews: Abraham in Early Christian Controversy* (Louisville: Westminster / John Knox, 1991); Hanson, *Abraham in Galatians.* See also F. F. Bruce, "Abraham Our Father," in *The Time is Fulfilled: Five Aspects of the Fulfillment of the Old Testament in the New* (Grand Rapids, Mich.: Eerdmans, 1982), 57–74.

90. Loader, *A Tale of Two Cities,* 119.

91. See Nils Dahl, "The Story of Abraham in Luke-Acts," in *Studies in Luke-Acts,* eds. L. Keck and J. L. Martyn (Nashville: Abingdon, 1966).

92. The harsh language about the Jews probably reflects early conflicts about the continuing relationship between Christians and Jews (see the discussion in Siker, *Disinheriting the Jews,* 128–43). Kuschel (*Abraham,* 116) refers to the Gospel of John as the beginnings of the "Christianization of Abraham," who is detached from Judaism and used to sustain Christian claims. This direction of thought is carried on in the Letter of Barnabas, Ignatius, Justin, and Augustine (117–29).

93. Among the many studies of Paul's use of the Scriptures, see the commentaries on these verses in Richard B. Hays, *Echoes of Scripture in the Letters of Paul* (New Haven: Yale University Press, 1989); John L. White, *The Apostle of God: Paul and the Promise of Abraham* (Peabody, Mass.: Hendrickson, 1999); James W. Aageson, *Written Also for Our Sake: Paul and the Art of Biblical Interpretation* (Louisville, Ky.: Westminster / John Knox, 1993); E. P. Sanders, *Paul, the Law, and the Jewish People;* Siker, *Disinheriting the Jews,* 28–76; Ernst Kasemann, "The Faith of Abraham in Romans 4," in *Perspectives on Paul* (Philadelphia: Fortress, 1971); Roy A. Harrisville, Jr., *The Figure of Abraham in The Epistles of St. Paul: In the Footsteps of Abraham.* We are not concerned here with the question of the dependence or nondependence of Paul on existing literature. For such concerns, see Harrisville, who seems overly concerned to claim that Paul was not in any way dependent on sources other than the Old Testament.

94. In what follows we do not deal with every aspect of Paul's argument; we focus on the issues related to Abraham.

95. See Hays, *Echoes of Scripture,* 165–73.

96. Hays, *Echoes of Scripture,* 54.

97. This is also a key concern in Gen. 22 (see above, chapter 7).

98. For discussion and bibliography, see Brian J. Abasciano, *Paul's Use of the Old Testament in Romans 9:1–9: An Intertextual and Theological Exegesis* (London: T&T Clark, 2005).

99. This is also a point made by the Old Testament itself (see above p. 149).

100. The continuing importance of Ishmael for Paul should not be neglected: "Paul does not include Ishmael in the promise in so many words. But he does include gentiles, for whom Ishmael serves as the first representative, shown by the fact that the

themes Paul develops in Rom. 9 are embedded in Ishmael's story." So T. W. Berkley, *From a Broken Covenant to Circumcision of the Heart: Pauline Intertextual Exegesis in Romans 2:17–29* (Atlanta: SBL, 2000), 169. The response of Abasciano (*Paul's Use of the Old Testament*) that Ishmael was "the pattern for non-believing Israel" (194) insufficiently takes into account God's repeated promises to Ishmael (unique for an "outsider") and his circumcision.

101. See the discussion in Aageson, *Written Also for Our Sake*, 53–54; Hays, *Echoes of Scripture*, 65. At the same time, God is *not* free to exclude faithful Jews.

102. We have seen that the story of Abraham is a prefigurement for later Israelite history (see chapter 2). This Pauline usage of Abraham means that he prefigures *two* histories, the children of the flesh and the children of promise.

103. NRSV translates "sons" as "descendants." See also "seed" as collective in Rom. 4. See also the representative use of Christ in Gal. 2:20.

104. See Hays, *Echoes of Scripture*, 121 and 85. See the discussion in Aageson, *Written Also for Our Sake*, 73–88.

105. The sense of "seed" as a singular descendant is used in the Old Testament *only* with reference to the immediately following generation; when "seed" refers to descendants beyond that next generation, it *always* has reference to a collective entity.

106. If our analysis above is correct, texts such as 1 Macc. 2:52 and Sir. 44:20–21 do not stand over against such a claim.

107. Or, possibly, Gentiles who wish to "Judaize."

108. The Old Testament never appeals to circumcision as a guarantor; indeed, judgment may come upon circumcised ones who have an "uncircumcised heart" (Jer. 4:4; 9:25; cf. Deut. 10:16; 30:6; cf. Rom. 2:29).

109. Among the many studies of this text, see J. G. Janzen, "Hagar in Paul's Eyes and in the Eyes of Yahweh (Genesis 16): A Study in Horizons" *HBT* 13 (1991): 1–22; C. K. Barrett, "The Allegory of Abraham, Sarah, and Hagar in the Argument of Galatians," in *Essays on Paul* (Philadelphia: Westminster, 1982), 154–70; Hays, *Echoes of Scripture*, Aageson, *Written Also for Our Sake*. Note that, once again, Christ is not mentioned in this pericope, except for the final summation in 5:1.

110. This contrast has no known parallels in Jewish literature. In *Jub.* 16.17–19 Isaac embodies the Jews and Ishmael (and the other sons of Abraham) the Gentiles. Notably, *Jubilees* associates Isaac with the promise and not the law.

111. The stark contrast drawn does not sufficiently take into account that the Sinai covenant was God initiated and presupposed the continuing Abrahamic covenant (as Moses knows, Exod. 32:13).

112. See Hays, *Echoes of Scripture*, 86, 114–15.

113. The persecution of Isaac by Ishmael (Gal. 4:29) is based on a reading of Gen. 21:9 in Paul's time, wherein Ishmael's "playing" could mean "mocking" (or even worse). And the "so it is now also" refers to Paul's opponents as present persecutors of Christians. Sarah's response to Ishmael's behaviors (Gen. 21:10; Gal. 4:30) is recommended as the

appropriate response to Paul's opponents so as not to be tempted to submit to their understanding of law and promise. Unfortunately, this text has been used as biblical grounding for driving out persons descended from Hagar and Ishmael and identified with Muslims in some way.

114. See Janzen, "Hagar in Paul's Eyes."

115. For studies of Abraham in James, see the commentaries, for example, Luke T. Johnson, *The Letter of James,* (New York: Doubleday, 1995) especially 58–64.

116. James "*never* connects *erga* to the term 'law' (*nomos*)" (Johnson, *James,* 30, 60).

117. The common translation "justified" in James 2:21 and 2:24 is better translated "shown to be righteous" (see Johnson, *James,* 242).

118. See our discussion of this text above (chapter 7).

119. See Johnson (*James*), "The perceived contradiction between Paul and James on the question of righteousness or justification . . . has little, if any, basis" (62).

120. Among other commentaries, see Craig Koester, *Hebrews: A New Translation with Introduction and Commentary* (New York: Doubleday, 2001).

121. Walter Brueggemann, *An Introduction to the Old Testament: The Canon and Christian Imagination* (Louisville: Westminster / John Knox, 2003), claims: "This dismissive judgment of the new covenant promised to Israel thus enshrines in the NT a piece of unembarrassed supersessionism that affirms that the Christian faith—faith in Christ—has superseded Judaism and made Judaism 'obsolete' . . . Such a supersessionist reading is an astonishing misreading . . . for the text in Jer. 31 looks not to a displacement of Judaism but to a reconstitution of Judaism in a mode of glad obedience to the God of the Torah" (285). The last sentence is, actually, quite close to the argument of Hebrews.

122. See Koester, *Hebrews.* Hebrews assumes that God's promises to Abraham "express commitments that remain in force for all of Abraham's heirs, including the followers of Jesus" (111).

123. See S. Spiegel, *The Last Trial on the Legends and Lore of the Command to Abraham to Offer Isaac as a Sacrifice: The Akedah* (New York: Pantheon Books, 1967).

124. The similarities with the Christian relationship to Abraham might be noted.

125. For a recent and modestly successful popular effort to use the Abrahamic texts in this way, see Bruce Feiler, *Abraham: A Journey to the Heart of Three Faiths* (New York: W. Morrow, 2001). For a more scholarly attempt to use the Abrahamic traditions to find a way, see Kuschel, *Abraham.* For a helpful response to Kuschel and related issues, see Levenson, "The Conversion of Abraham." For discussion of Quranic history of interpretation of Abraham, see works by Reuven Firestone (p. 222).

126. For the role of Abraham in the Qur'an, see John Kaltner, *Ishmael Instructs Isaac: An Introduction to the Qur'an for Bible Readers* (Collegeville, Minn.: Liturgical Press, 1999), 87–131.

127. Kaltner, *Ishmael Instructs Isaac,* 87, 90.

128. Several themes regarding Abraham's worship of the one God and his exemplary faithfulness are also present in the Jewish tradition, as we have seen (e.g., *Jub.* 17.15–18; 18.14–16; 19.9; 21.2–4; 23.10; *LAB* 6.1–18; *Apocalypse of Abraham*).

129. This tradition no doubt has its roots in Josh. 24:2–3, which witnesses to idolatry among members of Abraham's family (though, uncertainly, with him). As we have seen, later Jewish tradition also lifts up this role for Abraham.

130. Difficulties in the relationship between Hagar and Sarah/Abraham are not dealt with in the Qur'an.

131. Already in the second century B.C.E., *Jubilees* anticipates later developments regarding the future of Ishmael: "And Ishmael and his sons and the sons of Keturah and their sons went together and they dwelt from Paran to the entrance to Babylon in all of the land which faces the east opposite the desert. And these mixed with each other, and they are called Arabs or Ishmaelites" (20.12).

132. We only attempt to be suggestive here.

133. See Kaltner, *Ishmael Instructs Isaac,* 107–11.

134. For a detailed comparison, see Kaltner, *Ishmael Instructs Isaac,* 92–103. Compare also Suras 15:51–77 and 51:24–37 for similar accounts.

135. Kaltner, *Ishmael Instructs Isaac,* 103.

136. See Kaltner, *Ishmael Instructs Isaac,* 126–29.

137. Levenson, "The Conversion of Abraham," 18.

138. See Kuschel, *Abraham,* 204–5. Kuschel seeks a basis for a critique of the three religions in Genesis. Levenson, "The Conversion of Abraham," helpfully notes that in efforts to use the Bible to critique the Qur'an, one has to remember that the Bible does not have the status of Scripture for Muslims.

139. Levenson, 38.

140. Levenson, 38–39

141. Levenson, 40

SELECT BIBLIOGRAPHY

For a bibliography of books and articles up to 1980, see Claus Westermann, *Genesis 12–36* (with each section); up to 1985, see G. J. Wenham, *Genesis 1–15;* and up to 1995, see G. J. Wenham, *Genesis 16–50* (with each section). In addition, see bibliographies in the studies below by Edward Noort (on Genesis 22) and by John Reeves (the Bible and the Qur'an).

COMMENTARIES

Alter, Robert. *Genesis: A New Translation with Commentary.* New York: W. W. Norton, 1996.

Baldwin, Joyce. *The Message of Genesis 12–50: From Abraham to Joseph.* Downers Grove, Ill.: InterVarsity Press, 1983.

Borgman, Paul. *Genesis: The Story We Haven't Heard.* Downers Grove, Ill.: InterVarsity Press, 2001.

Brodie, Thomas. *Genesis as Dialogue: A Literary, Historical and Theological Commentary.* Oxford: Oxford University Press, 2001.

Brueggemann, Walter. *Genesis.* Atlanta: John Knox Press, 1982.

Cotter, David. *Genesis.* Collegeville, Minn.: Liturgical Press, 2003.

Fretheim, Terence E. "The Book of Genesis." *NIB,* vol. 1. Nashville: Abingdon, 1994.

Gowan, Donald. *From Eden to Babel: A Commentary on the Book of Genesis 1–11.* Grand Rapids, Mich.: Eerdmans 1988.

Gunkel, Hermann. *Genesis.* Translated by M. Biddle. Macon: Mercer University Press, 1997.

Hamilton, Victor. *The Book of Genesis, Chapters 1–17.* Grand Rapids, Mich.: Eerdmans, 1990.

———. *The Book of Genesis, Chapters 18–50.* Grand Rapids, Mich.: Eerdmans, 1995.

Janzen, J. G. *Abraham and All the Families of the Earth: A Commentary on Genesis 12–50.* Grand Rapids, Mich.: Eerdmans, 1993.

Rad, Gerhard von. *Genesis.* Rev. ed. Philadelphia: Westminster, 1972.

Roop, Eugene. *Genesis.* Scottsdale, Pa.: Herald, 1987.

Sarna, Nahum. *Genesis=Bereshith.* Philadelphia: Jewish Publication Society, 1989.

Towner, W. Sibley. *Genesis.* Louisville, Ky.: Westminster / John Knox, 2001.

Vawter, Bruce. *On Genesis: A New Reading.* Garden City, N.J.: Doubleday, 1977.

Wenham, Gordon. *Genesis 1–15.* Waco, Tex.: Word, 1987.

———. *Genesis 16–50.* Waco, Tex.: Word, 1995.

Westermann, Claus. *Genesis 12–36: A Commentary.* Translated by J. J. Scullion. Minneapolis: Augsburg. 1985.

STUDIES OF SPECIAL ISSUES RELATING TO GENESIS 12–25

Aageson, James. *Written Also for Our Sake: Paul and the Art of Biblical Interpretation.* Louisville, Ky.: Westminster / John Knox, 1993.

Abasciano, Brian J. *Paul's Use of the Old Testament in Romans 9:1–9: An Intertextual and Theological Exegesis.* London: T&T Clark, 2005.

Abramovitch, H. *The First Father: Abraham: The Psychology and Culture of a Spiritual Revolutionary.* Lanham, Md.: University Press of America, 1994.

Albertz, Rainer. *History of Israelite Religion in the Old Testament Period,* vol. 1. Translated by John Bowden. Louisville, Ky.: Westminster / John Knox, 1994.

Albright, W. F. *The Biblical Period from Abraham to Ezra: An Historical Survey.* New York: Harper & Row, 1963.

Alexander, T. D. *Abraham in the Negev: A Source-Critical Investigation of Genesis 20:1–22:19.* Carlisle, U.K.: Paternoster Press, 1997.

———. *From Paradise to the Promised Land: An Introduction to the Main Themes of the Pentateuch.* Carlisle, U.K.: Paternoster Press, 1995.

Allison, Dale. *Testament of Abraham.* Berlin: de Gruyter, 2003.

Alter, Robert. *The Art of Biblical Narrative.* New York: Basic Books, 1981.

Bal, Mieke, ed. *Anti-Covenant: Counter-Reading Women's Lives in the Hebrew Bible.* Sheffield, U.K.: Almond Press, 1989.

Balentine, Samuel. *Prayer in the Hebrew Bible: The Drama of Divine-Human Dialogue.* Minneapolis: Fortress, 1993.

———. *The Torah's Vision of Worship.* Minneapolis: Fortress, 1999.

Barton, John. *Reading the Old Testament: Method in Biblical Study.* Philadelphia: Westminster, 1984.

Berkley, T. W. *From a Broken Covenant to Circumcision of the Heart: Pauline Intertextual Exegesis in Romans 2:17–29.* Atlanta: Society for Biblical Literature, 2000.

Berman, Louis. *The Akedah: The Binding of Isaac.* Northvale, N. J.: Aronson, 1997.

Beyerlin, Walther, ed. *Near Eastern Religious Tests Relating to the Old Testament.* Philadelphia: Westminster, 1978.

Blenkinsopp, Joseph. *The Pentateuch: An Introduction to the First Five Books of the Bible.* New York: Doubleday, 1992.

Brenner, Althalya, ed. *A Feminist Companion to Genesis.* Sheffield, U.K.: Academic Press, 1993.

———. *Genesis.* Sheffield, U.K.: Academic Press, 1998.

Brenner, Althalya, and Carole Fontaine, eds. *A Feminist Companion to Reading the Bible: Approaches, Methods and Strategies.* Sheffield, U.K.: Academic Press, 1997.

Brown, William P. *The Ethos of the Cosmos: The Genesis of Moral Imagination in the Bible.* Grand Rapids, Mich.: Eerdmans, 1999.

Bruckner, James. *Implied Law in the Abraham Narrative: A Literary and Theological Analysis.* Sheffield, Academic Press, 2001.

Brueggemann, Walter, and H. W. Wolff. *The Vitality of Old Testament Traditions.* 2nd ed. Atlanta: John Knox Press, 1982.

Calvert-Koyzis, Nancy. *Paul, Monotheism and the People of God: The Significance of Abraham Traditions for Early Judaism and Christianity.* London: T&T Clark, 2004.

Carr, David. *Reading the Fractures of Genesis: Historical and Literary Approaches.* Louisville, Ky.: Westminster / John Knox, 1996.

Caspi, Mishael, and Sascha Cohen. *The Binding: Akedah and Its Transformation in Judaism and Islam, the Lambs of God.* Lewiston, N.Y.: Mellen Biblical Press, 1995.

Charlesworth, James, ed. *The Old Testament Pseudepigrapha,* 2 vols. New York: Doubleday, 1983, 1985.

Childs, Brevard. *Introduction to the Old Testament as Scripture.* Philadelphia: Fortress, 1979.

Clements, Ronald. *Abraham and David: Genesis 15 and Its Meaning for Israelite Religion.* London: SCM, 1967.

Clines, D. J. A. *The Theme of the Pentateuch.* Rev. ed. Sheffield: JSOT Press, 1997.

———. *What Does Eve Do to Help? And Other Readerly Questions of the Old Testament.* Sheffield: JSOT Press, 1990.

Coats, George. *Genesis: With an Introduction to Narrative Literature.* Grand Rapids, Mich.: Eerdmans, 1983.

Cohen, Norman. *Self, Struggle and Change: Family Conflict Stories in Genesis and Their Healing Insights for Our Lives.* Woodstock, Vt.: Jewish Lights Publications, 1995.

Crenshaw, James. *Defending God: Biblical Responses to the Problem of Evil.* Oxford: Oxford University Press, 2005.

———. *A Whirlpool of Torment.* Philadelphia: Fortress, 1984.

Cross, Frank M. *Canaanite Myth and Hebrew Epic.* Cambridge, Mass.: Harvard University Press, 1973.

Darr, Katheryn P. *Far More Precious Than Jewels: Perspectives on Biblical Women.* Louisville, Ky.: Westminster / John Knox, 1991.

Davies, Philip, and David Clines. *The World of Genesis: Persons, Places, Perspectives.* Sheffield, U.K.: Academic Press, 1998.

Davis, Ellen. *Getting Involved with God: Rediscovering the Old Testament.* Cambridge: Cowley Publications, 2001.

Day, Peggy, ed. *Gender and Difference in Ancient Israel.* Minneapolis: Fortress, 1989.

Delaney, Carol. *Abraham on Trial: The Social Legacy of Biblical Myth.* Princeton, N.J.: Princeton University Press, 1998.

Dennis, Trevor. *Sarah Laughed.* Nashville: Abingdon, 1994.

Dreifuss, Gustav, and Judith Riemer. *Abraham: The Man and the Symbol: A Jungian Inter-pretation of the Biblical Story.* Wilmette, Ill.: Chiron Publications, 1995.

Ebach, Jurgen. *Gott im Wort: Drei Studien zur biblische Exegese und Hermeneutic.* Neukirchen-Vluyn: Neukirchener, 1997.

Feiler, Bruce. *Abraham: A Journey to the Heart of Three Faiths.* New York: W. Morrow, 2001.

Fields, W. W. *Sodom and Gomorrah: History and Motif in Biblical Narrative.* Sheffield, U.K.: Academic Press, 1997.

Firestone, Reuven. *Journeys in Holy Lands: The Evolution of the Abraham-Ishmael Legends in Islamic Exegesis.* Albany: State University of New York Press, 1990.

———. "The Qur'an and the Bible: Some Modern Studies of Their Relationship." In *Bible and Qur'an: Essays in Scriptural Intertextuality,* ed. John Reeves. Atlanta: Society of Biblical Literature, 2003. 1–22.

Fokkelman, J. *Narrative Art in Genesis: Specimens of Stylic and Structural Analysis.* Assen, The Netherlands: van Gorcum, 1975.

Fretheim, Terence E. *Deuteronomic History.* Nashville: Abingdon, 1983.

———. *Exodus.* Louisville, Ky.: Westminster / John Knox, 1991.

———. *God and World in the Old Testament: A Relational Theology of Creation.* Nashville: Abingdon, 2005.

———. *The Pentateuch.* Nashville: Abingdon, 1996.

———. *The Suffering of God.* Minneapolis: Fortress, 1984.

Fretheim, Terence E., with Karlfried Froehlich. *The Bible as Word of God in a Postmod-ern Age.* Eugene, Ore.: Wipf & Stock, 1998.

Gellman, Jerome. *Abraham! Abraham! Kierkegaard and the Hasidim on the Binding of Isaac.* Burlington, Vt.: Ashgate, 2003.

Goldingay, John. *Old Testament Theology: Israel's Gospel,* vol. 1. Downers Grove, Ill.: InterVarsity Press, 2003.

Gossai, Hemchand. *Power and Marginality in the Abraham Narrative.* Lanham, Md.: University Press, 1995.

Geifenhagen, F. V. *Egypt on the Pentateuch's Ideological Map: Constructing Biblical Israel's Identity.* Sheffield, U.K.: Academic Press, 2002.

Gunn, David, and Danna Nolan Fewell. *Gender, Power and Promise: The Subject of the Bible's First Story.* Nashville: Abingdon, 1993.

———. *Narrative in the Hebrew Bible.* Oxford: Oxford University Press, 1993.

Halpern-Amaru, Betsy. *The Empowerment of Women in the Book of Jubilees.* Leiden: Brill, 1999.

Hanson, Walter. *Abraham in Galatians: Epistolary and Rhetorical Contexts.* Sheffield: JSOT Press, 1989.

Harrisville, Roy A., Jr. *The Figure of Abraham in the Epistles of St. Paul: In the Footsteps of Abraham.* San Francisco: Mellen Research University Press, 1992.

Hays, Richard B. *Echoes of Scripture in the Letters of Paul.* New Haven, Conn.: Yale University Press, 1992.

Heard, R. Christopher. *Dynamics of Diselection: Ambiguity in Gen 12–36 and Ethnic Boundaries in Post-Exilic Judah.* Atlanta: Society of Biblical Literature, 2001.

Hendel, Ronald S. *Remembering Abraham: Culture, Memory, and History in the Hebrew Bible.* Oxford: Oxford University Press, 2005.

Hess, Richard S., et al., eds. *He Swore an Oath: Biblical Themes from Genesis 12–50.* Carlisle: Paternoster Press, 1994.

Jacobson, Howard. *A Commentary on Pseudo-Philo's LAB.* Leiden: Brill, 1996.

Jeansonne, Sharon. *Women in Genesis: From Sarah to Potiphar's Wife.* Minneapolis, Minn.: Fortress, 1990.

Johnson, Luke T. *The Letter of James: A New Translation with Introduction and Commentary.* New York: Doubleday, 1995.

Kaltner, John. *Ishmael Instructs Isaac: An Introduction to the Qur'an for Bible Readers.* Collegeville, Minn.: Liturgical Press, 1999.

Kessler, Edward. *Bound by the Bible: Jews, Christians, and the Sacrifice of Isaac.* Cambridge: Cambridge University Press, 2004.

Koester, Craig. *Hebrews: A New Translation with Introduction and Commentary.* New York: Doubleday, 2001.

Kugel, James L. *Traditions of the Bible: A Guide to the Bible as It Was at the Start of the Common Era.* Cambridge, Mass.: Harvard University Press, 1998.

Kugel, James L., and Rowan A. Greer. *Early Biblical Interpretation.* Philadelphia: Westminster, 1986.

Kuschel, K-J. *Abraham: Sign of Hope for Jews, Christians, and Muslims.* New York: Continuum, 1995.

Letellier, Robert I. *Day in Mamre, Night in Sodom: Abraham and Lot in Genesis 18–19.* Leiden: Brill, 1995.

Levenson, Jon. *The Death and Resurrection of the Beloved Son: The Transformation of Child Sacrifice in Judaism and Christianity.* New Haven, Conn.: Yale University Press, 1993.

Lipton, Diana. *Revisions of the Night: Politics and Promises in the Patriarchal Dreams of Genesis.* Sheffield, U.K.: Academic Press, 1999.

Loader, J. A. *A Tale of Two Cities: Sodom and Gomorrah in the Old Testament, Early Jewish and Early Christian Traditions.* Kampen, The Netherlands: J. H. Kok, 1990.

Loning, Karl, and Erich Zenger. *To Begin With . . . God Created: Biblical Theologies of Creation.* Translated by Omar Kaste. Collegeville, Minn.: Liturgical Press, 2000.

Luther, Martin. *Luther's Works: Lectures on Genesis,* vols. 2–4. St. Louis: Concordia, 1960–64.

Lyons, W. J. *Canon and Exegesis: Canonical Praxis and the Sodom Narrative.* London: Sheffield Academic Press, 2002.

McKane, William. *Studies in the Patriarchal Narratives.* Edinburgh, Scotland: Handsel, 1979.

Milgrom, Jo. *The Binding of Isaac: The Akedah—A Primary Symbol in Jewish Thought and Art.* Berkeley: BIBAL Press, 1988.

Millard, A. R., and D. J. Wiseman, eds. *Essays on the Patriarchal Narrative.* Winona Lake, Ind.: Eisenbrauns, 1983.

Miller, Alice. *The Untouched Key: Tracing Childhood Trauma in Creativity and Destructiveness.* New York: Doubleday, 1990.

Miller, Patrick D. *The Religion of Ancient Israel.* Louisville, Ky.: Westminster / John Knox, 2000.

Moberly, R. W. L. *The Bible, Theology, and Faith: A Study of Abraham and Jesus.* Cambridge: Cambridge University Press, 2000.

———. *The Old Testament of the Old Testament: Patriarchal Narratives and Mosaic Yahwism.* Minneapolis, Minn.: Fortress, 1992.

Moyers, Bill. *Genesis: A Living Conversation.* New York: Doubleday, 1996.

Niditch, Susan. *Underdogs and Tricksters: A Prelude to Biblical Folklore.* San Francisco: Harper & Row, 1987.

Nickelsburg, George W. E. *Jewish Literature between the Bible and the Mishnah.* 2nd ed. Minneapolis, Minn.: Fortress, 2005.

Nissinen, Marti. *Homoeroticism in the Biblical World: A Historical Perspective.* Translated by K. Stjerna. Minneapolis, Minn.: Fortress, 1998.

Noort, Edward, and Eibert Tigchelaar, eds. *The Sacrifice of Isaac: The Aqedah (Genesis 22) and Its Interpretations.* Leiden: Brill, 2002.

———. *Sodom's Sin: Genesis 18–19 and Its Interpretations.* London: Brill, 2004.

Oates, Wayne. *The Bible in Pastoral Care.* Philadelphia: Westminster, 1953.

Pagolu, Augustine. *The Religion of the Patriarchs.* Sheffield, U.K.: Academic Press, 1998.

Patai, Raphael. *The Seed of Abraham: Jews and Arabs in Contact and Conflict.* Salt Lake City: University of Utah Press, 1986.

Peachey, Paul., G. McLean, and J. Kromkowski, eds. *Abrahamic Faiths: Ethnicity and Ethnic Conflicts.* Washington, D.C.: Council for Research in Values and Philosophy, 1997.

Peters, F. E. *Children of Abraham: Judaism, Christianity, Islam.* Princeton, N.J.: Princeton University Press, 1982.

Public Affairs Television. *Talking about Genesis: A Resource Guide.* New York: Doubleday, 1996.

Rad, Gerhard von. *Das Opfer des Abraham.* Munich, Germany: Kaiser, 1971.

———. *Old Testament Theology,* vol. 1. New York: Harper, 1962.

Reeves, John, ed. *Bible and Qur'an: Essays in Scriptural Intertextuality.* Atlanta: Society of Biblical Literature, 2003.

Rendsburg, Gary. *The Redaction of Genesis.* Winona Lake, Ind.: Eisenbrauns, 1986.

Sanders, E. P. *Paul and Palestinian Judaism: A Comparison of Patterns of Religion.* Philadelphia: Fortress, 1977.

———. *Paul, the Law, and the Jewish People.* Philadelphia: Fortress, 1983.

Sandmel, Samuel. *Philo's Place in Judaism: A Study of Conceptions of Abraham in Jewish Literature.* New York: KTAV, 1971.

Sarna, Nahum. *Understanding Genesis.* New York: Schocken, 1966.

Schneider, Tammi J. *Sarah: Mother of Nations.* New York: Continuum, 2004.

Seters, John van. *Abraham in History and Tradition.* New Haven, Conn.: Yale University Press, 1975.

Shanks, Hershel, ed. *Abraham and Family: New Insights into the Patriarchal Narratives.* Washington, D.C.: Biblical Archaeological Society, 2000.

Siker, Jeffrey. *Disinheriting the Jews: Abraham in Early Christian Controversy.* Louisville, Ky.: Westminster / John Knox, 1991.

Spiegel, Shalom. *The Last Trial on the Legends and Lore of the Command to Abraham to Offer Isaac as a Sacrifice: The Akedah.* New York: Pantheon Books, 1967.

Spina, Frank A. *The Faith of the Outsider: Exclusion and Inclusion in the Biblical Story.* Grand Rapids, Mich.: Eerdmans, 2005.

Steinberg, Naomi. *Kinship and Marriage in Genesis: A Household Economics Perspective.* Minneapolis, Minn.: Fortress, 1993.

Steinmetz, Devora. *From Father to Son: Kinship, Conflict, and Continuity in Genesis.* Louisville, Ky.: Westminster / John Knox, 1991.

Steins, Georg. *Die "Bindung Isaaks im Kanon" (Gen 22): Grundlagen und Programm einer Kanonisch-intertextuellen Lekture.* Freiburg, Germany: Herder, 1999.

Sternberg, Meir. *The Poetics of Biblical Narrative: Ideological Literature and the Drama of Reading.* Bloomington: Indiana University Press, 1985.

Tate, W. R. *Biblical Interpretation: An Integrated Approach.* Peabody, Mass.: Hendrickson, 1991.

Teubal, Savina. *Hagar the Egyptian: The Lost Traditions of the Matriarchs.* San Francisco: Harper & Row, 1990.

———. *Sarah the Priestess: The First Matriarch of Genesis.* Athens, Ohio. Swallow Press, 1984.

Thompson, Thomas L. *The Historicity of the Patriarchal Narratives: The Quest for the Historical Abraham.* Berlin: de Gruyter, 1974.

Toorn, Karel van der. *Family Religion in Babylonia, Syria, and Israel: Continuity and Change in the Forms of Religious Life.* Leiden: Brill, 1996.

Trible, Phyllis. *God and the Rhetoric of Sexuality.* Philadelphia: Fortress, 1978.

———. *Texts of Terror: Literary-Feminist Readings of Biblical Narratives.* Philadelphia: Fortress, 1984.

Turner, Lawrence. *Announcements of Plot in Genesis.* Sheffield: JSOT Press, 1990.

VanderKam, James. *The Book of Jubilees.* Sheffield, U.K.: Academic Press, 2001.

Weems, Renita. *Just a Sister Away: A Womanist's Vision of Women's Relationships in the Bible.* San Diego: LuraMedia, 1988.

Wenin, A., ed. *Studies in the Book of Genesis: Literature, Redaction, and History.* Leuven, Belgium: Leuven University Press, 2001.

Welhausen, Julius. *Prolegomena to the History of Israel.* Edinburgh: Black, 1995.

Westermann, Claus. *Blessing in the Bible and the Life of the Church.* Translated by Keith R. Crim. Philadelphia: Fortress, 1978.

———. *The Promises to the Fathers: Studies in the Patriarchal Narrative.* Philadelphia: Fortress, 1980.

White, Hugh. *Narration and Discourse in the Book of Genesis.* Cambridge: Cambridge University Press, 1991.

White, John L. *The Apostle of God: Paul and the Promise of Abraham.* Peabody, Mass.: Hendrickson, 1999.

Whybray, R. N. *Introduction to the Pentateuch.* Sheffield, U.K.: Academic Press, 1995.

———. *The Making of the Pentateuch.* Sheffield: JSOT Press, 1987.

Wiesel, Elie. *Messengers of God: Biblical Portraits and Legends.* New York: Random House, 1976.

Williams, Delores. *Sisters in the Wilderness: The Challenge of Womanist God-Talk.* Maryknoll, N.Y.: Orbis Books, 1993.

Williamson, P. R. *Abraham, Israel and the Nations: Patriarchal Promise and Its Covenantal Development in Genesis.* Sheffield, U.K.: Academic Press, 2000.

ARTICLES OF SPECIAL INTEREST REGARDING GENESIS 12–25

Alexander, T. D. "Abraham Re-assessed Theologically." In *He Swore an Oath.* Edited by R. Hess et al. Carlisle, U.K.: Paternoster Press, 1994. 7–28.

———. "The Hagar Traditions in Genesis XVI and XXI." In *Studies in the Pentateuch.* Edited by J. Emerson. Leiden: Brill, 1990. 131–48.

Alt, Albrecht. "The Gods of Our Fathers." In *Essays on Old Testament History and Religion.* Oxford: Blackwell, 1966. 3–77.

Alter, Robert. "Sodom as Nexus: The Web of Design in Biblical Narrative." In *The Book and the Text.* Edited by R. Schwarz. Oxford: Blackwell, 1990. 146–60.

Anderson, Bernhard. "Abraham, the Friend of God." *Interpretation* 42 (1988): 353–66.

Auerbach, Erich. "Odysseus's Scar." In *Mimesis: The Representation of Reality in Western Literature.* Princeton, N.J.: Princeton University Press, 1953. 1–19.

Baird, William. "Abraham in the New Testament." *Interpretation* 42 (1988): 367–79.

Barrett, C. K. "The Allegory of Abraham, Sarah, and Hagar in the Argument of Galatians." In *Essays on Paul.* Philadelphia: Westminster, 1982. 154–70.

Bechtel, Lyn. "A Feminist Reading of Genesis 19:1–11." In *A Feminist Companion to the Bible.* Second Series. Edited by A. Brenner. Sheffield, U.K.: Academic Press, 1998. 108–28.

———. "Boundary Issues in Genesis 19:1–38." In *Escaping Eden: New Feminist Perspectives on the Bible.* Edited by H. Washington et al. Sheffield, U.K.: Academic Press, 1998.

Ben Zvi, Ehud. "The Dialogue between Abraham and YHWH in Gen. 18:23–32: A Historical-critical Analysis." *JSOT* 53 (1992): 27–46.

Bettenhausen, Elizabeth. "Hagar Revisited: Surrogacy, Alienation, and Motherhood." *CC* 47 (1989): 159.

Biddle, Mark. "The 'Endangered Ancestress' and Blessing for the Nations." *JBL* 109 (1990): 599–611.

Blenkinsopp, Joseph. "Abraham and the Righteous of Sodom." *JJS* 33 (1982): 119–32.

Bodoff, Lipmann. "The Real Test of the *Akedah:* Blind Obedience versus Moral Choice." *Judaism* 42 (1993): 71–92.

Borgman, Paul. "Abraham and Sarah: Literary Text and the Rhetorics of Reflection." In *The Function of Scripture in Early Jewish and Christian Tradition*. Edited by Craig A. Evans and James A. Sanders. Sheffield, U.K.: Academic Press, 1998.

———. "Letting Go of Fear: The Love of Abraham." *Perspectives* 17 (2002): 21–23.

Breithart, Sidney. "The Akedah: A Test of God." *Dor le Dor* 15 (1996): 19–28.

Brett, Mark. "Abraham's 'Heretical' Imperative: A Response to Jacques Derrida." In *The Meaning We Choose: Hermeneutical Ethics, Indeterminacy, and the Conflict of Interpretations*. Edited by C. Cosgrove. London: T&T Clark, 2004. 166–78.

Bruce, F. F. "Abraham our Father." In *The Time Is Fulfilled: Five Aspects of the Fulfillment of the Old Testament in the New*. Grand Rapids, Mich.: Eerdmans, 1982. 57–74.

Brueggemann, Walter. "'Impossibility' and Epistemology in the Faith Tradition of Abraham and Sarah (Gen. 18:1–15)." *ZAW* 94 (1982): 615–34.

Capps, Donald. "Abraham and Isaac: The Sacrificial Impulse." In *The Destructive Power of Religion: Violence in Judaism, Christianity, and Islam*, vol. 1: *Sacred Scriptures, Ideology, and Violence*. Edited by J. H. Ellens. Westport, Conn.: Praeger, 2004. 170–89.

Carr, D. M. "Genesis in Relation to the Moses Story. Diachronic and Synchronic Perspectives." In *Studies in the Book of Genesis: Literature, Redaction, and History*. Edited by A. Wenin. Leuven: University Press, 2001. 273–95.

Castelli, E. A. "Allegories of Hagar: Reading Genesis 4:21–31 with Postmodern Feminist Eyes." In *The New Literary Criticism and the New Testament*. Edited by E. Malbon and E. McKnight. Valley Forge, Pa.: Trinity Press International, 1994. 228–50.

Clements, Ronald. "Abraham." *Theological Dictionary of the Old Testament*. Grand Rapids, Mich.: Eerdmans, 1974. 1:52–58.

Clines, David. "The Ancestor in Danger, but Not the Same Danger." In *What Does Eve Do to Help? and Other Readerly Questions to the Old Testament*. Sheffield, U.K.: Academic Press, 1990. 67–84.

Coats, George. "Abraham's Sacrifice of Faith: A Form-critical Study of Genesis 22." *Interpretation* 27 (1973): 389–400.

Coats, G. "Lot: A Foil in the Abraham Saga." In *Understanding the Word*. Edited by J. Butler et al. Sheffield: JSOT Press, 1985. 113–32.

Cohen, J. M. "Was Abraham Heartless?" *JBQ* 23 (1995): 180–81.

Cohn, Robert. "Negotiating (with) the Natives: Ancestors and Identity in Genesis." *HTR* 96 (2003): 147–66.

Cooper, Alan. "Hagar in and out of Context." *USQR* 55 (2001): 35–46.

Cranford, Michael. "Abraham in Romans 4: The Father of All Who Believe." *NTS* 41 (1995): 71–88.

Cross, F. M. "Yahweh and the God of the Patriarchs." *HTR* 55 (1962): 225–59.

Dahl, Nils. "The Story of Abraham in Luke-Acts." In *Studies in Luke-Acts*. Edited by L. Keck and J. L. Martyn. Nashville: Abingdon, 1966. 139–58.

Dahlberg, B. "On Recognizing the Unity of Genesis." *TD* 24 (1977): 360–67.

Daly, Robert. "The Soteriological Significance of the Sacrifice of Isaac." *CBQ* 39 (1977): 45–75.

Davies, G. I. "Genesis and the Early History of Israel: A Survey of Research." In *Studies in the Book of Genesis: Literature, Redaction, and History*. Edited by A. Wenin. Leuven: Leuven University Press, 2001. 104–34.

DeSilva, David. "Why Did God Choose Abraham?" *BR* 16 (2000): 16–21, 42–44.

Dijk-Hemmes, Fokkelien van. "Sarai's Exile: A Gender-Motivated Reading of Genesis 12:10–13:2." In *A Feminine Companion to Genesis*, vol. 2. Edited by A. Brenner. Sheffield, U.K.: Academic Press, 1993. 222–34.

Eichler, Barry. "On Reading Genesis 12:10–20." In *Tehillah le-Moshe: Biblical and Judaic Studies in Honor of Moshe Greenberg*. Edited by M. Cogan, B. L. Eichler, and J. H. Tigay. Winona Lake, Ind.: Eisenbrauns, 1997. 23–38.

Eisen, R. "The Education of Abraham: The Encounter between Abraham and God over the Fate of Sodom and Gomorrah." *JBQ* 28 (2000): 80–86.

Exum, Cheryl. "The Mothers of Israel: Patriarchal Narratives from a Feminist Perspective." *BR* 2 (1986): 60–67.

———. "Who's Afraid of 'The Endangered Ancestress'?" In *Women in the Hebrew Bible: A Reader*. Edited by A. Bach. New York: Routledge, 1999. 141–56.

Fewell, Danna. "Changing the Subject: Retelling the Story of Hagar the Egyptian." In *Genesis: The Feminist Companion to the Bible*. Second Series. Edited by A. Brenner. Sheffield, U.K.: Academic Press, 1998. 182–94.

Firestone, Reuven. "Abraham's Son as the Intended Sacrifice (al-Dhabih, Qur'an 37:99–113)." *JSS* 34 (1989): 95–131.

Fretheim, Terence E. "Christology and the Old Testament." In *Who Do You Say That I Am? Essays on Christology*. Edited by Mark A. Powell and David R. Bauer (Louisville, Ky.: Westminster / John Knox, 1999). 201–15.

———. "Divine Judgment and the Warming of the World." In *God, Evil, and Suffering: Essays in Honor of Paul R. Sponheim*. Edited by Fretheim and Curt Thompson. St. Paul: Word and World, 2000. 21–32.

———. "God, Abraham, and the Abuse of Isaac." *W&W* 16 (1996): 49–57.

———. "Is Anything Too Hard for God? (Jeremiah 32:27)." *CBQ* 66 (2004): 231–36.

————. "The Plagues as Historical Signs of Ecological Disaster." *JBL* 110 (1991): 385–96.

————. "The Reclamation of Creation: Redemption and Law in Exodus." *Interpretation* 45 (1991): 354–65.

————. "Salvation in the Bible vs. Salvation in the Church." *W&W* 13 (1993): 363–72.

Frymer-Kensky, Tikva. "Hagar, My Other, Myself." In *Reading the Women of the Bible: A New Interpretation of Their Stories.* New York: Schocken, 2002. 225–37.

Gaiser, Frederick J. "Why Does It Rain? A Biblical Case Study in Divine Causality." *HBT* 25 (2003): 1–18.

Goldingay, John. "The Patriarchs in Scripture and History." In *Essays on the Patriarchal Narratives.* Edited by A. Millard and D. Wiseman. Winona Lake, Ind.: Eisenbrauns, 1983.

————. "'You Are Abraham's Offspring, My Friend': Abraham in Isaiah 41." In *He Swore An Oath: Biblical Themes from Genesis 12–50.* Edited by R. Hess et al. Grand Rapids, Mich.: Baker, 1994. 29–54.

Goshen-Gottstein, M. "Abraham and 'Abrahamic Religions' in Contemporary Interreligious Discourse: Reflections of an Implicated Jewish Bystander." *Studies in Interreligious Dialogue* 12 (2002): 165–83.

————. "Abraham—Lover or Beloved of God." In *Love and Death in the Ancient Near East.* Edited by J. H. Marks and R. M. Good. Guilford, Conn.: Four Quarters, 1987. 101–4.

Hackett, J. A. "Rehabilitating Hagar: Fragments of an Epic Pattern." In *Gender and Difference in Ancient Israel.* Edited by P. Day. Philadelphia: Fortress, 1989. 12–27.

Hayward, C. "The Sacrifice of Isaac and Jewish Polemic Against Christianity." *CBQ* 52 (1990): 291–306.

Haywood, R. "The Present State of Research into the Targumic Account of the Sacrifice of Isaac." *JJS* 32 (1981): 127–50.

Helyer, L. "The Separation of Abram and Lot: Significance in the Patriarchal Narratives." *JSOT* 26 (1983): 77–78.

Hendel, Ronald S. "Dating the Patriarchal Age." *BAR* 21, no. 4 (1995): 56–57.

Holmgren, Frederick. "Faithful Abraham and the *'amana* Covenant: Nehemiah 9:6–10:1." *ZAW* 104 (1992): 249–54.

Jackson, M. "Lot's Daughters and Tamar as Tricksters and the Patriarchal Narratives as Feminist Theology." *JSOT* 98 (2002): 29–46.

Janzen, J. G. "Hagar in Paul's Eyes and in the Eyes of Yahweh (Genesis 16)." *HBT* (1991): 1–22.

Jenzen, Robin. "The Offering of Isaac in Jewish and Christian Tradition: Image and Text." *Biblical Illustrator* 2 (1994): 86–120.

Kahl, Brigitte. "Hagar between Genesis and Galatians: The Stony Road to Freedom." In *From Prophecy to Testament: The Function of the Old Testament in the New.* Edited by C. A. Evans. Peabody, Mass.: Hendrickson, 2004. 219–32.

Kahn, Pinchas. "The Mission of Abraham: Genesis 18:17–22:19." *JBQ* 30 (2002): 155–63.

Kaltner, John. "Abraham's Sons: How Bible and Qur'an See the Same Story Differently." *BR* 18 (2002): 16–23.

Kaseman, Ernst. "The Faith of Abraham in Romans 4." In *Perspectives on Paul.* Philadelphia: Fortress, 1971.

Kitchen, K. A. "The Patriarchal Age: Myth or History?" *BAR* 21, no. 2 (1995): 48–57, 88–95.

Klein, Ralph. "Call, Covenant, and Community." *CurTM* 15 (1988): 120–27.

Kohn, M. J. "The Trauma of Isaac." *JBQ* (1991–1992): 96–104.

Kramer, Phyllis S. "The Dismissal of Hagar in Five Art Works of the Sixteenth and Seventeenth Centuries." In *Genesis: The Feminist Companion to the Bible.* Second Series. Edited by A. Brenner. Sheffield, U.K.: Academic Press,1998. 195–217.

LaHurd, Carol. "One God, One Father: Abraham in Judaism, Christianity, and Islam." *Dialog* 29 (1990): 17–28.

Lapsley, Jacqueline. "Friends with God? Moses and the Possibility of Covenant Friendship." *Interpretation* 58 (2004): 117–29.

Lasine, Stuart. "Guest and Host in Judges 19" *JSOT* 29 (1984): 37–59.

Levenson, Jon. "Abusing Abraham: Traditions, Religious Histories, and Modern Misinterpretations." *Judaism* 47 (1998): 259–77.

———. "The Conversion of Abraham to Judaism, Christianity, and Islam." In *The Idea of Biblical Interpretation: Essays in Honor of James L. Kugel.* Edited by H. Najman and J. Newman. Leiden: Brill, 2004. 3–40.

Leviant, Curt. "Parallel Loves: The Trials and Traumas of Isaac and Ishmael." *BR* 15 (1999): 47.

Liptzin, Sol. "Princess Hagar." In *Biblical Themes in World Literature.* Hoboken: KTAV, 1985. 39–53.

Lundbom, J. R. "Parataxis, Rhetorical Structure and the Dialogue over Sodom in Genesis 18." In *The World of Genesis.* Edited by P. R. Davies and D. J. A. Clines. Sheffield, U.K.: Academic Press, 1998. 136–45.

Macdonald, Nathan. "Listening to Abraham—Listening to Yahweh: Divine Justice and Mercy in Genesis 18:16–33." *CBQ* 66 (2004): 25–43.

———. "Abraham's Purchase of the Cave of Machpelah and Anthropological Theories of Exchange." In *Anthropology and Biblical Studies: The Way Forward.* Edited by M. I. Aguilar and L. J. Lawrence. Leiden: Deo, 2004.

Mann, Thomas. "All the Families of the Earth: The Theological Unity of Genesis." *Interpretation* 45 (1991): 341–53.

Martyn, J. L. "The Covenants of Hagar and Sarah." In *Faith and History.* Edited by J. Carroll et al. Atlanta: Scholars Press, 1990. 160–92.

Matthews, V. H. "Hospitality and Hostility in Genesis 19 and Judges 19." *BTB* 22 (1992): 3–11.

McConville, J. Gordon. "Abraham and Melchizedek: Horizons in Genesis 14." In *He Swore an Oath: Biblical Themes from Genesis 12–50*. Edited by R. Hess et al. Carlisle, U.K.: Paternoster Press, 1994. 93–118.

Millard, A. R. "Abraham." In *ABD*. New York: Doubleday, 1992. 1:35–41.

Mleynek, S. "Abraham, Aristotle, and God: The Poetics of Sacrifice." *JAAR* 62 (1994): 107–21.

Moberly, R. W. L. "The Earliest Commentary on the Akedah." *VT* (1988): 302–23.

Moltz, Howard. "God and Abraham in the Binding of Isaac." *JSOT* 96 (2001): 55–69.

Moster, Julius. "The Testing of Abraham." *Dor le Dor* 17 (1989): 237–42.

Newman, J. H. "Lot in Sodom: The Postmortem of a City and the Afterlife of a Biblical Text." In *The Function of Scripture in Early Jewish and Christian Tradition*. Edited by C. A. Evans and J. A. Sanders. Sheffield, U.K.: Academic Press, 1998. 34–44.

Nikaido, Scott. "Hagar and Ishmael as Literary Figures: An Intertextual Study." *VT* 51 (2001): 219–42.

Phillips, Elaine. "Incredulity, Faith, and Textual Purposes: Post-Biblical Responses to the Laughter of Abraham and Sarah." In *Function of Scripture in Early Jewish and Christian Tradition*. Edited by Craig A. Evans and James A. Sanders. Sheffield, U.K.: Academic Press, 1998. 22–33.

Polzin, Robert. "The Ancestress of Israel in Danger." *Semeia* 3 (1975): 81–98.

Reis, P. T. "Hagar Requited." *JSOT* 87 (2000): 75–109.

Reiss, Moshe. "Ishmael: Son of Abraham." *JBQ* 30 (2002): 253–56.

Rodd, C. S. "Shall Not the Judge of All the Earth Do Right?" *ExpTim* 105 (1994): 211–12.

Roshwald, M. "A Dialogue between Man and God." *SJT* 42 (1989): 145–65.

Ruiten, J. van. "Lot versus Abraham, the Interpretation of Genesis 18:1–19:38 in *Jubilees* 16:1–9." In *Sodom's Sin: Genesis 18–19 and Its Interpretations*. Edited by Edward Noort and Eibert Tigchelaar. Leiden: Brill, 2004. 29–46.

Rulon-Miller, Nina. "Hagar: A Woman with an Attitude." In *The World of Genesis: Persons, Places, Perspectives*. Edited by P. R. Davies and D. Clines. Sheffield, U.K.: Academic Press, 1998. 60–89.

Schoeps, H. "The Sacrifice of Isaac in Paul's Theology." *JBL* 65 (1946): 385–92.

Scudder, Lewis. "Ishmael and Isaac and Muslim-Christian Dialogue." *Dialog* 29 (1990): 29–32.

Segal, Alan. "The Sacrifice of Isaac in Early Judaism and Christianity." In *The Other Judaisms of Late Antiquity*. Atlanta: Scholars Press, 1987.

Seters, John van. "The Religion of the Patriarchs in Genesis." *Biblica* 61 (1980): 220–23.

Sutherland, D. "The Organization of the Abraham Promise Narratives." *ZAW* 95 (1983): 337–43.

Tamez, Elsa. "The Woman Who Complicated the History of Salvation." In *New Eyes for Reading: Biblical and Theological Reflections by Women from the Third World*. Edited by J. Pobee et al. Geneva: World Council of Churches, 1986. 5–17.

Taylor, Katy. "From Lavender to Purple: A Feminist Reading of Hagar . . . in Light of Womanism." *Theology* 97 (1994): 352–62.

Tonson, Paul. "Mercy without Covenant: A Literary Analysis of Genesis 19." *JSOT* 95 (2001): 95–116.

Trible, Phyllis. "The Other Woman: The Hagar Narratives." In *Understanding the Word: Essays in Honor of Bernard W. Anderson.* Edited by J. Butler et al. Sheffield: JSOT Press, 1985. 221–46.

————. "Genesis 22: The Sacrifice of Sarah." In *'Not in Heaven': Coherence and Complexity in Biblical Narrative.* Edited by J. Rosenblatt and J. Sitterson. Bloomington: Indiana University Press, 1991. 170–91.

Waldman, Marilyn. "New Approaches to 'Biblical' Material in the Qur'an." In *Studies in Islamic and Judaic Traditions.* Edited by William Brinner and Steven Ricks. Atlanta: Scholars Press, 1986. 47–64.

Waters, John. "Who Was Hagar?" In *Stony the Road We Trod: African-American Biblical Interpretation.* Edited by Cain Hope Felder. Minneapolis, Minn.: Fortress, 1991. 187–205.

Wenham, G. J. "The Religion of the Patriarchs." In *Essays on the Patriarchal Narratives.* Edited by A. R. Millard and D. J. Wiseman. Leicester: IVP, 1980. 157–88.

Whybray, N. "Shall Not the Judge of All the Earth Do What Is Just?: God's Oppression of the Innocent in the Old Testament." In *"Shall Not the Judge of All the Earth Do What Is Right?": Studies in the Nature of God.* Edited by D. Penchansky and P. L. Redditt. Winona Lake, Ind.: Eisenbrauns, 2000. 1–19.

Wiesel, Elie. "Ishmael and Hagar." In *The Life of Covenant; The Challenge of Contemporary Judaism.* Edited by Joseph Edelheit. Chicago: SCJ, 1986.

Wilken, Robert. "The Christianizing of Abraham: The Interpretation of Abraham in Early Christianity." *CTM* 43 (1972): 723–31.

————. "Melito, the Jewish Community at Sardis, and the Sacrifice of Isaac." *TS* 37 (1976): 53–69.

Williamson, P. R. "Abraham, Israel, and the Church." *EvQ* 78 (2000): 99–118.

Wood, J. Edwin. "Isaac Typology in the New Testament." *NTS* 14 (1968): 583–89.

Yeres, Moshe. "The Meaning of Abraham's Test: A Reexamination of the Akedah." *Dor le Dor* 19 (1990): 3–10.

SUBJECT INDEX

SCRIPTURAL INDEX